D0849660

Principles
of
Property and Liability
Underwriting

Principles
of
Property and Liability Underwriting

J. J. LAUNIE, Ph.D., CPCU
Professor of Finance and Insurance
California State University, Northridge

J. FINLEY LEE, Ph.D., CLU
Julian Price Professor of Business Administration
University of North Carolina

NORMAN A. BAGLINI, Ph.D., CPCU, CLU, AU
Executive Vice President and Deputy Director
Insurance Institute of America

Third Edition • 1986

INSURANCE INSTITUTE OF AMERICA
720 Providence Road, Malvern, Pennsylvania 19355-0770

Foreword

Over the years, the American Institute for Property and Liability Underwriters and the Insurance Institute of America have responded to the educational needs of the property-liability insurance industry by developing new programs.

The American Institute maintains and administers the program leading to the Chartered Property Casualty Underwriter (CPCU) professional designation.

The Insurance Institute of America offers programs leading to the Certificate in General Insurance, the Associate in Claims (AIC) designation, the Associate in Management (AIM) designation, the Associate in Risk Management (ARM) designation, the Associate in Underwriting (AU) designation, the Associate in Loss Control Management (ALCM) designation, the Accredited Adviser in Insurance (AAI) designation, the Associate in Premium Auditing (APA) designation, the Associate in Research and Planning (ARP) designation, and the Associate in Insurance Accounting and Finance (AIAF) designation as well as the Introduction to Property and Liability Insurance (INTRO) course and the Supervisory Management (SM) courses.

Throughout the development of this series of texts it has been—and will continue to be—necessary to draw on the knowledge and skills of Institute staff members. These individuals will receive no royalties on texts sold, and their writing responsibilities are seen as an integral part of their professional duties. We have proceeded in this way to avoid any possibility of conflicts of interests.

We invite and welcome any and all criticisms of our publications. It is only with such comments that we can hope to provide high quality texts, materials, and programs. Comments should be directed to the Curriculum Department of the Institutes.

Edwin S. Overman, Ph.D., CPCU
President

Preface

This book is one of a series of four—all of which are written specifically for students working toward the Insurance Institute of America Associate in Underwriting (AU) designation. The authors have written this book for all persons who are involved in the business of placing and underwriting insurance—company underwriters and field representatives, agency underwriters, and producers. The primary objective of this book is to improve underwriting decision making through mastery of the basic underwriting tools that are common to all lines of insurance and to all types of insurers. The three remaining books (*Personal Lines Underwriting, Commercial Liability Underwriting,* and *Commercial Property and Multiple-Lines Underwriting*) build upon these principles and apply them to the major lines of property and liability insurance.

Through the years, the development of underwriting knowledge and skills has followed the apprentice system. Young, inexperienced underwriters have absorbed knowledge and developed skills under the supervision of seasoned underwriters. This day-to-day, on-the-job experience is absolutely necessary in the acquisition of sound underwriting judgment. However, on-the-job experiences are more fruitful if they can be tied to a solid foundation of principles and a structured approach to underwriting fundamentals.

Although the debate continues, it is generally agreed that underwriting, as we know it today, is more an art than a science. Any art is a skill in performance acquired through mastery of the tools of the art and practice under the supervision of a skilled practitioner. Thus, successful underwriting performance requires the right combination of both—a study of the basic principles developed through the years by veteran underwriters and an opportunity to make underwriting decisions under simulated conditions.

There are some inherent difficulties in writing a principles book—the major one being the inability to delve into detail in the interest of keeping the book simple. The examples and illustrations in this book are drawn from both personal and commercial lines to show the widespread application of the principles. However, the magnitude and complexity of the property and liability insurance business often present exceptions to the basic principle, and sometimes regional variations may further amend the usefulness of the principle being discussed. These obstacles should serve to stimulate thought as to why these basic principles need to be modified, and the reader is referred to the three remaining books in this set for discussion of the differences in the major lines of insurance.

This book was written with the assumption that the reader would have a basic knowledge of insurance principles and coverages. It was designed to focus on underwriting decision making rather than on an in-depth analysis of insurance coverages. No review exercises or discussion questions are included. These appear in a companion study aid—the AU 61 Course Guide. The Course Guide contains a set of educational objectives and an outline of the study material for each assignment, as well as key terms and concepts, review questions, discussion questions, and cases in underwriting.

It is impossible to list all of the persons who contributed to this textbook writing project. A large number of underwriting executives and company education directors shared with us their views on what is needed in a countrywide educational program for underwriters. Special thanks are extended to the AU Advisory Committee (listed in the Course Guide) that meets regularly to review national examination questions and to advise us on the curriculum and study materials.

Each manuscript chapter was reviewed by a group of insurance educators and practitioners. The authors deeply appreciate the critical reviews submitted by the authors of the other three underwriting texts in this program: Larry D. Gaunt, Ph.D., CPCU, Professor of Insurance, Georgia State University; G. William Glendenning, Ph.D., CPCU, Professor of Risk Management and Insurance, Temple University; E. P. Hollingsworth, CPCU, ARM, Vice President, Frank B. Hall & Co., Inc.; Robert B. Holtom, CPCU; and Numan A. Williams, Ph.D., CPCU, CLU, Professor of Finance and Insurance, Ball State University. Sincere thanks are also extended to Edward L. Henninger, Assistant Vice President, State Farm Insurance Companies; Peter R. Kensicki, D.B.A., CPCU, CLU, Vice President, Insurance Institute of America; and Ralph E. King, CPCU, Professor of Insurance, State University of New York, Agricultural and Technical College, who read and commented on the entire manuscript.

In addition, many capable individuals critically reviewed portions of the text in the areas of their specialty. The authors wish to thank all of these individuals, especially Deborah J. Conley, CPCU, AU, Senior Technical Specialist, PMA Group; Diane Curtiss, AU, Underwriting Technical Assistant, Fireman's Fund Insurance Company; Robert E.

Dietz, CPCU, Training Director, Pennsylvania National Insurance Group; Edward J. Fitzgerald, CPCU, AU, ARP, Underwriting Manager, CIGNA; Sherman O. Fjalstad, CPCU, AU, Underwriting Training Manager, Federated Mutual Insurance Company; M. Eugene Garthwaite, CPCU, AU, Assistant Vice President, Johnson & Higgins of Delaware, Inc.; Richard S. Griffith, CPCU, Assistant Director, Commercial Insurance Division, The Hartford Insurance Group; Robert A. Gwinn, AU, ALCM, Commercial Property Underwriter, Kemper Group; Duane L. Manns, AU, Senior Business Accounts Underwriter, Continental Insurance Company; Barry J. McCall, AU, AIM, Personal Lines Underwriting Supervisor, Kemper Group; Robert J. Miller, FIIC, Property Underwriting Manager, Federated Mutual Insurance Company; William T. Nebraska, CPCU, PE, CSP, Vice President, Loss Control, The Hartford Insurance Group; Raymond M. Normann, CPCU, AIM, Commercial Training Director, Allstate Insurance Company; Frank J. Pellegrino, CPCU, Director, Motors Re Management Corporation; John A. Quinlan, FCAS, Actuary, The Hartford Insurance Group; Penny L. Quinn, AU, Senior Account Underwriter, Allstate Insurance Company; James Rugh, AU, Manager, Sales Promotion, The Hanover Insurance Companies; Jack L. Spring, AU, Senior Underwriter, Horace Mann Educators; David C. Sterling, CPCU, CLU, ChFC, CIC, AU, AIM, ARM, ALCM, APA, AAI, ARP, AIC, Secretary, The Hartford Insurance Group; Thomas C. Tenerowicz, CPCU, AU, Underwriting Manager, Eastern Casualty Insurance Company; Kent Van Schoonhoven, CPCU, ARM, AIM, ARP, Commercial Underwriting Training Manager, Allstate Insurance Company; and William L. Venable, CPCU, AU, AIM, Consultant.

Three of the above-mentioned reviewers also assisted in the rewrite of several sections of the text in the third edition. The authors gratefully acknowledge this assistance by Deborah J. Conley, James Rugh, and Kent Van Schoonhoven.

The authors wish to offer their thanks to those members of the Institute staff who have been involved in this project. They literally transformed a rough manuscript into a book.

Finally, special acknowledgment goes to contributing authors who are listed elsewhere in this text.

The authors accept full responsibility for all errors and omissions. It would be greatly appreciated if readers would send us their criticisms and suggestions so that the next edition can be improved.

J. J. Launie
J. Finley Lee
Norman A. Baglini

Contributing Authors

The Insurance Institute of America and the authors acknowledge, with deep appreciation, the help of the following contributing authors of the first edition whose position papers and ideas were used as the basis of several chapters and whose contributions made this book possible:

Ellis H. Carson, FCII (Deceased)
Author and Consultant

Bob A. Hedges, Ph.D., CPCU, CLU
Chairman and Professor of Risk
Management and Insurance
Temple University

E. P. Hollingsworth, CPCU, ARM
Vice President
Frank B. Hall & Co., Inc.

Paul J. Kelley, CPCU
Senior Vice President
Johnson & Higgins of Virginia, Inc.

Raymond M. Normann, CPCU, AIM
Commercial Training Director
Allstate Insurance Company

R. B. Reynolds, Jr., RHU, FLMI
Assistant Vice President
The Centennial Life Insurance Company

William H. Rodda, CPCU
Editor
Best's Underwriting Newsletter

Table of Contents

The Underwriter's Role in Rate Making ~ *Development of Data; Development of Certain Rates; Rate Analysis*

Summary

Chapter 8—Pricing, Continued 279

The Rating Process ~ *Rate Manuals; Classification: A Critical Part of the Process; Factors Not Included in Rates*

Property and Liability Insurance Pricing: The Differences ~ *Introduction; Regulatory Controls; Rating in Property Insurance; Rating in Liability Insurance; Deductibles; Expenses*

Individual Rating Plans ~ *Background; Experience Rating; Schedule Rating; Retrospective Rating; Expense Modification; Participating Plans; Composite Rating*

Rate Making and Pricing Problems and Their Impact on Underwriting ~ *The Data; Inflation; Territorial Imbalances; Improper Classification Systems; The Long Tail Problem; Regulatory Constraints; Credibility of Loss Data*

Summary

Chapter 9—Analysis of Underwriting Information/Financial Analysis 315

Information Needs ~ *Identification of Crucial Risk Characteristics or Hazards; Determination of Possible Measurements; Acquisition of the Necessary Information*

Data Requirements: Personal Lines Versus Commercial Lines ~ *Physical Inspection Reports; Moral Reports; Financial Reports*

Evaluation of Information ~ *Utility Analysis; Cost-Benefit Analysis*

Financial Data as an Underwriting Variable ~ *Indicator of Potential Moral and Morale Hazard; Indicator of Ability to Pay Premiums; Indicator of Financial Strength and Sound Management; Indicator of Potential Growth and Possible Future Desirability from an Underwriting Standpoint.*

CHAPTER 1

Underwriting Objectives, Activities, and Organization

INTRODUCTION

Most definitions of insurance contain two fundamental ideas: first, insurance involves a transfer of risk for a consideration; second, insurance seeks to achieve a spread of similar risks subject to the same peril to increase predictability of losses. These basic insurance concepts produce the need for underwriters.

To understand the implication of these ideas, it is necessary to consider several terms, two of which have already been used, risk and peril. Perhaps the most troublesome insurance term is risk. Risk is used in many ways, depending on the context in which the term is being used. In this book, "risk" will have one of three meanings and the context in which the term is used will determine its precise meaning.

First, risk means the subject of insurance—the person(s) or object(s) insured. For example, a reference to improving the "risk" means improving the subject of insurance, an insured building, perhaps. A reference to investigating the "risk" means investigating the applicant for insurance. This usage conflicts with most textbook definitions of risk, but a book written for underwriters must use terms as they are used in the field.

Second, risk means the variability in future losses, not the chance of loss. If it were certain that a specific building would burn next month, the owner of that building would not be subject to risk, but would be confronted with the certainty of a loss. The greater the variability in future outcomes, the less certainty one has about what the outcomes will be, and the riskier the situation becomes. Thus,

1

absence of certainty is sometimes given as a definition of risk and is another way of looking at this second definition. (A later chapter will discuss the measurement of risk.)

Third, risk means an exposure to potential occurrences that could result in economic loss or human suffering.[1] This is the way the term risk is used in risk management. Thus, the duty of the risk manager is to "manage risk" and work to avoid or reduce loss or suffering.

A peril is a cause of loss. In property, common perils are fire, lightning, windstorm, explosion, and smoke. Although peril has been used throughout the history of insurance, some newer property insurance policies use the term "cause of loss" in lieu of "peril." Perils may be defined in the insurance contract or determined by common or statutory law.

Two additional terms which will be used throughout this book are loss exposure (or simply exposure) and hazard. *A loss exposure is a condition of susceptibility or vulnerability to loss—that is, the possibility of loss.* Persons purchase insurance because they have a loss exposure. If there were no loss exposure, there would be no need for insurance. The term loss exposure includes both the probability of a loss occurring (frequency) and the dollar amount of a loss should it occur (severity). A loss exposure exists if there is a possibility of a loss occurring and if such an occurrence would cause a financial loss.

A hazard is anything that tends to increase the probable frequency or severity of losses. The hazards of concern to underwriters are those that are related to losses caused by insured perils.

Some insurance practitioners use the terms "peril" and "hazard" interchangeably. An example will illustrate the terms as used in this book. A commercial building is subject to the *peril* of fire. The practice of storing oily rags in cardboard boxes inside that building is a *hazard:* this practice tends to increase the probable frequency or severity of losses caused by the peril of fire. Hazards can be divided into three classes: physical, moral, and morale. (These hazards are examined fully in a later chapter.)

Originally, underwriters were individuals who accepted risk transfers and backed them with their own fortunes: the underwriter was the insurer. Lloyd's of London, a collection of individuals who accept risks on their own account, preserves this practice. With the formation of corporate rather than individual insurers came the ability to (1) achieve a spread of similar risks subject to the same peril and (2) increase the predictability of losses. Top management began to delegate underwriting to specialized underwriting departments. Nonetheless, in any insurer, regardless of size or type, ultimate underwriting responsibility and the determination of underwriting policy rest with top management. *As used in this book, underwriting is defined as deciding which risks are acceptable, determining the premium to be charged and the terms and conditions of the insurance contract, and the monitoring of those decisions.*

There are many persons involved in underwriting. They range from the producer to the Senior Vice President of Underwriting for an insurer. A producer is often called the front (or first) line underwriter. (The underwriting performed by the producer is covered in more detail later in this chapter.) The extent to which the persons in this range are involved in underwriting varies. Although this book is written primarily from the viewpoint of an underwriter with an insurance company, anyone involved in underwriting can benefit from this book.

UNDERWRITING OBJECTIVES

An insurance company can fulfill its commitments to its insureds, stockholders, employees, and the community at large only if it is financially sound. Underwriting, as one of the major departments of the insurance company, does its part to see that the insurer meets its survival goal. *Specifically, the major goal of underwriting is the selection and maintenance of a profitable, growing book of business.* A book of business, or simply book, is the set of all the policies currently in force with an insurer of a particular kind of insurance (for example, personal auto or workers' compensation), a certain class of business or perhaps all the policies written by the insurer. An example would be the national book of general liability insurance for an insurer that could be subdivided into regional books by branch office. Another example might be the book of business of all construction contractors.

There are a number of underwriting objectives or subgoals related to this major goal: (1) to provide proper coverage; (2) to maintain selection standards; (3) to maintain pricing standards; and (4) to maintain high standards of professional competence. Attainment of these objectives is not reached without obstacles and hard work. One such obstacle occurs when these objectives conflict with the insurer's social responsibility objectives.

Just as the underwriter has the objective of providing coverage, the insurer, in order to be responsible to society, has a similar but broader objective of providing coverage to as wide a range of persons as possible without jeopardizing the financial stability of the insurer. In some cases, the insurer's social responsibility to provide coverage to persons conflicts with the underwriter's objective of maintaining selection standards. For example, auto insurance is compulsory in many states. Insurers, being part of the industry responsible for providing insurance, are asked to insure some persons who have been rejected in the normal underwriting process (sometimes described as having been *denied access to the voluntary market*), but who must get coverage somewhere since it is required. This dilemma led to the establishing of auto insurance (assigned risk) plans as part of the shared or residual market (that is, the market for those risks who have been denied coverage through normal channels).

Provide Proper Coverage

Providing proper coverage is a primary underwriting objective. Proper coverage can be said to be providing insurance protection at a profit while meeting the wants and needs of the insurance buying public. Often, these needs can be met by providing a fairly standardized coverage. However, the underwriter must remain flexible enough to meet the needs of insureds with unique hazards.

Every firm must have something to offer the public. For insurers, the product is insurance coverage. Underwriters must keep this in mind when they are dealing with producers and insureds. The underwriter's creativity should be used to find ways to *accept* business. Although this "creativity" is limited at times by rate filings, insurance company rules, and so on, there is often some leeway.

The objective is to provide the *proper* coverage. (This coverage must also be provided "at the right price," an objective that will be addressed shortly.) Underwriters must always be aware of what is happening in the environment and make sure that the coverages offered reflect those changes. Some specific examples are coverage (or exclusions) for citizen band radios in autos and for home computers.

Underwriters must offer a product that is wanted or needed by the insurance-buying public. For many coverages, the public buys a fairly standard set of coverages with minor modifications. On the other hand, some insureds have unique exposures that require special attention.

An underwriter may, at first glance, think that providing very narrow coverage to only a few select insureds would be desirable since the loss ratio would be very favorable. However, if coverage is too narrow, very few persons will purchase it. Narrow coverage and strict selection standards would inhibit the development of a sizable volume of business. An insurer needs business to survive. This is not to say that underwriters should give everyone the broadest possible coverage, but underwriters should remember that if they do not provide proper coverage, the applicant will go elsewhere.

Maintain Selection Standards

Another underwriting objective is to maintain proper selection standards. Underwriters make the accept or reject decision. With that decision comes a lot of responsibility, including the responsibility to maintain selection standards. This does *not* mean that underwriters should accept only "perfect" risks. If the insurance product is priced properly, the "average" risk will also generate a profit for the insurer in the long run.

Maintenance of selection standards should cause an insurer to avoid the consequences of adverse selection. *Adverse selection means there is a disproportionately large share of applicants for insurance who have an above average probability of loss compared to those with an average or below average probability of loss.* Adverse selection is more prevalent for some types of insurance, such as flood, than others. For example, when insurers offer flood insurance as a separate policy, only those persons with serious flood exposures are likely to purchase the coverage. Those near the top of Mount St. Helens do not want flood coverage while those along the Mississippi River in New Orleans do. (But offer volcanic action coverage and watch the opposite occur.)

Because of adverse selection, an underwriter must "select or be selected against." Otherwise, the business written will be primarily "worse than average" risks from a probability of loss standpoint. The results could be disastrous.

Maintain Pricing Standards

Although rates are usually determined by a rating bureau, underwriters still have input into the rate-making process. *A rate is the price per exposure unit for an insurance coverage. The exposure unit is the fundamental measure of the possibility of loss assumed by an insurer.* Underwriters classify risks and apply rates. Any errors will be reflected in future rates. The term "garbage in - garbage out" used in conjunction with computers is appropriate here. If risks are misclassified or misrated, future rates and premiums will be incorrect.

Underwriters have some leeway in granting rate debits and credits. Underwriters should be judicious in the application of these, but a competitive environment will influence their use. If other insurers offer rate credits, it is not likely that insureds will accept a debit. Still, if rate credits are abused and are applied strictly for competitive reasons and not to reflect actual differences in exposure as intended, the credibility of future rates is undermined.

The balance between proper use of credits and debits and their use in response to competition is difficult for an individual underwriter to achieve. Much will depend on competition at the time and the insurer's short run objectives. A later chapter will go into more detail about the underwriting cycle which aggravates this problem.

By consistently maintaining the proper pricing standards, underwriters are able to provide a relatively stable market. Producers and insureds are confused and sometimes angered by wide fluctuations in underwriting policy and the prices charged. It gives little assurance to an insured about the soundness of an underwriter's decision when the insured is told, "Your business has been profitable and therefore deserves a rate credit," and a year later is told, "Your business is no longer acceptable even though you had few or no losses during the year." Similarly, giving a 50 percent rate credit one year and then doubling the rates the next, regardless of individual experience, is quite unsettling to producers and insureds. To the extent possible, reductions in the availability of coverage and fluctuations in premiums for that coverage unrelated to experience should be kept to a minimum.

Maintain A High Level Of Professional Competence

Many persons have attempted to define "professional" or "profession." While there is usually agreement that doctors, lawyers, and accountants are professionals, there is not agreement on the specific characteristics or traits necessary for professional status. Dr. Ronald C. Horn has described one set of characteristics of a profession as:

1. A Commitment to High Ethical Standards
2. A Prevailing Attitude of Altruism
3. Mandatory Educational Preparation and Training
4. Mandatory Continuing Education
5. A Formal Association or Society
6. Independence
7. Public Recognition as a Profession[2]

Although there is debate on the characteristics of a profession and whether the insurance industry should be considered a profession, there is little doubt that the persons within the industry vary in the degree of "professionalism" they exhibit. Underwriters should strive at all times to be more professional in their activities by staying current on insurance topics, continuing their education, conducting their duties and handling problems in a professional manner, approaching the job with a professional attitude, and by accomplishing their objectives.

This professional conduct and attitude will likely be rewarded in the long run with a more professional and honest relationship with producers and insureds. Underwriters must "service what they sell."

This service begins the moment an application is completed and continues throughout the period of time that the person or firm is insured. Professionalism in this service includes prompt action on the application, accurate and prompt policy issuance, prompt and accurate answers to questions, and so on.

Professionalism in an underwriter's service to producers is broader than that to insureds. Underwriters answer producers' questions, explain underwriting guidelines, review producer results and recommend prompt and reasonable corrective action. In each of these dealings with producers, underwriters have an opportunity to display professionalism.

UNDERWRITING ACTIVITIES

The activities performed by underwriters to meet these objectives are many. Underwriting activities can be divided into two groups. First, some activities are common or universal to all underwriters. Second, there are additional activities performed by some, but not all, underwriters.

Activities Performed by All Underwriters

Hazard Identification and Evaluation Underwriters must identify and evaluate the hazards associated with the loss exposures of applicants. That is, underwriters must first determine those conditions that will increase the frequency or severity of losses. For example, if an applicant for auto insurance owns an auto which has defective brakes, that hazard is likely to increase the frequency or severity of a loss. Manufacturers using dangerous chemicals, such as lead, present a serious possibility of a workers' compensation loss through employees suffering lead poisoning. Once such a hazard is identified, the underwriter must then evaluate how dangerous the chemical is, the ways it can escape, the precautions taken to prevent overexposure, employee training in the use of the chemical, and so on. Each of these factors affects the probable frequency and severity of employee lead poisoning and, therefore, of workers' compensation losses.

The underwriter must evaluate the totality of the situation and determine whether all of the hazards, in combination, raise the probability of loss to an unacceptable level. What is unacceptable? Once the hazards are identified and evaluated, the underwriter must compare these hazards with similar risks. How does this manufacturer compare with other manufacturers of the same product? What is the workers' compensation loss experience throughout the industry for manufacturers of the same product? This comparison should determine whether the risk in question is above or below average—one indication of acceptability.

While the definition of hazard is seemingly negative in that it is defined as something that would increase the probable frequency or severity of losses, a hazard evaluation also looks at those positive steps the applicant has taken to try to control these hazards. An applicant for commercial insurance may be considered "above average" if it has implemented a sound loss control program, is financially strong, and the owners have a sound reputation. Conversely, a similar risk may be considered "below average" because it has not undertaken any loss control measures, has lost money for the last five years, and the owners have questionable reputations.

Pricing Another underwriting activity that leads to the selection decision is the pricing of insurance. A below average risk may be made acceptable and profitable because of premium increases. On the other hand, there may be no pricing flexibility if the premium is established by a rating manual for all of the risks of this type. If the premium is adequate only for risks which are average or better, those risks which are below average are not likely to be written.

In the majority of cases, pricing involves the proper classification of the applicant's exposures and the application of rates to the exposure units (rating). *The premium is the product of the rate times the number of exposure units* (for example, a rate times each $1,000 of payroll for general liability insurance).

Proper classification is of utmost importance. Part of the risk selection decision is based on a comparison of the premium developed with the exposures and hazards presented. Proper classification is also important since future rates are based on the experience under current rates and rating classifications.

A second aspect of pricing is the proper application of rates to the exposure units. Exposure units must be accurately determined and the proper rate applied to these units. While computerization has helped with this process and reduced mathematical errors, the computer only uses the information it is given. If the classification code is input incorrectly, the error will not be detected by the computer. If any individual rating plan (for example, experience rating) applies, it must be used only with the eligible applicants.

As risk characteristics or hazards change over time, rating classes must be modified to reflect those changes. For example, the introduction of high impact plastics for car bodies as well as unibody construction have affected auto physical damage classification and rate making. Likewise, the changing legal environment in products liability and environmental pollution have had an effect on acceptability and rating classes as well as policy wording. Underwriters play a crucial role in seeing that loss statistics are accurately reported by rating class and that risks are properly classified so that appropriate adjustments can be made.

While actuaries determine the rates to be used, underwriters are still an important part of the process. The manner in which current premiums are determined will affect future rates based on these premiums. Additionally, for some unusual loss exposures or risks, underwriters actually determine the rates to be used based on experience, judgment, and guidelines established by the insurer (these rates are called judgment rates). In this case, the underwriter is the ratemaker as well as the rater.

Determination of Policy Terms and Conditions Closely intertwined with the pricing and risk selection decision is the determination of policy terms and conditions. In some cases this is simply a matter of providing the applicant with the requested coverage through use of a standard form and attachments with no modifying endorsements. In other cases, extensive negotiations with the applicant over policy coverages, conditions, requirements, deductibles, exclusions, and endorsements might be involved. The final result may be coverage which is very different from that offered by a standard policy.

Risk Selection Decision When making the risk selection decision, the underwriter must simultaneously consider the exposures, hazards, policy terms and conditions, and the premium. These factors should not be considered in isolation except in extreme cases where perhaps one factor is so bad that the underwriter will not accept the application, no matter how "favorable" the other factors. The reverse is not true in that no one factor can be so good as to make the applicant acceptable regardless of the other factors.

Given all necessary information about the exposures, the hazards, the premium, and the policy terms and conditions, the underwriter must make a decision. Yes or no are obviously two choices, but often the underwriter will say, "no, unless ..." or "yes, if ...." It could be that a request for some loss control device will make the risk acceptable. In these cases, the underwriter has basically said, "If you do this, the coverage will be provided." It is important that underwriters be willing and able to make a decision and, if nothing changes in the meantime, stand by that decision. If the underwriter says "yes, if ...," he or she should not back out on that agreement once the "if" is fulfilled.

Every effort should be made to determine all "ifs" early and spell them out in the first communication. Additional conditions or requests are little more than an effort by the underwriter to avoid making a decision.

Selection serves two major purposes. First, without risk selection insurers would be adversely selected against by applicants who present loss exposures greater than those assumed in the rate (or premium). Second, risk selection helps insurers achieve production and underwriting goals. It enables them to obtain a profitable and proper spread of business by geographical area and by class of business. (Class of business should be distinguished from rating class. *A class of business is a grouping of insureds possessing the same characteristic[s].* Some examples would include contractors, youthful drivers, and restaurants. Often a class of business will encompass more than one rating class.) This spread helps insurers avoid catastrophic losses and also permits the sale of insurance to a large segment of the market.

If every risk were either obviously "good" or obviously "poor," and if the probability of loss could be easily predicted for each, selection would be an easy matter and no doubt could be computerized (in some cases, obviously poor and obviously good risks are identified by computer already). However, the vast majority of risks fall between the extremes of "good" and "poor," and the probability of loss for an individual risk cannot be predicted with mathematical precision. Consequently, there is a definite need for underwriters to determine and maintain a profitable spread of business through risk selection.

Risk classification systems are used by many insurers to guide underwriters in the selection of business. Some insurers group classes of business such as long-haul truckers or restaurants according to the degree of acceptability (that is, good, average, or poor) while others rely primarily on a "decline" list which outlines the classes of business that should not be written. *The procedure of categorizing classes of business according to acceptability has been called class underwriting.*

This is in contrast to considering each submission on its own merits regardless of the class of business in which it belongs. The majority of underwriters and insurers employ a combination of these two approaches for several reasons. On one hand, pure class underwriting fails to consider the above-average risks present in each class of business. Above-average risks present loss exposures that are less severe than expected in the class and may be profitably underwritten. On the other hand, underwriting each risk individually fails to consider the experiences of previous underwriters handling the class of business. Each class of business has particular hazards and unique characteristics that cannot be totally disregarded in an evaluation of a single risk. The same errors may be made over and over during the evaluation process if the underwriter fails to compare the individual risk to the "average" risk for the class.

Monitoring and Servicing the Account Once a decision is made to accept a risk, the underwriter's task is not complete. The policy(ies) must be issued properly and the account must be serviced and monitored. *An account is the set of insurance coverages held by an insured.* Servicing might include processing endorsements, making required filings with the state, assistance in explaining coverages, and so on. At renewal time, the account must sometimes be underwritten again to see if there have been any changes in exposures or hazards or changes in the coverage being provided that would affect the acceptability of the account. In other cases, the account is renewed automatically with no new underwriting taking place.

The underwriter must also monitor the loss experience for the account both at renewal and during the year. The monitoring may require that the account be canceled or nonrenewed, that there be a change in coverage and/or premiums at renewal, or that the risk be reunderwritten. If reunderwriting is indicated at renewal, the underwriter repeats the entire underwriting process that was performed when the account was first submitted. This time, the underwriter has additional information available on premiums and losses to help in the renewal decision.

Activities Performed by Some Underwriters

The following activities are those performed by some underwriters but which are not common or universal to all underwriters. This is not to say that these activities are not important. Their importance will vary by insurer. It may also be that these activities are the ones that distinguish one insurer from another in terms of services offered—that is, the competitive advantage. Also, some of these activities may be more common at the underwriting management level.

Risk Management Services As will be described in a later chapter, underwriting is very closely related to risk management. Much of underwriting involves making coverage recommendations. In some cases, if the recommendation had been made by the risk manager of the firm, the decision would have been labeled a risk management decision and not an underwriting decision. Deductibles are a good example. To assist in maintaining a profitable book of business, underwriters often recommend self-insured retentions and the creative use of deductibles. Many medium- to large-sized property and liability risks now utilize various types of retention programs and an assortment of different types and amounts of deductibles. Regardless of who initiated the recommendation, the judicious use of retention and deductibles can aid significantly both in providing adequate coverage at an appropriate price and in solving many underwriting problems. Their use also aids insureds in meeting their risk management objectives.

Risk management services involving underwriters also include loss control and claims management provided primarily to large accounts. These services are either offered without charge in an attempt to acquire and hold new business, or on a fee basis to generate income independent of insurance coverages sold. A large account, for example, might retain or "self-insure" its workers' compensation exposure, but purchase both loss control and claims management services from insurers (perhaps in combination with some form of excess insurance).

The broadening range of risk management services offered by insurers has caused underwriters to become more actively involved in these areas. In some cases, the underwriter may work with a firm's risk manager, helping make risk management decisions regarding the handling of various exposures (for example, reduce the exposure or retain the exposure).

The implementation of the loss control program however is still primarily the responsibility of the insurer's engineering department (sometimes called the safety engineering or loss control department). The fundamental purpose of loss control is the reduction in the total cost of losses. Insurers are obviously most interested in the total cost of *insured* losses and the prevention of losses in the first place. To assist in providing this service, underwriters must be conversant with the impact of loss control programs and techniques and be able to recognize and explain this impact on losses. Underwriters may also be called upon to assist in monitoring the loss control programs implemented by the engineering department, possibly through some type of claims review.

Marketing All underwriters have some indirect marketing responsibility. In general, an underwriter's attitude towards prospective business should be a positive one. Underwriters do *not* look for ways to decline business but to find ways to make marginal business acceptable by creatively suggesting improvements or changes in the form, conditions, loss control, physical characteristics, or rates applicable to the submission. In this sense, underwriting plays a vital role in marketing and in the production of properly priced business.

In addition to this indirect marketing responsibility, some underwriters are now becoming much more directly involved in the marketing of business. These underwriters have production or marketing goals to meet and these goals are considered just as important as any profitability goals the underwriter might have. In fact, the title of some underwriters has been changed to "account representative," "account manager" (note that the term *underwriter* is not even used), or "production underwriter." The position of "special agent" or "field representative" may have been eliminated and the duties combined with those of the underwriter.

This change in emphasis has met with mixed reaction within the insurance industry. Some experienced underwriters feel that it is important that underwriters recognize their marketing responsibilities, and giving the underwriter specific marketing goals is one of the best ways to do so. Others agree that marketing is important, but that the primary emphasis of the underwriter should be on "underwriting" and not marketing. In their opinion, combining the two only dilutes each function.

Regardless of whether the underwriter has specific marketing goals, underwriters in many insurers are spending more and more time in the field with producers both at the initial prospecting stage and as part of account servicing. Observing a risk in person may help the underwriter make a more accurate evaluation of the risk's acceptability. Further, the underwriter's expertise can often be of use to the producer in making a sale. Finally, although underwriting is primarily accomplished in the office, encouraging the underwriters to get out into the field helps them to better understand what producers do and helps them to visualize the operations and hazards of the accounts they underwrite.

Product Design Another underwriting activity deals with the creation of special policies to fit particular needs, such as drafting an unusual contract for unique exposures. This insurance contract is called a manuscript policy. *A manuscript policy is one written specifically for a particular risk or risks.* Manuscript policies are most often used in inland marine insurance and with large accounts.

Not all underwriters issue manuscript policies but most are involved in product design in the sense of the earlier description of "determining policy terms and conditions." A manuscript policy might be viewed as the "ultimate" determination of policy terms and conditions. In general, product design is highly specialized and requires a great deal of expertise and knowledge in contract language, law, and state insurance department regulations. Creating a policy "from scratch" is much more difficult than piecing together a policy from forms and endorsements already created by others.

Another aspect of product design is the periodic modification of standard forms. As laws change, there is a need to alter current policies or create new ones. For example, the preference for claims-made liability forms by Lloyd's of London underwriters and other reinsurers necessitated the revision of standard general liability policies.

The design of products is very important from two standpoints. First, the wording obviously determines what coverage is being offered, whether intended or not. Secondly, the design of the product will influence its marketability. If coverage is too narrow, there may be no market and if it is too broad, there may be more demand for the product than intended, possibly creating a servicing problem. Procedures for the use of policies and forms must also be created.

Creation of Rating Programs   Although many insurance companies use rating programs created by bureaus, competition often forces them to develop special rating programs of their own. Insurers sometimes prepare and, where necessary, file their own rating programs with the state insurance departments. Insurers deviating from bureau rates must determine the amount of the deviation. Actuaries work with underwriters in determining the deviations, given the insurer's underwriting policy.

Preparation of Underwriting Manuals   Established underwriting policy must be communicated to the field, usually in the form of underwriting manuals or guides (guidelines). These manuals describe underwriting selection standards as well as required procedures and often list factors which the underwriter must evaluate, such as the insured's financial standing. Underwriting manuals generally tell what to look for, but the final judgment of acceptability is left to an underwriter.

While the preparation of these manuals is usually by a home office underwriter, field underwriters participate in their preparation through feedback to underwriting management. If underwriters find some requirement or procedure unrealistic, given current marketing conditions, they can inform higher level underwriters of the problem. In addition, as underwriters discover unusual underwriting problems, they should be invited to inform underwriting management so other underwriters can be alerted through the underwriting manual.

Participation in Bureaus and Associations   Each insurer has an industry commitment it must meet. The combined thinking of many qualified people often produces solutions to common problems such as the residual or shared market programs that offer coverage to those who are not able to obtain coverage through "normal channels." In addition, there are many committees and bureaus at both the national and state levels which meet to discuss common problems and solutions.

Formulation and Monitoring of Broad Underwriting Policy   To meet an insurance company's growth and profit objectives, markets must be selected carefully. This selection is often handled jointly by the underwriting and marketing departments. One important consideration would be what geographical areas provide the most profitable business opportunities. Another consideration would be the establishment of selection standards at current rate levels within various lines of insurance such as the number of auto accidents and violations that would be acceptable in personal auto insurance applications.

While this is primarily a management activity, the underwriter again participates through noting trends, opportunities, or problems and passing this information along to management. It is the underwriter who implements the underwriting policy and, thus, it is the underwriter who makes it work.

Underwriting policy must be monitored once it is implemented. Underwriting management must determine if the policy is being followed. Often insurers will use field review teams to visit local underwriting offices to "audit" or review their operations. Individual files may be reviewed to determine if files are properly documented, if the selection standards are being followed, and if underwriting procedures are being followed. Often this review becomes a part of the underwriter's performance appraisal.

COOPERATION WITH OTHER DEPARTMENTS

An insurer's efficiency depends in large part on the successful cooperation of its different departments. Underwriters must deal with other departments frequently, and it is essential that sound working relationships be maintained. This relationship benefits both parties as well as the insurer as a whole.

Marketing

The marketing department is responsible for the insurer's production goals. However, these goals cannot be reached if the underwriting department becomes overly selective and declines much of the business submitted. The underwriting department should be cognizant of production goals and should participate in the achievement of them. The list of underwriting activities given earlier points out that, in some cases, underwriters themselves are being held responsible for production goals. Additionally, the marketing and underwriting departments usually work together in establishing underwriting and marketing policies for the insurer.

In cases where additional information is needed to issue a policy or endorsement or where a policy must be canceled, the underwriter and the producer must work together. While underwriters are not usually considered salespeople, they must "sell" their decisions to producers to maintain a working relationship. If an underwriter makes no effort to sell decisions and convince the producer that they are correct, the producer may in turn make no effort to submit further business.

Also, the underwriting department contributes to the training of the sales force by communicating selection standards to producers. These standards aid producers in the submission of profitable, acceptable business and should reduce the number of risks that must be declined. A later chapter describes this in more detail. The achievement of production goals requires that producers and underwriters work together as both sales and underwriting partners.

Actuarial

The actuarial department, which in some cases is an integral part of the underwriting department, is responsible for gathering the data necessary to evaluate how the insurer's rates and rating plans are performing in practice. If changes are necessary, the actuarial department is responsible for making those changes and assuring that the changes are indicated by the results. In addition, the actuarial department is responsible for reporting statistics regarding the filed rates and rating plans to the rating bureaus and to the regulatory authorities, as well as for use in the insurer's annual statement. Thus, the interest of the actuarial department is primarily in how the insurer's entire book of business is performing rather than how individual risks are performing.

There is little regular communication between the underwriter and the actuarial department. Most of the communications between underwriting and actuarial personnel is at the upper management levels. Once a rate is offered to the public (promulgated is the term used), the underwriter is responsible for applying that rate. It is the underwriter who puts the rates and rating plans developed by the actuary into practice. If the underwriter fails to use the systems as intended, the data given back to the actuarial department will be faulty. Similarly, if the rates or rating systems themselves have flaws, it is the underwriter who is often the first to discover these flaws. Underwriters are also in the best position to see the marketing impact of new rates and rating plans.

There are occasions when direct communication between actuaries and the underwriter is necessary. If an underwriter desires further information about the statistics behind a certain rating plan, it is to the actuarial department that the underwriter often turns. Although underwriters should understand the basics behind the rating plans used, more specific details can be obtained from the actuarial department. On occasion, actuarial personnel conduct studies on a particular subject that requires information found in the underwriting file. It may be necessary for the actuary to work with underwriters to understand some of the information in the file.

Claims

The claims and underwriting departments work very closely servicing accounts. Claims representatives often ask underwriters to clarify the intent of certain coverages as part of an overall review of losses or with regard to a specific claim. This might be to determine what items are insured or to look for supporting records such as appraisals which might be in the underwriting file. For example, if the producer believes that collision coverage was requested on a specific car, but the policy does not show such coverage, the underwriter can assist by reviewing the application or correspondence to see what coverages were requested and provided.

On the other hand, the claims department is the source of loss data that are used to formulate underwriting policy and determine the renewal premium to be charged to some insureds. Claims personnel can be a valuable source of monitoring information during the policy term. For example, an adjuster settling a workers' compensation claim may notice that safety rules are not being followed. When this is communicated to the underwriter, corrective follow-up action can be taken. Additionally, adjusters might observe significant exposures of which the underwriter is unaware involving several lines of insurance and not just the specific line of insurance under which the claim was filed. (*A line of insurance or line of business means a major segment of insurance coverages such as commercial auto liability or general liability.*) Improved underwriting results and better service to producers and insureds result from cooperation between the claims and underwriting departments.

Premium Audit

Many commercial insurance policies are issued on an estimated premium basis. That is, the premium paid by the insured at the beginning of the policy period is a deposit premium only and the final premium is not determined until after the policy period has ended. The final premium (also known as the audited premium) is usually the rate (which is expressed per exposure unit in the manual) times the number of exposure units. In some cases the exposure unit might be each $1,000 of sales, while in others it might be each $100 of remuneration.

For example, workers' compensation premiums are based upon the insured's remuneration (the exposure unit being $100 of remuneration). *Remuneration is therefore called the exposure base, or simply the denomination in which the exposure unit is expressed.* An exposure base should be an accurate measure of the exposure to loss, should be easy for the insurer to determine, and should be difficult for the insured to manipulate.[3]

Remuneration is a good indicator of the workers' compensation exposure presented by an insured (workers' compensation benefits are often based on a worker's salary). For general liability, payroll and gross sales are the predominant exposure bases.

Insureds cannot know in advance the precise amount of remuneration, payroll, or gross sales they will have during the upcoming policy period. Therefore, they estimate these figures at the beginning of the policy period and after the policy has expired, the insurer usually sends its premium auditors out to "audit" the insured's books and determine the exact amount of payroll or gross sales during the policy period. In some cases with smaller accounts, the insurer may send a form to the insured to complete with the necessary information rather than incurring the expense of a visit by a premium auditor. If the initial estimate was too low, the insured is billed for an additional premium. If the estimate was too high, the insured receives a return premium.

Underwriters can help premium auditors perform their jobs by making sure that the proper rating classifications are shown on the policy and that estimates are as accurate as possible. The policy should clearly reflect what exposure base (often called a *premium base* in the manual and policy) is being used to determine the premium. While it is primarily the producer's job to make sure that the insured understands that the policy is on an audit basis, that an auditor may visit the insured's premises after the policy expires, and that the insured's books should be available, the underwriter should be sure this is the case.

In turn, the premium auditor like the claims adjuster, is able to observe firsthand some of the insured's operations and the condition of the insured's premises. If the auditor observes any unsafe practices or conditions, he or she can alert the underwriter. More importantly, the auditor may observe exposures that have been overlooked or misclassified when the policy was written and can report any changes or contemplated changes in operations. Although the changes that have taken place are shown in the audit, the auditor can make a note to the underwriter about the changes that might be about to occur or any trends noted that might not be obvious from just looking at the audit figures. In this way, the underwriter can take any necessary action to handle the new exposures (perhaps through loss control or an endorsement to the policy). For example, the audit may show a small amount of sales for a new classification indicating the manufacture of a new product. The underwriter might consider this insignificant until the auditor points out that the insured intends this new product to replace the old product entirely.

In some cases, the underwriter may wish to ask a premium auditor to visit the insured's premises with the loss control representative and determine the proper rating classifications and estimates to use for a new insured. This might be necessary when there is a question about the proper rating class, or the estimates to use, or perhaps as more of a service visit to give the insured instructions on how best to keep its books (this type of visit also saves many headaches when the actual audit is conducted).

Finally, once the audit is completed, the underwriter uses the information in the audit to evaluate the estimates made on the renewal policy. Rating classes may have changed and the audit may reveal substantially different payrolls or gross sales from that shown on the renewal policy. If warranted, the underwriter may wish to endorse the renewal policy to reflect the correct figures or rating classes.

Loss Control

The inspector or loss control representative is often called the "eyes" of the underwriter. Quality loss control service is needed to obtain the information necessary for proper evaluation of submissions. Requests for surveys should be clear and accurate—specific requests usually produce the best information. For a restaurant risk, a request for a check on "housekeeping," for example, is not as effective as a request to "check for grease accumulation in the hood and ducts over the range."

Risks that do not meet the company's underwriting standards may be made acceptable through the proper use of loss control services. Underwriters are in a position to aid the loss control representative by noting any obvious trends in losses from a particular cause or in a particular location. These should be mentioned in the request for loss control service. Loss control representatives also become very familiar with the operations of the insured and can answer many of the underwriter's questions about the risk which will help in selection, classification, and pricing.

Data Processing

With the vast number of policyholders in the United States today, recordkeeping would be more cumbersome without computerized methods of storage and retrieval. Often the underwriting department is the major source of data for the computer. If the computer outputs are to be reliable, information must be relayed accurately from the underwriting department to the data processing (or electronic data processing—EDP) department.

Computer programs can be designed to meet underwriting requirements once these are made known. Working with data processing people, insurers can obtain loss and hazard information quickly and accurately. As computer programs are established, it is essential that the EDP department work closely with the users of that program (often the underwriter) to see that the appropriate information is collected in a manner to be of the greatest use by the end user. For example, computer programs storing policy data should be set up so that information can be accessed by both policy number and by the insured's name. Underwriters, in turn, must be aware of the limitations as well as the capabilities of the computer so that they can better relay reasonable requests to the programmer.

With increasing loss frequency and severity in such coverages as products liability, immediate access to loss data is critical. Underwriters should become familiar with their data processing facilities in order to use them effectively.

Policyholders' Service

In large insurance companies, work is subdivided into specialty units. In some, premium computation (rating), policy writing, and statistical coding activities are a part of the underwriting department while in others, these activities are handled outside the underwriting department. In either case, these "service" functions are dependent on instructions from underwriters. Therefore, the *accuracy* of this work will often depend on the underwriting department.

UNDERWRITING ORGANIZATION

Centralization versus Decentralization

Initially, underwriting was centralized in the home offices of insurers. As insurance companies expanded their operations geographically, many found it advantageous to move underwriting closer to the "action," and an era of decentralized underwriting began. More recently, however, there appears to be a move back toward partial centralization of the underwriting function. One cause seems to be the greater use of data processing equipment. With large amounts of business handled in a single location, the computer can be used more efficiently, and the cost is justified by adequate use.

Another cause of centralization is scarcity of experienced people in some lines. With a limited number of truly capable underwriters available, insurers tend to group them together to form functional departments. The underwriting of specialty lines, such as surety bonding, has traditionally been centralized for this reason.

An insurance company's operations are sometimes divided geographically because of differences in state insurance laws. These differences might result in it being necessary to use different policies in different states.

In addition, risks differ widely throughout the country, and this fact requires that underwriters be familiar with the territory in which they underwrite. The importance of various perils also vary by territory (for example, earthquake). The factors involved in underwriting one-story, fire resistive factories in the Midwest are significantly different from those of multi-story, multiple-occupancy "mill-construction" factories in New England. These territorial differences encourage some degree of decentralization.

One of the major factors in the centralization decision is technology. The data processing and communications advances in the recent past have made possible extremely rapid transmission of data from producer to underwriter and from underwriter to home office. This rapid transmission serves to counter the argument that an insurer needs to be centralized for reasons relating to communications among underwriters.

More importantly, however, these advances also counter the argument that underwriters need to be decentralized or near the producer in order to give faster service to the producers. Mail delays are not of concern when the information is being sent via phone lines or satellite. If a producer has the computer capability in his or her office to issue policies, it makes little difference to the producer whether the underwriter giving the OK to issue the policy is located fifteen or fifteen hundred miles away. Many insurers are now trying to take advantage of this by having large regional processing centers for most data processing work related to underwriting.

Delegation of Underwriting Authority Underwriting authority is delegated from the home office to the field in a variety of ways, depending on the type of marketing system being employed, the line and class of business, and the experience and capability of the underwriters and producers. Over the years, underwriting authority has moved back and forth with underwriting results.

In some insurance companies, the degree of authority granted the individual underwriter is slight—the underwriter may simply decide whether a particular risk fits a list of criteria. In others, some underwriters may be given authority to make recommendations for risk improvement (the risk management services activity mentioned earlier) which will, when complied with, make the risk acceptable. Decisions regarding reinsurance may also be within an underwriter's authority. Also, many insurance companies have moved toward giving producers more underwriting authority. But most insurers still have "referral" programs which require that certain classes of business or amounts of insurance be referred by the producer to an underwriter.

Regardless of the amount of authority, one of the most important tools of the underwriter is the underwriting manual. Correct use of it and thorough knowledge of its contents are essential to the proper underwriting of business. It tells in detail the procedures to be followed and the authority given for each type of risk. Therefore, provisions for interpretation and updating must be made.

Underwriting by the Producer

A producer is a marketing person—a person who sells insurance. Producers may be independent agents, exclusive agents, sales personnel of direct writers, or field representatives (special agents). The relationship of the underwriter and producer is a crucial one in the operation of any insurance company. The only insurance marketing system without producers is direct response (mail or telephone).

Even though the primary concern of producers is marketing, they also have an underwriting function to perform. Producers should in effect be field underwriters, recognizing the relative desirability of various types of business. The universality of the underwriting role can be inferred from the fact that the professional designation in the property and liability industry is Chartered Property Casualty *Underwriter.*

A knowledge of underwriting as well as production is essential to the success of any producer, whether in an independent agency, exclusive agency, or direct writing organization. If a producer is unable to recognize undesirable or unacceptable business, then that producer will waste valuable time and resources developing submissions that will ultimately be declined. The producer derives no revenue from business that cannot be placed.

Many insurance companies attempt to motivate producers to emphasize underwriting through the use of reward agreements. Under the terms of such an agreement, the producer may receive additional underwriting authority or compensation above the basic commission based upon the loss ratio of the producer's agency (often there are premium volume requirements). A producer's most important asset is a strong *market* (insurers with which to place business) and failure to properly pre-underwrite business may badly weaken the relationship between producer and insurer.

Producers are very much involved in the underwriting functions of selection and classification. Much time is wasted if producers submit proposals under a rating plan or form for which the risk is not eligible. A producer may submit a workers' compensation risk for retrospective rating, spending a great deal of time developing data, only to learn that the risk is too small to be eligible for that rating plan. Similarly, ill will toward the producer, and the insurance industry in general, may be created if the producer gives an insured a private passenger auto quote based on "safe driver" rates when the insured is not eligible for that type of rating plan.

Producers differ greatly in their interest in and their ability to perform these underwriting functions. Some producers have proven their mature judgment and ability to submit only desirable business, but others have not. Therefore, many underwriters tend to underwrite the producer, as well as the risk itself. Those following this practice must be alert to possible changes in producers' methods of operation or personnel. A producer who formerly submitted only outstanding auto risks may start a newspaper advertising campaign to increase volume, changing the character of his or her submissions drastically; or a producer may add a new salesperson who may submit substandard business through inexperience. The company underwriter has an important role in training and guiding the underwriting activities of the producer.

One final aspect of the underwriting role of producers is their ability to feed back important information to underwriters. Since producers deal with individual risks on a firsthand basis, they are in a unique position to observe and report changes in the risk which may have serious underwriting consequences. Similarly, producers may discern areas where current forms could be adapted to provide coverage more precisely tailored to the changing needs and requirements of insureds. The producer is a vital part of the insurance company's underwriting department and an important contributor to its success.

SUMMARY

Insurance involves a transfer of risk for a consideration and seeks to achieve a spread of similar risks to increase the predictability of losses. For these reasons, there is a need for underwriters.

Before beginning any study of a subject, a person must be able to understand the terminology used in that subject area. The same is true for underwriting. There are many terms that have specific meanings as well as many terms that have several meanings. Risk is a good example. Its primary use in underwriting is its use to mean the subject of insurance—the person or object insured. There are many additional meanings of risk which the underwriter should recognize, however. Other important terms include peril, loss exposure, and hazard.

The major goal of underwriting is the selection and maintenance of a profitable, growing book of business. Under this major goal are many objectives, such as providing proper coverage; maintaining selection standards, maintaining pricing standards; and, maintaining a high level of professional competence.

In order to meet these objectives, underwriters perform many activities. Some of these are universal to all underwriters while others are performed by a few underwriters. These universal activities include hazard identification and evaluation, pricing, the determination of policy terms and conditions, the selection decision, and the monitoring and servicing of those accounts that are accepted. Activities performed by some underwriters include risk management services, marketing, product design, creation of rating programs, preparation of underwriting manuals, participation in bureaus and associations, and formulation of broad underwriting policy.

Underwriting is only one of many departments within an insurance company. To successfully perform their jobs, underwriters must cooperate with other departments such as marketing, actuarial, claims, premium audit, loss control, data processing, and policyholders' service.

There are many factors which impact on the decision to centralize or decentralize the underwriting department. These factors include the availability of personnel, the location of producers, variations by state, and technology. Similarly, the decision as to where underwriting authority should rest and the extent of that authority depend on many factors.

Even though the primary concern of producers is marketing, they also have an underwriting function to perform. They have sometimes been called the front line underwriters. Insurers use different methods to encourage producers to fulfill this underwriting function. Underwriters play an important role in helping the producer understand underwriting.

Chapter Notes

1. "The Definition of Risk," *Business Insurance*, 9 May 1983, p. 41.
2. Ronald C. Horn, *On Professions, Professionals, and Professional Ethics*, 1st ed. (Malvern, PA: American Institute for Property and Liability Underwriters, 1978), pp. 8-39.
3. Bernard J. Webb, J. J. Launie, Willis Park Rokes, and Norman A. Baglini, *Insurance Company Operations*, 3rd ed., Vol. II (Malvern, PA: American Institute for Property and Liability Underwriters, 1984), p. 25.

CHAPTER 2

The Underwriting Decision-Making Process

INTRODUCTION

The basic objective of this chapter is to analyze the underwriting decision-making process. An organized approach to decision making is as applicable to underwriting decisions as it is in a general business setting. The same procedure may be applied either to individual decisions on a single risk or to managerial decisions affecting an entire book of business.

The Pervasiveness of Decision Making

Decision making is a familiar part of everyday life. Trivial decisions such as the selection of a tie or other item of apparel are followed by slightly more momentous decisions, such as the route to be taken driving to work and which restaurant to select for lunch. Minor decisions such as these are made without much analysis. Habit, or routine, has the advantage of making some decisions automatic. Other routine decisions are made after a brief consideration of past performance. For example, an alternate route for driving to work may have taken ten minutes longer than the freeway. The inexpensive coffee shop with the fast service that was selected for lunch may have resulted in mid-afternoon heartburn. Future decisions in these areas may be improved through a consideration of past experience. On the other hand, major decisions such as the purchase of a house or auto deserve a much more thorough analysis.

Business and Scientific Decision Making In one sense, business and scientific decision making is very similar to personal decision making. Each day sees a mix of trivial decisions to be made on the basis of routine or habit along with those of greater substance. The busy underwriter cannot afford to spend a great deal of time deciding in which order he or she will dictate the day's letters or which underwriting file will be opened first. These decisions are made on the basis of routine, with a minimal amount of analysis. In any event, much more analysis must go into the underwriter's decisions with respect to the new and renewal business reaching his or her desk.

Decision making, as part of the selection process, is the very heart of underwriting. Whether an auto underwriter is reviewing a batch of applications, a commercial property underwriter is considering a large package submission, or an underwriting manager is rewriting the underwriting manual, the most important part of the task is making decisions.

In a general business context, decision making is the very essence of management. The various schools of scientific management that have been developed over the years have had as their main purpose the improving of the quality of management *decision making*. At one time, it was generally believed that management was an art and that successful managers were born with that talent. However, the major schools of business have been successful in improving managerial skills through study and analysis.

Decision Making as a Process. A process is defined as a series of actions or operations directed toward a particular result. Decision making can be viewed as a creative process combining knowledge, experience, and thought. In analyzing decision making, students of management have focused on the various steps in the process by which decisions are reached. How managers make decisions, the factors considered in reaching their decisions, and the time and resources devoted to those decisions have been the subject of a great deal of study.

Underwriting decision making is a process that deserves analysis. It involves the underwriter's making decisions repeatedly on the acceptance, rejection, and modification of new and renewal business. The fact that the quality of these daily underwriting decisions will have a great bearing on the overall results of the insurance company is almost too obvious to mention. Thus an underwriter is faced with the task of making a large number of important decisions daily. An underwriter may make more decisions in a day than a noninsurance counterpart would make in a week or even a month.

The goal of management scientists studying decision making is to achieve better outcomes (results) of decisions by improving the process of decision making. Their study has provided valuable insights into the mechanism of arriving at a decision—that is, of making a choice among alternatives as well as providing some tools which can be used by the decision maker. The techniques that have proved to be successful in improving the quality of general business decisions can also be applied to underwriting decisions.

Steps in the Decision-Making Process. Joseph W. Newman has defined decision making as a process that includes the following steps:[1]

1. recognition of a situation that calls for a decision about what action should be taken,
2. identification and development of alternative courses of action,
3. evaluation of the alternatives,
4. choice of one of the alternatives, and
5. implementation of the selected course of action.

In applying this process to insurance underwriting, it is necessary to add an additional step—the gathering, organizing, and analysis of information. While this may be implicit in the first and second steps of Newman's procedure, information analysis is of such vital importance in underwriting decision making that it is best to explicitly include this step in the process.

An additional modification of Newman's procedure is necessary in the final step of the process. In general business, decision making as well as in insurance underwriting, implementation alone is not sufficient. Underwriters must monitor those risks upon which a decision has been made to ensure that the actual fact situation corresponds to their perception of it at the time of the decision and that no material changes have taken place.

Underwriting decision making, then, is a process including the following steps (the italicized parts are where this process differs from the one above):

1. recognition of a situation that calls for a decision about what action should be taken,
2. *gathering, organizing, and analyzing information pertinent to the decision,*
3. identification and development of alternative courses of action,
4. evaluation of the alternatives,
5. choice of one of the alternatives, and
6. implementation *and monitoring* of the selected course of action.

The remaining chapters in this text will look at various aspects of this process.

Decision Making and the Underwriting Function

The Myth of Intuition   Specialists in almost every major field find it difficult to articulate how or why they carry out many of the activities of their professions. The inability to explain fully how specific skills are learned does not mean, however, that those skills have not been acquired through a form of learning.

Underwriting has been referred to as an art that cannot be taught. The decision-making process which the experienced underwriter applies to the task of risk selection involves the application of his or her knowledge and experience in a manner which has long ago become habitual (unconscious). Thus, to the observer, and perhaps even to the underwriter, it appears that the selection of the proper alternative is arrived at by intuition. What is taking place is not so much intuition as an internalization of decision making.

Computers are being used more and more to assist in underwriting. One of the most ambitious uses of the computer is in the area known as *expert systems* and *artificial intelligence*. In this area, the computer essentially is used to emulate or copy the thought and decision-making process of underwriting "experts." While the computer does not have the final say, it is very helpful in making sure that the underwriter considers all factors and considers them logically. For example, if an underwriter is having a bad day, he or she might be more likely to decline a borderline risk or fail to get all the necessary information. Through the use of the expert system, the computer will list the information that should be gathered and allow the underwriter to consider what others would do when faced with similar facts. One of the consequences of the setting up of an expert system is the "experts" are required to think about and put into writing their decision-making process. If they were unable to do this, the expert system would not work.

Certainly, skill in making underwriting decisions can be gained by long years of experience, just as skill in making general management decisions can be gained through experience. But experience is a costly teacher; it gives the test first and the lessons later. Experiencing a fire loss to an unprotected restaurant is not the only way to learn that this class of business must be carefully underwritten, if it is to be written at all. The case study approach to learning represents, in effect, a distillation and compression in time and space of real world decisions in order that the important elements of the decision-making process can be brought into focus. In a short space of time, the experience of many years is simulated.

Therefore, in this text underwriting decision making will first be analyzed and then applied to cases which represent a simulation of real world experiences. In this manner, insights that might otherwise be obtained only through years of underwriting may be available. Just as experienced managers have found great value in advanced management training in the classroom, so the experienced underwriter can gain a better understanding of the decision-making process, enabling him or her to make better decisions in the future.

Optimal Alternatives The best decision cannot be made unless the best alternative course of action is among those being considered. If the best alternative has never occurred to the underwriter, it is clear that the decision made will be somewhat inferior to the best one. The creative part of underwriting involves the ability to recognize and develop all of the available feasible alternatives, including the best alternative.

Information Efficiency The time and money allocated and the accuracy required in a decision should be appropriate to its importance. The choice of a restaurant for lunch does not justify a staff study of the food service industry. An auto underwriter considering an individual auto insurance application would not hire Pinkerton's Detective Agency for two days to observe the prospective insured in order to develop information on moral character and reputation in the community. The premium involved clearly would not justify such an expenditure. Even more to the point, the information obtained would likely add very little to the quality of the decision to be reached.

This concept is referred to as information efficiency. Before allocating time and money to the development of additional information to be considered in making a decision, the decision maker should contemplate how much of an improvement in the decision the new information is likely to make possible. For example, the underwriter, prior to writing a letter asking for additional information, should assume that he or she has already obtained that information. The underwriter could then consider what effect that information would have on the final decision. If the answer is none or little, then perhaps it is time to close the file and make the decision.

Underwriting decisions are made under conditions of uncertainty. Seldom, if ever, is it possible for the underwriter to obtain all of the possible information regarding the physical and moral characteristics of a particular risk. One of the most difficult and important calculations underwriters must make is to ascertain the point in time at which sufficient information is available on which to base a decision. The objective is to use information efficiently. A more in-depth discussion of the usefulness of information is found in a later chapter.

Underwriting goals can be achieved only through effective and efficient decision making. When goals conflict with one another, the corresponding decisions are made more complex. Underwriting decisions should be viewed not in isolation but as an important part of an ongoing activity which is striving to meet the goals of the firm.

THE PROCESS OF
MAKING UNDERWRITING DECISIONS

Recognition of the Need for a Decision and Information Development

In underwriting, recognition of a situation calling for a decision is frequently quite simple. When a submission reaches an underwriter's desk, the need for a decision is to accept, reject, or accept with modification is obvious. The situation is more complex with respect to underwriting management, such as the need to determine when the underwriting manual requires rewriting, for example.

The first activity that takes place when a decision situation has been recognized is the gathering of information. The underwriter's initial task in decision making, then, is to collect information that is necessary in order to make a decision.

Decisions under Uncertainty Most business decisions are made under conditions of uncertainty in that the decision maker does not know what the outcomes (results) of the various alternative courses of action will be. Uncertainty, as it is used here, means lack of knowledge, either about future outcomes or about some of the salient characteristics of the matter under consideration.

Underwriting is simply a special case of decision making under uncertainty. One major area of uncertainty exists because the underwriter does not know what the outcome will be with respect to future losses for the particular risk being considered. Since one of the alternatives available to the underwriter may be to modify the risk in some manner, the problem is complicated since the outcomes of each of the possible modifications are also unknown.

A second area of uncertainty arises because the underwriter's knowledge of the physical and moral characteristics of the risk under consideration is imperfect. Regardless of whether the underwriter has only a written description of the risk or has inspected it personally, it is impossible to collect and assimilate all of the physical and other characteristics which have some bearing on the acceptability of the risk for the coverage desired.

Perfect knowledge has been defined as complete information about all of the outcomes, obtained without cost. It is clear that this is a theoretical abstraction. It does, however, provide a means of estimating the value of information. If one had perfect information, clearly the best decision *could* always be made. No matter how much information is gathered in a real world situation, the value of perfect information has set an upper limit; the decision cannot be improved beyond that point.

When gathering additional information, underwriters try to narrow the gap between the imperfect information and the unattainable ideal of complete knowledge. Some solace may be gained in the realization that most general business decisions are made in this same setting.

Sources of Information Information is not useful for its own sake in an underwriting setting. The only purpose for information gathering is to enable the underwriter to improve decision making. The underwriter should weigh the improvement in the decision that will be made possible by the gaining of additional information against the cost in time and money of obtaining that information. This is a difficult task in that it is not easy to quantify the improvement in the decision.

Sources of information may be either external or internal. External sources of underwriting information originate from outside the insurance company. A disadvantage of external sources is that they are essentially uncontrollable by the underwriter with regard to the quality and reliability of the information, and must be evaluated in that light. Internal sources of underwriting information emanate from within the insurance company and are more controllable because the underwriter may ask for specific information from insureds or applicants. In addition, internal sources may provide information more quickly and can be tailored to the underwriter's needs.

Information gathering, whether from internal or external sources, always has some cost attached to it in terms of time, money, or both. If the information sought is going to be useful in terms of the underwriting decision, then it should be obtained, provided the cost is commensurate with its value. It would hardly be appropriate for the underwriter to ask a loss control representative to make a physical inspection of the premises on a homeowners risk developing a $300 annual premium if the only information sought is the housekeeping on the premises. On the other hand, if it is important to know if the house is exposed to the brush hazard, and the proximity of brush is a controlling factor in the acceptance decision, a trip by the technical representative might be cost efficient if the information could not be obtained less expensively.

The internal/external distinction is not absolute. What is external for one insurance company may be internal for another. For example, the producer in some insurance distribution systems is an employee of the insurance company while in others he or she may be an independent agent. Some insurers are large enough to employ salaried loss control representatives, while others hire independent consultants to perform this function.

The important point of this distinction is whether the source is external or internal to an underwriter's own company and the advantages and limitations therefore applying to the source. This section briefly examines the major sources of information, both internal and external, available to insurers.

The Application/Underwriting File. The basic source of information for new business is the application itself. For renewal and mid-term underwriting, the major source of information is the underwriting file which usually contains the application, loss information, and all of the reports received on the insured (such as MVRs). Applications differ somewhat, not only from insurer to insurer but from one type of insurance to another. Only in a few cases is the application a formal one that becomes part of the contract. The most familiar of these formal applications is the jeweler's block application, which is extremely detailed and provides underwriting and rating information as well as the data needed to complete the declarations page of the policy. Indeed, the application clearly states that it is warranted to be a part of the policy. Other applications, such as commercial property, private passenger auto, and workers' compensation are typically less formal and contain much less information. The more information contained in the application, the fewer the alternate sources of information that must be consulted for descriptive information.

The Producer. The producer is a source of supporting and supplemental information on a new submission or existing business. Often the producer can attest to the business and personal reputation of the insured. If the producer has had business dealings with the applicant for several years and can state that the applicant has an unblemished reputation, this is certainly useful information. However, this is only one input and does not eliminate the underwriter's need for corroborating information from other sources. Sometimes a producer's enthusiasm leads to a more optimistic assessment of a particular risk than might be warranted by an objective appraisal of the information. Through experience, either personal or that of associates, the underwriter must develop a feeling for the validity and objectivity of the data supplied by a particular producer.

Government Records. Governmental records provide information such as motor vehicle records (MVRs), records of mortgages and liens, lists of business licenses, records such as bankruptcy filings. In private passenger auto underwriting, the MVRs of the operators are a fundamental source of information. In commercial property insurance, it is frequently useful to check that there are no unreported encumbrances (such as a mortgage) on the property under consideration. At best, an unreported encumbrance on real property would indicate an insurable interest that should be covered by endorsement that was inadvertently omitted; at worst, it might represent an attempt by the applicant to conceal an adverse financial condition.

Financial Rating Services. Financial rating services such as Standard and Poor's, Dun & Bradstreet, and others provide data on credit ratings, and industry averages for purposes of comparison. These services provide a great deal of financial information regarding the strength and stability of business enterprises. They help to corroborate financial statements supplied by the applicant or insured to support an application for a surety bond, for example. The financial strength of a potential insured is of great significance in commercial property underwriting as well as in commercial liability underwriting. The possible moral hazard in a financially shaky business is familiar to all property and liability underwriters.

Additional sources of financial information are the financial statements and accounting records of the insured. These records provide more detailed information on the insured's financial strength than reports from financial rating services. (An analysis of financial statements is discussed in a later chapter.)

Consumer Investigation Reports. Individual consumer investigation reports obtained from firms such as Equifax, Inc., provide background information concerning applicants for personal lines insurance. The consumer investigation report can provide information on the insured's general reputation in the community, the general appearance of the home and neighborhood, and similar data. Some consumer investigation reports also include a check of the MVRs on auto applications and a review of appropriate court records if available. A felony conviction or a series of nonauto-related misdemeanor convictions may come to light in a consumer investigation report. A poor reputation or undesirable associates, which could be indicated in an investigation report, is a matter of grave concern to the underwriter of all personal lines. On a homeowners submission, the consumer investigation report may indicate that the premises are poorly maintained and in a state of disrepair. It may be useful to check adverse information from the report with additional input from another source.

New underwriters should be aware that the costs of these reports have increased and the usefulness and completeness of the information on the reports have declined in the last decade or so. Privacy laws, the Fair Credit Reporting Act, and regulations regarding what information can or cannot be used by underwriters have reduced the information that can be obtained by the reporting firm. As fewer underwriting decisions are based on the reports, the value of the reports, compared with their cost, must be reexamined. Some insurers now use the reports on an exception basis only rather than using them for every personal lines submission.

Previous Insurers. Underwriters sometimes obtain important information from the insured's previous insurer. This may range from a short list of losses and premiums (to confirm those given on the application) or a phone call giving further insight into the insured and the insured's operations. Privacy laws and potential liability make many insurers hesitant to give out much information.

Inspection Reports. Inspection reports prepared by technical personnel provide data on the physical and other characteristics of the risk under consideration. The impressions obtained by technical representatives (loss control representatives, engineers, etc.) about the insured's attitude, cooperativeness, and moral tone are helpful to the underwriter. Inspection reports typically are used for commercial property and liability risks. Occasionally, a personal lines submission will be of sufficient size or will possess some unique characteristic calling for an inspection by a loss control representative (but more common in personal lines is an inspection by the special agent or field sales personnel). In areas prone to brush fires, for example, the published brush maps do not always accurately indicate the presence or degree of brush exposure for an individual homeowners risk. In these cases, an on-site inspection can clearly indicate the distance of the structure from the nearest brush and also provide the basis for an informed opinion about the severity of the brush hazard.

It is customary in inspection reports of commercial risks to make a list of mandatory recommendations and follow this with a list of suggested recommendations. Compliance with mandatory recommendations is required for writing or continuation of the coverage. The willingness of the insured to follow the suggested recommendations provides a useful insight into the degree of cooperation that can be expected of the insured.

Field Sales Personnel. Field sales personnel (referred to as special agents, marketing representatives, or similar names) can provide both specific and general information. If the application from the producer is lacking in specific information, frequently the field representative in the area can obtain the necessary data for the underwriter. In some insurance companies field sales personnel provide simple inspection reports in territories that are sparsely populated or in other situations when a loss control representative may not be available. The sales force can also provide background information on insureds or on producers if the underwriter is unfamiliar with them. The underwriter may wish to know how familiar the producer is with the type of insurance that is being submitted. This could be a legitimate area of concern with respect to an ocean marine submission or a surety bond proposal. The special agent or field representative could supply this information.

Claims Department. Review of a claim file can sometimes provide insights into the character and moral tone of the insured. A claims adjuster visiting a commercial risk to settle a small fire loss may discover a poor housekeeping situation together with a careless attitude toward loss control on the part of management. A questionable claim or a hostile and uncooperative attitude on the part of the insured would be of interest to the underwriter. Not all information developed by claims personnel and relevant to the underwriter is of a negative nature. The claims adjuster may be able to report that an older vehicle about which the underwriter has been concerned is maintained in the finest mechanical condition and shows pride of ownership. Similarly the adjuster's visit to the insured's business premises may bring back a glowing report of outstanding housekeeping and eager management cooperation on a risk located in an older building. This positive information can enable the underwriter to identify and retain the superior risks just as the adverse information can single out the less desirable insureds.

Production Records. Insurance company records are usually available on the producer with respect to loss ratio, volume of business, length of service, mix of business, and supporting business, if any exists. This information indicates the experience and familiarity of the producer with the type of business under consideration. The producer's loss ratio, volume, and length of association with the insurance company provide a means of assessing the overall quality of the producer's previous business. The acceptance of marginal business as an accommodation to the producer is a difficult area at best. An underwriter faced with that situation should carefully assess the producer's record to verify that he or she merits further consideration. On the other hand, if the producer has a large volume of desirable business, an historically low loss ratio, and considers the underwriter's company as his or her leading company, the underwriter should weigh these factors while making a decision on the submission at hand.

Insurer Underwriting Manuals and Guides. Underwriting manuals and guides are especially helpful when writing a new or unfamiliar line of business. When reviewing a package policy application on a metallurgist, for example, an underwriter may ask, "What does a metallurgist do? Of what peculiar exposures to loss should I be aware?" Most insurers have some form of underwriting manual that provides basic information on the loss exposures of many types of businesses. In addition, the manual states the insurer's position on the class of business in general and the deviation that is allowed from company policy. In effect, an underwriting manual is a method by which the experience of a large number of underwriters can be passed along to the less experienced ones.

Other Underwriting Manuals. In addition to the insurer's underwriting manuals, underwriting manuals of a more general nature are available from commercial publishers. These manuals usually describe a number of different types of businesses. For each business, the typical operations are identified, along with the exposures and hazards to be expected. In some cases, various insurance coverages are rated on a scale to show the "seriousness" of the exposures or hazards.

Other Underwriters. Like underwriting manuals, information can be obtained directly from other underwriters. The bond underwriter just a few desks away may have already written or rejected submissions from the same prospective insured. Senior underwriters who may have written risks of this nature are perhaps the single most fruitful internal source of information.

Informal Information Sources. There are various informal channels of communication that can provide information to the underwriter. The underwriter is in daily contact with producers and other members of the business community. Underwriters, as members of the community, frequently obtain information pertaining to present or potential insureds both during and after business hours. Local trade organizations frequently hold meetings that provide contacts with underwriters from other insurers. Most of this informal information consists of what may be referred to as "hearsay." Some of the information obtained in this fashion is of questionable value, and the underwriter should carefully evaluate the information sources in this category. On the other hand, occasionally the underwriter will hear something of significant importance by this means which warrants further investigation through other information sources of greater validity.

Types of Information Information is also classified by type. One such classification is objective versus subjective information.

Objective information needs only to be verified as to its validity. Subjective information, however, must be weighed with respect to bias, imperfect perception, or distortion on the part of the person or organization from which it originates. Both internal and external sources must be examined and classified as to objectivity and subjectivity. Information from a single source may be both objective and subjective. For example, a single report may give the year and condition of a car—the year is objective while the condition is subjective.

Objective Information. Objective information consists of facts that can be verified and that have been recorded in some manner. While it is theoretically possible for an objective fact to exist although it has not been written down anywhere, as a practical matter such information would be difficult or impossible to verify, causing the fact to lose some of its value from an informational standpoint. To illustrate the characteristics of objective information, this section deals with a few of the major types.

Motor Vehicle Records. The State Department of Motor Vehicles or similar state agency maintains records regarding a number of important aspects of an individual's driving record. Information is usually filed by name and driver's license number and includes reported accidents, citations, and suspensions. These data provide an excellent example of verifiable, objective information. Occasionally there is confusion with respect to individuals with the same or similar names, and a driver will be charged with a citation or accident in which he or she was not involved.

Financial Statements. The financial statements of a business, especially an income statement and a balance sheet, contain a detailed summary of the financial condition of the firm. These financial statements may be separated into two categories, audited and unaudited statements. An *audited financial statement* contains an opinion of an outside Certified Public Accountant (CPA) regarding the degree to which the statement in fact reflects the actual condition of the firm. This opinion may be either qualified or unqualified. In an *unqualified opinion,* the CPA states that he or she has examined the books and records of the firm and determined that the values set forth in the statement have been arrived at following "generally accepted accounting principles." (In accounting discussions, this is frequently abbreviated as GAAP.) A *qualified opinion,* which is becoming more commonplace, states that the CPA has examined the books and records of the firm and has some reservations with regard to the manner in which a particular fact or facts have been accounted for. The CPA may not agree with the manner in which certain assets have been valued, for example.

Unaudited financial statements are simply the financial statements that have not been audited by a CPA. They may be viewed by the underwriter as a set of unverified objective facts. The audited statement, on the other hand, represents a set of objective facts which have been verified by an outside firm. This increases the extent to which the underwriter can rely on the information.

Court Records.   Both civil and criminal courts maintain records with regard to actions filed in the courts and the disposition of these actions. Criminal court records might show, for example, that an individual was indicted for a felony offense; later the charge was reduced to a misdemeanor, and the individual was subsequently convicted of the misdemeanor and received a suspended sentence. The only verification required in this case is to determine that the court record is in fact that of the particular individual under consideration and that it has been reported accurately.

Civil court actions include the filing of liability damage claims for torts or breach of contract, for example. These records will indicate the final disposition of such an action or whether it is still pending. A search of these court records might present the commercial liability underwriter with the fact that two premises claims are now pending against the applicant. Filings for bankruptcy or reorganization are another example of civil court records of interest to the underwriter.

Mortgages and Liens.   Local records of recorded encumbrances are maintained, usually at the county level, on both real and personal property. The information contained in these records includes the description of the property, the date and amount of the encumbrance, and the name and address of the creditor. Provided the property description is accurate, the only modification the underwriter has to make with respect to data obtained from these records is to consider the possibility of recent, unrecorded changes in the status or amount of the debt.

Loss Data.   A loss history from insurer records is an example of objective, easily verified information. When the loss history is contained within the company, the underwriter can usually obtain detailed loss information. Loss information provided with a submission is usually unverified. Sometimes, it can be corroborated in some manner, usually by previous insurers although previous insurers vary in their willingness to provide such information.

Loss data must be organized systematically before it can be analyzed efficiently. The loss frequency, loss severity, the cause or type of loss, and the date of the loss are all significant. There may be one peril causing a majority of the losses and indicating the possibility for either loss control or modification of the coverage provided. The date of the loss may indicate either seasonality in the incidence of a loss or a trend toward improvement or deterioration of the loss experience. Countrywide loss experience in the class of business should be considered, especially if it has changed markedly in recent years.

Subjective Information. Subjective information consists of opinions or impressions about relevant characteristics of the risk. The subjective data received by the underwriter runs the gamut from extremely valuable information to inputs that are worthless or possibly even counterproductive. Although not all-inclusive, the following are some major types of subjective information.

The Producer's Opinion Or Evaluation. A producer's evaluation of the qualitative aspects of the risk is an example of subjective information. Underwriters are confronted with the task of estimating not only the value of the information but the plausibility of the source. Some producers are quite candid and forthright in providing background data while others may overemphasize the desirable qualities of a risk and minimize its shortcomings. The underwriter naturally seeks a flow of new and renewal business from producers who are as proud of their low loss ratios as are the insurance company underwriters. From such producers has come the old adage that "a good producer is the company's first line underwriter."

The Observations of Claims Personnel. Along with the statement of the objective facts concerning a particular claim, claims personnel frequently include their impressions of possible moral hazard based upon interviews and contacts with the insured. The fact that the adjusters are trained professionals whose comments are based upon observations in an area in which they have experience gives their statements greater credence than would otherwise be the case. Claims personnel may also include observations on the general physical condition or hazards inherent in the particular risk as well as the cooperativeness of the insured. This type of subjective information is frequently of great value to the underwriter.

Investigation Reports. Almost any investigation report contains a mixture of objective and subjective information and each must be weighed accordingly. For example, in a personal lines report, the investigator may report that although there are no derogatory facts, the general tone of the insured's environs and associates nevertheless leaves an adverse impression. The evaluation by the underwriter of "soft" information of this nature is a difficult mission, but a necessary one.

Statements and Rumors.   Statements and rumors from a variety of sources may reach the underwriter regarding an insured's reputation in business or in the community as a whole. Corroboration of subjective information from any source is desirable, but this type of vaguely defined data must definitely be substantiated before it can be given any credence whatsoever. On the other hand, the mere fact that the information cannot be attributed to a specific source does not warrant dismissing it without further investigation.

For example, assume that a commercial property underwriter has heard a rumor (the most unreliable type of subjective information of all) that a firm for which the underwriter has written a large package policy is in serious financial difficulty. By itself, this unverified bit of information is of little value. The underwriter, however, has available a variety of other information sources that can and should provide objective data to substantiate or dismiss the original suspicion. Mature judgment is clearly called for in this area.

Hazard Evaluation   A hazard has previously been defined as a factor or condition that tends to increase the probable frequency and severity of a loss due to an insured peril. Hazards can be classified as physical, moral, and morale hazards.

Physical Hazards.   Physical hazards are the tangible characteristics of the insured property, persons, or operations that affect the likelihood and severity of loss due to one or more perils. They can be characteristics of the risk itself, or characteristics of the environment in which the risk is located. Examples of physical hazards considered here are:

- occupancy and operations on premises
- protection of premises and persons
- geography, and
- housekeeping.

Occupancy and Operations on Premises.   Occupancy hazards arise from the use to which a structure has been employed. A frame building used as an office presents quite different hazards with respect to the peril of fire than an identical building occupied by a restaurant. Inherent in the restaurant occupancy is the likelihood of grease fires in the flues, something that is not present in an office. The flammability and damageability of the contents in a particular occupancy are also of concern with respect to the peril of fire. In manufacturing plants, the various processes may require flammables which increase the likelihood of a loss. From the standpoint of commercial liability, premises utilized for an amusement park present many hazards which would not be found in premises of the same size and which are employed for manufacturing, with no public access allowed.

Protection. The presence or absence of private or public fire and burglary protection is an important element to be considered with respect to both personal and commercial property lines. Inadequate fire protection may come from a lack of local fire stations, poor equipment or training, the lack of an adequate water supply, or the absence of an adequate sprinkler system. Occasionally, in the industrial area of a large city, there will be a small area that has railroad tracks on all sides with no fire hydrants located inside the area. Newly constructed limited access highways in cities have inadvertently isolated existing risks from previously available public water supplies. Infrequent or ineffective police patrol and protection can increase the hazard of all of the crime perils significantly.

This protection is not only for the property but also the persons on the premises. The more quickly a fire can be detected and extinguished, the less chance there is someone will be injured either from the fire itself or the by-products of the fire (for example, toxic gases). Police protection as a deterrent to crime decreases the chance someone will be injured during the commission of a crime. If employees and customers know that there is someone "handling the situation" during a crime, they are less likely to try to stop the crime, possibly causing injury to themselves and others due to improper training.

Geography. The topography of the terrain on which the risk is located is of interest to the underwriter. A warehouse located on low land next to a river is an example of a risk where the geography is an important consideration if the peril of flood is to be covered. Similar geographic considerations include the presence of a building on a steep, sandy hillside where landslide and subsidence are a strong possibility, or the presence of underground limestone caves which might collapse, causing subsidence. Geography may be a factor in a simple fire application if fire-fighting equipment is not able to reach the property promptly. Earthquake damage is frequently more severe when the structure is built on filled land. On a risk that is large enough to justify the expense, an aerial photograph can supply a great deal of information with respect to the topography surrounding the risk under consideration. Topographic maps are published by the U. S. government and can also provide data regarding the contours of the terrain in which the risk is located. Being inaccessible to local ambulance service can present problems with respect to workers' compensation and bodily injury coverages since long delays could develop in getting seriously injured persons to a location where they could receive proper medical care.

Housekeeping. The quality of the housekeeping and general maintenance of a particular risk is of significance for both property and liability underwriting. Poor housekeeping can be responsible for serious fires as well as for persons' being injured on the premises. Hazards in this category include poor storage of wastes and oily rags, slippery substances permitted to remain on the floors, and wiring that does not meet the building code. While many physical hazards are difficult, inordinately expensive, or impossible for the insured to alter, the reverse is true with respect to housekeeping and maintenance. If the insured is not self-motivated to improve standards in this area, the underwriter can sometimes provide the incentive for the insured through a restriction in coverage and/or an increase in the rate. Information with respect to housekeeping and maintenance should be obtained, not only when a risk is first underwritten, but periodically as long as the risk remains part of the book of business. Housekeeping hazards can fluctuate over time. A business that kept a very high standard of maintenance in the past might cut back on maintenance expenditures and postpone needed repairs in response to a downturn in economy. The premium auditors, claims personnel, and loss control representatives who visit the insured premises are often in the best position to note changes in housekeeping.

Moral Hazards. Moral hazard can be defined as a subjective characteristic of the insured that tends to increase the probable frequency or severity of a loss due to an insured peril. The hazard arises from the possibility that the insured may intentionally cause a loss. One of the requisites of an insurable risk is that the event insured against be fortuitous and outside the control of the reasonably prudent insured. When significant moral hazard exists, this condition is violated. Moral hazard is not amenable to prediction by the statistical techniques upon which insurance is based; therefore, the existence of moral hazard cannot be compensated for by increasing the rate.

Financial Condition. A weak financial condition may increase the likelihood of intentionally caused losses. In a prosperous business, even a complete insurance program will leave some uninsurable losses that will have to be borne by the firm. A failing business, on the other hand, may find an intentionally caused fire to be the "solution" to its financial difficulties. Overinsurance similarly may lead an insured to attempt to profit from an intentionally caused loss. The financial condition of a business can change very quickly. A style change, innovation, or a change in consumers' tastes can leave a business with a sizable obsolete inventory. A formerly successful roadside restaurant might find its business drastically reduced by the opening of a new freeway or major highway which changes patterns of travel. Economic downturns may cause postponement of essential maintenance to vital services such as electrical, plumbing, and heating systems as well as safety features such as machine guards and employee safety meetings. The underwriter needs up-to-date financial information to guard against the existence of moral hazard arising from deteriorating financial conditions of the insured.

Associates. The fact that the insured or potential insured is known to associate with unlawful elements of the community indicates a potential moral hazard. This is not guilt by association but merely a reflection of the fact that a business which is frequented by members of the underworld or other undesirable elements in the community does not indicate a high moral tone on the part of the proprietor. Undesirable associates of the insured would be of particular concern to the underwriter considering a sizable jewelry and fur schedule on a homeowners policy, for example.

Moral Character. Moral hazard may arise directly from the immorality of the insured independently of financial condition or associates. The moral character of the insured may be deduced from such evidence as previous questionable losses, a police record, and other evidence of moral turpitude. A recent fire of suspicious origin or a reputation in the community for unethical or illegal business practices are examples of information that may indicate the presence of moral hazard. Insurance contracts are based on utmost good faith. If the insured is of poor moral character, this condition may be violated.

Morale Hazards. Morale hazards arise out of carelessness or indifference to loss. This carelessness or indifference often results from the presence of insurance. Morale hazard is usually much more subtle and difficult to detect than moral hazard, but its presence does tend to increase the frequency or severity of loss. Two major indications of morale hazard are personality traits and poor management.

Personality Traits. Personality traits, such as carelessness with valuable property, can be an indication of morale hazard. An example would be a wealthy woman who thoughtlessly leaves valuable jewelry and furs strewn about the house where they easily could become lost or stolen. While the woman may be of high moral character and have no intention of defrauding the insurance company, her attitude toward her valuable possessions increases the probability of loss. Pride of ownership is the characteristic that is desired; its lack may be evidence of morale hazard.

Poor Management. Poor or ineffective management may lead to morale hazard. Slovenly housekeeping and slipshod bookkeeping are overt indications of an undesirable management attitude. Management that is indifferent to loss may neglect to service fire extinguishers or may have such poor control over tools and inventory that theft losses become extremely likely. A disdain for the protection of property frequently results in its loss. This type of morale hazard can increase the likelihood of liability losses as well. Careless management can result in the tolerance of dangerous conditions that result in the injury of customers, or perfunctory quality control inspection techniques that lead to products liability problems. In these cases, it is not that management is intentionally attempting to cause losses; it is simply that it is uninterested in the prevention or reduction of loss.

Identification and Development of Alternative Courses of Action

In the previous section, we looked at the *first two* major steps in the underwriting decision-making process: recognition of a situation that calls for a decision about what action should be taken; and gathering, organizing, and analyzing information pertinent to the decisions.

In this section, we will look at the *third* step in the process: identification and development of alternative courses of action. As stated previously, the best decision cannot be made if the best alternative course of action is not among those under consideration. Underwriting judgment and experience come into play in the determination of feasible alternatives for the modification of a risk under consideration. Modern decision techniques provide the decision maker with tools that make the development of alternatives both clearer and easier. When the alternatives and their possible outcomes can be clearly defined, the probability of making a good decision is greatly enhanced.

The Decision Tree

Definition. The decision tree is a graphic presentation of the anatomy of a decision.[2] A diagram is drawn with a branch designating each of the alternatives available to the decision maker. These main branches may have subsidiary branches illustrating possible chance outcomes. Usually a decision point is represented by a square; a chance outcome is shown as a circle.

The usefulness of the decision tree is that a complex set of alternatives leading to an even more complicated set of possible chance outcomes can be explicitly drawn up in a form that makes the implications of each alternative clear. The entire decision process can be visualized more readily with the aid of this tool, and valuable insights can be gained.

One of the drawbacks of the decision tree is that it is too time-consuming to be employed on many decisions. Probably the best use of the decision tree is in training underwriters to see all of the possible alternatives available for a decision, and in some cases, the results of those alternatives. Using the tree, a person can see how one decision can lead to an entirely new set of decision alternatives, each of which must be considered.

An Example. Exhibit 2-1 shows a simple decision tree in which the underwriter is faced with three alternatives—accept the risk, accept it with modification, or reject it. It is assumed that if the underwriter accepts the risk, the rate and form will remain the same. Other insurance companies are also attempting to write this risk; therefore, the underwriter is not certain of obtaining the business, even if it is accepted without modification.

If some modification of the risk is insisted upon, the chances of obtaining the business will decrease, but the likelihood of the business being profitable if it is obtained should increase. The decision tree traces the decision through its various alternatives to the final outcome—the underwriting results on that particular piece of business.

As an example of a situation in which the decision tree could be desirable, consider the following example of a commercial property submission. The fact situation is as follows:

- The submission is from a profitable producer.
- The submission is for all of the business or nothing, since the producer wants to place all of the business in one insurance company.
- Coverage is to be on a "broad form" with a package discount requested.
- The quote is needed quickly since the producer is giving you the first shot at the business but must have an answer so that other markets can be approached if necessary.
- The risk consists of ten locations, seven desirable and three undesirable.
- A review of the file and D&B (Dun & Bradstreet) shows a good financial picture. You presently have one of the best locations insured.
- Review of rating information shows that the HPR (Highly Protected Risk) locations develop a very low premium.
- One non-HPR location has high values.

The decision tree should be applied to the evaluation of alternatives only after the necessary information has been developed. In this case the alternatives are as follows:

1. To accept the submission on the basis presented;
2. To accept with modifications:

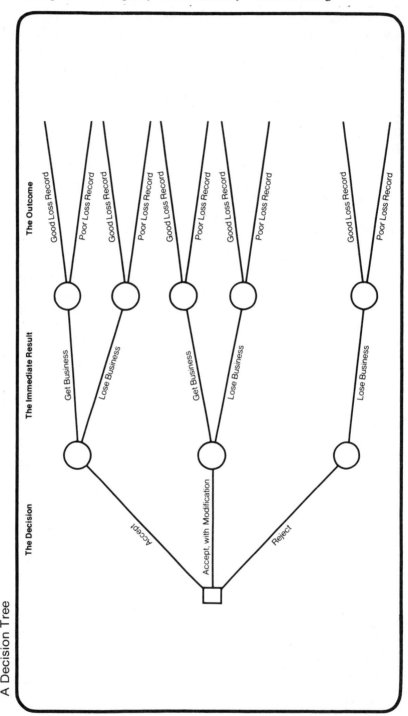

Exhibit 2-1
A Decision Tree

a. Change the rating plan and offer to write it at standard rates rather than at a discount (it is important to note that a change in rating plans does not always mean a surcharge; a lower rate might be offered to improve the probability of obtaining a particularly desirable piece of business);

b. Reinsure part of the high valued location on a facultative basis;

c. Modify the contract to make the risk more acceptable, such as using the broad form for the HPR locations and offer less broad coverage on the poor locations; and

d. Insist that the three undesirable locations be brought up to acceptable standards.

3. To reject the submission

The first step in applying the decision tree is to draw in each of the alternatives. In this case, that would consist of six branches. If you accept the submission as is, you might get the business or you might lose to another proposal with a lower rate or broader coverage. Therefore, the next step in the process is to consider the probability of getting the business or losing the business. You might evaluate the probability of getting the business on the terms offered as 90 percent with a 10 percent probability of losing it.

Next you estimate the probability of getting or losing the business under each of the four modifications under consideration. All of these probabilities are placed on the tree.

The final step is to consider what effect the modifications, or lack of them, could have on the probability of obtaining a good or poor loss ratio on the submission. These estimates are also placed on the tree. The resulting tree is shown in Exhibit 2-2. As can be seen, the decision tree makes the alternatives quite specific and facilitates careful analysis. It should be noted that outcome in an underwriting sense refers not only to loss frequency but to the combination of both frequency and severity.

Alternative Courses of Action for Individual Risks

Accept Without Alteration. One of the available alternatives with respect to a new submission or a present policy being reviewed for renewal is to accept the business without alteration in rate, form, or engineering (loss control). This happens quite frequently on renewals, but with new submissions the frequency with which this alternative will be selected depends upon the quality of the submissions being processed.

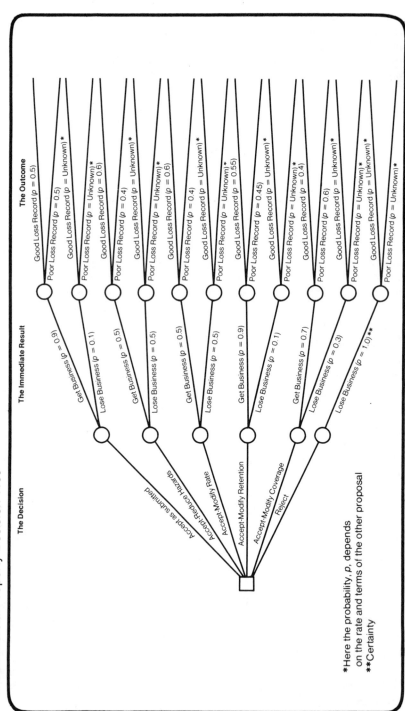

Exhibit 2-2
A Commercial Property Decision Tree

*Here the probability, p, depends
on the rate and terms of the other proposal
**Certainty

Accept Subject to Modification. When a risk which has been submitted is unacceptable in its present form, often modifications can be offered to make it acceptable. The more complex the submission, the greater the variety in changes that can be made. The variables with which the underwriter has to work are:

- the hazards in the risk itself;
- the rate;
- the coverage; and
- the retention (amount retained before reinsurance).

Reduce Hazards. Examples of hazard reduction through loss control include sprinklers or security guard service, improvements in housekeeping and maintenance, clear space requirements, or installation of guards on machinery. Sometimes a relatively simple and inexpensive solution is available for the problem submission, while other changes such as the installation of sprinklers require major modifications of the building. The economic feasibility of the suggested changes and the willingness of management to institute them will determine the viability of this type of modification. In some types of insurance, such as boiler and machinery, where there is a required pre-inspection, mandatory modifications which must be implemented before coverage can be bound are quite commonplace. From the viewpoint of society as a whole, this is one of the most desirable activities the underwriter can undertake. From the insured's viewpoint, recommendations may have a very positive long-term effect on ultimate costs of doing business or be viewed as wholly unnecessary.

Modify Rate. A change in the rate or rating plan may make the risk acceptable. A rate surcharge or modification may be required. On a private passenger auto submission, for example, while the risk may not qualify for a preferred risk plan, it might be acceptable in the standard auto program. In inland marine insurance where rates are not filed with the regulatory authorities, rate increases to adjust for the underwriter's perceived need for additional premium are quite commonplace. In liability insurance, modifications based on past experience or expected losses may provide enough additional premium to make the risk acceptable.

Modify Coverage. A change in coverage from that originally requested or presently provided may make the risk acceptable. A policy on which renewal is doubtful under the present contract may be retained if the coverage is modified to remove the peril causing the problem losses. The degree of flexibility available to the underwriter varies considerably from line to line. In those lines where the forms are filed (subject to approval by state regulatory bodies) and cannot be deviated from (except within prescribed limits), fewer options are present than with respect to "uncontrolled" lines where essentially any facet of the coverage can be changed.

A contractor's equipment floater which is presently unacceptable as written on an "all-risks" form may become much more attractive when converted to a named perils basis. Risks that have a poor loss history due to a large number of small losses may be greatly improved by the introduction of or increase in the deductible. By and large, as the size and complexity of the risk increases, it may be necessary to change all three variables, i.e., coverage, rate, and hazards, in order to make the risk acceptable.

Modify Retention. Changes in the retention provide another set of alternatives. These include "splitting the line" (sharing the business) with other insurers, obtaining reinsurance on a facultative or treaty basis, or obtaining other types of reinsurance arrangements. Reinsurance is dealt with in a later chapter. These changes in retention generally represent a method of dealing with a risk that is otherwise acceptable except for size. Quite frequently a large fire line will be split among two or more insurers enabling each one to remain within the limits set by its line guide for that type of risk. This method of dealing with a large risk has the advantage of avoiding reinsurance expense.

Occasionally a submission will entail an exposure that makes the underwriter reluctant to retain the entire line contemplated in the normal reinsurance treaties. In this case, facultative reinsurance will enable the underwriter to reduce the exposure on that risk to the level deemed to be appropriate.

Reject. With some submissions, no alternative remains but rejection. This should be considered as a last resort because it is costly to reject business. A submission the underwriter has considered and analyzed represents an expenditure of underwriting time at the very least. In addition, there may be information-gathering expenses and clerical expenses as telephone calls and letters are exchanged regarding the submission, and possibly even the expense of an on-site inspection by technical representatives. It is an obvious but important fact that the rejected risk generates no premium. This does not mean that an unacceptable risk should be written but that every effort should be expended to find a way in which a risk can be made acceptable before it is rejected. No amount of loss control or coverage modification will remove moral hazard, but risks with other types of deficiencies frequently can be modified to make them acceptable.

Alternative Courses of Action for a Line of Business or a Territory

The preceding discussion of alternative courses of action has focused upon individual risk underwriting. The underwriting decision-making process is also applied to those decisions that affect an entire book of business for the firm. The process itself is essentially the same whether the decision pertains to an individual risk or to an entire book of business.

It is the current practice in the industry to use the term "book of business" interchangeably to refer to the total business in a particular line or territory and also to refer to the total business of the insurance company as a whole.

The Line of Business. Underwriting review of the underwriting manual involves the same process of identification and evaluation of alternatives as does individual risk underwriting. A property underwriting manager involved in the revision of the property underwriting manual needs to carefully develop and weigh the alternative courses of action available. These alternatives can be developed by using experience and judgment in a review of loss data and other underwriting information. Frequently, one alternative is to make no changes and to continue to use the existing underwriting manual. There is a great difference between arriving at this conclusion after the thorough study and analysis of the alternative courses of action and the same result stemming merely from a reluctance to alter the status quo. The former represents a decision arrived at through a logical process, the latter the absence of decision.

The Territory. Similarly, underwriting review of the geographic spread of business and the mix of business (distribution among classes of risks) within various territories involves the same process as does individual risk underwriting. Examples of these decisions are the decision to enter or retire from a particular state or where additional producers should be appointed. Information gathering and analysis play a particularly important role in this type of decision. The insurance company's present spread of business over the various territories under consideration is the starting place. Physical and market conditions in new territories and the most likely trends in terms of the growth and development of areas are other considerations.

The regulatory environment within a state is also of prime concern since an insurer might not be allowed to withdraw from a state in just one line and not in all lines. This is a type of underwriting decision made at the highest levels in the firm. While the alternatives are more difficult to identify and more complex in their development, the decision-making process involved is the same as that employed at the underwriting desk with respect to a private passenger auto submission. The experience, judgment, and expertise required for this type of decision are immeasurably greater than required for the individual auto submission, but the underlying decision process is the same. In summary, "book of business" underwriting decisions can be viewed as strategic, while individual risk underwriting decisions represent tactical implementation.

The Evaluation of Alternatives

Once the alternative courses of action have been identified and developed, the relative merits of each course of action must be evaluated. For example, in an individual risk submission, the alternatives may be:

1. to accept,
2. to reject,
3. to accept with an increase in the rate, or
4. to accept, maintain the rate, and increase the deductible.

In this simple example, the underwriter has four alternatives to evaluate. A major part of the evaluation process involves the underwriter's assessment of the hazards which the particular risk under consideration presents contrasted with the hazards that are contemplated for the "average" risk in that particular rate classification for which the rate is appropriate.

In those cases when the risk is clearly much better or much worse than the average in its class, the evaluation process is relatively easy. On a commercial property submission, for example, assume that the underwriter determines that the risk is far below the average in its class due to its physical condition. If the condition is such that loss control engineering is not feasible as a means of improving the risk, and the modifications in rate and coverage which are possible will not, in the underwriter's judgment, improve the risk materially, the rejection alternative appears to be the best course of action.

In addition to the evaluation of the risk itself, certain other factors impinge upon the decision process. These factors include:

- the degree of underwriting authority required for the decision,
- the presence of supporting business,
- the mix of business in the underwriting book,
- producer pressure, and
- regulatory constraints

Underwriters must decide if they have the authority to make the final decision with respect to the submission under consideration or whether their task is to develop the underwriting file for referral to higher authority. Chester I. Barnard in his work *The Functions of the Executive* stated: "The fine art of executive decision consists in not deciding questions that are not now pertinent, in not deciding prematurely, in not making decisions that cannot be made effective, and in not making decisions that others should make."[3] Underwriters can waste a good deal of time evaluating alternatives in those cases when the choice of the course of action is going to be or should be made by someone else.

Supporting business may make a marginal submission acceptable. Underwriters should consider the desirability of the entire account. For example, a marginal personal lines submission may become acceptable when considered together with a sizable commercial account for the same insured. Mere premium volume alone is not sufficient, however. The supporting business should be better than the average in its particular classification if it is going to justify the acceptance of a risk that is slightly below the level of normal acceptability.

The mix of business in the underwriting book must be considered. *The mix of business refers to the distribution of individual risks among the various lines or classifications within a certain line.* For example, a book of auto business includes risks from the various territories and rate classifications. If young drivers represent 10 percent of the total driver population in the territories under consideration and 30 percent of the book of auto business consists of young drivers, the mix of business with respect to the age category is out of balance. Acceptance of even more young drivers will further unbalance the book of business.

With respect to property insurance, the same concept applies. The book of commercial property insurance should reflect the characteristics of the population of risks from which it is drawn. If a particular occupancy class, such as restaurants, is heavily over-represented in the book of business, the book is unbalanced. One exception to this situation occurs when the insurer, because of its expertise in the area or because of an attractive class rate, has a program to emphasize a particular occupancy class.

Particularly (but not exclusively) when marketing through independent agents and brokers, pressure from producers must be weighed in the decision. This is usually not a consideration for those risks that are clearly acceptable or clearly unacceptable, but producer pressure typically occurs on marginal submissions. The first factor to be considered is the volume of business the producer is placing with the company. The second factor is the quality of the producer's business as evidenced by the loss ratio and mix of business. Producer accommodation is one of the most difficult factors for the underwriter to assess. A marginal submission from a highly professional producer with a large volume of profitable business usually merits a "second look." If the underwriter is to develop a profitable book of business, this factor must be kept in perspective as simply one of the considerations that go into the final decision.

Regulatory constraints may inhibit the underwriter's freedom to decline or refuse to renew a submission. Particularly in auto insurance, but also in some property lines, regulations have been enacted in many states limiting rejection or refusal to renew to a few stated cases. An example would be a property submission under the FAIR plan (a residual market for substandard property risks). The regulations in this case set forth the manner in which the submission must be considered and delineate conditions under which it can be rejected. The regulatory constraints may be the controlling consideration on those risks to which they apply.

Choice of Alternatives

This is the decision itself. After carefully weighing all the alternatives which have been identified and developed, the underwriter chooses one of them. One of the keys to efficient decision making is to determine when sufficient information has been gathered, when the proper amount of analysis has been performed, and when the decision should be made. There is a natural tendency, which should be resisted, to postpone difficult decisions. Perfect information is not attainable in an underwriting situation; therefore, the decision must be made on the basis of information that can be reasonably obtained. Insurance underwriting consists of the taking of calculated risks by selection of the best course of action from the set of available alternatives.

Implementing and Monitoring the Decision

When the decision has been made, the underwriter's task is not completed. The decision must be implemented by communication to the producer and then monitored to determine its outcome.

Communication of the Decision In many cases, it is necessary for the underwriter to telephone or write the producer to pass along the decision that has been reached with regard to the submission. In other cases, particularly when a policy is going to be issued on the same terms as requested, no communication is required and the implementation of the decision is the issuance of the policy. That is, from the producer's standpoint no news is good news.

When the decision is to accept the submission subject to a modification of the rate, deductible, or other policy provision, the first step in implementation of the decision is to inform the producer. If the rate is to be increased, for example, the underwriter should tell the producer the reason for the increase. If the producer understands the reasoning behind the requested modification, the underwriter is more likely to obtain the business. In the case of a rate increase, it is more useful to enumerate the hazards which are greater than those contemplated in the standard rate than to indicate that the higher rate is due to "company policy." Once the offer is made to accept subject to modification, the underwriter must then wait for the applicant or insured to accept this proposal.

With a rejection, the underwriter has the task of selling the negative result. The underwriter should effectively communicate not only the rejection of a risk but also the reasons which led to that rejection. Good communication contributes to the education of the producer for future submissions. For example, if a commercial property submission has been declined due to the physical condition of the structure, one approach might be to return the submission to the producer with the notation, "rejected due to substandard condition." While this is true, it does not convey enough information. A better approach would be to list those particular features of the risk that are substandard. This provides the producer with a guide for future submissions and contributes to his or her education as a field underwriter.

There is an element of diplomacy in the communication of a rejection. Frequently the goodwill of the producer can be maintained by presenting convincing arguments that show the decision to be a reasoned one rather than an arbitrary rejection.

Monitoring the Decision One aspect of monitoring underwriting decisions involves the evaluation of the results of those decisions. The premium volume and the loss ratio indicate the results of underwriting decisions. The second aspect of the monitoring deals with the periodic review of the risks underwritten to determine that recommendations have been implemented and that the hazards have not increased.

Evaluation of the underwriting decisions would be simple if the outcomes or results always reflected the quality of the decisions. This is not the case. It is possible to have a good decision with a bad outcome. When a bad outcome does occur, a review of the underwriting file will usually indicate if the decision was the best one that could have been made, based upon the information that was or should have been available at the time the decision was made. If that is the case, then the flaw is not in the decision making. Rather, the underwriter has again been subjected to the whimsical vagaries of "Lady Luck."

Another factor complicating the assessment of the quality of decisions based on results is that a bad decision can result in a good outcome. The decision may appear to be better than it was. A commercial fire underwriter, for example, may have shown poor judgment in writing a risk that is in poor physical condition. If there are no losses, the decision appears to be a good one, judging from the results to date, when in fact the decision was a poor one. In the long run, these poor risks will produce more losses than contemplated in the rate. Cases of this type are difficult to uncover since the lack of losses decreases the likelihood that the file will ever be reviewed. Frequently the file will not be reviewed until renewal. There is a tendency for the review of an account with good loss experience to be perfunctory. When reviewing such a file, it would be useful to consider whether the favorable experience was due to a good decision that was previously made or whether it is simply the case of a bad decision that has had good results to this point.

Monitoring a Book of Business

The results of a series of decisions can be monitored for an entire class or book of business. The better the quality of the individual risk decisions, the better the results on the book of business should be, assuming the number of policies is of sufficient size. Both the volume and the loss ratio should be considered in this review. An overly restrictive underwriting policy may hold down the loss ratio but at the cost of greatly restricting the premium volume. This may result in a premium volume that is too small to support the fixed and overhead costs, thus causing an unsatisfactory combined ratio (that is, loss and expense ratio). Furthermore, overly restrictive underwriting may produce a low loss ratio but, because of small volume, a small profit as well.

For the purpose of analysis, the book of business in a particular line such as commercial property or auto coverage can be subdivided in several ways. These examples include:

1. rating class and class of business
2. territory
3. producer

An analysis of the book of business on the basis of rating class will show if the individual risk decisions have resulted in an imbalance in the book of business. This would occur if a disproportionately large amount of the volume was in one or several rate classes. The loss ratios by class of business may indicate classes with poor or deteriorating experience. Loss ratio analysis of this type should be tempered by a consideration of whether the volume is sufficient for the results to be credible.

An analysis of the book of business on the basis of territory will show the degree of geographic dispersion present. In property lines, too much concentration in a particular area or territory may result in an unanticipated conflagration (a raging destructive fire) hazard. In certain parts of the country, the same holds true with respect to windstorm. In auto insurance, territorial imbalance may result in an overexposure in high accident areas.

Analysis of the book of business by producer will indicate the volume and loss ratios of the individual producers. The mix of business between personal lines and commercial accounts can also be determined and compared to the mix that is desired. This information is useful not only to the underwriter but also to the marketing department as an indication of areas where attention is needed.

Each individual risk represents an underwriter's assessment that the physical hazards contained within the risk are commensurate with the premium being charged. The underwriter should periodically monitor those hazards to determine that the situation remains unchanged. If recommendations were made at the time of the acceptance of the risk, follow-up is necessary to determine that they have been carried out. Particularly with respect to large commercial lines, monitoring activities will determine whether any changes have taken place in the physical, moral, and morale aspects on which the original decision was made. A business reversal or a change in the social or economic climate can change a desirable risk into one with unacceptably high hazards.

PROSPECTIVE AND RETROSPECTIVE UNDERWRITING

Prospective Underwriting

Prospective underwriting is defined as that situation where the underwriter has no past experience to draw on and there are no similar exposure units. This would occur, for example, if the underwriter is called upon to provide coverage for a business or venture that is new or unique. As an illustration, a large gas utility once ordered a fleet of large tankers to transport gas from Alaska and Indonesia to Southern California. What was unique about this risk was that the tankers, which were slightly under 1,000 feet long, were transporting the gas in a compressed, super-chilled form. The ships were in effect large thermos bottles. The characteristics of this fleet differ considerably from the ordinary oil and gas tankers. The underwriter considering this risk employed prospective underwriting.

Since, by definition, the risks to which prospective underwriting is applied are new or unique, the underwriter will not have a body of loss data to draw upon. What can be done is to search for analogies. This is an attempt to discern similarities between this risk and others with which the underwriter is more familiar. When wild animal parks were first introduced, they represented some new and unique problems for the commercial liability underwriter. In the search for analogies the underwriter considered those elements that the wild animal park had in common with a zoo with which the underwriter was already familiar. In both risks there are animals both able and willing to bite or claw the patrons. The analogies, when they are found, enable the underwriter to place the new risk in perspective relative to what is more familiar.

The second step in prospective underwriting is to study those characteristics of the risk that are different. This analysis represents an attempt to assess the hazards inherent in this risk and not present in any other. The underwriter dealing with the compressed gas tanker had to obtain data on what would occur if the tanker were involved in a collision. The probable frequency and severity of explosion, pollution, or contamination had to be assessed. The liability underwriter considering the wild animal park had to determine the differences between the park and a zoo. In a zoo, the wild animals are in cages or compounds, and the people roam freely about the grounds. In the wild animal park, the people are confined to their automobiles while the wild animals roam freely about the grounds. This represented a different set of hazards. The proper assessment of hazards that have no close analogies is one of the most challenging tasks faced by the property and liability underwriter.

Retrospective Underwriting

Retrospective underwriting is defined as that situation in which the underwriter has adequate loss history and sufficient similar exposure units for purposes of comparison. (This term should not be confused with retrospective *rating*, which is a pricing technique described in a later chapter.) Virtually all auto underwriting is retrospective in nature.

One technique employed in retrospective underwriting is the analysis of individual risk and class loss experience. Since the underwriter has data available on the loss history of similar risks, the analysis of this history can help predict the likelihood of future losses. Characteristics that are highly correlated with losses can be identified. One example is the relationship between accidents and traffic violations. Exhibit 2-3 shows the results of a study by the State of California Department of Motor Vehicles. It clearly shows that those drivers with one or more convictions for moving violations over a three-year period have more accidents than the drivers with no violations. This is retrospective information since it is based upon an analysis of the loss

Exhibit 2-3
Number of Convictions vs. Accident Rate — Three-Year Period*

Number of Total Convictions	Relative Increase in Accident Rate Over "0" Convictions (Times-As-Many Factor)	Percent of "Accident Free" Drivers
0	1.00	89.44%
1	1.95	80.09
2	2.70	73.74
3	3.54	66.81
4	3.98	64.44
5	5.17	57.75
6	5.34	55.95
7	6.72	48.12
8	8.11	44.94
9+	9.03	39.56

*Adapted from *The California Driver Fact Book*, State of California, Department of Motor Vehicles, April 1981, Report No. 29, p. 5.

history of exposure units similar to those the underwriter is currently writing. The loss history of the individual risks represents another type of retrospective data. The credibility of this information must be carefully considered.

ILLUSTRATIVE CASES

The cases in this section illustrate the application of the decision-making process. While the cases are kept fairly simple, each shows how the underwriting of an individual risk or a book of business is a step by step process. While few underwriters think in terms of step one, step two, and so on, most will recognize the process.

A Homeowners Submission

The underwriter has received the following homeowners submission from producer A. W. Smythe. Name of insured: L. V. Jones. Address: 101 High St., Bigtown. Coverage desired: HO-3, $100,000 coverage A on the dwelling, $300,000 coverage E, personal liability.

First State Bank of Bigtown holds a mortgage on the property in the amount of $60,000 and there are no other liens of the property.

The underwriter applies the six steps of the decision-making process to this application. The first part of the process, recognition of a situation that calls for a decision, is quite simple since the producer does not have binding authority and has asked for an answer soon. Therefore, the underwriter moves on to the second step, gathering, organizing, and analyzing information. From conversation with the producer, the following information is gathered regarding this risk.

The house in question is three years old and located in a quiet residential neighborhood. The area is rated as protection class 4. (The protection class measures the public fire protection. Class 1 is highly protected; class 9 is unprotected.) The house is of frame stucco construction with a tile roof, and the amount of insurance requested reflects 90 percent of current replacement cost. The applicant is an accountant with the local office of a national firm and is well thought of in the community. He has a large swimming pool which is fenced and a Doberman pinscher which is reportedly well-mannered and gentle. The underwriter orders an inspection report to verify this information. This completes step two.

The underwriter determines that the following courses of action are available:

1. Accept the risk on the terms requested.
2. Accept the risk with a modification in the coverage. Possible modifications include writing the risk on HO-2 with more limited coverage, or writing the risk on HO-3 as requested but holding the liability limits to $100,000 because of the dog and swimming pool.
3. Reject the submission.

Identification and development of these alternative courses of action completes step three.

In step four, the underwriter evaluates the alternatives that have been identified. The risk appears to be above average in its class; therefore, the underwriter determines acceptance of the risk on the terms requested to be the best available alternative. In step five, the underwriter actually makes the decision to accept the risk on the terms requested.

Step six implements the decision that has been reached. The underwriter calls the producer to communicate the fact of the acceptance. This does not complete the process. The underwriter must still issue the policy and then monitor the decision to determine its quality and to ascertain that the hazards in the risk are as described by the producer and remain unchanged. Based upon the information given, the policy is prepared and delivered to the bank with a copy to the insured.

One week later, the inspection report arrives. The report confirms that the insured is well thought of in the community and that the neighborhood and environs of the risk are excellent. The investigator had no opportunity to observe the dog but heard no adverse comment about the dog in the neighborhood. The report adds that while the swimming pool is in fact fenced, the fence is a decorative one, eighteen inches high. A call to the producer determines that the producer asked the insured if the pool was fenced, but it had not occurred to the producer to inquire about the height.

Through this monitoring activity, the underwriter has determined that one material aspect of the risk is not what the underwriter assumed it to be when writing the risk. The underwriter informs the producer of the severe liability exposure inherent in a swimming pool that is inadequately fenced. The producer is informed that if the condition is not corrected, it will be necessary to retire from the risk on a homeowners basis but that the underwriter would be willing to write dwelling fire and extended coverage, without the liability exposure.

The producer calls back, one hour later, and states that the insured was extremely cooperative when informed of the problem and that the insured has already called a fence contractor to install a proper six-foot fence surrounding the swimming pool. The underwriter, upon verification from the producer that the fence has been installed, returns the risk to the files.

When is step six, monitoring the decision, completed? The answer is that it is not completed as long as the risk remains on the books. The monitoring process is a continual one, whether on an individual risk or on a book of business.

Decision Making on a Book of Business

A national fire underwriting manager is making a review of fire underwriting loss history. One particular class, lumber yards, has had poor experience. This leads into the first step of the decision making process, recognition of a situation that calls for a decision. Once this has occurred, the process of information gathering and the organization and analysis of information begins. It is determined that the loss ratio on this class has steadily deteriorated in recent years. The premium volume is sufficiently large, and company experience is felt to be credible. The underwriter next obtains the industry experience on this class over the same time period. The same pattern of deterioration in results is noted.

The next step is to identify and develop alternative courses of action. The underwriting manager develops the following alternatives:

1. Prohibit any further writing in this class.
2. Place this class in a restricted category in that all submissions must be referred to the home office for approval.
3. Reduce the fire line (retention) in the class from $100,000 to $50,000
4. Change the reinsurance arrangements for this class.
5. Take no action.

In step four, the underwriting manager evaluates the effect of each of these alternative courses of action. The effect of each action upon the producers, upon the insurer's competitive position, and upon premium volume and losses is considered.

Entering into step five, the underwriting manager decides to reduce the fire line in this class.

In implementing this decision, which is step six, the underwriting manager sends a bulletin to the underwriters setting forth the change in the underwriting manual. This action completes the communication portion of implementation. Monitoring the decision remains. The underwriting manager continues to watch the premium volume and losses in this class particularly closely to determine the outcome of the decision. Over the next two years, the premium volume in the class drops slightly, but the loss ratio exhibits gradual improvement.

In the examples above, the decision-making process was applied to an individual homeowners submission and to a problem involving an entire book of business. In the case of the submission, the recognition of a situation that called for a decision was a trivial part of the process. This was not the case with respect to the decision on the entire book of business. Once that step was reached, the gathering, organizing, and analyzing of information was similar for both decisions. The only difference here relates to the type of information required for the different decisions.

Steps three, four, and five, involving the identification, evaluation, and choice of the alternative, are similar in both cases. The major element of difference arises from the relatively wider range of alternatives available with respect to the decision on the book of business.

In these cases, step six illustrates different facets of the communication and monitoring activities. The manner in which the individual risk decision was implemented was quite different from the implementation appropriate to the decision on the book of business. This follows from the wider scope of the decision on the book of business. The only difference in monitoring the two decisions is in the scope of the monitoring process.

In both of these examples, the same decision-making process has been applied. A decision involving the overall insurance risk portfolio of the insurance company would entail the same procedure.

SUMMARY

Decision making is a pervasive facet of everyday life. Modern methods of decision making provide a systematic approach which has as its goal better outcomes (results) to be achieved through better decision making. The results of underwriting decision making are seen in the volume and loss experience of the insurance company. The analysis of how decisions are made in order to improve the results is analogous to a golfer analyzing the components of the swing in order to lower the score. One of the problems in evaluating the quality of decisions is that it is possible to have a good decision and a bad outcome or a bad decision with a good outcome. (However, over the long run, the better the decisions, the better the results will be.)

The time and money devoted to a decision should be appropriate to its importance. This is an application of the concept of information efficiency. Underwriting is a special case of decision making under uncertainty. The two areas of uncertainty are that the outcomes of each of the possible alternative courses of action are unknown and the underwriter's knowledge of the characteristics of the risk under consideration is imperfect. Decision scientists have developed the concept of perfect knowledge. Time and cost considerations preclude the attainment of perfect knowledge with respect to the characteristics of the risk under submission; therefore, the underwriter must work with varying degrees of imperfect knowledge.

The first step in the decision-making process is the recognition of a situation that calls for a decision. The second step is the gathering, organizing, and analyzing of information pertinent to the decision. There are both internal and external sources of information. Sources of information include the application, the underwriting file, the producer, governmental records, financial rating services, the claims department, inspection reports, sales personnel, and underwriting guides. The information which flows to the underwriter should be divided into its components of objective facts and subjective impressions. It is also necessary for the underwriter to determine the physical, moral, and morale hazards inherent in the risks under consideration.

The third step in the decision-making process is the identification and development of alternative courses of action. Underwriting has been termed both an art and a science. An important part of the art of underwriting is the creative process of developing innovative alternatives. The best decision cannot be made if the best alternative course of action is not among those under consideration. The decision tree is a technique that enables the decision maker to structure the alternatives and their outcomes in a systematic fashion in order to obtain valuable insights.

The fourth step in the decision-making process is the evaluation of the alternatives. This step involves weighing the relative merits of each course of action. This is followed by the selection of the best alternative, which is the fifth step in the process.

The final step in the decision-making process is the implementation of the decision. The first portion of implementation is the communication of the decision to those affected by it. This is followed by monitoring the decision. The monitoring function continues as long as the risk or class affected by the decision remains on the books. Whether a decision affects an individual risk or an entire book of business, the same process is employed. On decisions affecting an entire book of business, the scope of the decision is wider and the means of implementing the decision are different from the individual risk decision, but the decision-making process is identical.

Chapter Notes

1. Joseph W. Newman, *Management Applications of Decision Theory* (New York: Harper & Row, 1971), p. 3.
2. For a detailed presentation of decision trees see John F. Magee, "Decision Trees for Decision Making," *Harvard Business Review*, Vol. 42, No. 4, July-August 1964, pp. 126-138.
3. Chester I. Barnard, *The Functions of the Executive (Cambridge, MA: Harvard University Press, 1968), p. 194.*

CHAPTER 3

Coverage Analysis

INTRODUCTION

Analysis of relevant information is crucial to sound underwriting decisions. An underwriter must develop the ability to dissect and examine the essential elements of any insurance contract with emphasis upon the underwriting significance of these contract (or policy) terms and conditions.

A logical starting point is a thorough examination of the scope and limits of coverage provided by the contract in question. In time, underwriters may become very familiar with the major clauses of the policies they underwrite daily, and the need to refer to sample forms may diminish. But underwriting takes place in a rapidly changing environment. Legal, social, and technological developments create or alter potential losses, requiring frequent checks with the contract itself to be certain that the coverage provided is the coverage intended. As the person charged with committing and protecting the insurer's assets, the underwriter must be aware of all policy provisions that may affect coverage.

The skill of analyzing coverages and the knowledge accompanying it are often acquired through experience. Some underwriters suggest facetiously that the best way to learn the extent of coverage is to experience a covered loss. Although effective, this learning experience can be extremely expensive to the insurer, and it still does not guarantee that all potentially severe losses will be brought to the underwriter's attention. A study of past errors in judgment made by other underwriters can be a valuable learning tool.

An underwriter's knowledge of coverages is useful at two levels—

individual risk underwriting and book of business underwriting. In the first case, applicants are evaluated for their loss-causing potential. Each of these potential insureds and the property or situation to be insured is a unique blend of exposures to loss. An old cliche among underwriters is, "No two risks are exactly alike." The peculiar characteristics of each risk must be related to policy provisions that deal with these potential loss characteristics.

In the second case, underwriters including department managers and supervisors manage entire books of business composed of many somewhat similar risks which, because of their similarity, may be insured through the same standard contract. At times, modifications are necessary, for example, adding or removing exclusions to entire classes of business or attaching a special form to "tailor" the coverage to a class of insureds. Thus, knowledge of coverages and their relationship to an entire book of business is essential to successful underwriting management.

At this point, it should be stressed that contract analysis is not always a defensive action by the underwriter to avoid an undesirable situation. It is often a positive activity directed toward meeting consumer needs. Producers and insureds look to the underwriter to determine if the policy requested is proper for the insured. For example, suppose an applicant has requested very limited property coverage on contents including stock at the manufacturing location. Upon reviewing the nature of the insured's operations in the inspection report, the underwriter may discover a transportation exposure to stock that is not covered by the policy requested. If the transit exposure is acceptable, the underwriter may bring this exposure to the attention of the insured or producer and offer to provide coverage. This type of activity exemplifies the *positive* approach to underwriting.

Knowledge of insurance contracts and the ability to relate contract provisions to individual risks are important in another way. Often, producers request broader coverage on a particular risk than the underwriter is willing to provide. Rather than decline the application altogether, the underwriter may offer a more limited form of coverage. The producer then has an opportunity to provide some form of protection to the client, and the role of the underwriter is enhanced. Knowledge of the various alternative insurance policies and skill in applying those policies to an individual risk are necessary to provide a high degree of professional service.

ANALYSIS OF INSURANCE CONTRACTS

The primary objective of this chapter is to develop a *procedure* for underwriters to use in determining the *underwriting significance* of insurance contract clauses and provisions. New underwriters or experienced practitioners handling a new class of business may ask themselves, "What is the extent of coverage I am providing through this contract?" To answer this question, the numerous agreements, exceptions, statements, extensions, and limitations must be organized into a framework for study and analysis.

Virtually every insurance policy provision can be classed as one of the following:

1. Declarations
2. Insuring agreement
3. Exclusions
4. Conditions

These categories provide a convenient way in which to study insurance clauses, but more importantly they also indicate the particular function performed. Although many insurance contracts may not use these four terms as headings, they are useful in understanding the content of any insurance contract and in relating any endorsement (or any document that amends a basic policy) to the section of the contract affected.

Declarations

The *declarations page* (also called a "dec" page, "schedule," "information page," or a "daily") contains information about the insured, the property or locations insured, the types of coverage, and the limits of liability. The information unique to the insured (name, address, and description of property or location) is contained in the declarations section and "personalizes" the coverage to the insured. The underwriting files of many insurers simply consist of the declarations page and any special endorsements to the policy rather than a complete copy of the entire contract.

The declarations page provides, at a glance, the major items of underwriting information referred to when reviewing the policy during its term or when the policy is being renewed. The "dec" page may also provide the underwriter with rating information such as classification, territory, experience rating factor, and so on. Additional information regarding the producer and the forms and endorsements attached to the policy will be shown on the declarations page. Under the Insurance Services Office (ISO) commercial package policy, there are two "dec" pages. The first is common to all coverages and the second is specific to each line of coverage. The second is the "dec" page which would show the rating information described.

Insuring Agreement(s)

The *insuring agreement* is a statement of the insurer's commitment under the contract. In many insurance policies there is more than one insuring agreement, with each coverage part or section clearly stating the insurer's agreement under that section. All insuring agreements, whether relatively brief or somewhat lengthy, are modified or clarified by declarations, conditions, or exclusions. When considering applications or submissions for insurance, underwriters must carefully equate the intent of the insuring agreement with the potential losses presented by the applicant and the amounts that may be paid in the event of a loss. To do this, the underwriter must analyze the insuring agreement in the light of definitions stated in the policy itself, court interpretations, and, most important, conditions and exclusions that amend the insuring agreement.

Exclusions

Exclusions are used to clarify the meaning of terms in the policy or to limit coverage. For purposes of contract analysis, the terms "exclusions" and "exceptions" may be considered as synonymous. Some contracts include a list of terms or events that are excluded, while other sections of the contract provide broad coverage and specifically eliminate some items or events through exceptions. The two have the same effect.

Exclusions that restrict or eliminate may pertain to:

- losses, perils, or certain hazards that are not generally considered to be commercially insurable (such as war);
- losses, perils, or hazards that are more appropriately covered under another type of policy (such as the aircraft liability exclusion in the commercial general liability policy [CGL]);
- losses that are wholly or partially in the control of the insured and are therefore not considered fortuitous (such as the marring or scratching exclusion in the fine arts floater);
- loss of property that is difficult to verify or to value yet significant enough to warrant separate treatment (such as currency or manuscripts);
- losses that occur with frequency, are generally small in amount, and are relatively expensive for the insurer to process (such as damage to trees, plants, and shrubs caused by vehicles owned or operated by a resident of the premises in the homeowners policy.)

These categories should be helpful to underwriters in that the exclusions can be grouped into classes according to the type of exposure they are designed to control. There is some overlap between these classes; a particular exclusion may exist to perform more than one function and consequently would fall into more than one of these classes. In that case, however, the underwriting implications are even less likely to be overlooked.

Conditions

In a legal sense, the *conditions* of an insurance contract are the provisions with which the insured must comply in order to hold the insurer to its obligations.

An example of a condition that imposes an obligation on the insured is the following from the business auto policy:

A. YOUR DUTIES AFTER THE ACCIDENT OR LOSS.
1. You must promptly notify us or our agent of any accident or loss. You must tell us how, when and where the accident or loss happened. You must assist in obtaining the names and addresses of any insured persons and witnesses.
2. Additionally, you and other involved insureds must:
   a. Cooperate with us in the investigation, settlement or defense of any claim or suit. No insured shall, except at his or her own cost, voluntarily make any payment, assume any obligation or incur any expense.
   b. Immediately send us copies of any notices or legal papers received in connection with the accident or loss.
   c. Submit at our expense and as often as we require to physical examinations by physicians we select.
   d. Authorize us to obtain medical reports and other pertinent medical information.

Examples of general conditions which have underwriting implications are contained in the standard homeowners policy:
1. **No Benefit to Bailee.** We will not recognize any assignment or grant any coverage that benefits a person or organization holding, storing or moving property for a fee regardless of any other provision of the policy.
2. **Severability of Insurance.** This insurance applies separately to each insured. This condition will not increase our limit of liability for any one occurrence.

The "no benefit to bailee" clause protects the underwriter from unintentionally providing coverage to other persons or firms such as trucking companies (called carriers) or warehouses (called bailees) through the policy. Quite often, coverage would be willingly provided to such other firms if proper underwriting information is obtained and an appropriate premium is paid. This clause, then, is necessary as a control device to prevent an unintended extension in coverage. Every condition can be illustrated in this way to bring out its purpose, and most will have significance to underwriting.

The second clause is another example of clarification of policy intent through conditions. Through this clause, the insurance applies to each insured separately, but the limit of liability applies to all if more than one insured is named in the same lawsuit. Again, the control function of underwriting is apparent, and if broader limits of liability are needed by the insured, these should be negotiated with the underwriter.

A PROCEDURE FOR CONTRACT ANALYSIS

In the analysis of any insurance contract, a framework or procedure is necessary to make certain that a systematic approach is followed and that no provisions are omitted in the analysis.

A framework gives the underwriter a checklist of items to look for and helps to develop a general pattern of insurance contract provisions. With this pattern, deviations are easier to discern, and the contract analysis procedure can be accomplished more quickly with less chance of error.

For example, having studied the underwriting significance of the standard subrogation clause in one policy, there is no need to embark on an intensive examination of the same clause in another. The underwriter has only to verify that the clauses are the same; if so, the underwriting implications should be the same unless amended by other policy conditions. Underwriting experience with one policy can thus be transferred to others.

If the two clauses are dissimilar, it would be necessary to compare the two, analyze the difference, and decide whether the differences are significant in the risk being underwritten. In this way, an underwriter becomes familiar with a standard pattern and looks for deviations from that pattern.

Every policy clause must be examined *as it relates to, is amended by, or is suspended by* other policy clauses. Serious underwriting errors can be made if a careless underwriter reviews only the major policy section pertaining to the item being analyzed. Other policy sections may alter or delete the coverage provided elsewhere, and endorsements that are no longer attached may change the coverage significantly.

In general, the objective of insurance contract analysis is to determine if coverage exists and to what extent the underwriter is providing the coverage. This objective can be achieved by answering the following specific underwriting questions:[1]

1. What persons or interests are insured?
2. What property, activity, or situation is insured?
3. What places or locations are insured?
4. During what time period is coverage provided?
5. What perils are insured?
6. What kinds of losses are insured?
7. What are the limits on the amounts of coverage?
8. What *miscellaneous* clauses affect the coverage provided?

Many veteran underwriters have developed their own checklists for policy analysis. The checklist discussed here is only one of several possible lists. It is important, however, that some systematic procedure be used in analyzing the underwriting implications of insurance contracts.

What Persons or Interests Are Insured?

Insurance contracts exist to protect persons from the financial consequences of a covered loss. It is customary for underwriters to refer to the "property which I have insured," although it is actually the *person* who is being insured. An underwriter *insures* the person against loss but *covers* the property. Similarly, in liability insurance, it is the persons covered in the policy who are being insured for the payment of sums for which they may be legally liable.

In analyzing any insurance contract, a distinction must be made between the *named insured* and *persons insured*. In many cases, the extent of coverage provided by the contract is substantially broader to the named insured. Consequently, there may be reason to investigate further and evaluate underwriting information pertaining to the persons named in the policy. In general, the named insured is simply the person(s) or organization named in the declarations. For example, a policy could be issued to John E. Barrett, John E. and Patricia M. Barrett, John E. Barrett doing business as Barrett's Hardware, or John E. Barrett, Inc.

Insurance on businesses is often written in the name of a corporation or corporations. For example, a policy may be written for the "Alpha Products Company, Inc.; APC Realty Co.; and Alpha Products Sales Co., Inc." Because the corporate name often does not reveal the identity of the persons who are being insured, underwriters sometimes require that the persons who own or control the corporation be identified prior to the issuance of a policy and periodically thereafter. A corporate name may be used to shield the identity of individuals who may be undesirable risks. Legitimate businesses have been purchased by criminals to provide a "cover" for their illegal operations. Knowledge of the breadth of the policy provision pertaining to persons insured is a reminder to investigate carefully the identity and interests of those being insured.

A questionable situation that should be investigated by underwriters would be a corporate name that does not indicate any parties at interest. An example would be a blind trust in the name of a bank where the identity of the parties is concealed, or where some other situation exists which seems to have as its purpose the concealment of the identities of the owners.

In addition to the named insured, coverage is extended to other "persons insured" whose exposures to loss must be carefully evaluated by the underwriter. For example, when underwriting a private passenger auto application, it is important to note that the typical personal auto policy extends liability coverage under various circumstances to the following in *addition* to the named insured:

1. the named insured's spouse, if a resident of the same household;
2. relatives of the named insured or spouse who are residents of the same household as the named insured or spouse;
3. any other person using the covered auto; and
4. any other person or organization legally responsible for the use of the covered auto by persons in 1, 2, and 3.

The extension of coverage to the other persons was deemed in the best interests of the named insured to cover losses from customary practices such as loaning a car.

In property insurance, the same distinction between the "named insured" and "persons insured" exists, and the underwriting implications are similar. For example, most homeowners policies extend coverage for property belonging to relatives living with the named insured, and if the named insured desires, property belonging to guests and residence employees is also covered.

Extensions of coverage to persons other than the named insured can complicate the problem of determining whether the applicant is acceptable. Moreover, the decision on whether the risk should be considered average, above average, or below average is made more difficult because of the presence of other persons insured.

Other classes of persons insured are mortgagees (a bank or other financial institution that holds a mortgage loan on the property), legal representatives and assignees. In property insurance, underwriters routinely extend coverage to include the mortgagee's interest. In many property insurance contracts, the mortgagee clause provides for a continuation of coverage of the mortgagee's interest even if the insured has suspended coverage by violating a policy condition such as by increasing the hazard. That is, a violation of a policy condition might suspend coverage to the named insured, but the mortgagee's interest is not affected unless it had knowledge of the violation. Some peculiar underwriting problems can arise if the insured abandons the property, and the mortgagee, due to more pressing problems, cannot adequately protect it.

Some underwriters feel that the existence of a mortgage reduces the need for an investigation of the property and the owner since this was done by the mortgagee. Often, however, the mortgagee's investigation is of a different nature than that needed for underwriting purposes. Moreover, government guarantees of mortgages have influenced some lenders to curtail or limit their investigations.

The term legal representatives refers to executors or heirs under a will and receivers in bankruptcy. In general, legal representatives simply act on behalf of the named insured, and underwriters should realize that the coverage provided to these representatives is no broader than that provided to the named insured. These legal representatives serve with court consent or by court appointment and generally present little, if any, moral hazard.

An assignee is a person to whom an insurance contract has been assigned (transferred with the property sold, for example). To illustrate, this would be the case if Randall sells his home to Wiening and "assigns" (transfers) the homeowners policy to Wiening at the time of sale. Most property and liability insurance policies require the written consent of the insurer before an assignment is binding on the insurer. Accordingly, underwriters are protected from the undesirable situation of covering persons they have not investigated. A property insurance contract insures the *owner* of the property against loss. The policy does *not* insure the property. If the property is sold, the insurance remains in effect on the previous owner to the extent of his or her insurable interest. It does not follow the property unless the underwriter agrees to an assignment. A basic principle of underwriting is the right of selection of policyholders. This right should not be used unfairly to discriminate among insureds with the same loss potential, but it is necessary to reduce the number of fraudulent losses. An underwriter cannot be forced by means of an assignment to insure anyone who happens to acquire an insurable interest in the property.

Assignment clauses apply only to assignments *before* a loss. After a total loss, the right to receive the loss payment may be assigned by the insured without the underwriter's consent. This type of assignment does not increase the loss potential facing the underwriter. When a total loss has occurred, a settlement must be made, and the assignment only changes the person who is paid for the loss. But in the case of a *partial* loss, the remainder of the policy *cannot* be assigned without the consent of the underwriter.

The question, "What persons or interests are insured?" is a crucial one for underwriters, and the answer may be complicated by the many classes of insureds and interests described above. In commercial lines, all of the corporations and organizations owned and controlled by the named insured must be underwritten. None of these additional insureds should be ignored by the underwriter on the assumption that investigation of the named insured is sufficient.

What Property, Activity, or Situation Is Insured?

Property insurance contracts do not cover every item of property owned by the insured, and liability insurance contracts do not cover every conceivable situation which could lead to a claim against the insured. The property or situations insured are generally defined in the policy to limit or extend the coverage to meet the needs of most insureds and to control premium costs.

In property insurance or the property section of a package policy, most types of real and personal property can be covered under one form or another, and underwriters must be familiar with the definitions and exclusions of property under the form being underwritten. Additionally, they must develop the skill of comparing the coverage of property intended in the policy to the coverage of property requested in the application. That is, the property covered should consist of the property stated in the declarations as amended in the policy jacket, form, and endorsements.

Property may be covered in three general ways: schedule (sometimes called specific), blanket, and, in the case of inland and ocean marine insurance, on an open basis. If the property is insured on a schedule basis, the items are specifically listed in the policy or on an attached schedule kept in the underwriting files with an amount of insurance for each of them. For example, a property policy may be requested to cover:

1. $75,000 on the one-story brick and masonry building occupied as a machine shop and situated at 426 Winter Street;
2. $15,000 on equipment situated in the above-described building.

In this case, different amounts of insurance are to apply to scheduled items of property.

In a typical general property form, buildings are defined as follows:

A—BUILDING(S): Building(s) or structure(s) shall include attached additions and extensions; fixtures, machinery and equipment constituting a permanent part of and pertaining to the service of the building; yard fixtures; personal property of the named insured used for the maintenance or service of the described building(s), including fire extinguishing apparatus, outdoor furniture, floor coverings and appliances for refrigerating, ventilating, cooking, dishwashing and laundering (but not including other personal property in apartments or rooms furnished by the named insured as landlord); all while at the described locations.

The breadth of coverage provided for "buildings" in this policy should alert underwriters to ask pertinent questions such as:

- Does the building occupied as a machine shop have any of the above-listed items of property (such as equipment constituting a part of the building)?
- If so, does the amount of insurance applied for include the value of these items?

These questions are representative of the kinds prompted by an examination of contract clauses when underwriting a particular risk. Similar questions may be posed when analyzing the definition of equipment, stock, or contents. These definitions are precise and sometimes include property that is not anticipated by the underwriter or the insured. Thus, the definitions should be analyzed carefully *with a particular risk in mind.*

A second method of insuring the property is on a *blanket* basis, in which more than one item of property or more than one location may be "blanketed" or grouped under a single amount of insurance. For example, a building, equipment and stock blanket form, covers "all property of an insurable nature, both real and personal, now existing or hereafter acquired, except 'Stock' as defined...."

This approach avoids some of the underwriting problems inherent in schedule coverages, but the broad nature of the wording presents other potentially serious exposures. When underwriting blanket coverage as just described, questions such as the following must be satisfactorily answered:

- What is meant by "property of an insurable nature" in the building, equipment and stock blanket form?
- What controls, if any, does the underwriter have to prevent this policy from covering extremely hazardous or damageable property that might be "hereafter acquired?"
- Does the machine shop in question present unusual exposures to loss to property that is "high valued" or difficult to replace?

Answers to these questions may be found in the experience of senior underwriters, underwriting files on similar risks, *F.C. & S. Bulletins* (Fire, Casualty & Surety Bulletins—National Underwriter Company), *Best's Underwriting Guide,* and similar sources. The answers to questions pertaining to the specific machine shop itself may be obtained from the producer, from an inspection report, or from the insured.

The *open* approach to insuring property is used in inland and ocean marine insurance. For instance, an "open cargo" policy is issued by an underwriter to cover all shipments made within a specified period of time and over predetermined shipping routes. A unique feature of this form is that insureds are given the privilege of issuing certificates of insurance on their own property for an amount of insurance that is within the policy limits. These certificates may be transferred or assigned to other parties somewhat like negotiable instruments. In this situation, the primary concern of an underwriter is the loss of control over the type of property being insured. To some degree, the underwriting functions of determining what property is insured, and in what amounts, are delegated to the insured.

In liability insurance, the "situations covered" by the policy are parallel to the "property covered" in property insurance. Like property insurance, liability policies can be limited (scheduled) to premises and operations only, or comprehensive (blanket) such as the commercial general liability policy—CGL. The types of situations to be covered indicate the kinds of information needed to make underwriting decisions. Careful analysis of the declarations, insuring agreement, exclusions, and conditions are essential to determine the intended scope of the policy. For example, the CGL is designed to cover most liability situations arising from the use of "mobile equipment," as defined. However, the definition is sufficiently broad to include many loss exposures not generally envisioned by underwriters. Among the items included in the definition of mobile equipment are the following:

1. bulldozers, farm machinery, forklifts and other vehicles designed for use principally off public roads,
2. vehicles maintained for use solely on or next to premises owned or rented by the named insured, and
3. vehicles that travel on crawler treads.

Although by no means all-inclusive, the above illustration points out the detail into which contract analysis may delve. Moreover, the analysis should be undertaken with the loss exposures of a particular risk in mind. A high degree of imagination is required by the underwriter in associating an applicant's exposures with the exposures envisioned in the policy.

What Places or Locations Are Insured?

An insurance contract carefully written in regard to persons insured and property (or situations) insured may be inadequate if some locations are omitted. Similarly, failure to ascertain the territorial scope of a policy could result in an unexpected loss. Both situations underline the importance of matching the applicant's needs for coverage in various locations with the proper policy form.

Many property insurance policies cover primarily at a single location, and this location then becomes the object of the underwriter's attention. However, the underwriting investigation should not be limited to the primary location because some loss exposures are presented from other locations covered in the policy.

Virtually all property insurance contracts have extensions of coverage away from the location stated in the policy. For example, a typical building and contents form extends a limited amount of insurance applicable to contents to cover the described property, other than stock, that is temporarily at a location not owned, leased, or operated by the named insured. Additional information pertaining to these off-premises locations may be necessary.

Multiple locations owned or operated by the insured may be listed on one policy using one of the multiple-location forms which provide for movement of property among the locations. Consequently, an underwriter must investigate the desirability of providing coverage at each of the locations, which may range from highly desirable to unacceptable. In such a situation, underwriters should weigh the risk characteristics of all locations and view the account as a whole.

Some types of property are so often in transit that the approaches discussed so far are inadequate. Instead of limiting coverage at stated locations and temporarily elsewhere, it may be preferable to cover the property wherever it is located. This is called *floater* coverage and is most commonly used in inland marine insurance, which often give worldwide coverage. The territorial clause may read as follows: "Unless otherwise provided hereinafter or endorsed hereon, this insurance covers wherever the property may be located."

The geographical scope of coverage should signal the underwriter to examine the characteristics of the territory where the insured property is expected to be located. The acceptability of a risk often depends on the presence and seriousness of certain hazards within a particular territory. For instance, an application covering motor truck cargo or contractor's equipment may be evaluated primarily on the basis of the location or even the terrain where the property is located, transported, or used. Contractor's equipment in a hilly area is generally more susceptible to damage than similar equipment used on level ground.

Many insurance contracts provide coverage principally at a described location but also provide "floater" coverage on certain types of property. This is true of homeowners policies which cover primarily at the location named in the policy but also cover personal property "anywhere in the world." Similar provisions exist in many commercial package policies.

From an underwriting standpoint, there are substantial differences between "floater" coverage that applies to property wherever it may be located, and temporary off-premises coverage which is an extension of a fixed location policy. In the former case, the transit exposure may be the most serious exposure to loss, and the policy limits may be at stake. In the latter case, the amount of insurance applying away from the named location is generally limited in commercial policies to from 2 to 10 percent of the amount of insurance applying to the class of property, and often transportation perils are not covered.

In liability insurance, the activities or situations covered are also subject to limitations on places or locations insured. Some comprehensive liability policies extend coverage "anywhere in the world" or "within the United States of America, its territories or possessions, and Canada." On the other hand, the locations covered may be limited to operations in the states listed in the declarations (as in a workers' compensation policy).

In addition to the definition of policy territory, an underwriter must carefully review the declarations and all endorsements pertaining to location. For example, the business auto policy provides coverage in the United States of America, it territories or possessions, Puerto Rico, or Canada. This means that, unless endorsed, a trucking firm has countrywide coverage even if the premium charged reflects a local, noncongested traffic exposure. Endorsements designed for a specific class of applicant should be studied to determine what peculiar risk characteristics prompted the drafting of the endorsement and whether those risk characteristics are present in the applicant being underwritten.

During What Time Period Is Coverage Provided?

At first glance, the duration of coverage question seems to refer simply to the policy period. However, cancellation provisions (and the laws restricting them) and provisions extending coverage beyond the policy term are also pertinent to an analysis of duration of coverage.

Termination of insurance policies has become increasingly restrictive. State laws and state insurance department regulations must be consulted to determine the underwriter's prerogatives in canceling or nonrenewing policies. In some states, an underwriter must provide continuous auto liability coverage on a policyholder as long as the premium is paid and the insured has a valid driver's license, in spite of a policy clause allowing for cancellation.

In most lines of property and liability insurance, advance notice of cancellation by the insurer is required, and the required length of time is stated in the policy. In addition, cancellation procedures dictated by the insurer or by state regulations must be followed to assure that the policy is terminated legally.

A practice that is gaining wider acceptance is the issuance of *continuous* policies. There are savings in the expense portion of the premium by issuing one policy with periodic renewals by certificates. Coverage under these policies does not expire, and policies are terminated only by cancellation, in compliance with applicable laws and policy provisions.

Occurrence versus Claims Made Although the policy term applies to losses or incidents that occur (or begin to occur) during that period, losses are not always reported promptly. A peculiar characteristic of liability insurance is the time lag between the occurrence of the alleged negligent act and the report of the claim. Although professional medical liability and products liability are particularly affected by this loss development delay, underwriters are aware of its effect on most liability polices. Because a claim may be presented several years after an incident has occurred, an especially heavy burden is placed on underwriters in their efforts to adequately price the coverage. To alleviate this situation, some policies have been changed from an *occurrence* basis to a *claims-made* basis.

The Insurance Services Office (ISO) commercial general liability (CGL) policy form gives insureds the option of choosing between coverage on an "occurrence" or a "claims-made" basis. Consequently, underwriters and producers must be thoroughly familiar with the advantages and disadvantages of each form *as it pertains to the insured in question.*

If a policy is written on an occurrence basis, the underwriter provides coverage on those losses which occur during the policy period even if claims are not actually brought against the insured for years after the coverage has expired. If a policy is written on a claims-made basis, the underwriter provides coverage on only those "claims made" against the insured *during* the policy period. An analysis of the contract would reveal whether the coverage afforded is on a "claims-made" or "occurrence" basis. The major difference between the two forms is what activates or "triggers" coverage. Under the "occurrence" form, the policy in effect when the bodily injury or property damage occurs responds to the claim. If the injury or damage occurs over several policy periods, all the policies in effect during these periods may be called upon to pay part of the total losses. Under the "claims-made" form, the policy in effect when the claim is made (usually required to be in writing) responds to the claim.

Similarly, in property insurance, consideration must be given to those policy provisions that may extend coverage beyond the expiration date of the policy. Business income policies generally cover the reduction in net income during the period of time required to restore normal operations, and the duration of loss may extend well beyond the expiration date. This may be the case when highly specialized machinery is being replaced.

It should be evident to underwriters that the duration of coverage under an insurance contract is not simply a matter of the time that elapses between the inception and expiration dates. Policy provisions regarding cancellations and state regulations and statutes are factors that must be weighed in making an underwriting decision. These "time" factors affect the overall acceptability of the risk and assist in determining a premium commensurate with the exposure to loss.

What Perils Are Insured?

As defined in Chapter 1, a "peril" is a cause of a loss. In fact, the property forms under the ISO commercial package policy do not use the term perils but use "causes of loss." In property insurance, common insurable perils include fire, windstorm, explosion, smoke, theft, collision, and similar perils. In liability insurance, the peril insured against is the legal liability (actual or alleged) of insureds. In both cases, insurance contracts can provide coverage either on a specified perils (or named hazards) basis, or on a comprehensive "all-risks" (or all hazards) basis. The term "all-risks" is a misnomer. In property insurance, "all-risks" really means "all-*perils,*" and refers to fire, explosion, windstorm, etc., with certain exclusions. In liability insurance, the term "comprehensive" or all-risks refers to the *hazards* insured, such as auto, premises, products, etc., which tend to increase the frequency or severity of a loss. Because of the problem of concurrent causation, the term "all risks" is disappearing from insurance policies. Concurrent causation is described in detail in a later chapter.

To the novice underwriter, or an underwriter entering a new field, one of the most important preliminary steps in contract analysis is defining and interpreting the perils insured against. Unfortunately, all of the needed information cannot be found in the policy itself. Some perils are not defined in the insurance contract but have been defined and interpreted through law and legal precedent. For example, fire is not defined in the commercial property forms. Underwriters must be aware that, due to changes by litigation, interpretations of any perils not defined in the policy may vary in different states at different times. Accordingly, company underwriting bulletins, subscription services such as *F.C.&S. Bulletins* or *Policy Form and Manual Analysis*, and information from other underwriters should be consulted and recorded in reference files.

In the policies that define perils, great care has been taken to assure that the coverage provided is the coverage intended. The insurance meaning of a term sometimes may differ from the more common usage, and this may cause misunderstandings with insureds. In many cases, the definition of a peril is somewhat limited in the specified perils contracts but is broadened in the comprehensive policies.

To illustrate, in a common general property form, "smoke" is restricted to:

> sudden and accidental loss or damage from smoke other than smoke from agricultural smudging or industrial operations.

The detail in this policy definition gives underwriters a clear picture of the types of losses to expect and can be related to the physical condition of the risk to assist in determining its acceptability. Here, any smoke damage that is "sudden and accidental" (except smoke from agricultural smudging or industrial operations) is covered.

With regard to perils, the most difficult forms to underwrite are "all-risks" (or all hazards) contracts. In these forms, the burden of proof is on the insurer that a loss which occurs is not covered within the meaning of "all-risks." In reviewing applicants for "all-risks" coverage, a high degree of imagination is needed to answer the question, "What causes of losses am I insuring?" Here, again, the exclusions must be analyzed to determine the intent of the contract.

In the "all-risks" approach, the coverage of smoke damage is much broader. A typical special causes of loss form insures against "risks of direct physical loss," unless the loss is excluded or limited. In the exclusions sections it is stated that the policy does not insure against "loss or damage caused by ... smoke, vapor or gas from agricultural smudging or industrial operations."

Thus, unlike the earlier form, it is not required that the smoke damage be "sudden and accidental." Therefore, losses caused by a gradual exposure to smoke would be covered under the special form.

In liability insurance, the underwriter's attention shifts to the *hazards* which may cause a liability claim. The major hazards consist of liability arising out of autos, premises, operations, elevators, independent contractors, products, completed operations, contracts, and professional, personal, and employer's liability. As in property insurance, the policy definitions as well as related court interpretations should be consulted and retained on file for future reference.

What Kinds of Losses Are Insured?

In the analysis of a property insurance contract, the types of losses covered are either *direct* or *indirect.* Direct losses are the physical loss of or damage to the objects insured. Indirect losses are caused by some direct damage but occur over a period of time. These indirect losses can be divided, for policy analysis, into *consequential* losses (such as spoilage of meat in a freezer that was without power because of a direct damage loss); and *net income losses,* which result from a reduction in the net income of the insured caused by either a reduction in gross revenue or an increase in expenses. Time element coverages were designed to meet this loss exposure, and they include business income, extra expense, rents and rental value insurance, tuition and fees insurance, and so on.

Originally considered a "fringe" or optional coverage, insurance covering indirect losses is now considered by many corporate risk managers to be essential. A review of actual claim files reveals that time element losses often exceed direct damage losses.

Because insurance contracts provide for both the loss of profit and continuing expenses and the extra expenses incurred to continue in business or just the latter, the needs of the applicant must be known so that the appropriate policy form can be chosen. For example, a newspaper publisher has almost no need for business income because any shutdown will most likely be permanent due to the loss of market to competitors. However, a publisher would need extra expense coverage to absorb the additional cost of renting substitute printing presses and overtime compensation for employees.

The underwriting implications of certain clauses in business income insurance should be noted. For example, a common business income form covers: "... the actual loss of Business Income you sustain due to the necessary suspension of your 'operations' during the 'period of restoration.'" Period of restoration is defined as beginning the date of the direct physical loss or damage and ending "on the date when the property at the described premises should be repaired, rebuilt or replaced with reasonable speed and similar quality."

The breadth of this insuring agreement is a caution sign to the underwriter who, for instance, is considering an applicant who depends upon obsolete machinery or highly specialized inventory which would require considerable time to replace. Such risks should not necessarily be avoided, but it is up to the underwriter to recommend appropriate loss control techniques or practices (such as sprinkler systems, security measures, or carrying an inventory of spare parts) to make the risk acceptable. The starting point in this process is contract analysis with the potential losses of the applicant in mind.

In liability insurance, the kinds of losses covered are generally bodily injury (sometimes expanded to include personal injury) and property damage losses. The relative importance of each type of loss will vary considerably from one risk to another. Bodily injury liability may be the more serious loss exposure to a school district, whereas property damage liability may be more important to a building contractor. The terms "bodily injury" and "property damage" liability are defined in the policy and are fairly standardized. Definitions of "personal injury," however, are not standardized, and some contracts may be extended to cover discrimination and humiliation. Underwriters should be aware of the policy definitions and evaluate submissions in light of those definitions.

Underwriting in a changing legal environment has caused changes in policy provisions. For example, auto liability policies now extend to cover benefits under the various no-fault statutes which, like medical payments, cover losses without regard to negligence. Thus, liability policies must be examined in terms of changing legal conditions in each jurisdiction where losses may occur.

What Are the Limits on the Amounts of Coverage?

Perhaps the most complex aspect of coverage analysis is the determining of the amounts of coverage a policy provides. Most insurance contracts have numerous clauses, and when more than one clause applies to a given situation, the underwriter must decide in a systematic way which clause takes precedence. Although the contract provisions relating to amounts of coverage are primarily dealt with in the claims adjusting process, underwriters, in evaluating the potential losses presented by applicants and insureds, must base their decisions to some extent upon the contract limitations pertaining to the amounts of recovery. Some underwriters refer to this as "adjusting the loss in advance."

Every insurance policy must have limitations on amounts, and the amount of insurance is generally related to the premium paid by the insured. Often, insureds who are dissatisfied with claim payments could have collected substantially more if they had paid a higher premium for higher limits since they were acceptable from an underwriting stand-point. Insurers' loss payments must be matched to premium income to assure that financial stability is maintained and that all insureds are treated equitably.

The major contract limitations on the amounts of recovery in a loss are:

1. extent of insurable interest;
2. valuation of the loss itself;
3. policy limits (including "inside" limits or sublimits);
4. insurance-to-value requirements (such as coinsurance, contribution, and average clauses); and
5. deductibles.

Each of these major categories has an effect on the underwriting decision. Based upon these contract clauses and their relation to the potential losses of the applicant, the underwriter has information regarding the acceptability of the risk, the premium that should be charged, and the terms or conditions that should be attached to the policy to broaden or restrict the amounts of recovery.

Extent of Insurable Interest The maximum reimbursement for losses is subject to the interest of the insured. That is, if an insured owns 50 percent interest in a building and a total loss occurs, the insured is entitled to 50 percent of the loss proceeds. For obvious underwriting reasons, insureds must be prevented from collecting more than they lose. The insurable interest provision is written into many property insurance policies but also has been upheld in court decisions involving policies without such specific wording.

Valuation of the Loss Itself Both property and liability losses must be adjusted according to the "value" of the damaged or lost property and the "value" (cost of settling) of the bodily injury liability claim against the insured.

Some property insurance contracts are written on an *actual cash value* basis, but actual cash value is not defined in the policies. Custom and a long list of court cases support the general rule that actual cash value means replacement cost minus depreciation (*physical* depreciation, not *accounting* depreciation) or obsolescence. This requires that replacement cost be determined and that depreciation be measured. These computations are crucial to claims adjusting, but underwriters often find themselves in situations where the determination of actual cash value is an important factor in the underwriting decision. Although underwriters are not expected to compute the actual cash value of the insured property, there are many situations where underwriters will compare the amount of insurance to the estimated actual cash value, to discover if coinsurance penalties might be applicable at the time of a loss and to determine if the property is insured to value. Likewise, indications of overinsurance, a possible hint to moral hazard, can be confirmed only by a determination of the actual cash value of the property.

The increasing use of *replacement cost coverage* creates similar problems for underwriters. If the policy provides replacement cost coverage on buildings only with actual cash value applying to contents, an appraisal may be sufficient to answer questions concerning the amount of insurance. If the replacement cost provision extends to contents as in the homeowners policy of some insurers, several more specific questions must be answered, such as:

- When was the property purchased and for how much?
- Can the insured personal property be replaced?
- If the value is unusually high or if the property is irreplaceable, can coverage be provided on another form, using different valuation terms?
- What has inflation done to the replacement cost of the property?

These general questions can and should be made more specific to each particular risk. This is done by analyzing the valuation clause and determining the extent to which it applies to the risk.

Occasionally, underwriters are asked to deviate from the actual cash value concept or the replacement cost approach. Businesses sometimes request that merchandise be insured for its *selling price.* The selling price includes the profits that would be earned if the goods had been sold. Similarly, some property is customarily insured on a *valued* basis and the value is agreed upon between the insured and the underwriter at the time the policy is issued. These deviations from the actual cash value concept are fairly consistent with the intent of the concept of indemnity but do present some challenges to underwriters.

In some states called *valued policy states*, the insurer is required to pay the face amount of the policy if there is a total loss to real property. To overcome the possibility of overinsurance, some underwriters believe all property in valued policy states should be appraised before the policy is written. However, since relatively few losses are total losses, other underwriters believe that it is less expensive to pay an infrequent excessive claim than to absorb appraisal costs on all properties. Underwriters should carefully study the applicable valuation clauses of any policy that deviates from the actual cash value or replacement cost basis because the specific wording will vary between policy forms or may be amended by endorsement.

In liability insurance, the valuation of the loss is determined either by negotiation between the insurer and the claimant, or by litigation. If the claim is litigated, the verdict generally will include the actual cash value of the damaged property and compensation for bodily injury (including pain and suffering) incurred by the claimant. When a property damage liability claim is litigated, the court often instructs the jury to determine the actual cash value of the property, add a reasonable amount for the loss of use of the property and, at times, add the loss of profits as well. Thus, the concept of actual cash value is also involved in the valuation of liability claims. Most liability contracts cover "loss of use"—a factor that can greatly increase the potential loss—and underwriting decisions on pricing should not overlook this factor.

Policy Limits   The amounts of recovery under both property and liability policies are always restricted by some policy limits. Property insurance recoveries almost never exceed the face of the policy, and some losses are limited to lesser amounts on certain types of property or certain types of losses (for example, the limit on theft of unscheduled jewelry in most homeowners policies). In liability insurance, the cost of defense, premiums on bonds, the cost of investigation, and other expenses are usually paid in addition to the limits of liability. The extension of coverage under these various clauses should be of concern to underwriters in determining whether the applicant presents too great an exposure to loss and in determining an appropriate premium.

The use of policy limits, either maximum limits or "inside limits," is an outgrowth of the control function of underwriting management. Some applications for property insurance, such as unprotected frame restaurants, may be acceptable only if the exposure of the insurer is limited to a small amount and the premium made to reflect the probable frequency and severity of loss. The inability to obtain adequate policy limits for both property and liability insurance has provided the motivation for the loss control devices or programs of many below-average risks.

The control function is also apparent in the use of aggregate limits. *An aggregate limit is the maximum loss payment per unit of time, per type of loss, or per policy.* Aggregate limits may apply to both bodily injury and property damage liability, depending on the form used.

Property underwriters are faced with some loss of control when writing coverage on a blanket basis or on a reporting form. On a blanket basis, the policy form provides for the amount of insurance to apply to multiple locations without specific limits per location. Many businesses have a mix of good, average, and poor locations, and under blanket insurance the total amount may be applied to the poor location. Blanket forms are sometimes required when property is moved regularly from one location to another.

When writing reporting form coverage, underwriters are protected by the policy limit, which is often set at 20 to 30 percent above the maximum expected values. Since the insured pays a premium based upon reported values (which are within the insured's control), the policy stipulates that the insured may be penalized in the event of a loss if reports are late, inaccurate, or if no reports are made. Many underwriters are reluctant to issue reporting coverage to an insured who is expected to be late in reporting values to the insurer.

The amount of insurance on the face of the policy does not always indicate the underwriter's total exposure to loss. In determining the maximum acceptable "line" for an insured, it is necessary to total the amounts of insurance under each of the insuring agreements. For example, under the homeowners policy, the amounts applying to other structures, personal property (contents), and loss of use are paid in addition to the amount covering the dwelling. Thus, the total exposure to be underwritten under a homeowners policy with a $100,000 limit on the dwelling exceeds $180,000. If the total amount at risk is too great for the insurer to absorb, reinsurance may be sought.

Insurance-to-Value Requirements Loss payments may be limited in still another way. Many standard policies stipulate that the insured must carry an amount of insurance equal to or greater than a predetermined percentage of the value of the property insured. These "insurance-to-value" requirements are necessary to make certain that the premiums collected are commensurate with the amount at risk as well as to provide equity in rates. It is estimated that only 2 percent of all property losses are total losses, and an underwriter insuring a building valued at $300,000 under a policy providing $100,000 of coverage could pay several losses within the policy limit. The premium collected, however, reflects an exposure of only $100,000.

Insurance-to-value requirements include coinsurance clauses, prorata distribution clauses, agreed-amount endorsements, and full reporting clauses in reporting forms. A detailed analysis of the underwriting implications of each of these clauses is beyond the scope of this chapter. An underwriter should, however, be able to apply the terms of such clauses to particular risks to determine their effect upon the underwriting function. To illustrate, suppose an underwriter is reviewing an application for property coverage on an institution that comprises fifteen buildings varying in age from two to forty-five years. To avoid the possibility of a coinsurance penalty, the applicant (through the producer) requests an *agreed-amount* endorsement whereby the insured and the insurer agree that the amount of insurance satisfies the insurance-to-value requirement. In this case, the underwriter must collect and analyze appraisals and other cost information to assure that the amount of insurance is sufficient compared to the total exposed values. Since there are many differences in the wording of agreed-amount clauses, the policy clause in question should be examined at the outset.

Although chiefly associated with direct damage insurance coverages, insurance-to-value requirements are applicable in indirect (net income) property insurance. *Coinsurance* clauses, also called contribution clauses, exist in most business income policies. To some extent, the use of graded premium rates (lower rates for higher limits) in liability insurance achieves this same objective of motivating insureds to carry adequate coverage against severe loss.

Deductibles The use of deductibles is the fifth category of policy clauses affecting amounts of recovery. In most property lines, deductibles are used to eliminate small losses which are relatively expensive to settle, and to reduce rates. Underwriters often use deductibles as an incentive for an improved loss control program by the insured. The acceptability of renewal coverage on an insured with an unusually large number of small losses may hinge upon the insured's consent to participate in losses through some form of deductible. Deductibles are not widely used in liability lines because insureds require claim service even on small claims and the underwriter needs prompt reporting of all claims regardless of size.

The use of deductibles is not always within the control of underwriters. Some policy forms or insurance company filings dictate the type and sometimes the amount of the deductible that applies. This is common in homeowners and commercial package policies, as well as auto physical damage insurance. If the underwriter has flexibility, as one does in large commercial lines, the choice of deductibles must be considered in the light of (1) the types of deductibles available to the class of business and (2) the underwriting problem to be solved.

In summary, the limits on amounts of recovery are found in contract clauses that fall into the five categories explained herein. Underwriters must be aware of the *interaction* among these many provisions and their cumulative relationship to the loss exposures of the insured. It is helpful to list on a sheet of paper all of the terms that affect the amounts of recovery, beginning with the basic policy, the forms or coverage parts, and endorsements. Viewed in this way, underwriters can compare this intended scope of coverage to the specific risk in question. Then, situations calling for special attention such as a potential coinsurance penalty or an expensive piece of property which exceeds the policy's inside limits will be more apparent, and appropriate underwriting action can be initiated.

What Miscellaneous Clauses Affect the Coverage Provided?

There are several miscellaneous clauses that may have strong underwriting implications but do not fall into the seven categories examined previously and might be overlooked. The reason these miscellaneous clauses may be ignored is that they are part of all policies and thus do not seem to affect the decisions regarding the acceptability or pricing of individual risks. However, all of the following clauses are significant to the underwriter and to the underwriting manager of a book of business. This brief summary covers only the major types or classes of miscellaneous clauses. Of course, the reader is strongly urged to refer to the actual policy being underwritten to ascertain the specific extent of the clause discussed here in a general way. A review of these clauses with a particular risk in mind may suggest questions or items of information necessary to assure that the insurer is not unduly exposed to loss and that the policy is the proper one for the insured.

Subrogation   Subrogation is a common law right of an insurer that has paid a loss to a policyholder. Although the right of subrogation is a well-established principle of equity, many contracts state that the insurer may require from the insured an assignment of all rights of recovery against any party for loss to the extent that payment is made by the insurer. To permit the insured to collect the proceeds of the policy from the insurer and then to collect again from the person responsible for the loss would be contrary to the principle of indemnity.

The rights of the insurer under subrogation are only as good as the rights of the insured. Thus, underwriters need to know what, if any, actions by the insured (such as releasing a common carrier of liability) affect the insurer's right of subrogation. An example is the practice of using a "released" bill of lading in connection with shipments of property via common carrier. In the released bill of lading the shipper (property owner) "releases" the goods to the carrier (trucking company, for example) for a given value and therefore limits the amount a shipper can recover from the carrier in case of loss. Consequently, the right of an insurer or the owner to collect from the negligent carrier is similarly limited. Underwriters may rectify this condition by either requiring that the goods be shipped under a bill of lading with no release or by charging a higher rate to reflect the reduced potential for subrogation recovery from the common carrier.

In liability insurance, the opportunity for subrogation arises when the insured is held liable for the negligence of another and proceeds against the negligent third party. For instance, a workers' compensation insurer can proceed against a third party who negligently causes injury to a covered employee. The subrogation clause may also require that the insured cooperate fully in any action against a third party. The subrogation clause of the standard workers' compensation policy states:

> Recovery from Others
>> We have your rights to recover our payment from anyone liable for an injury covered by this insurance. You will do everything necessary to protect those rights for us and to help us enforce them.

These contractual provisions in the policy go beyond the common law principle of subrogation. They strengthen the rights of an insurer to recover from the third party responsible for the loss. Thus, underwriters are somewhat shielded from the full financial impact of the loss if the subrogation clause is in effect and if the insurer successfully exercises its rights.

Defense and Defense Costs In most liability insurance, as previously mentioned, the costs needed to defend the insured must be added to the limits of liability to indicate the total loss potential facing the underwriter. These supplementary payments not only impose additional costs on the insurer, but they may also impose a duty to defend. Although some policies such as umbrella liability, which is not standardized state that "the company *may* defend," the majority of liability policies specify that "the company *shall* defend" the insured "even if any of the allegations of the suit are groundless, false, or fraudulent."

Policy clauses specify the types of expenses included in defense costs. In some liability lines such as professional liability, directors' and officers' liability, or products liability, the costs to defend may present a greater loss potential than the amount of the settlement.

Of concern to underwriters is whether the allegations of the lawsuit are within the coverage of the policy. There can be a question of coverage under personal injury for allegations such as invasion of privacy, wrongful eviction, defamation of character, or humiliation. Underwriters should note that these coverages expose the insurer to defense costs even if the suit can be successfully defended.

Provisions for Other Insurance Almost all property and liability insurance contracts contain policy provisions, known as *other insurance provisions*, which specify or limit the insurance company's liability if other insurance exists. At first, it may seem that these provisions have importance only in loss adjustments. However, many commonly encountered other insurance provisions were developed to lessen the moral or morale hazard as much as, or more than, to limit insurer liability.

The major categories of other insurance provisions are:

1. *contributing* (cover a proportionate share of the loss);
2. *primary* (pay up to its limit without regard to the other insurance);
3. *excess* (pay only the part of the loss not covered by the other insurance); or
4. *no-liability* (not pay at all if other insurance exists).

Contributing Provisions. Other insurance clauses that are "contributing" provisions include *pro-rata* (by policy limits) and *equal shares* provisions. A common pro-rata provision is:

> You may have other insurance subject to the same plan, terms, conditions and provision as the insurance under this Coverage Part. If you do, we will pay our share of the covered loss or damage. Our share is the proportion that the applicable Limit of Insurance under this Coverage Part bears to the Limits of Insurance of all insurance covering on the same basis.

This is an example of an other-insurance provision calling for contribution by policy limits in determining the insurer's liability if other insurance exists. Historically, this clause or one like it was inserted by fire insurers to prevent insureds from picking one of several insurers on the risk, collecting a loss from that insurer only, and forcing that insurer to seek "contribution" from the other insurer(s) on the risk. It also was, and is, compatible with the common underwriting need of individual insurers to limit loss exposure on a risk and at the same time participate on an equitable basis with other insurers covering the same risk.

Under contribution by equal shares, losses are shared dollar for dollar up to the point at which the policy with the smaller face amount is exhausted. Any excess is then borne by the other contract(s).

Primary Provisions. There are few types of contracts that specifically state their intent to be primary insurance. There are many that state their intent that *other* insurance be primary, but among commonly encountered coverages only general liability and ocean marine contracts agree in explicit terms to be primary insurance and then only under certain conditions. Primary insurance pays first when other insurance exists unless, of course, the other insurance contains the same provision. Applicable wording from a typical general liability policy reads:

> This insurance is primary except when b. below applies. If this insurance is primary, our obligations are not affected unless any of the other insurance is also primary. Then, we will share with all that other insurance by the method described in c. below.

Paragraph b. is the excess provision and paragraph c. is the contributing provision.

An underwriter may feel that a risk can be successfully written only if the other policy is considered primary. The underwriter's contract may make *its* intent clear, but this is not binding on the other insurance company that issued the contract intended to be primary. Thus, the alertness to review the type of clause in the other policy when analyzing the risk can be an important factor in making an underwriting decision.

Excess Provisions. An excess provision intends that other insurance exhaust the limits of its obligation for the loss before any liability attaches to the policy with the excess provision. Excess provisions are commonly found in many property insurance policies and auto insurance policies as they apply to nonowned, hired, and temporary substitute autos. A typical excess provision is the following, taken from a commercial inland marine policy:

> *Other Insurance* If you have other insurance covering the same "loss" as the insurance under this Coverage Part, we will pay only the excess over what you should have received from the other insurance. We will pay the excess whether you can collect on the other insurance or not.

Contracts with excess other insurance provisions should be distinguished from contracts written on an excess basis. The latter by design are tailored and priced to be excess over underlying insurance or a specified retention by the insured. These will or should always make clear their intent to provide excess coverage *only*. Such a contract obviously cannot be regarded by an underwriter of basic coverage as a potential loss sharer of any loss within the limits of the basic coverage. The pricing structure of insurance written on an excess basis assumes insulation from losses below its attachment point and typically would require much less premium than the same protection written as basic coverage.

Contracts with excess other insurance provisions make no such assumption. Their intent is to provide basic coverage, and they usually are priced accordingly. The excess status is sought *only if* there is other insurance.

No-Liability Provisions. This final category is hard to title appropriately, but its intent is to cover all policy language that denies coverage if other insurance exists. In liability insurance, particularly auto, these provisions are sometimes known as "escape" clauses. Escape clauses are not found in standard liability coverages except indirectly through an exclusion in personal auto coverages, where coverage is denied on newly acquired autos if the named insured has purchased other applicable auto liability insurance for which a specific premium charge has been made.

In property coverages, there are three principal variations of no-liability provisions. One prohibits other insurance, thus making the existence of other insurance a violation of an explicit policy condition. The other two common forms of no-liability provision found in property insurance contracts are: (1) an exclusion of property that is otherwise insured and (2) a simple statement that the policy does not apply if other insurance exists. The former could be viewed as part of the policy language dealing with "property covered"; the latter is a straightforward application of a no-liability provision.

Duties of the Insured When analyzing an insurance contract to arrive at an underwriting decision, reference should be made to the clause dealing with the insured's duties. Initially, it may be felt that little or no underwriting information can be obtained from this provision. However, the specific duties of the insured either before or after a loss are outgrowths of the control function in underwriting management. At times, these may suggest that the applicant would be better off if another policy form were used.

To illustrate, suppose that a reputable producer has requested a reporting form "A" to cover the stock of a paper goods manufacturer at three locations. This application is the first coverage to be submitted from this potentially profitable account, and the producer is most anxious to provide the best service possible and to avoid any situation that might irritate the insured. The value reporting clause of the reporting form imposes a duty on the insured to report values promptly and accurately. It states:

Reports of Values

You must file with us a report, within 30 days of each "reporting period" and at expiration, showing separately at each location the values of Covered Property. Each report must show the values on the dates required by the "reporting period." These dates are the report dates.

The clause goes on to stipulate the restriction in coverage for failure to report promptly. If it is expected that the applicant will be delinquent in reporting, it may be preferable to avoid the reporting situation and issue a policy on a nonreporting basis.

With respect to the duties of the insured after a loss, underwriters must be concerned with the insured's ability to fulfill these obligations. Accepting a risk and issuing a policy are based upon the expectation that the insured will cooperate fully and do everything possible to minimize the loss. The clause dealing with the duties of the insured is important to the underwriter because it assists in minimizing the amount of the loss. There is no way to underwrite profitably insureds who would deliberately allow further loss to occur; accordingly, underwriters must attempt to ascertain the integrity of insureds and their ability to carry out the duties required by the policy.

Conformity to Statutes It is customary for a policy to include a provision stating that "policy terms which are in conflict with statutes within the state are amended to conform to such statutes," or some similar phrase. State legislatures have passed many laws relating to insurance coverage. The provision that the policy shall conform to these statutes is a legal requirement that should caution the underwriter to check any statute affecting the contract. For example, some states require that the time within which suit may be filed must be specifically amended. The contention of the state insurance department in such cases is that policyholders cannot be familiar with all of the statutes and that they should be specifically told of important differences between a standard policy and one written according to the provisions of a particular state.

Likewise, it is useless to issue a named driver exclusion to an auto policy if a state law or state insurance regulation prohibits such exclusions.

Fraud, Misrepresentation, and Concealment Fraud may be defined as a false representation or concealment of a material fact *with the intent and result* that it be acted upon by another party.[2] A concealment amounts to a false representation if active steps are taken to prevent a discovery of the truth. A misrepresentation is also a false representation.

The provision of the homeowners policy relating to concealment and fraud is an example of such a provision:

> Concealment or Fraud. We do not provide coverage for an insured who has:
> a. intentionally concealed or misrepresented any material fact or circumstance; or
> b. made false statements or engaged in fraudulent conduct;
> relating to this insurance.

In connection with underwriting, note that the insured cannot be considered to have committed fraud unless there was an *intent* to defraud. The effectiveness of the fraud and misrepresentation provision in the policy depends upon the questions asked in the application. If the insured is not required to give information about the condition or ownership of the property, he or she cannot be held to have committed fraud if the actual situation differs from that expected by the underwriter.

A defense on the basis of fraud or misrepresentation may be thrown out by the courts if the underwriter knew or should have known of some situation about which the insured has made a misstatement. Knowledge by an agent usually is considered knowledge by the insurance company.

Two important points relating to fraud and misrepresentation must be kept in mind by the underwriter. Fraud or misrepresentation generally can be maintained as a defense only:

1. if the insurer has asked questions which have been answered fraudulently by the insured;
2. where the insurer has been induced to write the policy by the fraud or misrepresentation and the insurer did not have the information available to it.

Warranties A warranty is a stipulation in the policy relating to the nature of the risk insured which conditions the liability of the insurer. A breach of warranty by the insured may void the policy even if the insured gave the information to the best of his or her knowledge.

The effectiveness of warranties varies from one line of insurance to another, depending upon the wording of the warranty and court decisions. Warranties that are signed by the insured and attached to the policy are more likely to be upheld in the courts than are cases where warranties are not signed. The statements made by the insured on an application for a jeweler's block policy are examples of warranties upon which underwriters rely to determine acceptability and pricing. In situations where underwriters exercise some control over contract terms, it may be preferable to attach a mutually acceptable warranty to the policy and ask the insured to sign it. For example, suppose a substantial rate credit is given because the building is equipped with an automatic sprinkler system which, in the underwriter's opinion, significantly reduces the probable severity of a loss. To emphasize the importance of this loss control device to the insured, the underwriter may attach a warranty providing that the sprinkler system and its water supply must not be changed in any way without the consent of the insurer and that due diligence shall be used to maintain the system in good working order.

In summary, the procedures just discussed in general should be applied specifically to an applicant requesting a policy with which the underwriter is not familiar. In this way, the essential elements of the insurance contract are clearly delineated and may be compared to the loss exposures presented by the applicant. The underwriter can then decide if the coverage provided is the coverage intended.

Exhibit 3-1 is a matrix which may be used as a reference. The matrix is filled in when an underwriter analyzes a particular contract for the first time and may be referred to when applications for that particular contract are being evaluated.

Exhibit 3-1
Coverage Analysis Matrix

	Policy Jacket	Coverage Part or Form	Other Coverage Part or Form	Endorsements Broadening Coverage	Endorsements Restricting Coverage	Regulatory Endorsements (State Exceptions)	Other
Persons or Interests							
Property, Activity, or Situation							
Places (Locations)							
Period							
Perils							
Losses							
Limits							
Miscellaneous							

One of the benefits of this matrix is that the important *amendments* or changes can be seen at a glance. For example, if a definition in the policy jacket is altered by the policy form (or coverage part) and further amended by an endorsement, the underwriter can see the ultimate effect on the coverage provided at once, rather than having to refer to the actual jacket, form, and endorsement themselves.

The usefulness of the matrix is limited in two important ways. First, it should be used only to analyze *standard printed* forms that provide identical coverage to all insureds. Manuscript endorsements or printed endorsements that require some typed information unique to each insured must be analyzed directly from the endorsements themselves. Secondly, the matrix is useless if it is not updated. As forms and endorsements are revised, the matrix must be changed to reflect the changes in coverage.

PRODUCT DESIGN AND DEVELOPMENT

Insurance contracts provide the foundation for the underwriting function. Consequently, the policy clauses and conditions must be carefully designed and periodically updated to assure that the coverage provided is the coverage intended. Although most underwriters use printed policy forms prepared by others, every underwriter is involved to some extent in product design, usually in one of two ways.

First, home office underwriters and some underwriting managers frequently work with other departments to develop new policies to cover new risks. Additionally, existing contract forms must be brought up to date periodically to reflect the changing social, legal, and economic environment. Second, virtually all underwriters are involved in product development when they "tailor" a policy to meet the insured's needs through the attachment of endorsements. Often, suggestions for policy revisions made by line underwriters provide the impetus for major product changes.

In order for underwriters to be thoroughly familiar with the coverage provided under various insurance contracts, they should know how the contracts are developed. This knowledge enables underwriters to better comprehend the intent behind the wording of the contract, the particular design of the policy, and the need for periodic changes.

Standard Forms

Almost every major line of insurance is based on a standard contract form used by a large number of insurance companies. Generally, the standard forms are prepared, amended, and distributed by rate-making organizations or bureaus responsible for promulgating rates as well as developing policy forms. The Insurance Services Office (ISO) is the largest of these rating organizations. In this text, the term "bureau" will be used to refer to any rating organization such as ISO and the remaining national or regional rating bureaus or boards.

A large number of insurers use bureau forms almost exclusively, although there has been a trend in the last several years toward the use of "independently filed" forms by many of the larger insurance companies.

Advantages of Standard Forms There are six major advantages to using standard forms:

1. *Economy.* The use of standard forms eliminates the need for each insurer to spend money to develop insurance contracts to cover risks with similar loss exposures. Without standard forms it would be necessary for every insurance company to have its own experts develop its own policies, resulting in duplication of effort and unnecessary costs.

2. *Expertise.* Standardization permits a concentration of experts in policy design. Since each insured pays a share of the cost, sufficient resources are available to attract capable people and assemble them in one area.

3. *Pooling of statistics.* The problems inherent in insurance rate making would be complicated materially if rates had to be established in relation to hundreds of different policies instead of being related to standard policies. Rates must be developed in accordance with the coverage provided by the policies. Insurers that modify the standard policies for their own use must evaluate the effect of differences in coverages so that they can adjust their rates to reflect those differences.

4. *Concurrency.* Insurance policies are said to be "concurrent" if both (or all) contain identical clauses; that is, if the coverage provided is the same under all policies. Many large property risks are covered by insurance provided through several insurance companies. Concurrency of insurance policies is essential in order to provide uniformity of coverage among all of the insurers.

5. *Education.* It is easier for insurance personnel to learn a standard form and then study the deviations from the standard. Producers representing more than one insurer and underwriters competing for business can quickly learn another insurance company's coverage if they are familiar with the standard form and can recognize nonstandard clauses.

6. *Court tested.* The provisions of standard forms that are not new are likely to have been tested in court and the interpretations known.

Advantages of Nonstandard Forms Nonstandard (or independent) policy forms are developed to accomplish objectives or solve problems requiring special consideration. In practice, these independent policy forms are generally variations of the standard forms. The major advantages of independent forms are:

1. *Flexibility.* Flexibility is greater with independent (nonstandard) forms. It is noteworthy that most of the new policies developed in the past were developed independently. A bureau, by its size and nature, requires more time and study to develop

new coverages. An insurance company using independently filed forms can "tailor" its policies to its own method of operation or to the specific territory in which it operates. For instance, it may be able to package auto and homeowners coverages more economically, and improve its efficiency; or if the standard exclusions are not applicable in one particular state or part of a state, an independent form can be developed for use there.

2. *Competition.* Competitive advantages can be gained by the use of independent forms. If, for example, most other insurers exclude windstorm damage to television antennae, an individual insurance company might gain a sales advantage by including such coverage. Replacement cost coverage for personal property under homeowners policies is another example of a competitive advantage brought about through independent forms.

The choice between using standard or independent forms depends upon the underwriting philosophy of the insurer. It is not even necessary to adopt one program exclusively. For example, an insurance company could use standard forms for dwelling and commercial property, and independent forms for commercial packages. The underwriter whose company uses standard forms will have more educational material for use and will be certain that policies are concurrent with those of other insurers using standard forms. On the other hand, the underwriter whose company uses independent forms will have more opportunity to innovate, and changes which could improve the coverage or enhance competitive advantage are more likely to be developed.

Form Revisions

Insurance policies and forms, both standard and independent, must be revised constantly in order that they be kept up to date.

Changes are needed for various reasons. First, as laws and regulations change, contracts must be revised to reflect those changes. Should cancellation laws change, for example, a standard cancellation clause "regarding advance notice to the insured" may need to be changed to a longer period of time, and cancellation may be limited to the few situations permitted according to the statutes. Second, competition may force a change, particularly if an independent form is used. If a standard form broadens coverage, an independent company may feel competitive pressure to follow suit. Third, changes may be necessary as a result of loss experience. Loss figures may show that the coverage provided is broader than intended by those who drafted the policy and is also broader than is assumed by the rates. An example is the broad earth movement revision that was prompted by the payment of earthquake claims under the peril of collapse in California. The "concurrent causation" doctrine resulted in a rewording of the earth movement exclusion.

Underwriters can have substantial influence in achieving such revisions by identifying uninsured loss exposures in which insureds and producers have expressed an interest. This type of information can be gained from conversations with producers and insureds, and it illustrates one of the benefits to the insurance company of having underwriters meet with both producers and insureds.

Underwriters may also recognize potential problems and recommend revisions in coverage to control them. For example, soon after stereo tape players became popular as added equipment in autos, a serious theft problem developed. Underwriters who reviewed individual claims and claims statistics detected a rapid increase in theft losses. Consequently, most insurers responded by excluding coverage for tape players except those permanently installed in the auto. Coverage was available to those who desired it and agreed to pay an additional premium reflecting the additional exposure to loss. Consequently, the theft premium was not increased for the majority of insureds who did not install tape players.

Recommendations of this sort by underwriters often result in major changes and occasionally may result in the development of totally new coverages. More often, the underwriter sees smaller, individual changes which are needed for a particular client, not changes influencing the business as a whole. In these cases, the underwriter may need to endorse the policy to "tailor" it to the needs of the insured. The needs of insureds are often similar, and standard printed endorsements are available for these common needs. The underwriter may draft an endorsement which makes a change in perils, exclusions, persons covered, or other provisions, such as excluding coverage for a dilapidated tool shed on the premises of a covered property. Such adaptation of the policy may permit a risk which would otherwise be rejected to be written. For this reason, the ability to modify a specific contract is an important underwriting tool.

Problems Associated with Form Revisions An underwriter must consider several problems when modifying an insurance policy. These problems may be grouped into four broad categories—legal, regulatory, statistical, and training.

Legal problems consist of the obstacles presented through the body of court decisions (common law) which have been made in the past. The courts' interpretations of the various words, phrases, and provisions in the policy affect underwriting and claims handling. This is a common problem with all contracts but is more pertinent to insurance because of the great number of similar contracts that have been interpreted. A problem peculiar to insurance contracts is the fact that most ambiguities will be interpreted against the insurer, since the insured usually has no opportunity to modify the details of the policy. These legal considerations must be carefully weighed before revising existing forms or issuing new ones.

Regulatory requirements are particularly stringent in the insurance field. Most businesses can enter into any contracts (as long as they are legal) with no prior governmental approval needed. In most states, however, insurance policies must be approved by the state regulatory agencies. Often, these regulations also apply to endorsements and forms. In some states, a specific filing must be made of individual contracts that have been restricted to afford less coverage than the standard policy.

Statistical problems arise when policy forms are changed. Insurance rate making relies heavily on the comparison of past statistics to current statistics. If substantial changes are made in the contracts, it may be difficult or impossible to make proper comparisons. This factor alone has a severe dampening effect on changes in insurance policies. Unless the situation is serious, it may be better to delay making changes for several years until the effects of past changes are known and the impact of proposed changes can be measured.

Training problems arise from the need to teach underwriters, claims adjusters, and producers the coverage provided by the new form. Producers must be able to explain to their clients the differences between the old and new forms. The change from occurrence to claims-made forms is an example of the training problem associated with form revision.

DEVIATING FROM PRINTED FORMS

Although most insurance policies are written on printed forms, there are occasions when underwriters deviate from them, and judgment must be exercised to avoid improper deviations. The major instances of deviation from printed forms are discussed in this section.

Request for Coverage Not Widely Written

Every line of insurance includes some risks which are unusual and may require special treatment for which printed forms are inadequate. The underwriter must analyze the exposures of such risks and determine which contract provisions are to be used, which are to be deleted, and what individual endorsements must be prepared.

The first question to be answered is whether the risk should be accepted by the underwriter. The insurer's underwriting guide needs to be consulted, which, particularly in personal lines, may answer the question immediately. For example, the risk may be of unusual design, such as a geodesic dome construction, or an antique auto which has been completely rebuilt for use in parades and shows. If such unusual houses or cars are not among those considered eligible, there is no need for further consideration. Printed forms may be inappropriate for such risks, and an insurer may decide that it prefers not to write a personal lines policy where substantial modifications in the standard forms are necessary.

If the risk is acceptable, the underwriter next must decide on the contract to use. In the cases just considered, the underwriter may need to endorse the policy to fit the risk; for example, to cover special engineering costs in the rebuilding of a house.

In commercial lines, the applicant sometimes submits the proposed contract. Large multiple-location risks, both commercial and public, often use this approach. Risk managers request bids for insurance and will specify some, or all, of the contract provisions they desire. The underwriter must, of course, analyze those terms carefully. He or she may accept them, and quote a rate on that basis, or accept only some of them, modify others, and submit a bid taking such changes into consideration.

The determination of the contract wording must be based on a comparison of the loss potential of the risk and the proposed wording. Whether the underwriter accepts the contract as offered, modifies its terms, or writes a new contract, the essential consideration is the relationship of the wording to the exposure to loss. To assist in this evaluation, the loss history of the risk should be reviewed, and experienced underwriters as well as underwriting files on similar risks should be consulted. These sources have the advantage of providing the underwriter with examples of actual experiences under similar conditions.

Request for Removal of an Exclusion

Every insurance policy has exclusions, and occasionally an underwriter is requested to remove some of them. The insured, applicant, or producer may make such a request to cover an excluded peril such as earthquake, or an excluded item of property such as manuscripts.

Several factors must be considered and evaluated before such requests can be approved. The underwriter may feel that the exposure is acceptable and that the exclusion can be eliminated as a service to the client or as an accommodation to the producer. In any case, additional premium should be charged for the removal if there is any additional exposure. Some standard exclusions are commonly eliminated, and premium charges are fairly uniform throughout the industry. The removal of other exclusions is less common, and the additional premium to be charged must be determined by the underwriters. Factors to be weighed in computing the premium are the probable frequency and severity of the additional loss exposure, probable additional premium charged by competing insurers, and the reactions of the producer and the insured.

In addition to obtaining additional premium for the increased exposure to loss, the underwriter should try to minimize the exposure. Every exclusion exists because there would be added exposure without it, and an insured will request the removal of an exclusion when a need for the coverage is perceived. This presents a good opportunity for the underwriter to insist upon loss control measures such as safety devices, alarms, or other measures that will reduce the probable frequency or severity of a loss. Thus, an increase in premium is only a limited underwriting response and should be coupled with steps to minimize the loss exposure.

Finally, if an exclusion is removed, the underwriter should set up controls to monitor the decision. The underwriting file should be "flagged" so that the underwriter will be alerted to any incident or claim that arises from the broadened coverage. In this way, a judgment can be made regarding the adequacy of the additional premium and the effectiveness of the loss control measures. From this experience, the underwriter may decide to discontinue the exception and decide against similar exceptions in the future.

SUMMARY

Contract or coverage analysis is the starting point in underwriting all lines of insurance. Analysis of coverages is important to line underwriters handling individual risks as well as underwriters advising top management on the company's entire book of business. In all cases, some procedure or format is essential to determine the underwriting significance of the contract clauses and provisions. These diverse clauses and provisions may be categorized in the following manner:

1. Declarations
2. Insuring agreements
3. Exclusions
4. Conditions

These categories indicate the particular function performed by the policy clause.

Although there are several procedures or checklists for contract analysis, the one used in this text is based upon eight questions:

1. What *persons* or *interests* are insured?
2. What *property, activity,* or *situation* is insured?
3. What *places* or *locations* are insured?
4. During what *time period* is coverage provided?
5. What *perils* are insured?
6. What *kinds of losses* are insured?
7. What are the *limits* on the amounts of coverage?
8. What *miscellaneous* clauses affect the coverage provided?

The full value of this contract analysis exercise is realized when applied to specific applicants or insureds. By associating an applicant's or insured's loss exposures with the coverage envisioned in the policy, the underwriter is provided with information essential to the decision-making process. While the illustrations provided help to demonstrate the usefulness of the procedure and the matrix, they are not intended to be all-inclusive. They are provided mainly to emphasize the *underwriting* implications of certain policy provisions.

Underwriters should know how the various contracts are developed; in fact, they are often involved in this process. While many insurers use standard forms or contracts prepared by rate-making bureaus, there is a recent trend toward the use of independently filed (nonstandard) forms.

The six major advantages of the use of standard forms are: economy, expertise, pooling or statistics, concurrency, education and court tested. The advantages of the use of nonstandard (independent) forms are flexibility and the ability to meet competition.

Insurance forms need constant revision due to changes in laws and regulations, competition among firms, and loss experience. Underwriters, through their recommendations for revisions, may affect the development of totally new coverages. Problems associated with form revisions include legal obstacles, regulatory requirements, statistical considerations, and training problems.

Cases that call for underwriters to deviate entirely from printed forms may include requests for coverage not widely written, and an insured's desire for the removal of certain exclusions.

Chapter Notes

1. Robert I. Mehr and Emerson Cammack, *Principles of Insurance*, 7th Edition (Homewood, IL: Richard D. Irwin, 1980), p. 147.
2. David L. Bickelhaupt, *General Insurance*, 10th Edition (Homewood, IL: Richard D. Irwin, 1979), p. 98.

CHAPTER 4

Risk Management for Underwriters

INTRODUCTION

Before the term "risk management" was first used in the late 1950s, underwriters were managing risks. For years, underwriters have been identifying hazards, encouraging loss control, and asking insureds to bear a portion of their losses. More recently, risk management has become widely accepted for humanitarian and economic reasons.

What, then, is risk management? *Risk management is the process of making and carrying out decisions that will minimize the adverse effects of accidental losses upon an organization.*[1] Although large businesses often employ risk managers, risk management activities are not limited to these individuals. Agents, brokers, loss control representatives, claims adjusters and, of course, underwriters are heavily involved in risk management.

In many ways, risk management and underwriting are very similar. A comparison of objectives, skills, activities, and decision making emphasizes the importance of underwriters' being knowledgeable of risk management. Risk management and underwriting are similar in:

1. Objectives. Both seek to prevent or reduce losses and to settle the losses that do occur in the most efficient manner.
2. Needed skills. The ability to make decisions, to monitor them, and to apply knowledge of loss control, retention (sometimes called self-insurance), insurance contracts, and rating plans to a variety of risks is essential to risk managers as well as to underwriters.

Exhibit 4-1
Decision-Making Process in

Underwriting	Risk Management
1. Recognition of a situation that calls for a decision about what action should be taken	1. Discovering the firm's loss exposures
2. Gathering, organizing, and analyzing information pertinent to the decision	2. Evaluating and measuring the loss potential
3. Identification and development of alternative courses of action	3. Developing alternative methods for dealing with these exposures
4. Evaluation of the alternatives	4. Choosing the best method or combination of methods for dealing with these exposures
5. Choice of one of the alternatives	5. Implementing the chosen method(s)
6. Implementation and monitoring of the selected course of action	6. Monitoring the results to control and coordinate all risk management activities.

3. Activities. Both are heavily involved in discovering and evaluating potential causes of loss; selecting, implementing, and monitoring loss control systems and safety programs; and negotiating the terms, conditions, limits and rating plans of various types of insurance contracts.
4. The process of decision making. The process of making risk management decisions is very similar to the underwriting decision-making process discussed in Chapter 2. (This is shown in Exhibit 4-1.)

This chapter is divided into two major sections. The first is a brief introduction to risk management with emphasis on the various methods or techniques for treating risks. The second is a more in-depth study of loss control—the risk management technique in which underwriters are most likely to be involved.

THE RISK MANAGEMENT PROCESS

As a branch of general business management, risk management shares some activities with other business functions. Any person involved in risk management must plan, organize, staff, direct, and control risk management activities. The steps in the risk management decision-making process shown in Exhibit 4-1 are an adaptation of the basic problem-solving process used in many fields including management.

Risk Discovery

The first and most critical step in this process is the discovery of the loss exposures and related hazards facing the firm. This step raises the question, "What can possibly cause a loss?" Imagination plays a key role here since previously unperceived loss exposures must be anticipated. The term "discovery" is used rather than the more widely used term "identification" because the latter connotes pre-existing known exposures while risk managers occasionally discover an unprecedented and therefore unperceived risk. Surveys have supported the notion that risk discovery and evaluation (collectively called risk analysis) are the most time-consuming responsibility of risk managers. The time involved in risk discovery is well spent. Failure to uncover all the potential causes of loss prevents the firm from dealing with all exposures.

To assist in discovering the various sources of loss, several aids or systematic approaches have been developed—risk questionnaires or checklists, insurance surveys, personal inspections, financial statements, flow charts, and others. Each of these aids has advantages and disadvantages, and no single aid is comprehensive enough to discover and evaluate all of a firm's loss exposures. In fact, most risk managers use a combination of these approaches. Each approach provides some additional information from a different perspective and helps to present a snapshot of loss exposures at one point in time.

One of the most common risk discovery aids is the risk questionnaire or checklist available from insurance brokers, insurance companies, or commercial publishers. The contents portion of such a form is shown in Exhibit 4-2.

Checklists help risk managers to avoid overlooking some loss exposures. They provide a means to discover systematically all or most of a firm's property, liability, and other loss exposures. In large firms where the risk manager is unable to visit all locations on a regular basis, a risk checklist sent by the parent corporation may be used by the local manager. Although this method has some serious flaws, primarily the local manager's lack of risk management training and preoccupation with other duties, this technique may alert the risk manager to the existence of a potential loss that has not been satisfactorily treated. Some larger firms have designated regional or

Exhibit 4-2
Contents Schedule

Schedule number: _____

Location number: _____

Building number: _____

1. Machinery, equipment, tools, and dies:

   a. Replacement cost new_____

   b. Actual cash value   _____

   c. Basis for (b)—obtain appraisal if available _____

   _____

   d. Any chattel mortgage? _____

   Name _____

   Address_____

   _____

2. Furniture and fixtures, equipment, and supplies:

   a. Replacement cost new_____

   b. Actual cash value   _____

   c. Basis for (b)—obtain appraisal if available _____

   _____

   d. Any chattel mortgage: _____

   Name _____

   Address_____

   _____

3. Improvements and betterments:

   a. Date installed   _____

   b. Original cost_____

   c. Replacement cost_____

   d. Actual cash value   _____

   e. Describe   _____

   f. Obtain appraisal if available _____

4. Stock (raw, in process, and finished):

   a. Maximum—at cost _____   at selling price _____

   b. Minimum—at cost _____   at selling price _____

   c. Average—at cost _____   at selling price _____

   d. Present—at cost _____   at selling price _____

   e. How and when inventoried   _____

   _____

   f. Any fluctuations between buildings_____

5. Property of others for repair, processing, or other purpose (including goods held on consignment): _____

6. Is there any agreement covering your responsibilities for these values?_____

7. Property of concessionaires: _____ Consignors: _____

8. Employee's belongings: _____

9. Valuable papers or drawings:_____

    a. Value _____ Reproduction cost _____

    b. Where kept _____

    c. Description _____

10. Value of exhibits—sales office: _____

11. Describe type, size and value of signs:

    a. On premises_____

    b. At other locations _____

12. Care, custody, or control problems:

    Property in bailment_____

    Any warehouseman's legal liability?_____

    Innkeeper's legal liability? _____

13. Water damage and sprinkler leakage exposure, including flood exposure, distance from nearest mass of water and height above water, and percentage of contents value subject to loss: _____

    _____

14. Earthquake exposure and amount subject to loss: _____

    _____

15. Any unusual cameras, scientific equipment or valuable instruments? _____

    _____

16. Any fine arts in office? _____ If so, secure appraisals.

17. Any data processing equipment? _____

    a. If owned, indicate value_____

       If leased, secure copy of rental agreement _____

    b. If leased, who is responsible for damage or destruction?_____

       _____

       _____

    c. Cost to replace data stored in destroyed units _____

       _____

    d. Are duplicate cards and tapes maintained? _____

       Where?_____

       _____

    e. Any potential business interruption exposure? _____

    f. Any use by others? _____ If so, qualifications of senior personnel _____

       _____

       _____

       _____

    g. Secure copy of contract form used and estimate liability exposure _____

       _____

local risk managers and have charged them with this task. They may report to either the corporate risk manager or the operating unit manager. In any case, these "on-the-spot" regional risk management representatives can play a major role in risk analysis. Checklists and questionnaires do little beyond reminding the user that such a loss exposure may exist. A checklist by itself, is limited; but when combined with other tools it assists in the task of risk discovery.

Insurance surveys by insurance agents, brokers, or insurance company loss control representatives also help to discover unperceived exposures through inspection visits. Generally, these are the methods used by small firms that do not have the services of a full-time risk manager and depend upon outside sources for this service. For the firms that are large enough to employ a risk manger, one of the chief risk discovery methods is the personal fact-finding visit to the operating locations.

Personal inspections provide risk managers with the opportunity to "see and feel" the risk situation first hand, although they are time consuming and expensive if many scattered locations must be visited. The inspection is also helpful in implementing and monitoring the risk management program by gathering support for the program from persons at the various locations.

Another widely used risk discovery technique is the analysis of readily available financial statements. The types of assets exposed to loss, the location of these assets, and the methods of protecting them can be developed from financial statements and related documents.

For example, a balance sheet reveals a firm's cash position and raises such questions as:

1. How much cash is kept in banks, how much is kept overnight in safes, and how much is elsewhere, perhaps unprotected?
2. What loss control measures are being taken, such as making daily deposits, stamping checks "for deposit only," and so on?
3. Are amounts of insurance adequate to cover losses even during peak periods?

Similarly, a balance sheet would identify the amount of accounts receivable (money owed by customers)—sometimes a substantial loss exposure. Among the risk management questions raised in analyzing this item are:

1. Are accounts receivable records on computer disc, paper file, or both?
2. Are duplicate copies of accounts receivable kept off-premises in order to reconstruct records if a loss occurs?

3. If accounts receivable insurance is purchased, is the amount adequate, given the fluctuations during the year?

Flow charts trace the firm's activities from the purchase of raw materials through the production process, the transportation process, and the sales process, to the ultimate consumer. By following all of the operations and activities of the firm in an orderly manner, the various types of losses, causes of loss, and hazards can be discovered and, to some extent, loss control methods can be considered at the same time.

The flow chart method also identifies bottlenecks that could cause a serious business income loss. For example, if all manufactured products for various departments are painted and dried in one location, damage to that location could cause an interruption of the business. The flow chart method discloses what the firm does, the processes used, the sequence of activities, and the potential losses.

Risk Measurement

The second step in the risk management process is evaluation and measurement of the potential losses that have been discovered. This step asks the questions: "How significant is the loss exposure?" To evaluate the potential losses properly, an estimate must be made to determine the frequency, severity, and predictability of each exposure. Frequency is the number of times a loss occurs. Severity is the size or financial impact of a loss. *Frequency is a measure of the probability of loss; severity determines the seriousness of those losses that occur.* This measurement process is vital because it ranks loss exposures by seriousness to the firm and also singles out those requiring immediate attention.

Risk Management Methods (Techniques)

Once exposures to loss have been discovered and analyzed, the next step is to evaluate the available methods or techniques for dealing with these exposures. The major risk management techniques are:

- avoidance,
- loss control—prevention and reduction,
- transfer other than insurance,
- retention, and
- insurance.

Most risk management programs, even those of families and small businesses, consist of more than one technique. Underwriters often require that the insured accept a deductible (a form of retention) and comply with safety recommendations (a form of loss control). The adoption of one of these techniques is not an alternative to insurance but a complement to it. More than ever, underwriters tailor insurance programs through these risk management techniques to help meet the objectives of insureds.

Avoidance   Avoidance is the most effective way to handle risks, but it is not always possible. Avoidance means a family or firm avoids potential losses by choosing not to engage in certain activities or own certain property. Of course, the income or benefits arising out of such risks is necessarily lost. Avoidance is generally used when the frequency or severity of the potential loss is too great to be effectively treated by any other risk management method. To illustrate, suppose a pharmaceutical firm has planned to introduce a relatively new drug for the treatment of high blood pressure. Although the drug has been approved for use, a small number of potentially serious claims have been reported during a field test. Because of these claims, the risk manager may recommend that introduction of the drug be delayed.

Loss Control   Losses can be controlled through:

1. *loss prevention*—lowering the frequency or probability of loss,
2. *loss reduction*—lowering the severity of the losses that occur, or
3. a combination of the two.

Providing adequate safety training to employees and assigning responsibility for employee safety to supervisors are examples of loss prevention. The installation of a sprinkler system and the operation of a first-aid facility are examples of loss reduction. Many activities, such as keeping an inventory of spare parts for production machinery and making arrangements for substitute manufacturing facilities in the event of a loss at the main plant, involve both prevention and reduction. Unlike avoidance, loss control does not totally eliminate the possibility of loss. Some chance of loss remains although it may be minimized. Underwriters and risk managers share an interest in loss control since both have the same objective—preventing or reducing losses. Loss control systems and training programs can be expensive, however, and underwriters must be alert for loss control measures that are unrealistic and, therefore, unacceptable.

Transfer Other Than Insurance   Transfer of loss exposures can take place before or after a loss. *Some transfers are loss financing techniques since they simply transfer the obligation to pay for the loss to someone else.* Examples of loss financing transfers are:

- provisions in lease of premises obligating the landlord to repair any damage by fire, and so on,
- similar provisions in construction contracts; bailments, and sales, supply, or service contracts, and
- surety contracts.[2]

Some transfers are loss control techniques since they transfer more than the financial obligation after a loss. Examples of these control-type transfers are:

- subcontracting a part of a construction project to another contractor who takes over the corresponding loss exposures,
- sale of a product line to another firm, and
- hold harmless agreements.[3]

Under a hold harmless agreement or "exculpatory" agreement, the transferee agrees not to hold the transferor responsible for losses for which the transferor would otherwise be responsible. For example, a softball team may sign a hold harmless agreement absolving the team's sponsor from any liability for injury. The loss transfer may not be upheld in court, however.

Retention Retention means keeping or absorbing all or part of the financial impact of a loss. Retention may take the form of a collision deductible on the family car, a substantial retention of $100,000 per loss on a commercial property insurance policy, or the non-insurance of earthquake losses due to high premium cost. If a loss exposure is not avoided, controlled, transferred, or insured, it is retained. Retention is not a last resort, however. It is often the best way to treat high frequency-low severity losses that cannot be eliminated such as glass breakage or small homeowners' losses.

Retention can be either passive or active (see Exhibit 4-3). *Passive retention occurs when a firm or family is not aware that a loss exposure exists and makes no effort to deal with it, or when a loss exposure has been underestimated. This is not the same as planned non-insurance, the decision to absorb losses from the firm's or family's resources after considering other financing methods, that is, active retention.* Self-insurance is one type of active retention.[4] Self-insurance is appropriate when losses can be predicted fairly accurately so that some financing arrangements can be made to absorb the losses as they occur. Absorbing all auto collision losses or accepting a $100,000 deductible per loss on a property insurance contract are examples of active, planned retention. The broad term "retention" will be used in this book to refer to all programs for absorbing losses, including self-insurance and non-insurance.

Exhibit 4-3
Types of Retention

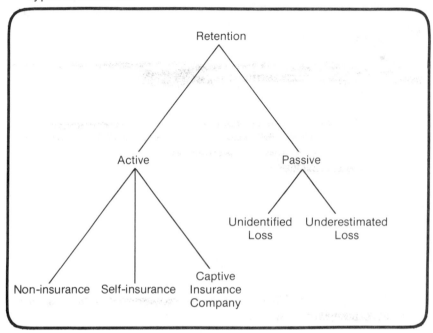

When Retention Should Be Used. Retention should be considered under the following conditions:

1. No other risk management technique is available or the cost of these other techniques is prohibitive.
2. The maximum possible loss can be safely absorbed by the firm or family.
3. The frequency and severity of losses are fairly predictable.[5]

When insurance capacity is shrinking due to heavy losses, retention may be the only way to handle high-risk exposures such as directors' and officers' liability. If premiums become unaffordable, as for some professional liability insurance, retention is forced upon the firm. In times of rapid inflation, when property values rise to heights beyond the capacity of the insurance market, retention of a portion of the loss exposure (usually the highest level) is necessary. Of course, certain uninsurable perils, such as war, are always retained. The size of the maximum possible loss and the financial position of the firm or family must be considered if retention is to be used alone or along with another risk management technique.

Finally, losses must be fairly predictable with relatively little variation from year to year if the retention program is to be successful. Low frequency-high severity losses such as hurricanes are not appropriate for retention because they are hard to predict and difficult to fund.

The potential advantages of retention are expense savings, lower loss costs, and improved cash flow. Perhaps the major attraction of retention is the savings in the *expense* portion of insurance premiums by eliminating duplication of effort by insurer and insured. Agent's or broker's commissions, loss control expenses such as inspection, and loss adjustment expenses are reduced if a firm performs the services these expenses purchase. These services may be provided by an outside source.

Another potential advantage of retention is the savings in the *loss* portion of insurance premiums through motivation for loss control. This applies only where losses are controllable through safety programs. If plant managers are charged with their own workers' compensation losses and their profit sharing is affected, the increased motivation for safety could reduce losses. Likewise, drivers of the family car may be more careful if father announces that the costs of damage to the car will be taken from the weekly allowance of the driver who causes the damage.

Finally, retention holds the promise of improved cash flow and additional income from the funds that would have been paid to an insurer. This presumes earmarked funds set aside and invested until needed to pay losses and loss adjustment expenses.

The potential disadvantages of retention are:

- the uncertainty of total annual costs due to the variation in losses from year to year,
- the possibility that losses will exceed funds, especially in the first few years, and
- regulations prohibiting retention, such as compulsory auto insurance.

An important consideration in comparing the costs of retention with commercial insurance is the direct and indirect expenses of loss adjustment. The cost of purchasing claims services from adjusting companies or insurers, if available, must be added to the indirect cost of the time spent by the risk management department, the safety department, the maintenance department, the purchasing department, and others.

Captive Insurers. One of the most significant developments in risk management is the formulation of captive insurance companies—a sophisticated form of retention. *A captive insurance company is an insurance or reinsurance company owned or controlled by a non-insurance parent company.* Captives are established in part to insure or reinsure the risks of its parent or affiliated companies.

Captives may be grouped into three categories: pure captives, profit center captives, or association captives. A *pure captive provides insurance only for the parent corporation or affiliated companies.* Since there is no true risk transfer in the case of pure captives, some (including the Internal Revenue Service) may not think of them as separate insurance entities but simply as a form of internal risk retention.

A *profit center captive* (sometimes called a broad captive) is *one that accepts risks other than those of its parent and is operated on a profit center basis.* Profit center captives have a better spread of loss exposures—a fundamental ingredient of the insurance mechanism that contributes to long-run loss stability if risks are prudently underwritten. The spread of loss exposures is accomplished by writing direct insurance or reinsurance of other captives and commercial insurers.

An *association captive* (or group captive) *is set up and controlled for limited purposes by and for a particular association and its members.* It is claimed that association captives can provide more technically skilled loss control services than any individually owned captive. Association captives are presently the fastest growing type of captive insurer.

Insurance Insurance is the cornerstone of virtually every risk management program. Historically, risk management evolved out of and is the successor to insurance management, and therefore the traditional emphasis has been to treat most potential losses (at least those meeting insurance requirements) through commercial insurance.

The widespread use of insurance is not solely due to the weight of tradition. In many cases, after considering all of the uncertainties and the lack of stability of noninsurance techniques, insurance often provides the most economical method to finance losses. In addition, some insurance coverages are purchased in order to benefit from corollary insurer services such as inspections, claim service, and legal assistance. Additionally, insurance is often required by law. Even the largest corporations purchase excess insurance to eliminate the possibility of an uninsured catastrophic loss and the resulting adverse reaction by the board of directors and stockholders. As will be seen later, underwriters work closely, often directly, with risk managers in the administration of the firm's insurance program, including:

1. determining which insurance contracts are best suited to each loss exposure and are acceptable to the underwriter,

2. setting the retention (deductible) on various policies at various locations,
3. negotiating rates and rating plans that recognize loss control efforts and the firm's risk-taking philosophy, and
4. setting up a system to monitor claims reports and payments that affect renewal premiums and even the acceptability of the risk itself.

Choosing the Best Method(s)

The fourth step in the risk management decision-making process is choosing the best method or combination of methods for dealing with the loss exposures that have been discovered. These decisions should not be made on a one-time basis, but rather it should be a continuous reevaluation of the risk management "mix" to assure that the combination of methods in effect is optimal for the firm at that point in time. The expense of loss control is related to the frequency and severity of the loss, its potential impact on the operating effectiveness of the firm, and the effectiveness of the loss control device or procedure in reducing the frequency and/or the severity of the loss. Expenditures such as retention and insurance are often the result of a least-cost analysis between the alternative methods.

Loss control, retention, and insurance decisions are related, since each has an effect upon the other. For example, a decision to construct buildings subject to rigid fire and wind-resistive standards is a loss control decision that often has the effect of lowering insurance premiums. Conversely, the decision to retain certain losses previously insured provides the incentive for a much-improved loss control program.

In selecting the optimum "blend" of risk management tools, the risk manager attempts to minimize costs. But alternatives are subject to constraints, which may or may not be controllable. Some of these constraints are:

- Risk management activities may be splintered among various corporate departments, such as safety, personnel, engineering, and others, and among the local managers. In effect, the risk manager in this situation cannot optimize the blend of risk management methods because of his or her lack of authority over all these activities.
- Senior management may seriously restrict the risk manager through budget constraints.

Implementing the Decision

Once the decision has been made, the risk management program must be implemented and communicated to all concerned parties. Other decisions must be made for proper implementation. For example, if certain losses are to be retained and charged to each department or division, this must be clearly communicated. On the other hand, if retained losses are to be paid from a central account, funds should be set aside or made available for that purpose and invested in highly liquid assets so that they can be easily converted into cash.

If loss control has been selected to be a technique used, the loss control service or system must be implemented or installed, and personnel trained in its use. When insurance is chosen, binders must be issued, applications completed, inspections ordered, and so on.

Implementation procedures can vary considerably because of the organizational structure of the firm (that is, centralized or decentralized), the risk management method involved, and the departments affected. For example, in a risk management oriented corporation with regional risk management representatives, implementation may be accomplished simply through a directive from the risk manager.

On the other hand, in a decentralized corporation that grants a high level of autonomy to its affiliates, the implementation may be extremely complicated and perhaps less effective. In this case, each local manager must be persuaded that the risk management program is in the best interests of the affiliate.

Implementation is less complex in those firms in which top management has taken a strong position in support of risk management; risk management manuals have been issued instructing each operating unit about its risk management duties; procedures for implementation have been established allowing for flexibility and monitoring; and channels of communication have been established.

Monitoring the Results

The final step in the risk management process is the monitoring of risk management activities to assure that coordination and control are achieved. Once again, it should be noted that this step, like the others, requires accurate up-to-date information on a continuous basis. It may be necessary and perhaps more efficient for some of this information to be developed by outside sources. Visits to some of the remote locations by the producer or insurance company representative might result in the collection of information not previously known to the risk manager. This information could cause an immediate revision in the existing program and could set in motion a series of related changes. Monitoring of any program or decision (described further in a later chapter) requires establishment of standards of performance, comparison of actual performance or experience against standards, and corrective action when necessary.

The dynamic nature of each firm leads to a continual reevaluation of the balance between risk management techniques to assure that the mix is optimal. In that regard, each risk management activity can be considered part of a "team." Each gives information or signals that affect the other activities calling for adjustment.[6] For example, changes in the loss control program may point to a need to reevaluate the existing retention or insurance programs. Likewise, a change in insurance policies or a change in insurers may carry with it a requirement to comply with some program of loss control or retention. The monitoring activity is not a self-adjusting system. It should be designed so that information flows are facilitated and communication problems minimized so that the adjustment process may operate speedily and efficiently.

LOSS CONTROL IN UNDERWRITING ACTIVITIES

Underwriters are most involved with the loss control aspects of risk management for two reasons. First, risk managers seek advice and assistance in controlling losses, and insurance companies and agencies have technical expertise to offer. Second, insurers often require compliance with loss control recommendations as a condition of providing insurance. Consequently, the balance of this chapter is directed toward an explanation of the essentials of loss control and how underwriters can use this information on the job.

Individual Risk Underwriting

The underwriter's use of loss control knowledge is not limited to hazard and loss evaluation. Suppose an evaluation shows an applicant is not acceptable at the premium available. If the premium cannot be increased, the risk must be improved, and both the applicant and the producer expect the underwriter to suggest ways in which improvement can be effected.

Similarly, the underwriter must be able to use the engineering or loss control department reports effectively. When requesting additional inspections or other engineering information, the underwriter should know what loss control specialists are trained to look for and evaluate.

In many types of insurance, and especially for large businesses, competition among insurers and among producers requires that insurance be provided as inexpensively as possible. An effective method of reducing insureds' premiums is to reduce their losses, and insureds who are aware that insurance claims payments never cover all their loss from damage or injury will favor underwriters who provide the most effective help in controlling losses. While such help is expected to come primarily from the insurer's or broker's loss control or engineering department, the underwriter responsible for the account and its renewal should make an effort to help to improve it and to keep it on the books.

When rates are negotiated, the underwriter may be expected to know how much of an improvement of a risk will affect the rate. The underwriter may not be able to confer with the engineering department when the question arises, so he or she should be able to supply the information based on personal knowledge of loss control.

Book of Business Underwriting Management

Underwriters also should be aware of loss control programs or systems that may improve the underwriting results of a particular class of business or territory. For example, a drivers' education program which improved a trucking account may be required on all similar accounts with poor loss records. Similarly, a double cylinder deadlock that was installed by a loss-control-conscious insured may be recommended by the underwriter to all accounts needing burglar protection.

The Cost of Losses

Each year, billions of dollars are paid by insurers for covered losses. Not reflected in these costs are the loss to society of valuable resources in the form of human lives and materials.

In addition, insureds and society bear the weight of *uninsured* costs resulting from an insured loss. Depending upon the type and extent of loss, these costs have been estimated to equal from three to ten times the cost of the insured loss itself. For example, in an industrial accident resulting in the injury of an employee, the indirect (and possibly uninsured) costs to the employer could include several or all of the following:

1. Cost of wages paid to workers not injured but who lost time because of disruption of schedule.
2. Cost of wages for injured workers not paid by insurance (time lost during the day for medical treatment and follow-up care).

3. Extra cost of overtime work (or production lost) to make up for lost time.
4. Cost of damaged product, raw material, or equipment involved in the accident.
5. Cost of wages paid to supervisors for time spent on accident-related activities (driving worker to clinic or emergency room, etc.).
6. Wage cost of decreased output by injured worker after return to work.
7. Cost of training new worker including cost of decreased output during training).
8. Cost of management and clerical personnel in investigating, reviewing, and reporting on accident.
9. Miscellaneous costs (renting replacement equipment, profits lost because of contract cancellation, and so on).[7]

The indirect and uninsured losses under other insurance coverages such as crime, fire, general liability, and commercial auto will vary, but their existence and cost to the insured also would be significant.

HOW ACCIDENTS ARE CAUSED

The Domino Effect

The first types of injuries to be thoroughly analyzed were work injuries caused by accidents. In 1931, H. W. Heinrich of Travelers Insurance Company published an analysis of work accidents called *Industrial Accident Prevention*. In summary, his philosophy was as follows:

1. An accident is usually the result of a sequence of factors which may include either the unsafe act of a person or a mechanical or physical hazard (unsafe condition).
2. The majority of accidents are caused by the unsafe acts of persons.
3. For every accident that actually occurs, there are hundreds of "near misses" which did not result in an accident.
4. Managers and supervisors should be responsible for the prevention of accidents.[8]

Although Heinrich's study dealt with the elimination or control of work injuries, these same principles, slightly modified, eventually became the basis for modern loss control activities. Substitution of the word "loss" for the word "accident" in each of the above principles

Exhibit 4-4
The Domino Effect in Loss Causation*

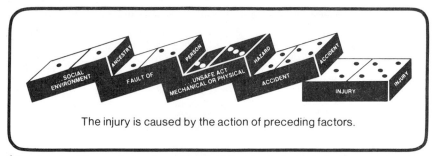

The injury is caused by the action of preceding factors.

*Reprinted with permission from H. W. Heinrich, *Industrial Accident Prevention*, 4th ed. (New York: McGraw-Hill Book Company, 1959), p. 15.

makes them applicable not only to workers' compensation but also to property, public liability, auto, and other losses.

Heinrich compared the loss causation sequence to a line of dominoes in which, when one falls, it knocks the next one over, and a chain reaction results. The five "dominoes" in the loss causation chain are:

1. Ancestry and social environment
2. Fault of person
3. Unsafe act and/or unsafe condition (hazard)
4. Accident
5. Injury or damage[9]

Exhibit 4-4 illustrates how injury is caused by the domino effect—the action of four preceding factors.

The accident itself is only one domino in the loss causation chain. Since each domino must fall to continue the chain reaction, the removal of *any* breaks the chain, as shown in Exhibit 4-5. Thus, some injuries and damage can be *prevented* by undoing the effects of ancestry and social environment, by correcting acquired faults, or by eliminating unsafe acts and conditions. Since human behavior is not easily altered, most loss control effects are directed toward eliminating the third domino—unsafe acts or conditions.

The Unsafe Act An unsafe act is an action or practice that violates standard or accepted procedures. An employee who refuses to wear protection while welding, a driver who fails to recognize hazardous road conditions and reduce speed, an electrician who installs the wrong type of outlet in a rush to complete the job, or a pedestrian who steps off a curb without looking all have committed unsafe acts. Some acts may have been committed with the knowledge or even the

Exhibit 4-5
Loss Control in Heinrich's Domino Theory*

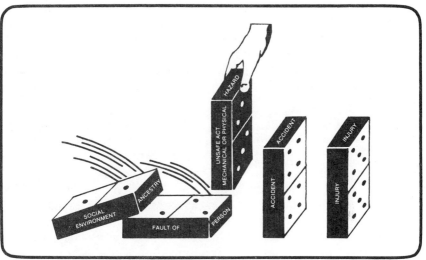

* Reprinted with permission from H. W. Heinrich, *Industrial Accident Prevention*, 4th
ed. (New York: McGraw-Hill Book Company, 1959), p. 16.

intent of the individual, while others were committed unknowingly or
unconsciously. All, however, have one factor in common—the potential
of producing an accident.

Heinrich identified four reasons for the commission of unsafe acts:

1. improper attitude,
2. lack of knowledge or skill,
3. physical unsuitability, and
4. improper environment.[10]

An unsafe act may be committed when behavior is affected by one
or more of the above factors. To identify each as a causal factor, and to
successfully eliminate or control the resultant accident potential, it is
necessary to understand the basic behavioral and physical deficiencies
causing each act.

Improper attitude includes various causal factors that can lead to
the commission of an unsafe act:

1. *Habit patterns* are developed by persons in any area of their
   lives where recurring actions or activities are required. Once a
   habit has been developed, the stimulus to initiate the action
   shifts from a conscious effort to an unconscious effort similar to
   a reflex. Employees who learn to lift incorrectly will continue to
   do so unless they are taught to override their bad habits.

2. *Incentives to commit unsafe acts* may encourage an individual to violate consciously a standard or accepted procedure if the benefit of doing so exceeds the danger involved. Pieceworkers, whose pay is determined by the number of units produced, may remove a critical safety device to increase production and take-home pay.

3. An unsafe act may also be committed to prove a point, get even, or simply to exercise one's independence.

Unsafe acts committed because of improper attitudes are difficult to identify and eliminate since they result from the behavioral patterns of the individual. And if, through accident analysis, one is able to determine that habit is the basic causal factor for an accident or series of accidents, elimination of this causal factor may be long and expensive, since extensive retraining and education, as well as temporary physical deterrents or safety measures, may be required. Lack of knowledge or skill is another reason why unsafe acts are committed. An individual who attempts to operate a new or modified machine without prior training may commit an unsafe act because of a lack of knowledge or skill. Even if the individual realizes that he or she lacks the required knowledge to perform a task or the skill to do a job, the unsafe act may still be committed unconsciously. Similarly, misunderstanding or poor communication may also result in unsafe acts.

Physical unsuitability includes both physical and mental impairments as causal factors. An individual with a diseased heart or an injured back commits an unsafe act when he or she exceeds the limitations that these conditions impose. Poor hearing or color-blindness may contribute to an unsafe act if the individual fails to respond to an audible signal or to color signals such as traffic lights.

Improper environment includes numerous causal factors in the environment. A monotonous job that promotes daydreaming or a work partner who is a practical joker may interrupt an individual's concentration on the job, resulting in an unsafe act. Also, environmental conditions such as glare from the sun or noise may cause an incorrect action to be taken.

In Heinrich's study, 88 percent of the accidents were caused by unsafe acts, 10 percent by unsafe conditions, and 2 percent were not determinable. Thus, 98 percent of these accidents were essentially "preventable."[11] Although other studies have shown slightly different results, it is widely accepted that unsafe acts are the major cause of accidents. It is, therefore, important to understand some characteristics of unsafe acts:

1. Unsafe acts are usually of short duration and may be committed at infrequent or irregular intervals.

2. Unsafe acts are usually not identifiable during an inspection visit since the chance of their occurrence at the time of the inspection is unlikely. Job safety analysis, accident investigations, or accident analyses must therefore be used.
3. Since the reasons for committing unsafe acts vary widely, they are difficult to eliminate, and efforts must be tailored to the precise cause of the act.
4. Unsafe acts involve people; people are unpredictable and, at times, illogical. The possibility of the recurrence of an unsafe act, even after corrective action is taken, remains a factor to be considered.

If the information about a risk is primarily from a physical inspection of the premises, the existence of an unsafe act as a causal factor cannot be determined with certainty, and much of the loss exposure may go unnoticed. Unsafe acts can be identified before an accident with a reasonable degree of reliability through the use of a job safety analysis. *A job safety analysis is a step-by-step study of a job to determine all recognizable unsafe acts on the particular job.* Accident and incident analyses are useful in identifying unsafe acts following an occurrence. (An incident is any event that could lead to a loss, such as the use of gasoline in an unventilated area.) The elimination or control of unsafe acts as causal factors cannot be accomplished satisfactorily through physical corrective measures, such as safety devices. While such measures may make the commission of unsafe acts more difficult, they usually will not reach the basic cause— a cause that requires direct supervisory involvement to train and to modify the behavior of the individuals concerned.

The Unsafe Condition A mechanical or physical hazard, commonly referred to as an "unsafe condition," is defined as any situation or arrangement of the environment that can cause an accident. An unsafe condition may be a physical and readily identifiable condition such as a pallet stored in an aisleway, a pothole in a parking lot, or a missing power press guard. An unsafe condition can also be a less conspicuous hazard such as an overloaded electrical circuit, air or water contamination, or a leak in an underground natural gas main.

Unsafe conditions may result from various causal factors such as the following:

1. an unsafe act or another accident;
2. normal wear and tear, such as a bald tire or a corroded pipe;
3. unintentionally poor design of an object or system, or a change in the object or system, such as exceeding the load capacity of a building floor, and

4. the environment.

Unlike unsafe acts which are created by people, unsafe conditions usually will not occur on their own but require the catalyst of a new causal factor.

Although Heinrich found that only 10 percent of accidents were caused by unsafe conditions, much progress in safety has been accomplished in this area. Heinrich noted that the engineering approach to safety, such as proper design of equipment and work areas, was the best way to prevent accidents.[12]

But the engineering approach to improving unsafe conditions is not limited to employee injuries. To reduce auto accidents, autos have been redesigned to include safety improvements; for example, disc brakes replaced hydraulic brakes, headlights were made more powerful, taillights were made more visible, and a third taillight added. To make highways safer, roads were widened, divided, or made limited-access, and warning signs were increased in size and number.

These measures are more noticeable than training to eliminate unsafe acts. Additionally, human behavior is not easily changed, and thus the quickest and most reliable loss control activities are those associated with unsafe conditions, although they only account for 10 percent of all losses.

Multiple Causation Modern loss control methods recognize that accidents usually result from a *combination of* or *multiple* causes and the removal of only one of the factors can be sufficient to break the chain. When a worker stuck his hand into an open gear train and was injured, Heinrich classified the principal cause as an unsafe act. But redesigning machines so gear trains are enclosed is more reliable and effective than attempting to control workers' behavior. Modern analysis makes this clear by noting that *both* the human act *and* the mechanical condition were required for the injury, so removal of *either* would prevent the loss. Consider the following investigation of a collision between a train and a school bus:

- The bus driver said he did not see the train approaching, even though it was readily visible (backing up, at five miles an hour) for at least a minute and a half before the collision, and the driver stopped the bus and opened the bus door (as required by law) just before going onto the tracks.
- The brakeman on the train apparently was not on the back platform of the caboose watching for traffic as the train backed into the intersection, although railroad rules required he be there and he claimed he was.

- The brakeman and engineer had no direct means of communication with each other, in violation of rules.
- The intersection was unprotected although it had been cited as unreasonably dangerous and the railroad and highway authorities so notified over a year earlier.

The apparent inattention of the bus driver and the failure of the brakeman to be where he was supposed to be were equal principal causes of this particular accident, and removal of either cause would have avoided it. But if the analysis stopped there, causes that would contribute to future accidents would remain—the lack of equipment for direct communication between brakemen and engineer, and the unprotected intersection. Uncovering additional causes is a major contribution of multiple causation theory to loss control.

Recognition of multiple causation led naturally to recognition of *depth* in causation. Between personal fault and accident, Heinrich placed only a single domino. This led him and others to refer repeatedly to *the* unsafe act or condition that directed attention away from the fact that there usually existed a sequence, often several sequences. For example, in the accident just described, the brakeman apparently was not on the platform because to communicate with the engineer he had to be in the middle of the caboose, where there was a radiotelephone. The brakeman's improper position, a cause of the accident, in turn had a cause—he carried no portable walkie-talkie. The *cause* of this cause had to be considered, and so on. Recognizing this type of complexity has produced two kinds of useful insights:

(1) the discovery of continuing underlying hazards in processes or procedures and
(2) the pinpointing of management responsibility.

In the school bus accident, tracing back the causes of the absence of the mandated communication equipment would produce the information that either: (1) procedure for its supply was lacking or inadequate or (2) someone was failing to see that the procedure was carried out. Either way, there was a *management* fault. Note that this process ends by making most accidents basically "people faults," but with the important difference that the "people" are now *management* people, rather than ordinary workers. Heinrich anticipated this development and had long since written that, "personal and mechanical hazards exist only because of the faults of persons", and "management through supervision controls man's failure…which causes or permits unsafe acts of persons [and] unsafe mechanical or physical conditions."[13] For as long as there has been serious study of safety, it has been emphasized that little will be accomplished in safety unless management is convinced that it should provide the necessary supervision.

Another example involving a work injury should help illustrate the concept of multiple causation and the role of management in loss control. Assume that an employee slips and falls onto a warehouse floor and that an investigation reveals an oil spot on the floor. The spot is traced to an oil leak in the hydraulic system of a forklift truck, and the cause of the accident appears to be eliminated by repairing the leak.

Although the factor that caused the slipping accident was eliminated, it is possible that the same accident could recur from a different cause or as the result of an *interaction* of factors—elimination of one factor may not always eliminate the loss. Present loss control philosophies indicate that, for every accident, numerous intermediate factors and causes exist that combine at random to cause the accident in question.

Further examination of the fall that resulted from the leaking forklift truck will make this concept more evident. In determining the intermediate causes of this accident, some possibilities are pointed up by the following questions:

1. Did anyone see the oil spill before the accident occurred?
2. Was the hydraulic fluid level low when the operator made the pre-operational inspection?
3. Did the operator make a pre-operational inspection?
4. Was routine maintenance being performed on this equipment?
5. Do maintenance records show that fluid has been found on internal parts, or that excessive fluid was being used?
6. When was the last time the hydraulic lines, fittings, and gaskets were changed?
7. Have similar spills occurred anywhere else in the warehouse? If so, what action was taken?
8. Are the present preventive maintenance schedules and pre-operational inspections adequate?

The initial corrective action was to repair the hydraulic fluid leak. As a result of the questions that a multiple-causation approach develops, several additional actions may be necessary, as follows:

1. The pre-operation inspection should be expanded to include checking hydraulic fluid level.
2. Preventive maintenance scheduling should include more frequent replacement of hydraulic system components.
3. Warehouse employees should receive training on incident reporting to advise supervisory personnel of possible loss causes.

4. Supervisors should spot-check equipment to verify its operational status.

Thus, a relationship exists between unsafe acts, unsafe conditions, and the management functions of supervision, education, training, and endorsement of loss control. In many instances, an accident will be the result of a combination of two or more of these causal factors. The elimination of an intermediate cause without identification of the basic cause, or the simple elimination of a fundamental cause while allowing intermediate causes to remain, will greatly reduce the effectiveness of a loss control program.

HOW ACCIDENTS ARE CONTROLLED

All loss control activities can be classified according to timing—whether they prevent a loss from occurring (loss prevention) or whether they reduce the effects of a loss that has begun (loss reduction).

The most effective method of control is to *eliminate* or *neutralize* the causal factors. The removal of a source of ignition or the use of a machine with properly guarded gears and drive belts eliminates two conditions that could result in a loss. A dip tank containing a flammable and toxic paint could present both a fire hazard created by nearby sources of ignition and an environmental hazard created by continued inhalation of the toxic vapors. The substitution of a noncombustible water-based paint will eliminate the environmental exposure by removing the causal factor, and eliminate the fire hazard by rendering the source of ignition harmless. All of these are loss prevention measures.

When it is not possible to eliminate causal factors, steps should be taken to reduce or minimize the extent of the loss. The requirement for drivers and passengers in motor vehicles to wear seatbelts and shoulder harnesses or that cars be equipped with air bags will not prevent an accident from occurring but will serve to limit the extent of injury to the occupants.

Fire walls and fire doors are two building construction features designed to contain a fire at or near its point or origin for a given period of time, allowing the fire department to locate and extinguish the fire before it spreads to other areas. Fire detection systems, now required by local and state codes in many residential (homes, hotels, and dorms), institutional (hospitals and nursing homes), educational, and high-rise office occupancies do nothing to extinguish a fire, but will notify the occupants or authorities that a fire exists, potentially minimizing the loss by rapid occupant and fire department response.

Loss control measures can be classified in another way. They may be oriented toward *engineering* or *human behavior*. The engineering orientation attempts to control losses by manipulating *things*, while the human behavior approach seeks to control losses by modifying human *behavior*. Engineering measures would include equipment design, traffic control, heat sensing devices, and burglar alarms. Human behavior measures would include defensive driving programs, employee safety meetings, training and retraining employees, and assigning responsibility for loss control to supervisors.

The Engineering Approach

The engineering approach, when it can be used, is usually the more reliable approach. Putting a good fence around electrical equipment is more reliable protection than an attempt to induce "keep off" behavior. For various reasons, people will often continue to do things they have been instructed not to do, and changing attitudes is difficult. It would be easier to design an interlock for a machine so that it is automatically shut off when it jams than it would be to change the attitudes of employees who believe that shutting the machine off before clearing it shows a lack of skill in its operation. The types of mechanical or automatic loss control devices vary greatly by type of loss.

The Human Behavior Approach

To provide complete safety by engineering requires that all possible variations of all possible emergencies be anticipated and provided for—including emergencies caused by failure of the automatic safety controls themselves. The more varied the environment, the greater the reliance necessarily placed on human controls. In a subway transit system, automatic controls can be and have been installed to determine the speed and the spacing of the trains, and even their stopping and starting at stations. However, the idea of managing the operations of a bus on city streets with the same degree of automated engineering control staggers the imagination. The human mind is still larger (in capacity) and more complex than any computer in existence.

In addition, as behavioral studies have shown, overly routine and automated jobs produce boredom and hostile attitudes in work forces. One antidote is more variety and challenge in jobs, requiring more skill and education—including education in safe performance.

In some situations, engineering is not the complete answer. There are situations in which virtually eliminating noxious elements (for example, minute solid particles, noise, extreme pressures) from the environment may be prohibitively expensive or impossible. When full redesign of the workers' environment is not feasible, education and enforcement must be used to produce behavior that conserves health in that deleterious environment. Major means are (1) conditioning and training to develop the bodily strength, skills, and mental attitude required for coping with a harsh environment (just as is required for expert performance in athletics); and (2) education in and enforcement of the use of effective safety practices, such as complete cleanliness for those who work with dangerous substances, and use of well-designed (engineered) protective equipment in hazardous environments.

Finally, however well designed, engineered objects themselves need checking. And if these are automatically checked by other objects, the automated checkers need checking. Eventually, *people* are at the root of everything, including the design, maintenance, and behavior of even the most automated systems. Studies of accidents in nuclear power plants have shown that it has been human behavior that has most often been critical—both in causing events and in controlling them. Hence, as long as humans are involved in any way in a system— including designing, building, and preserving it—unforeseen behavior will occur. And behavior intelligently adapted to the exact problem presented will be required for effective counteraction.

From time to time and from one class of business to another, the emphasis shifts from engineering to human relations. It is important to remember, however, that accidents or losses result from both unsafe acts of persons (human relations) *and* physical or mechanical hazards (engineering), and since many accidents involve an *interaction* of unsafe acts and physical hazards, knowledge of both approaches will be useful to underwriters in loss analysis.

Motivation for Loss Control

Loss control depends on the depth of commitment of top management, as middle management and line supervisors will not expend much effort in activities not required by top management.

Motivation of Top Management Historically, loss control specialists and underwriters have faced the problem of motivating top management to endorse loss control. Writers on the subject usually recognize two types of motives—humanitarian and economic—but differ as to the relative importance of the two. Some hold that only economic motives are strong and reliable enough, while others say that only humanitarian motives will produce the degree of safety that should be achieved.

There may be other motives, such as a manager's desire to be considered a competent member of the management profession. Laws that mandate standards of performance also exert an influence through the effects citations have on the manager's reputation and status, in addition to the economic effects of fines levied. Some health and safety laws provide criminal penalties for management—a significant motivating tool if enforced.

Underwriters have at their disposal some significant motivating forces, notably insurance premiums that reflect loss control effort, and the possibility of no insurance at all if loss control is too lax. But these strong motivators are not the only way that underwriters can stimulate management interest in loss control. Often, loss reports to insureds can be stated in terms that are apt to strike a responsive note with top management.

In a report to top management, a loss control specialist and an underwriter included some examples of the profit the firm would have to earn just to pay its workers' compensation losses. It was shown that the $319,000 of workers' compensation losses in the preceding three years would have produced 12,160 miles of rope—enough to reach halfway around the equator. This added another dimension to management's appraisal of the effectiveness of their operation and proved to be another tool for convincing supervisors to place greater emphasis on safety education and safety controls. It was not that the insured had not been working on safety before, but as the vice president noted, "Now, the safety efforts of our supervisors can be focused on a figure that holds more meaning for them and for our line people. It's a point of reference that everyone can understand." Relating the costs of accidents or the additional premium generated by the accidents to the production required to offset these costs can bring otherwise impersonal work accident statistics into better perspective in terms of the *real* cost of work accidents.

Motivation of Middle Managers and Supervisors Middle managers and supervisors are motivated when their effectiveness in implementing a policy clearly enters into evaluation of their performance. However, including an analysis of loss control in that evaluation is not always easy.

First, loss control has not traditionally been an important element, or even a standard ingredient, in managerial evaluation. Loss control receives little attention in texts or other published analyses of management functions and seldom appears in descriptions of good or superior managerial performance.

Second, unlike production, sales, or expenses, loss control effectiveness is seldom amenable to straight numerical measurement. As will be seen in a later chapter dealing with probability, most organizations do not have enough spread of loss exposures for their experience to be statistically credible. And even when the organization does have enough credibility, an individual manager's division, plant, or shop often does not. What is the significance of the record "no fires this year," in a single warehouse, or of "no major work injuries" in a work force of fifty? These numbers mean little by themselves, and even when loss frequency is great enough to have some credibility, its significance must be communicated in terms that have impact on management. Methods must be established to measure loss in terms that carry meaning to managers.

Some organizations and risk managers have devised systems that allocate accident loss costs to each division, plant, or department. This includes prorating insurance premium costs as well as noninsured costs such as first aid treatments, damaged equipment, medical costs, production line downtime, and so on. The growing use of computers and claims data has allowed more risk managers to exercise this technique.

Of course, a supervisor may be self-motivated for loss control. When this motivation comes from a superior, however, it may need additional reinforcement. Therefore, loss control specialists properly spend effort on direct motivation of all levels of management, providing the same reasons and using the same types of measures as for top management.

Motivation of Employees One of the puzzles of loss control is the frequent resistance of employees to procedures and rules intended to protect their own health, safety, and economic welfare. Much of the writing and materials in loss control are directed to this problem. On the other hand, employees and their unions do push for control of loss from work injuries under some circumstances. The difference seems to lie in whether the remedy proposed is one that requires action and outlay by the employer, or one requiring unpopular action by the employees (for example, acceptance of disciplinary actions, personal protective gear, or changes in accustomed work habits).

Generally, employees can be motivated through the following appeals (not necessarily in order):

- preservation
- profit
- pride
- punishment[14]

The appeal to preservation, sometimes called "'self-preservation," is effective in avoiding work injury situations and auto accidents by showing how unsafe acts and unsafe conditions can cause injuries, even death. This is communicated through safety meetings, training films, and brochures that increase safety awareness and offer advice on handling dangerous situations.

The profit motive is another strong appeal to motivate safety. Saving money on auto insurance premiums through safe driver discounts and receiving monetary rewards or time off with pay for employees who work safely are examples. If workers are rewarded for productivity but not for safety, they may bypass safety controls on equipment or safety procedures to increase productivity. Safety awards can save many times their cost through reduced accidents.

Appeals to pride may be accomplished through publicity and recognition for safety. Certificates and pins awarded to employees individually or as a group can stimulate healthy competition from others, especially if prominently featured at a banquet or in the company magazine.

Punishment or the threat of punishment should be used only as a last resort. Transfer to a less hazardous and lower paying job or revocation of driving privileges are forms of punishment that may provide motivation for loss control.

The Loss Control Process

In a manner similar to the risk management process, loss control is carried out by (1) identifying hazards, (2) evaluating hazards, (3) deciding on control measures, (4) implementing control measures, and (5) monitoring results.

Identifying Hazards　Hazards are identified by studying reports and descriptions of operations and plans for operations; by inspection of operations; by a job safety analysis or analysis of accident or incident reports and statistics; and by getting reports from operating personnel who note hazards.

Reports and descriptions of operations usually provide the bulk of the information. Normally it is from these that one learns building construction and arrangements, principal types of equipment, major types of materials and processes used, and products and services produced. Of course, the underwriter must have the knowledge to translate this information into hazard identification. When the description of materials includes urethane foam, the underwriter must know this presents a problem in fire loss control. And when the process is described as "machinery," the underwriter must know this means the use of metal lathes, and probably at least some presses, and the hazards such equipment presents (including the possibility of markedly increased hazards from poor housekeeping). When the location is given as Tuscola, Illinois, the underwriter must know that means an area with above average frequency of tornadoes.

The primary purpose of inspections by loss control specialists is hazard identification. Inspections uncover ongoing unsafe conditions and practices, such as crowded arrangements, bad lighting, poor housekeeping, and general disregard for safe procedures. Individual unsafe acts and intermittent unsafe conditions often can be missed.

Loss control programs should include requirements for reports on incidents or events of significance to loss control. Occupational Safety and Health Act regulations and most industrial safety programs call only for injury events to be reported, and in most operations, employee dishonesty other than petty thievery, and all burglaries and robberies will be reported, as will most if not all fires and explosions. More complete programs go beyond these and call for reports on many cases of property damage. Some even require reports on no-loss incidents that have serious loss potential. The underwriter can use these reports in hazard identification in two ways: (1) by analysis of individual reports to discover the specific causes behind each event reported and (2) by tabulating the information in the reports to see if there are patterns that point out particular problems.

Evaluating Hazards Evaluation of particular hazards requires appropriate technical training: for industrial accidents—safety (mechanical and chemical) engineers; for employee dishonesty—accountants and auditors; for liability exposures—lawyers; and so on. However, the fundamentals are represented in Exhibit 4-6. Examples of specific hazards, or potential sources of loss, are given in the first column. The immediate subject upon which each source may operate appears in the second column. In the third column, other areas to which damage or injury may spread are identified. The general size of resulting loss effect appears in the fourth column. (Other courses in the IIA Associate in Underwriting Program contain more detail of specific hazard evaluation by type of insurance.) Hazards are also evaluated on the basis of the loss experience they have already produced when that experience is statistically credible.

Deciding on Control Measures Decisions on control measures are accomplished by interaction between loss control specialists, underwriters, producers, and the insured firm's management. The specialists and underwriters recommend measures to use and estimate their costs and benefits. Management works these costs and benefits into the total cost and benefit picture and makes the decision. Illustrations of the kinds of things that might be done in engineering and in education and enforcement are presented in Exhibit 4-7 for the same set of hazards evaluated in Exhibit 4-6.

Implementing Control Measures Implementation is an operational matter generally directed by management. However, part of the program will consist of the activities of the various loss control

Exhibit 4-6
Examples of Hazard Evaluation

Source	Initial or Operating Subject	Damage, Injury Spread	Insured Loss Effect
Moving gears	Sleeve	Arm, shoulder	Medical expense Total permanent disability (all at present cost & wage levels)
Match	Wastepaper	Fire division	Property physical damage to or beyond 95% of amount subject Interruption to 8 months
		or Part of area	Property physical damage at PML Interruption to 6 months
Burglar	Cash in safe	Damage to premises and safe Other valuables in safe	$ _____
Machine out of adjustment	Components of product (defective)	Batch of products, customers' property	Up to $ _____ in claims, plus costs of defense
Dishonest employee	Tobacco products	X% of shipments for Y months	$ _____

specialists. The techniques of implementation—the setting of policy objectives and standards, their communication, the motivation of supervisors and workers, the use of manuals, and standard operating procedures—are those of effective management in general.

Monitoring Results   In well-established loss control programs, two important roles of the loss control specialists are planning and

Exhibit 4-7
Examples of Loss Control Techniques

Occurrence Step Dealt With	Engineering Approach	Human Behavior Approach
Example 1		
Moving gears	Interpose barrier (such as mechanical guard)	Turn off machine when adjusting
Sleeve	Clothing design	Proper movements by operator, rules about clothing
Arm, shoulder	Automatic trip	Train in shut-off procedures
Insured loss	Improved medical technology, e.g., emergency transportation, rehabilitation facilities	Planned emergency treatment procedures with training Movitation for rehabilitation
Example 2		
Match	None	No smoking; proper receptacles, use enforced
Wastepaper	None	No accumulation
Fire division	Fire doors, solid barriers, clear space	None
or Fire area	Automatic sprinklers, automatic alarms	Fire fighting, fire emergency procedures, sprinklers maintained, cutoffs operative
Insured loss	Standby equipment (for interruption loss)	Emergency plans; salvage operations
Example 3		
Burglar	Geographic location—low crime area; alarms; Quality of safe ("barrier")	Premises—well lit, highly visible
Cash in safe	None	Minimize amount
Damage to premises and safe, etc.	None	Advertise "no cash"; watchman
$ _____	None	None

Example 4

Machine out of adjustment	Machine design; automatic detection	Maintenance procedures; operator testing practices
Components of product	Automatic checking	Testing
Batch of products	Same	Same
Customers' property	None	Instructing customers in use and testing
$ in claims, defense	None	Effective recall procedures contractual defenses; claims adjustment

Example 5

Dishonest employee	None	Hiring and training procedures; employer attitudes and behavior
Tobacco products	Barriers to unauthorized access	Inventory and paperwork control systems and checks
X%, Y months	None	Same; rotate employees; audits
$ _____	None	Pursue subrogation

monitoring. In monitoring, the underwriter takes an active role in evaluating the effectiveness of loss control as it determines the acceptability of the risk and premium to be charged.

MEASURING LOSS CONTROL EFFECTIVENESS

The procedure for analyzing a loss control program will depend upon the purpose and the desired results of the analysis. From an underwriting standpoint, a loss control program should eliminate or mitigate insured losses. A loss control program that successfully eliminates or reduces insured losses, but which allows uncovered losses to continue, should still be considered a successful program from an underwriting standpoint. While this statement may appear to conflict with previous comments concerning the effect of insured and uninsured losses on the risk, the worker, or society, the underwriter should be concerned primarily with those aspects of the operations that have caused or have the potential to cause an insured loss under the policy.

This is not to say that loss control representatives totally ignore situations or hazards that are not related to the coverages provided. If an insurer provides all coverages except workers' compensation and during an inspection, a loss control representative notes a condition that could cause injury to an employee, the condition is likely to be brought to the attention of the firm. However, the correction of that condition would not be included among the loss control recommendations for the insured since it is unrelated to the coverages provided. Additionally, although the underwriter is primarily concerned with the effectiveness of the loss control program with regard to insured losses, the insured's attitude toward loss control and safety overall, regardless of whether the losses are insured or not, is an important determinant of the acceptability of a submission.

The loss control activity or program to be analyzed may be extremely complex in design and implementation, as would be expected in the aerospace industry or large industrial or manufacturing operations; or it could be basic and simple, involving only the installation of a fire extinguisher in a family-operated grocery store. Regardless of the size and complexity of the activity or program, the analysis can be completed by examining the administration of the program and its effect on both the loss potential and loss experience of the risk.

Reduction of Insured Losses

The most obvious and rewarding results of effective loss control activities can be found in the reduction of the frequency and severity of insured losses. An examination and detailed analysis of loss experience since the introduction of loss control activities may indicate whether specific loss control measures were effective in eliminating or controlling the fundamental causes of previous losses. A comparison of the incurred losses in dollars since loss control activities were initiated to the incurred losses during a similar period of time prior to the adoption of loss control measures will produce the dollar value of the loss control effort. This comparison should be tempered with the knowledge that there could be other factors affecting the losses such as plant closings.

If this comparative analysis indicates that a dollar savings has not been realized, a further analysis will be required to identify the reason. Commonly, the failure to achieve an improved loss experience will result from one of the following:

- The basic or fundamental causes of previous losses were *not identified,* and loss control efforts were ineffectively applied to irrelevant intermediate causal factors.
- Previous losses were the result of multiple causation, but loss control efforts identified and were directed to *only a part* of these factors.

- The loss control activities did control those losses that existed at the time, but *changes* in operations, materials, procedures, or personnel created new loss causes that were unaffected by the program.
- Proper loss control activities were implemented, but proved *ineffective* due to a lack of follow-up, management support and endorsement, communication to and motivation of first line employees, or the assignment of responsibility and accountability to supervisory and management personnel for program success.

Reduction in Loss Potential

While a decrease in incurred loss is indeed an encouraging sign, this is only a part of the overall analysis. On many risks, particularly in the property and personal lines, loss frequency may not have been a factor, and thus a reduction in frequency or in severity would be impossible. A frequency of fire losses on any one commercial or personal risk would indeed be unlikely, as would a frequency of public liability losses on a homeowners policy. In such cases, it would be necessary to analyze the effectiveness of the loss control activity based almost entirely on the decrease in loss *potential*.

The loss potential is an estimate of the losses that could occur considering the probable frequency and potential severity of all loss causes, and any intensifying or mitigating factors within the environment that could affect such losses. An increase or decrease in loss potential will affect not only those risks which do not have a frequency of losses, but all risks. In many cases, it may not be possible to place an exact dollar value on the effectiveness of this aspect of loss control activity since it is concerned with the prevention of a loss that has not yet occurred. A comparison of the insured risk with all other risks in the same class, however, will provide an estimate of the value of the activity. For example, an unfenced swimming pool on a commercial or residential property may never have been the scene of an accidental drowning, but accident statistics will document that most accidental drownings do occur where access to pools is unrestricted. The installation of a fence to prevent access to the pool, particularly by children, greatly reduces the probability of loss.

The replacement of a flammable paint with a nonflammable water-based paint, the initiation of a scheduled preventive maintenance program for a fleet of autos or trucks, the continued refinement of finished product testing and the maintenance of product recall and distribution records, or the installation of a central station robbery alarm in a jewelry store are all examples of loss control activities that document the relative effectiveness of a loss control program.

Administration of Loss Control Programs

The analysis of reductions in the loss experience or loss potential of a risk is not sufficient, since the ineffective administration of any loss control program or single activity can neutralize the benefit that has been gained. The installation of dual controls on a paper shear should, even without management support or endorsement, initially reduce the frequency of losses. However, if the operators are not properly indoctrinated as to the reason this safety device was installed, if maintenance personnel are not trained in its maintenance and repair, and if supervisory personnel are not charged with the responsibility of insuring that the devices are operational and used by all operators, few if any of these safety devices will remain operational and in use.

Thus, the final and, in many cases, the most important factor in an underwriting evaluation of the effectiveness of a loss control program will be the analysis of the administration of the program. The safety device for the paper shear provides only one example of what will probably occur unless loss control programs are properly administered and actively supervised. There are several "key" activities that need to be identified in analyzing the administration and supervision of a loss control activity or program:

1. Has top management endorsed the program and indicated that it will actively support and monitor its progress?
2. Has the program, and all specific activities within the program, been communicated to all personnel concerned? This would include employees in a plant, tenants in an apartment building, students in a school, the public in a place of assembly, or the user of a product.
3. Has the responsibility for the program or activity been assigned to a supervisor or person in authority who knows that he or she will be held accountable for the results?
4. Does the program or activity include provisions for follow-up and monitoring?
5. If losses occur, will the cause(s) be determined and further corrective action be undertaken?
6. Are adequate records being maintained to allow further analysis and review by the underwriter as the need arises?

While many loss control programs or activities could continue for weeks or even years without supervision or monitoring, the effectiveness of most would eventually be dissipated. The most difficult area in which to achieve satisfactory administration of loss control efforts is the personal lines. The average homeowner has little fear of fire, exercises limited respect for electricity, feels that his or her home would be the last in the neighborhood to be burglarized, and may or may not realize the benefit of wearing seat belts when driving the family auto.

Once the loss potential, loss experience, and administration of the loss control activities have been evaluated, the overall effectiveness of the activities can be determined. The actual results required to continue on the risk will depend on the coverage, the underwriting standards or objectives, the pricing, and the risk itself. While it is anticipated that a good system of administration, an improvement in loss experience, and a reduction in loss potential would be expected or desirable in most cases, the actual underwriting objective for a given risk may only be to prevent any deterioration in the desirability of the risk. Whatever the desired results may be, however, the importance of proper loss control administration by the risk manager or owner cannot be overemphasized.

The Underwriter's Loss Control Responsibilities

The philosophies and procedures of loss control can be effectively utilized by an underwriter to improve the book of business. The use of loss control as an underwriting tool requires careful planning, analysis, and implementation if the desired results are to be achieved. It is quite possible to expend considerable effort and resources and achieve only negligible results unless the concepts of loss causation are understood and applied in the formulation of loss control programs for every risk.

The sciences of safety engineering, fire protection engineering, vehicle design, and crime prevention are progressing rapidly, and as each area is further developed and refined, its value as an underwriting tool continues to increase. It is the responsibility of each underwriter to keep pace with these changes and to achieve maximum benefit from the resources available.

SUMMARY

Risk management is the process of making and carrying out decisions that will minimize the adverse effects of accidental losses upon an organization. It is similar to underwriting in terms of its objectives, needed skills, activities, and the process of decision making.

The risk management process is accomplished through the following six steps:

1. Risk discovery
2. Risk measurement
3. Developing alternative risk management methods—avoidance, loss control, transfer, retention, and insurance
4. Choosing the best method or combination of methods
5. Implementing the chosen method(s)
6. Monitoring the results

Avoidance is generally used when the loss potential is too great to use any other risk management method. Loss control can be directed toward lowering the frequency of losses (loss prevention) or lowering the severity of losses (loss reduction). Transfer of loss exposures to others (not including insurers) can be accomplished before a loss (lease of premises, for example) or after a loss (such as through a hold harmless agreement). Another widely used risk management method is retention, which is defined as keeping or absorbing all or part of the financial impact of a loss. Retention can be either passive or active including noninsurance, self-insurance, and captive insurance companies. Finally, insurance plays a major role in the risk management programs of families and firms, including large corporations.

An underwriter may on occasion be able to improve a risk by the application of loss control techniques. Underwriters should be aware of the orientation, techniques, and terminology of loss control personnel in order to analyze a risk's loss potential, to accurately interpret inspection reports, and to devise or approve recommended loss control procedures.

Although primarily concerned with work injuries, H.W. Heinrich's *Industrial Accident Prevention* provided an important analysis which, when modified, became the basis for modern loss control activities. Heinrich's philosophy was based on four major assumptions: (1) an accident is the result of a sequence of factors, possibly including unsafe acts or unsafe conditions; (2) most accidents are caused by unsafe acts; (3) for every accident that occurs, there are hundreds of "near misses"; (4) management and supervisory personnel must cooperate in order for a loss control program to be successful.

Heinrich formulated a loss causation sequence which he compared to the fall of a line of dominoes in that when one aspect of the sequence occurs, the others will follow in turn. This sequence has five steps: (1) ancestry and social environment, (2) fault of person, (3) unsafe act and/or unsafe condition, (4) accident, and (5) injury. Heinrich further postulated that the removal of any one of the first four elements should halt the sequence.

Loss control activities are directed either at *loss prevention* or *loss reduction*. They can also be categorized in another way—as being oriented toward the engineering approach or the human behavior approach. The engineering approach involves physical changes in the loss environment, while the human behavior approach involves changes in human behavior designed to reduce or eliminate future losses.

Top management, middle management, and supervisors must all be motivated to influence the success of any loss control program. Motivating factors include economic and humanitarian interests, personal pride, and legal requirements. In addition, the underwriter has significant powers of motivation in that premiums can be made to reflect loss control efforts, and no insurance may be made available if such efforts are too lax. Employees must also be motivated, which may be a more complex process.

The loss control procedure itself can then be carried out by (1) identifying hazards, (2) evaluating those hazards, (3) deciding on control measures, (4) implementing those measures, and (5) monitoring the results.

The procedure for analyzing the loss control program once it is established will depend upon the purpose and the desired results, but from an underwriting standpoint, the general criterion for a successful loss control program is that it should eliminate or mitigate insured losses.

Underwriters should make an attempt to keep up to date on recent developments that may affect the loss control effort so that they can offer their insureds the most efficient and effective program possible.

Chapter Notes

1. George L. Head and Stephen Horn II, *Essentials of the Risk Management Process*, Vol. I (Malvern, PA; Insurance Institute of America, 1985), p. 6.
2. C. Arthur Williams, Jr., George L. Head, Ronald C. Horn, and G. William Glendenning, *Principles of Risk Management and Insurance*, Vol. I, 2nd ed. (Malvern, PA: American Institute for Property and Liability Underwriters, 1981), pp. 92, 98, 99.
3. Williams, Head, Horn, and Glendenning, p. 92.
4. This term is widely used but is a misnomer. Self-insurance is not insurance because there is no transfer of risk to an outsider.
5. Williams, Head, Horn, and Glendenning, p. 125.
6. Tom C. Allen, *Risk Management Methodology: A New Journal of Commerce Report* (New York: The Journal of Commerce, 1973), p. 8.
7. "Hidden Costs—They Can Be Controlled," *NATLSCO Consultant*, September 1980.
8. H. W. Heinrich, *Industrial Accident Prevention*, 4th ed. (New York: McGraw-Hill, 1959), p. 13.
9. Heinrich, pp. 14-16.
10. Heinrich, p. 38.
11. Heinrich, p. 20.
12. Heinrich, p. 19.
13. Heinrich, pp. 19-20.
14. Bernard L. Webb, J. J. Launie, Willis Park Rokes, Norman A. Baglini, *Insurance Company Operations*, Vol. II, 3rd ed. (Malvern, PA: American Institute for Property and Liability Underwriters, 1984), p. 193.

CHAPTER 5

Reinsurance

INTRODUCTION

Underwriters are concerned with obtaining a safe and profitable distribution of risks. A safe distribution of risks, in turn, relies on those risks being free from concentration—not subject to catastrophe loss from a single peril and relatively homogeneous (similar dollar values exposed to loss). Accordingly, underwriters must be constantly alert in the selection of risks to obtain and maintain a safe and profitable distribution of business. One very important tool available to the underwriter in this connection is reinsurance.

Many underwriters may feel that decisions regarding the use of reinsurance are entirely within the realm of top management. This may be true in some insurance companies, but in others the underwriter is often given the authority to use some types of reinsurance.

Reinsurance may be of help in solving such typical underwriting problems as:

1. A homeowners application is received and meets all underwriting standards. The dwelling, contents, and jewelry schedule total $450,000, but the company's limit is $200,000 on any one homeowners policy.
2. A submission for a package policy on a computer operation shows property values of $4,500,000. The insurance company's limit is $1,000,000 at any one location, and reinsurance is currently available for another $2,000,000. The underwriter is still "short" $1,500,000 of coverage if this risk is to be accepted.
3. An application is received for builders' risk coverage on a housing development of some 150 homes. Clearly, insurance on

so many structures in one area would expose the insurance company to an undue concentration of risks.

4. Business has been so good (so much desirable new business has been accepted or rates have increased so much) that the underwriter is told to write only half the number of policies usually written so that there will not be a drain on the insurer's surplus (assets less liabilities), exposing the insurer to potential regulatory restrictions or insolvency.

While not exhaustive, these typical situations demonstrate that there are occasions when the underwriter's knowledge of reinsurance may help to further the best interests of the insurance company.

Reinsurance Terminology

Reinsurance is defined as "the transaction whereby the reinsurer, for a consideration, agrees to indemnify the ceding company (or primary insurer) against all or part of the loss which the latter may sustain under the policy or policies which it has issued."[1] Thus, reinsurance is "the sharing of insurance among insurers," whereby one insurer (the reinsurer) arranges with another insurer (the primary insurer) to be responsible for all or some part of an assumed policy or policies.

The insurance company that obtains reinsurance may be referred to as the original insurer, the ceding company, the cedent, the primary insurer, the insurer, or the reinsured. In this book, the terms *primary insurer* or *insurer* will be used. *The insurance company that provides reinsurance is referred to as the reinsurer.*

Reinsurance is transacted through a reinsurance agreement. The agreement stipulates the form of reinsurance and the type of "risks" to be reinsured, such as a single risk, a defined group of policies, or a defined class of business. Generally, the agreement provides for the primary insurer to reinsure a portion of a risk by *ceding* it (passing it on) to the reinsurer. This reinsurance transaction is called a *cession.* The primary insurer *retains* a portion of the risk for its own account. This is called the *retention.* The retention may be a percentage of the amount of insurance, or it may be a dollar amount. For example, the primary insurer may retain 30 percent and reinsure 70 percent of the policy limit. If expressed as a dollar amount, the primary insurer retains up to the dollar amount ($10,000, for example), and the amount of insurance above the retention (above $10,000 in this example) is ceded (or passed along) to the reinsurer.

The primary insurer (or ceding company) pays a reinsurance premium for the protection provided just as any insured pays a premium for insurance coverage. The reinsurer may, and will usually, pay a *ceding commission to the primary insurer* since the latter incurs all of the expenses of issuing the policy such as acquisition costs (compensation of producers), underwriting, inspection or servicing costs, taxes, and other expenses.

The reinsurer's protection takes the form of a retrocession, which is simply the "reinsurance of reinsurance." Just as the insurer must make the decision to cede a portion of the risk to the reinsurer, the reinsurer must make the same decision as to what risks can be retained within its own financial resources and what portion of the risks must be "retroceded." *The reinsurer that accepts reinsurance for the original reinsurer is called the retrocessionnaire.*

FUNCTIONS OF REINSURANCE

Reinsurance is used to provide six basic functions. The type of reinsurance used is often determined by the function needed by the primary insurer. These basic functions are as follows:

1. increased capacity—the ability to accept and issue policies for large amounts of insurance;
2. catastrophe protection—the need to protect against a single large loss or multiple losses;
3. stabilization—the need to minimize the fluctuations in loss ratios from year to year;
4. withdrawal—arranging for termination of a line of business, from a territory, or from producing sources;
5. financing (surplus relief)—the prevention of a drain on the insurance company's surplus (excess of assets over liabilities) when premium volume is expanding rapidly; and
6. underwriting guidance—the need to obtain underwriting information when introducing a new type of insurance or expanding operations in a new territory.

Quite often, the type of reinsurance arranged will perform more than one of the above functions, although the intent of the primary insurer may be to meet only one of them.

Increased Capacity

All insurers, regardless of size, occasionally need capacity greater than that which can be provided by their own financial resources. *Capacity problems may arise from the need for a large amount of insurance on one loss exposure, called large line capacity, or to support a larger volume of premiums, called premium volume capacity.* The need for capacity may arise from existing accounts or from new business.

For example, an underwriter may receive a submission for $10 million on a single warehouse which would be greater than the line limit for that class of business. Line in this context does not refer a "line of business" as used earlier in this book. *The line limit is the maximum amount of insurance that an underwriter may accept on a single risk.* The line limit is set with consideration of

- the amount and types of reinsurance available
- the maximum amount allowed by state insurance department regulations that prohibit an insurer from retaining for its own account (after reinsurance) an amount of insurance in excess of 10 percent of its surplus to policyholders on any one loss exposure
- the amount that management thinks the insurer can safely retain without impairing earnings or the financial statements.
- specific characteristics of the risk. That is, for a certain type of risk, the line limit may vary depending on whether or not the risk is sprinklered or whether there are certain hazards present.

Premium volume capacity is determined by the size of the policyholders' surplus of the insurance company. To assure solvency, insurance regulators in the various states prevent insurers from overextension by limiting their premium writings to a multiple of the insurer's surplus to policyholders. If surplus shrinks due to losses or financial market changes, a smaller amount of premiums must be maintained than before.

Catastrophe Protection

Reinsurance may also be used to protect the insurer from a single large loss or multiple losses from a single event. This is often referred to as protection against shock loss. An excessive accumulation of losses from industrial explosions, windstorms, plane crashes, release of toxic chemicals, and similar causes could result in both property and liability claims exceeding the insurer's capacity.

The most significant peril connected with catastrophic occurrences is wind—hurricane or tornado. Underwriters use reinsurance to obtain the necessary protection against an accumulation of small and medium-sized losses to the book of business. At the same time, reinsurance protection is available against any extremely large single loss. The underwriter must determine the exposure to loss and arrange to reinsure a portion of it under one of the types of reinsurance to be discussed in a later section.

In arranging reinsurance for catastrophe protection, primary insurers are concerned with the infrequent occurrence of severe losses, rather than with the frequent occurrence of low severity losses. It is usual for catastrophe reinsurance to become operative only after the primary insurer's retention and other reinsurance have been exhausted. In fact, catastrophe reinsurance is designed to absorb only the shock situations that may befall a primary insurer.

Stabilization

The purchase of reinsurance by an insurance company may be compared to the purchase of insurance by a consumer. An individual or business firm purchases insurance to reduce uncertainty and to protect against financial loss; an insurance company may purchase reinsurance for the same reasons.

Most business firms prefer a predictably stable level of earnings to an erratically fluctuating one. For this "smoothing out" of earnings, the business firm is willing to pay an insurance premium, just as an insurance company will seek to reduce the uncertainty of its losses by purchasing reinsurance. Consider the information in Exhibit 5-1. The total losses are $17,400,000 or an average of $1,740,000 each time period. The solid line that fluctuates dramatically in Exhibit 5-2 represents actual losses; the dotted line represents average losses.

Volatile loss experience can affect the value of an insurance company's stock; cause abrupt changes in management of under- writing, claims, and marketing; undermine the confidence of its marketing force (especially independent agents with other markets); and lead to insolvency in extreme cases.

Clearly, primary insurers would prefer stable loss experience to fluctuating loss experience, and this can be arranged by means of reinsurance. The price to be paid for this smoothing out is the reinsurance premium. The reinsurance program may be arranged for a line of insurance, class of business, or an entire book of business.

Withdrawal

When an insurer decides that underwriting results from a particu- lar class of business, a defined geographical area, or a producing source, is unprofitable or undesirable, it may either continue the insurance until all policies expire, cancel all policies (if allowed by insurance regulations in each state) and refund the unearned premium

Exhibit 5-1
Hypothetical Loss Experience of an Insurer
for a Line of Business

Time Period (Year)	Losses
1	$ 1,000,000
2	2,250,000
3	1,300,000
4	800,000
5	4,100,000
6	3,700,000
7	1,650,000
8	925,000
9	600,000
10	1,075,000
Total	$17,400,000
Average Annual Losses	$1,740,000

to each insured, or it may "sell" its retention under these policies to another insurer through portfolio reinsurance.

Portfolio reinsurance is a transaction in which an entire line of insurance, class of business, territory, or book of business of an insurer is reinsured. With portfolio reinsurance, the reinsurer assumes all of the liability of the primary insurer. For example, suppose that an insurer wishes to terminate its products liability business due to low volume and high loss ratio. By reinsuring its retention on the entire products liability book of business, the total liability of the primary insurer is transferred to the reinsurer. Similarly, an insurer may wish to discontinue all of its insurance activities in a certain state and arrange 100 percent reinsurance for the duration of the policies now on its books. Obviously, portfolio reinsurance is expensive because the reinsured business is generally unprofitable.

Financing (Surplus Relief)[2]

In most businesses, a rapidly expanding volume of business is regarded as a good sign of present or potential profitability. However, in property and liability insurance, a rapidly expanding premium volume can cause financial problems for an insurance company.

How can something as seemingly favorable as an increasing premium volume cause problems for an insurer? The problem arises because of the way insurers are required by statute to treat premiums on their financial statements. By statute, an insurer must maintain an

Exhibit 5-2
Loss Experience of an Insurer

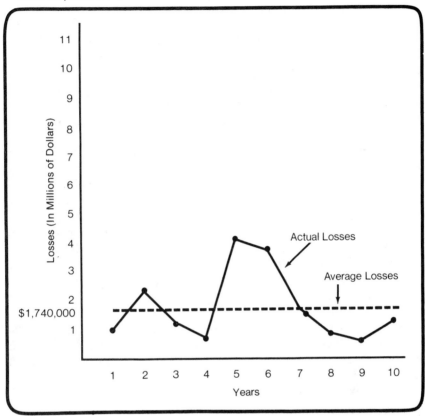

unearned premium reserve on the balance sheet as a liability. *Ignoring reinsurance for now, the unearned premium reserve is the amount the insurer would be obliged to return to its policyholders as return premiums for the unexpired terms of their policies, should the insurer wish to cancel every policy in force.* Thus, a $365 policy would be considered to be earned $1 per day. If canceled by the insurer after the first day, the policyholder would receive $364 as a return premium. The portion of the $365 that has not been earned (the return premium) must be carried in the unearned premium reserve.

Unfortunately for insurers, expenses are not incurred so evenly over the policy period. Producers' commissions must be paid when the policy is written. There are other expenses incurred when the policy is written such as inspection reports, the costs of issuing the policy, and so on. A "drain" on policyholders surplus is created equal to the amount by which these incurred costs exceed the expense portion of the premiums the insurer is statutorily allowed to show as earned.

If premium volume remains stable over a period of years, there is no additional drain. If an insurer begins writing a large volume of new business or increases rates significantly, there is a drain on surplus. The greater the increased premium volume from either cause, the greater the drain. Thus, if the increase in volume is large enough, what would seemingly make an insurer healthier could possibly cause the insurer to be declared technically insolvent. This is because insurers collect (or have available for their use) net premiums while the unearned premium reserve is based on gross premiums.

Where does reinsurance fit into this problem? If the primary insurer now reinsures part of this new business with an *admitted reinsurer* (an admitted reinsurer is one legally permitted to sell reinsurance in the state under consideration), the primary insurer is no longer obligated to maintain the unearned premium reserve for that part of the business that is reinsured. The obligation for maintaining that portion of the unearned premium reserve now falls upon the reinsurer. The reinsurer must now set aside a portion of its policyholders' surplus to recognize this obligation. (An example of how this is done appears later in this chapter.)

The surplus drain problem arises because of two conditions: the need to pay acquisition expenses when the policy is written; and the need to establish an unearned premium reserve which does not reflect heavy initial expenses. Reinsurance for this purpose is also said to provide *surplus relief.*

Underwriting Guidance

Finally, an insurer may wish to enter a new line of insurance in which it does not have any underwriting experience. This may be in an entirely new line of insurance for the insurer such as when an auto insurer expands into commercial lines, or when an insurer enters a new territory. By purchasing reinsurance, the primary insurer may avail itself of the knowledge and expertise of the reinsurer in this new type of insurance or territory. Part of the reinsurance arrangement may require the advice of the reinsurer in helping the insurer establish itself in this new market.

TYPES OF REINSURANCE TRANSACTIONS

There are two basic types of reinsurance transactions—*facultative* and *treaty.* A facultative reinsurance transaction is an "optional" one—

each party to the transaction has a faculty or power to act with free choice. In essence, under a facultative reinsurance arrangement, neither party has any ongoing obligation with regard to other reinsurance transactions. Therefore, facultative reinsurance is sometimes referred to as *nonobligatory reinsurance.*

On the other hand, a treaty reinsurance transaction obligates both the insurer to cede eligible insurance and the reinsurer to accept eligible business. Most, but not all, reinsurance treaties obligate the primary insurer to cede all eligible insurance governed by the treaty. The treaty is a contract that defines the eligible business and also prescribes the type of reinsurance.

Facultative

Under a facultative reinsurance transaction, the insurer offers an individual risk to the reinsurer which the latter is under no obligation to accept. Both the primary insurer and the reinsurer are free to act in a manner befitting their own best interests without regard to any prior contractual arrangements.

Each facultative transaction is complete in itself. Either party has the right to terminate the agreement at any time, subject to the advance notice specified in the facultative certificate.

Facultative reinsurance is used for its flexibility. Insurers facultatively cede risks in virtually every type of insurance they write, and will occasionally reinsure types of insurance not regularly written. Risks will be ceded to help support a treaty, to add to a treaty, or to bypass it. Facultative reinsurers are aware of how this facility may be used, and they recognize adverse selection as a fundamental concern.

Facultative reinsurance may fill several functions for a primary insurer:

1. Facultative reinsurance may be used to provide the needed large line capacity for risks that exceed the limits of the treaties. The underwriter may facultatively reinsure this excess amount to keep the insurer's commitment on the risk at the original retention level.
2. It may be used to reduce the primary insurer's exposure in a given geographical area. For example, an underwriter may have insured too many fire risks in a particular congested area. To reduce the concentration of risks in this area, the underwriter may select various ones and reinsure them on a facultative basis. Similarly, a marine underwriter could be faced with numerous shiploads of cargo stored in the same warehouse and belonging to different insureds. A solution

would be for the underwriter to reduce the possible maximum loss through a facultative reinsurance arrangement.

3. The primary insurer may use a facultative placement to reduce the exposure on a risk that is not typical of the insurer's book of business and therefore protect the favorable loss experience of its reinsurance treaties. For example, an insured may request coverage under a homeowners policy on a very expensive diamond ring or a schedule of high-valued jewelry items. Although this may be endorsed to the homeowners policy, the underwriter may be reluctant to do so because of the large increase in this special exposure. A facultative reinsurance placement of the jewelry exposure would eliminate the underwriter's concern by placing this exposure under the facultative agreement rather than under the treaty.

4. Generally, an underwriter may use facultative reinsurance for particular risks excluded under reinsurance treaties. Excluded risks are generally those subject to severe losses—losses greater than those expected in the treaty (automatic reinsurance agreement). This does not necessarily mean that these risks are undesirable. Instead, it means that if a loss does occur, it is likely to be severe, such as a chemical plant exploding and releasing toxic fumes into the atmosphere.

Facultative reinsurance has disadvantages primarily related to cost and possible adverse selection against the reinsurer. For facultative reinsurance to function, there must be an extensive exchange of information on each risk. Consequently, administrative costs are relatively high, as the underwriter must allocate a significant amount of time to completing each cession and notifying the reinsurer of any endorsements, cancellations, premium notices, or proofs of loss.

Of more importance is the possibility of adverse selection against the reinsurer. The volume of business under this type of reinsurance is not consistent, and the primary insurer controls the submission of the business. In some cases, the reinsurer might even quote a reinsurance premium higher than the primary insurer's premium to reflect this adverse selection.

Treaty

Treaty reinsurance has characteristics unique in the insurance industry. A treaty is an obligatory contract with respect to the reinsurer. The reinsurer *must* accept all cessions and has no power of selection. Thus, the reinsurer has little control over the general quality of the business transferred by the primary insurer once the treaty becomes operative.

The agreement may be just as binding for the primary insurer, depending on the type of treaty. If the primary insurer has some power of discretion on cessions granted, regular use could easily serve to negate the purpose or intent of the automatic treaty. Unless stated otherwise, the remainder of this chapter is based on the presumption that the contract is obligatory for both parties, the primary insurer being bound to cede every risk falling within the treaty terms and having no rights of distribution of cessions among others. The treaty is thus an arrangement by means of which, under one single contract, a large volume of risks is ceded over a period of time.

The most outstanding feature of the treaty lies in the assurances provided for both parties. For the primary insurer, there is a guarantee of reinsurance coverage for all its business reinsured, regardless of the actual merits of the risks ceded. For the reinsurer, there is a certainty of receiving a continuous and steady flow of business which should produce a profitable "average" risk over a period of time.

In the long run, the average risk reinsured should be comparable to the average risk on the books of the primary insurer, and consequently, the reinsurer should have almost the same experience (profit or loss) as the primary insurer. This is especially true if the treaty is quota share reinsurance; loss experience will be less comparable with surplus share and excess reinsurance because some risks written by the primary company are not reinsured. These terms will be defined later.

TYPES OF REINSURANCE CONTRACTS

Whether facultative or treaty, reinsurance contracts can be grouped into two broad categories: *pro-rata* (or proportional) and *excess* (or nonproportional). Under pro-rata reinsurance, the reinsurer shares losses in the same *proportion* as it shares premiums and policy amounts. The reinsurer shares in the fortunes of the insurer in such a way that in good years both make a profit and in bad years both incur a loss. Although the pro-rata treaty may take away a substantial portion of the primary insurer's premiums, it also takes away a substantial portion of the primary insurer's losses. In addition, the contract provides wider protection than the nonproportional (excess) cover because it is possible to recover on a large group of small losses.

In contrast, under excess reinsurance the reinsurer makes loss payments to the insurer when the latter's losses exceed a predetermined retention level. Almost all types of excess reinsurance

Exhibit 5-3
Pro-Rata Reinsurance

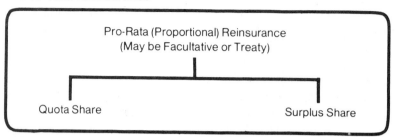

provide for the premium calculation of the reinsurance to be independent of the premium paid to the insurer. This type of reinsurance does not protect the insurer against a general deterioration in the loss experience, and it is possible for one party to make a profit while the other has a loss.

Another distinguishing characteristic is that pro-rata reinsurance is based on *sums insured*, while excess reinsurance is based on *losses*. That is, pro-rata reinsurance is applied to all losses (large and small) according to the *proportion* the reinsurance bears to the total amount of insurance. On the other hand, excess reinsurance is applied only to those losses in *excess* of a stipulated amount— the retention.

Finally, pro-rata and excess reinsurance are designed to perform differing functions. Pro-rata reinsurance is used primarily to provide increased premium volume capacity and financing (surplus relief). Excess reinsurance is suited for catastrophe protection, the stabilization of underwriting results, and large line capacity.

Pro-Rata Reinsurance

As shown in Exhibit 5-3 pro-rata reinsurance consists of two distinct types—quota share and surplus share.

In the past, pro-rata reinsurance was found most often in property insurance while excess reinsurance was the mainstay of the liability lines. Presently, it appears that these differences are disappearing; much property reinsurance is on an excess basis and pro-rata liability reinsurance is becoming more common.

Quota Share Quota share reinsurance is defined as a type of pro-rata reinsurance indemnifying the primary insurer against a *fixed* percent of loss on *each* risk covered in the reinsurance contract.[3] All liability and premiums are shared down to the first dollar. "Quota" share means "definite" share, and thus a fixed percent is stated in the reinsurance agreement. A typical quota share arrangement may be 50/50 percent, but other combinations are frequently used.

Although no two treaties are exactly alike, the insuring clause for a quota share agreement might read:

> The ABC Insurance Company is hereby obligated to cede and the XYZ Reinsurance Company is obligated to accept a quota share participation of _____% of ABC's ultimate net liability under any and all binders, policies and contracts of insurance issued or renewed during the term of this agreement for business classified as _____.

The blanks, of course, would reflect what had been agreed upon.

Additionally, the quota share usually includes a maximum dollar amount over which the reinsurer is not willing to be committed on any one risk, for example, "50 percent of every risk insured not to exceed $1 million on any one risk." As further protection for the reinsurer, the agreement customarily states that an agreed percentage *must* be retained by the primary insurer.[4] This is to deter the primary insurer from writing poor business and escaping all losses by facultatively reinsuring its share of the risk (its retention).

The primary function of quota share reinsurance is financing (surplus relief). When an insurer is faced with a decrease in surplus due to a rapid increase in unearned premium reserve or excessive losses in underwriting or investments, quota share reinsurance can correct this drain on surplus. The primary insurer may cede a percentage of its entire book of business or a specific line of insurance. The initial transaction (cession) is the unearned premium reserve on the business reinsured, and for this, the primary insurer receives a commission from the reinsurer. The insurer's assets are reduced by the amount paid the reinsurer for this cession *less* the commission allowance. The insurer's liabilities (reserves) are decreased by the amount of the unearned premium reserve assumed by the reinsurer. The decrease in liabilities is *greater* than the decrease in assets by the amount of the ceding commission. Thus, the insurer's surplus is increased by the amount of the ceding commission.

Quota share reinsurance may function as a single transaction (illustrated in the balance sheet examples) or as a continuing one. In the single transaction situation, the reinsurance remains in force until the unearned premium reserve that is ceded is fully earned. In the continuing transaction situation, the insurer cedes a quota share percent of new and renewal business until the reinsurance agreement is terminated.

To illustrate, assume that the IIA Insurance Company has developed unearned premium reserves of $2,000,000 at the close of business on December 31, 19X5. In order to increase its surplus from

Exhibit 5-4
IIA Insurance Company Balance Sheet As of 12/31/X5

Assets		Liabilities and Surplus	
Cash	$1,500,000	Unearned Premium Reserve	$2,000,000
Other assets	4,500,000	Other liabilities	3,000,000
		Surplus	1,000,000
Total assets	$6,000,000		
		Total liabilities and surplus	$6,000,000

Exhibit 5-5
IIA Insurance Company Balance Sheet As Of 1/31/X6

Assets		Liabilities and Surplus	
Cash	$ 900,000	Unearned Premium Reserve	$1,000,000
Other assets	4,500,000	Other liabilities	3,000,000
		Surplus	1,400,000
Total assets	$5,400,000	Total liabilities and surplus	$5,400,000

$1,000,000 to $1,400,000 (see the balance sheet example) it purchases a 50 percent quota share treaty applying only to business in force on that date. The reinsurance treaty will operate for one year only, and the ceding commission is 40 percent.

The balance sheet of the IIA Insurance Company *before* reinsurance can be seen in Exhibit 5-4.[5]

Through the 50 percent quota share reinsurance arrangement, the reinsurer assumes $1,000,000 (50 percent of $2,000,000) of the insurer's unearned premium reserve, and the IIA Insurance Company pays $600,000 to the reinsurer ($1,000,000 less 40 percent commission or $400,000). On the asset side, cash is reduced by $600,000 (paid to the reinsurer). On the liability and surplus side, the unearned premium reserve is reduced by $1,000,000, and surplus is increased by the amount of commission, which is $400,000.

The balance sheet of the IIA Insurance Company *after* the single cession quota share reinsurance is illustrated in Exhibit 5-5.

In the year following the effective date of the reinsurance, the reinsurer will pay 50 percent of the losses on those policies in force at the beginning of the treaty year for which the unearned premium

Exhibit 5-6
Reinsurer's Experience

Premiums ceded to the reinsurer	$1,000,000
(50% of unearned premium reserve of $2,000,000)	
Less 40% commission	400,000
Net payment to the reinsurer	$ 600,000
Less losses (56% of $1,000,000 in premiums earned during the year)	560,000
Reinsurer's gross profit (4% of earned premiums)	$ 40,000

reserve was $2,000,000. If we assume that all such policies expire during the year and also assume a loss ratio of 56 percent, the reinsurer's experience on this business is illustrated in Exhibit 5-6.

The $40,000 gross profit of the reinsurer represents the net cost of this transaction to the IIA Insurance Company. In return, the primary insurer has increased its surplus by 40 percent, thereby greatly improving its financial status and increasing its capacity.

Quota share reinsurance may be helpful for:

1. a new insurer with limited capital and policyholders' surplus and no experience in the line to be written;
2. a small insurer with limited capital and policyholders' surplus, some past experience in the lines to be written, and seeking to expand; and
3. a large insurer with ample surplus and experience, but requiring an adviser to help in a new territory.

With quota share reinsurance, selection against the reinsurer (adverse selection) is not as likely because every risk is shared. Also, if the loss ratio is favorable, more of the insurer's profits are ceded to the reinsurer than under other forms of reinsurance. The spread of business, as to both time and geography, is generally more favorable to the reinsurer; and consequently a more favorable ceding commission for the insurer may be allowed. Further, quota share provides more surplus relief than other forms of reinsurance because the reinsurer must share in every risk. For example, in the case of a 20 percent quota share contract, the primary insurer cedes 20 percent of its liability and premiums on every risk to the reinsurer, who must pay 20 percent of any loss sustained whether total or partial. The percentage is constant throughout and applies to both premiums and losses alike.

Assume the primary insurer has a 50/50 quota share treaty up to $50,000. If a risk is insured for $40,000, the premiums, disregarding

Exhibit 5-7
Illustration of Quota Share Reinsurance

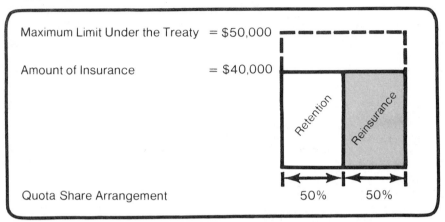

Maximum Limit Under the Treaty   = $50,000

Amount of Insurance   = $40,000

Retention   Reinsurance

Quota Share Arrangement   50%   50%

commissions, and losses are shared proportionately by the insurer and reinsurer. This is illustrated in Exhibit 5-7. The proportions are shown vertically to demonstrate that losses are shared down to the first dollar. This is in contrast to excess reinsurance, which is discussed later.

Quota share reinsurance is suitable for almost any line of insurance or class of business and may be applied on a gross basis (that is, before any other reinsurance is utilized), or may be applied to retained liability after deduction of other reinsurance.

Surplus Share   Surplus share reinsurance is a form of pro-rata reinsurance whereby the primary insurer cedes only the "surplus" liability above a predetermined limit. The reinsurer contributes to the payment of losses in *proportion* to its share of the total limit of coverage.[6] The primary insurer's minimum retention is a predetermined dollar amount which must be retained for its own account on any one risk before it may cede any amount to the surplus share reinsurers. A surplus share treaty is expressed in terms of the number of "lines" it contains. *A line is equal to the primary insurer's retention.* It is thus related to the "line limit" as described earlier. Thus, if an insurer's retention is $50,000 and it has a ten-line surplus share treaty, the capacity of the treaty to absorb amounts above the retention would be $500,000 (computed: 10 × $50,000).

Surplus share and quota share reinsurance operate identically in that both are forms of pro-rata reinsurance. That is, the reinsurer shares in the premium and losses *in the same proportion* as it shares in the total amount of insurance. The major difference between the two is that under quota share, every risk included in the treaty must be ceded according to the predetermined percentage. But under surplus share, only those risks where the amount of insurance is greater than the retention are ceded. The primary insurer is then able to cede as many "lines" as it wishes to the surplus treaties. The reinsurer is not involved at all unless the amount of insurance on the risk is greater than the retention set forth in the treaty. If the amount of insurance is below the retention, the primary insurer retains the entire amount and the reinsurer is not involved. If the amount of insurance is greater than the retention, the amount above the retention is ceded to the reinsurer in the proportion determined by the primary insurer subject only to the minimum retention and maximum number of lines.

Note that this discussion has mentioned only *amounts of insurance* and not *losses*. If a loss occurs on a risk covered by the surplus share treaty, the loss is shared by the insurer and reinsurer *in proportion* to the amount of insurance provided by each. This proportional sharing is applied to all losses regardless of size, even those below the retention (line limit).

In the following illustration, assume that the retention of the primary insurer is $20,000. This being the case, then:

1. if a policy is for less than the line limit ($20,000), no reinsurance will be involved and the primary insurer will retain the entire risk;

2. if a policy is for more than the line limit, the primary insurer will retain at least the line and cede any amount above the line limit, subject to the maximum limit. For example, if the policy is for $80,000 and the line is $20,000, the primary insurer may retain $20,000 and cede the $60,000 above the line. In this case, the primary insurer has 2/8 of the total risk, and the reinsurer has 6/8 of the total risk. As with quota share reinsurance, they will now share *premium* and *losses*, 2/8 and 6/8 respectively. If a loss of $16,000 occurs, the primary insurer pays $4,000 (computed: 2/8 × $16,000) and the reinsurer pays $12,000 (computed: 6/8 × $16,000). The loss *does not* have to exceed the retention before the reinsurer is involved in the loss. The retention of the insurer represents the basis for determining the amount and proportions of the cession. The primary insurer could choose to keep $40,000 and cede $40,000 or keep $60,000 and cede $20,000. The amount ceded is subject only to the minimum retention and the maximum limit.

A distinguishing characteristic of surplus share reinsurance, then, is that the percentage of the risk reinsured may vary from one account to another. This is because the retention of the primary insurer is set in *dollar amounts*. Therefore, with a fixed dollar amount of retention, the greater the total amount of insurance, the smaller the percentage of all losses retained by the primary insurer. This is in contrast to quota share reinsurance, in which the retention is a *fixed percentage*.

The surplus share method of proportional reinsurance permits the primary insurer to keep small policies for its own account and to cede the amount of potential loss on large policies that is above its retention level. Since the reinsurer does not share each risk on the same basis as the primary insurer, it is possible to have adverse selection against the reinsurer by the primary insurer. Surplus share generally provides more capacity than quota share.

Generally, a surplus share treaty may have several levels of retention. The size of the retention may vary in direct proportion to the quality of the risk being reinsured. The retentions may vary by class according to the probable frequency or severity of loss, not the type of risk. Class A, the highest quality risk, will often have a higher retention than Class D, the lowest quality risk. Every risk must be placed into a class, the appropriate amount being retained by the insurer and the "surplus" amount over the retention being ceded to the surplus share reinsurers.[7]

Surplus share reinsurance is often written in layers. The first layer of surplus share is referred to as a "first surplus," which means that if the surplus treaties are to be used, it is first. The first surplus could apply over a quota share treaty, an excess cover or above the amount retained by the primary insurer. There may be a second, a third, and even further surplus treaties to handle even larger risks.

The reinsurance treaties (layers) function identically like the first surplus treaty, but the capacity of each underlying surplus must be exceeded on a risk before the next surplus layer may be used. For example, assume the IIA Insurance Company has a net retention of $50,000 on fire business and has first, second, and third surplus treaties of three lines each (a "line" being equal to the insurer's retention). Exhibit 5-8 illustrates the distribution of $450,000 fire risk among the various surplus treaties.

Since this is a type of pro-rata reinsurance contract, the premium is allocated according to the proportion assumed by each reinsurer. Thus, the $6,000 premium (hypothetical) would be allocated as illustrated in Exhibit 5-9.

The premiums to the reinsurers are reduced by the amount of the ceding commission. For simplicity, this example assumes a 40 percent commission on each layer. Generally, there is a reduction in commission with each higher layer. The first surplus has the highest commission rate, while the percentage of commission would decrease by a few points on each succeeding layer (for example, second surplus—35

Exhibit 5-8
Illustration of Three Surplus Share Treaties

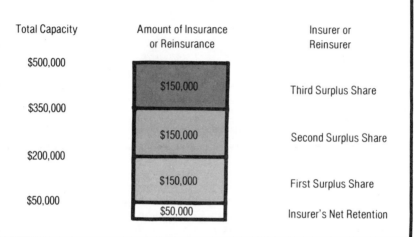

Example of total capacity provided by three surplus share treaties:

Total Capacity	Amount of Insurance or Reinsurance	Insurer or Reinsurer
$500,000		
	$150,000	Third Surplus Share
$350,000		
	$150,000	Second Surplus Share
$200,000		
	$150,000	First Surplus Share
$50,000		
	$50,000	Insurer's Net Retention

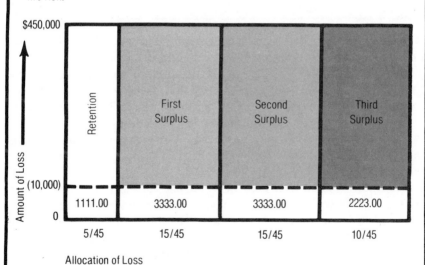

Example of loss allocation under the three surplus share treaties above, on a $450,000 fire risk:

$450,000

Amount of Loss

Retention	First Surplus	Second Surplus	Third Surplus
(10,000)			
1111.00	3333.00	3333.00	2223.00
0			
5/45	15/45	15/45	10/45

Allocation of Loss

Exhibit 5-9
Hypothetical Allocation of a $6000. Premium—Surplus Share

	Gross Premium	Less Commission	Net Premium
IIA (retention)	$6000 × 5/45 = $ 666.00	+2134.00	$2800.00
First Surplus	6000 × 15/45 = 2000.00	− 800.00	1200.00
Second Surplus	6000 × 15/45 = 2000.00	− 800.00	1200.00
Third Surplus	6000 × 10/45 = 1334.00	− 534.00	800.00
	$6000.00	0	$6000.00

Exhibit 5-10
Allocation of Loss—Surplus Share Reinsurance

	Share of Risk	Loss	Share of Loss
IIA	5/45	x 10,000	$ 1,111.
First Surplus	15/45	x 10,000	3,333.
Second Surplus	15/45	x 10,000	3,333.
Third Surplus	10/45	x 10,000	2,223.
	100.00%		$10,000.

percent third surplus—32.5 percent, and so on). Thus, the final allocation of premiums is shown in the net premium column.

Now assume that a $10,000 fire loss occurs. Since surplus share is a type of pro-rata reinsurance, premiums and losses are shared proportionately even if the loss is below the retention. The loss would be allocated as illustrated in Exhibit 5-10.

The above example illustrates that under surplus share reinsurance, all losses are shared proportionately on every risk insured for more than the retention of the insurer.

The spirit of the treaty is such that participating reinsurers to be treated alike should be subject to identical terms and conditions except in regard to the share allotted to them. The total number of lines to be carried by the reinsurers will reflect the needs of the ceding company. In establishing these lines, the primary underwriter will have first reviewed the present book of business; second, prospectively reviewed the potential and probable commitments to producers; third, studied the maximum multiple of the usual retention required to be insured by producers; and fourth, carefully analyzed the loss experience.

Exhibit 5-11
Surplus Share Reinsurance—An Illustration

Insurer:	IIA Insurance Company
Reinsurer:	Major Reinsurance Company
Form of Reinsurance:	Surplus Share Treaty
Perils:	All Broad Form Perils
Retentions:	Class A (highest quality) $50,000
	Class B (average quality) $30,000
	Class C (lowest quality) $15,000
Limits:	Five lines but no more than $150,000 on any one risk
Special Conditions:	The primary insurer may bypass the treaty or limit the reinsurer's liability if the loss potential warrants such action.

Generally, the first surplus layer is designed to be the only reinsurance that will be used to cover the normal needs of the primary company. If a second surplus is contracted, it would cover the unusually large risk or special groups of risks. Therefore, if the primary underwriter concludes that the maximum normal needs are within the range of eight times the retention, the reinsurance contract required is an eight-line treaty.

The use of surplus share reinsurance requires a judgment by the primary underwriter, since the retention usually varies with the quality of the risk. Although most underwriters may not design a reinsurance program or place reinsurance, many underwriters must decide into what class the risk must be placed for reinsurance purposes. The following examples are based on a common set of facts in Exhibit 5-11.

Situation 1. A property policy is requested on contents in a cinder block warehouse. The contents consist primarily of plumbing supplies, equipment, and tools, and the amount of insurance is $35,000. There are no exposing properties and the fire protection is Class 3.

The property underwriter classifies this risk as Class A and deems it satisfactory for complete retention. The file is so marked, and the treaty is not used since the amount of insurance is below the retention.

Situation 2. An application is received for property coverage in the amount of $60,000 on a two-story masonry building occupied as a grocery store and dwelling. The building is fifty-five years old but is well maintained. It is located in a stable neighborhood where the protection is Class 5.

The underwriter classifies the risk as low to average primarily due to the age of the building, the multiple occupancy, and the fire protection. It is decided that the potential for a total loss suggests that the safest situation ($15,000 retention) be taken and the remaining $45,000 be ceded to the surplus treaty.

Situation 3. A respected and profitable producer submits a frame hotel in a rural town with Class 8 protection. The hotel is "tied in" with a very profitable manufacturing account which IIA Insurance Company insures. The amount of insurance requested is $50,000 (part of $250,000).

The submission is clearly an accommodation. A declination is improper but full approval is impossible. The underwriter arrives at a compromise and offers to provide $20,000, which will be retained entirely. The treaty was intentionally bypassed to protect the treaty and its overall loss ratio.

Surplus Share and Quota Share Compared In summary, there are two major differences between quota share and surplus share. First, in quota share, the percentages are *fixed* for every risk included in the treaty, but in surplus share, the percentage varies from risk to risk. The retention, under a surplus share arrangement, is based on a dollar amount, and consequently the percentage varies with both the total amount of insurance and the quality of the risk.

Second, in quota share, every risk in the class covered by the treaty must be ceded to the reinsurer regardless of the amount of insurance. In surplus share, those risks that are below the retention (dollar amount) are not ceded.

The principal function of quota share is surplus relief, although increased capacity and stabilization of underwriting results are provided. Surplus share, on the other hand, is primarily used to increase capacity but can be used for catastrophic protection and stabilization.

Excess Reinsurance

Excess reinsurance refers to reinsurance that, subject to a specified limit, indemnifies the primary insurer against the amount of *loss* in *excess* of a specified retention.[8] As the name implies, excess reinsurance pays only that part of a loss exceeding a predetermined retention which is expressed as a dollar amount or a percentage. Unlike pro-rata (proportional) reinsurance, the reinsurer does not become involved until the *loss* is above the amount retained by the primary

Exhibit 5-12
Excess Reinsurance

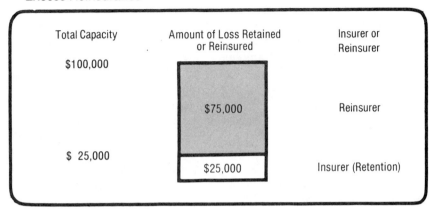

Total Capacity	Amount of Loss Retained or Reinsured	Insurer or Reinsurer
$100,000		
	$75,000	Reinsurer
$ 25,000		
	$25,000	Insurer (Retention)

Exhibit 5-13
Nonproportional (Excess) Reinsurance

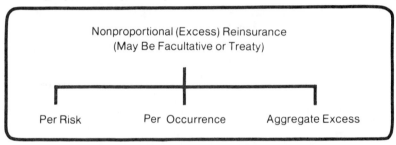

Nonproportional (Excess) Reinsurance
(May Be Facultative or Treaty)

Per Risk   Per Occurrence   Aggregate Excess

insurer. Thus, excess reinsurance is *nonproportional—losses* are shared, not amounts of insurance. Exhibit 5-12 illustrates the operation of excess reinsurance on a $100,000 risk. The retention of the insurer is $25,000, and the reinsurer provides the additional $75,000. A comparison can be made between excess reinsurance and deductible insurance coverage in that the excess reinsurer does not become financially involved in the loss until it becomes greater than the specified amount, and then only for the amount in *excess* of the specified amount up to the limit of the reinsurance agreement. Naturally, this deductible is quite substantial in comparison to the usual deductible amounts.

As illustrated in Exhibit 5-13, excess reinsurance is composed of three major types: *excess per occurrence, excess per risk,* and *aggregate excess of loss.* There are many combinations and modifications of these types of excess reinsurance.

Excess Per Occurrence This type of reinsurance provides indemnity against loss sustained beyond, or in excess of, the net retention of the primary insurer, subject to a reinsurance limit, regardless of the number of risks (number of separate policies, or specifically scheduled items) involved, in respect to one accident, occurrence, or event. The reinsurer becomes involved when a single occurrence causes the primary insurer to pay more than the specified amount (retention). For example, if as the result of a hurricane, the primary insurer should pay losses of $780,000 and the specified reinsurance is $750,000 excess of $100,000 per occurrence, the primary insurer bears the first $100,000 of loss, and the reinsurer is responsible for up to $750,000 in excess of $100,000. In this example, the loss share of the primary insurer is $100,000, and that of the reinsurer is $680,000.

The intent of excess per occurrence reinsurance is to afford protection against a shock loss. An important characteristic is that the loss be caused by a *single event* (one occurrence), no matter how many separate policies or specifically scheduled items are involved.

Excess Per Risk This type of reinsurance provides indemnity against loss sustained beyond, or in excess of, a specified retention *per risk* (a single policy or a single scheduled item in a policy), subject to a specified reinsurance limit applicable to each risk, and resulting from one event, accident, or occurrence.

The intent of excess of risk reinsurance is to give the primary insurer the necessary underwriting capacity in the line or class of risks reinsured. The reinsurer becomes financially involved when the *loss to a risk* is beyond the specified amount. The amount of reinsurance is available to each separately covered risk as defined for this purpose.

Most types of excess reinsurance use the concept of "ultimate net loss." The ultimate net loss is computed by summing:

1. total amount of the loss and
2. costs of litigation;

and subtracting:

1. recoveries from all underlying reinsurers and
2. salvage realized from the insured property.[9]

Thus, the "ultimate net loss" must exceed the retention before the reinsurer is involved in the loss.

The difference between *excess per occurrence* and *excess per risk* can best be explained through the use of an example.[10] Assume that the primary insurer uses excess per risk, on a facultative basis, for a property insurance situation involving four steel warehouses, commonly owned and operated, standing 200 feet from one another. There is no treaty reinsurance. Each of the four buildings is to be insured for $200,000 and the net retention is $20,000 *per risk*. (Each building is considered a risk for the purpose of excess per risk reinsurance.) Reinsurance of each of the buildings is for $180,000 excess of $20,000. Suppose a windstorm damages all four buildings to the total extent of $15,000. Under an excess per risk reinsurance contract, there is no reinsurance recovery, since no one loss was above the retention of $20,000 per risk. If a second loss occurs and *each* warehouse suffers damage in the amount of $15,000, for a total loss of $60,000 (computed: 4 × $15,000), there is still no recovery from the reinsurer because the retention applies *per risk*.

Now, let's change the reinsurance to excess per occurrence, with the reinsurance being set at $980,000 excess of $20,000. In the first loss above of $15,000 total, there is no reinsurance recovery since the loss is less than the $20,000 retention. In the second loss of $15,000 to each warehouse for a total loss of $60,000, the reinsurer is obligated to the primary insurer for $40,000, the loss in excess of the $20,000 retention per occurrence.

Excess reinsurance is often written in layers. The first layer is usually the "working excess." The working excess anticipates some loss frequency, and it allows the primary insurer to retain a majority of its premium but not expose itself to an adverse loss ratio. The working excess layer is primarily involved in the stabilization and capacity functions of reinsurance. It is designed to "average out" losses over a period of time and accordingly should not be exposed to peak limits of liability.

Aggregate Excess of Loss This form of excess reinsurance is also referred to as "stop loss reinsurance" and as "excess of loss ratio reinsurance." Aggregate excess of loss indemnifies the primary insurer against the amount by which the primary insurer's losses, incurred during a specific period, usually twelve months, exceed either:

1. a predetermined dollar amount *or*
2. a percentage of the insurer's subject premiums (loss ratio) for the specific period.[11]

Under this form of excess reinsurance, the reinsurer is liable for all losses, regardless of size, that occur after the specified loss ratio (or total dollar losses) has been reached. For example, an aggregate excess of loss program may stipulate that the reinsurer is liable for *all losses* in excess of the 70 percent loss ratio subject to a limit of 110 percent. If the loss ratio of the insurer exceeds 110 percent, the additional losses revert to the primary insurer or may be absorbed by another aggregate excess of loss program in a higher layer. For example, another aggregate excess of loss cover may absorb the losses in excess of the

Exhibit 5-14
Aggregate Excess of Loss (Excess of Loss Ratio) Written in Layers

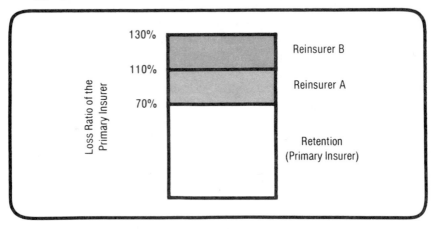

110 percent loss ratio up to 130 percent. This is illustrated in Exhibit 5-14.

Sometimes the reinsurer requires the primary insurer to act as a *co-reinsurer* for a portion of the excess to add the incentive for sound underwriting. The agreement might provide that the reinsurer is only liable for 80 percent of all losses in excess of the loss ratio of 70 percent up to its limit (110 percent in this example).[12] The primary insurer is then required to act as its own co-reinsurer for the remaining 20 percent.

When written for the dollar amount of loss to the primary insurer, this reinsurance is called *aggregate excess of loss reinsurance* or *stop loss reinsurance*. However, if it is written for the reinsurance to cover beyond an agreed loss ratio (ratio of incurred losses to earned premiums) during the calendar or fiscal year, or other time span, it is referred to as *excess of loss ratio reinsurance*. Whichever way this reinsurance is written, its purpose is to help stabilize the primary insurer's results from year to year within reasonable limits and is commonly used for those classes of business subject to rather severe cyclical losses. For example, crop hail and credit insurance experience may fluctuate markedly from year to year.

Excess and Pro-Rata Compared

Excess (nonproportional) reinsurance is more modern than pro-rata (proportional). Excess reinsurance is widely accepted by primary insurers, and its use by all types and sizes of insurers is steadily increasing. Excess reinsurance offers several advantages. First, it may

Exhibit 5-15
A $1,000,000 Risk with a Net Retention of $25,000 in Layers

Layer	Coverage	Cumulative (Aggregate) Coverage	Reinsurance Premium
First	$225,000 excess of $ 25,000	$ 250,000	$16,000
Second	250,000 excess of 250,000	500,000	3,500
Third	250,000 excess of 500,000	750,000	1,500
Fourth	250,000 excess of 750,000	1,000,000	1,000

be used in a variety of ways such as excess per occurrence, or aggregate excess. Second, it is economical, not only in pricing, but in the costs of administration. For many liability lines of business, it is the only available reinsurance cover.

The fundamental difference between excess and pro-rata reinsurance is that with excess reinsurance, there is no proportional sharing of risk or premium. The reinsurer has only a secondary exposure which does not begin until the primary insurer's retention is fully expended. The pricing of excess reinsurance, as actually practiced today, is not a difficult concept to understand. The greater the distance from the first level of loss expectancy, the lesser the loss potential and the lower the price. A risk valued at $1,000,000 with a net retention of $25,000 may be handled as illustrated in Exhibit 5-15.

In the above illustration, the uppermost layers may be thought of as the "disaster" or "catastrophe" reinsurance. The first layer, (called the "working layer") has a relatively low attachment point and will likely be involved in many losses. The higher layers (second, third, and fourth) are not expected to be called upon too frequently. Therefore, the higher layers are priced according to the probability of their being used. (The reader may want to compare the pricing of excess reinsurance with the pricing of higher limits of liability insurance. The additional premium for added levels of protection is significantly less than the premium for basic protection.)

In summary, excess reinsurance will pay on an *occurrence* basis (an accident, or event), on a *risk* (an item that is insured) basis, or on an *aggregate* basis. On an excess per occurrence basis, the primary insurer recovers losses in excess of the retention that applies to each occurrence, accident, or event regardless of the number of risks involved. In excess per risk reinsurance, the primary insurer recovers losses in excess of the retention that applies to each risk involved in a loss. Finally, on an aggregate basis, the primary insurer recovers losses that in the aggregate exceed a retention expressed as a loss ratio or an aggregate dollar amount over a period of time.

CASE STUDIES IN REINSURANCE

Various ways in which the different types of reinsurance can be used to solve underwriting problems can best be illustrated through case studies. The cases that follow also demonstrate how the combinations of various forms of reinsurance are useful in both property and liability lines.

Property reinsurance programs often combine both pro-rata and excess reinsurance to provide the required capacity, stabilization, financing, and catastrophe protection. On the other hand, liability reinsurance programs are usually composed of the excess method supplemented by facultative reinsurance in order to acquire the necessary capacity.

Property Reinsurance Program

Situation 1 The High Risk Insurance Company is a personal lines insurer with a countrywide marketing force. One of its agencies has cornered the homeowners market for high valued dwellings where the Section I limit (amount of insurance on dwelling, contents, other structures, and loss of use) is between $250,000 and $500,000. The company has written 200 of these large homeowners policies so far. The High Risk Insurance Company now faces a concentration of risks in addition to the fact that multiple $500,000 losses would seriously impair the financial strength of the insurer. Thus, the insurer decides to cede a portion of each homeowners policy as illustrated in Exhibit 5-16 to obtain the required capacity and eliminate the catastrophe exposure of this concentration of risks in a relatively small geographical area. In order to obtain maximum capacity over the $75,000 retention level per policy, the High Risk Insurance Company has used a combination of two reinsurance techniques: surplus treaties and a facultative agreement. The facultative arrangement is also on a pro-rata basis.

Assume a tornado rips through this area completely destroying ten homes with a total value of $5 million. The loss would be shared with $750,000 being retained; $1,500,000 in each surplus treaty; and $1,250,000 facultatively reinsured.

The reinsurance procedure in personal lines is generally simpler than in commercial lines. This is because commercial accounts are usually of higher value, and operations conducted on the premises may be more hazardous than those of a typical dwelling. A property

Exhibit 5-16
High Risk Insurance Company

	Assumption of Liability	% Assumption of Liability
1. Retention Level	$ 75,000	15%
2. First Surplus Treaty (capacity 2 lines)	150,000	30%
3. Second Surplus Treaty (capacity 2 lines)	150,000	30%
4. Facultative Reinsurance (surplus share)	125,000	25%
Total Assumption of Liability	$500,000	100%

reinsurance program for a commercial risk is illustrated by the following situation.

Situation 2 Assume that the High Risk Insurance Company insures the building and contents of the Data Specialists Company for $4,300,000 on an "all-risks" basis. A $4,300,000 risk is beyond the capacity of the High Risk Insurance Company. Therefore, it cedes this risk in the manner illustrated in Exhibit 5-17 according to previously arranged treaties and purchases a facultative reinsurance contract to obtain the extra capacity needed for this risk beyond the limits of the treaties.

Assume a fire strikes the computer section of Data Specialists Company causing a $2 million loss. This loss will be shared according to the percentages in Exhibit 5-17 with the primary insurer retaining 6.98 percent ($139,600); the first surplus treaty paying 41.86 percent ($837,200); the second surplus treaty paying 27.91 percent ($558,200); the third surplus treaty paying 13.95 percent ($279,000); and facultative reinsurance paying 9.30 percent ($186,000).

Note that the facultative reinsurance for the property risk is also on a pro-rata basis. Consequently, any loss adjustment expense is shared with the reinsurer in the same proportion as the loss. To obtain maximum capacity over the $300,000 retention level, the company has combined surplus treaties and the facultative method.

Exhibit 5-17

Risk Ceded by High Risk Insurance Company

	Assumption of Liability	% Assumption of Liability
1. Retention Level	$ 300,000	6.98%
2. First Surplus Treaty (capacity 6 lines)	1,800,000	41.86%
3. Second Surplus Treaty (capacity 4 lines)	1,200,000	27.91%
4. Third Surplus Treaty (capacity 2 lines)	600,000	13.95%
5. Facultative Reinsurance (surplus share)	400,000	9.30%
Total Assumption of Liability	$4,300,000	100.00%

Situation 3 The High Risk Insurance Company now has an additional problem. If it continues to write large risks of this nature, a retention level of $300,000 will restrict its underwriting capacity. To overcome this difficulty, it may use an excess per risk reinsurance treaty to provide protection for any loss in excess of $100,000 up to $300,000 where the proportional treaties assume the liability. This assumes there is no provision in the proportional treaties requiring High Risk to retain a minimum amount greater than $100,000.

Assume that the same fire strikes the computer section of the Data Specialists Company, again causing a $2,000,000 loss. The excess per risk recovery that the High Risk Insurance Company will be entitled to is computed in Exhibit 5-18. Note that the excess per risk reinsurance recovery is applied *after* the pro-rata reinsurance recovery.

Liability Reinsurance Program

The reinsurance coverages used for commercial liability risks are similar to those used for personal lines liability risks. Both situations have the inherent problems of rising legal fees, increasing jury awards, incurred but not reported losses (IBNR), and an increase in claim consciousness. The essential difference between the personal and commercial liability reinsurance plans would be the need for larger amounts of excess reinsurance to cover the generally higher liability limits in commercial lines.

Exhibit 5-18
High Risk Insurance Company—Excess Per Risk Recovery

		Loss
		Loss
Total Loss to High Risk Insurance Company		$2,000,000
Less: Total Loss Assumed by Proportional Reinsurers		
1. First Surplus Treaty 41.86% of loss	837,200	
2. Second Surplus Treaty 27.91% of loss	558,200	
3. Third Surplus Treaty 13.95% of loss	279,000	
4. Facultative Reinsurance 9.30% of loss	186,000	
		1,860,400
Subtotal		$ 139,600
Less: Retention level under excess per risk treaty		100,000
Loss assumed by excess per risk		$ 39,600

Facultative reinsurance is used in liability plans to provide additional capacity just as in property reinsurance plans, but in contrast to property facultative reinsurance, which is usually on a pro-rata basis, facultative reinsurance in liability lines is usually on an excess basis.

Assume that the High Risk Insurance Company purchases an excess per occurrence treaty that will pay in the event of a loss up to $1,000,000 in excess of a retention level of $100,000 per occurrence. In an effort to expand its underwriting capacity, the High Risk Insurance Company purchases facultative reinsurance that will provide coverage for $1,500,000 in excess of $1,100,000 on a particular risk it is insuring. Assume that the insured risk incurs a $1,800,000 loss. The loss recovery the High Risk Insurance Company will be entitled to is computed as illustrated in Exhibit 5-19.

The reinsurance situations presented above are intended to illustrate two points. First, reinsurance treaties and facultative placements are most often used in combination to provide the capacity, stabilization, financing, or catastrophe protection needed by each insurer. Second, the various reinsurance coverages may be programmed or set up in many varieties to achieve the optimum interrelationship.

Exhibit 5-19
Loss Recovery for High Risk Insurance Company

	Loss from Accident
Total Loss to High Risk Insurance Company	$1,800,000
Less: Facultative Reinsurance	700,000
Total Losses Subject to Excess Treaty	$1,100,000
Less: High Risk's Retention Level Under Excess per Occurrence Treaty	100,000
Loss Assumed by Excess Reinsurer	$1,000,000

SOURCES OF REINSURANCE

The reinsurance market consists of several types of reinsurers and different methods for accomplishing the reinsurance transaction. This section contains an overview of the reinsurance market.

The reinsurance marketplace can best be analyzed by examining the major types of reinsurers, which are:

1. reinsurance departments (or divisions) of primary insurers,
2. professional reinsurers, and
3. pools, associations, or syndicates.

Reinsurance Departments of Primary Insurers

Underwriters often have direct dealings with the reinsurance departments of other primary insurers on both facultative and treaty business. These reinsurance departments operate as a "reciprocal" market, as an "in-house" or "inter-group" reinsurance arrangement, or, less frequently, as a professional reinsurer owned or controlled by the primary insurer.

Reciprocal Arrangements Reciprocal reinsurance (reciprocity) involves one insurer exchanging an equal share of like policies with another insurer. Insurer X offers Insurer Y a 4 percent share of Insurer X's products liability business but with the condition that Insurer Y will reciprocate by offering Insurer X a share of its similar products liability business that has the same premium volume.

This reciprocal exchange of like policies should result in an equitable exchange of profit potential for these several reasons:

- If the shares of the exchanged policies have generally the same premium volume, each insurer's total premium volume will approximate the direct premiums written. The amount of premium volume lost through reinsurance is gained from other primary insurers through reciprocity. This exchange enables the insurer to retain more income for investment purposes than if the insurer were utilizing the services of a professional reinsurer and ceding much of its premium income to the reinsurer.
- Through reciprocity, just as through professional reinsurers, the insurer is able to spread its risks. Thus, the maximum liability the insurer has on any one risk is limited, which allows the "law of large numbers" to take effect and gives more stability to the loss ratio. In other words, the catastrophe exposure is significantly reduced.
- Under reciprocity, the profit transferred to the reinsurer (insurers through reciprocity) is about the same as the profits received by the primary insurer from these reinsurers. The insurer's cost of reinsurance is restricted to the cost of administering the various reciprocal treaties and does not have to include a profit margin for the professional reinsurer.

Although the advantages stated above are strong reasons favoring reciprocity, there are several disadvantages to consider:

- The insurer could very well find itself in the position of reinsuring risks that it would decline as direct business and at a rate lower than it deems adequate.
- By using reciprocity, the insurer forgoes any guidance that it could receive from a professional reinsurer.
- Reciprocity increases the number of reinsurers involved with a corresponding increase in the total administrative cost of handling numerous reinsurance (reciprocal) transfers.
- If the insurer requires "financing for growth," reciprocity is not the proper vehicle. Reciprocity does not provide the insurer with any surplus relief. If the insurer uses reciprocity, it will have to maintain the entire unearned premium reserve.

The type of coverage often desired, if not required, for the reciprocal arrangement is the surplus share treaty, largely in the property and marine lines. Excess reinsurance, being somewhat more specialized, is not felt to be totally suitable for reciprocity.

In-House or Inter-Group Reinsurance Arrangements   The in-house or inter-group reinsurance arrangement is the same as the reciprocal arrangement with one exception—all of the participating insurers belong to the same insurance company or group of companies. This type of operation probably has less influence in the marketplace, from the primary underwriter's point of view, than the other sources of reinsurance. The general characteristics of the in-house reinsurance arrangement are substantial net lines or net retention, along with the ability to accept risks with very large limits or values (capacity).

The in-house reinsurance arrangement has practically no publicity. The actual details of the in-house program or pool are well known only to a few executives of each insurance group.

Professional Reinsurers

The professional reinsurer is one whose total business activity is reinsurance.

Some advantages to the insurer of using professional reinsurers instead of reciprocity are:

1. Since reinsurance is its only business, the reinsurer is technically competent to provide the insurer with valuable underwriting advice. In addition, the cession should be accomplished in strict confidence, eliminating leakage of essential information to the insurer's competitors.
2. The professional reinsurer may offer one-stop reinsurance service to the insurer.
3. For the new or growing insurer, the professional reinsurer may provide financing under a proportional reinsurance contract. (Reciprocity does not provide surplus relief.)

The primary disadvantage in transferring risks to the professional reinsurer is that the primary insurer transfers potential profit as well. This is especially true in pro-rata reinsurance because the reinsurer shares in a percentage of the premiums collected by the insurer, who loses the underwriting profit (if any) on the reinsured business and also has less money to invest and thus relinquishes another potential source of earnings.

Reinsurance Pools, Associations, and Syndicates

A pool, association, or syndicate may be defined as a group of individual insurance companies who have as their objective the sharing of risks, usually through reinsurance. The size of the pool may vary from a few insurance companies to more than a hundred. In most cases, these insurers agree, according to pre-arranged proportions, to reinsure part of each risk written by member companies or otherwise ceded to the pool. The risks can be of a certain type or within a given geographical region. Generally, an insurance company shares in the premium and losses according to the proportion of each risk it assumes.

In the early years of reinsurance, an insurer contacted a number of other insurers in the area and placed the reinsurance facultatively. This method eventually gave way to the pooling technique whereby several insurers with similar problems formed a pool, association, or syndicate. In a technical sense, some "pools" cannot be considered reinsurance pools. Instead, they use the insurance principle of combining similar exposure units and sharing the premiums and losses among the member companies. Through this technique, many of the reinsurance functions (increased capacity, stabilization of results, catastrophe protection, and underwriting guidance) are achieved.

The factors that determine whether a pool is a reinsurance device are the organizational structure, type of contract issued, and the internal accounting procedures. The terms "pool," "association," or "syndicate" are often used interchangeably although there are some fine differences. Unfortunately, the title of an organization may contain one term while it actually operates under the definition of another.

In a *syndicate,* each member accepts a percentage of the risk and thus shares under a common name. The syndicate issues the policy under its name as a separate entity.

In a reinsurance *pool,* a policy for the full amount of insurance is issued by a member company and *reinsured* by the remainder of the pool members according to predetermined percentages. Sometimes the pool underwrites only the classes of business not written by the members. In this manner, the book of business of each member is unaffected by the pool experience.

The *association* category appears to be a catchall comprising those using both reinsurance or risk sharing techniques. In many cases, the member companies issue their own policies, but a reinsurance certificate is attached to the policy under which each company assumes a fixed percentage of the total amount of insurance. One of the member companies is responsible for inspection and investigation. Underwriting policy is established by an underwriting committee composed of underwriting executives of the member companies.

The basic idea behind organizations of this type is to provide a vehicle for sharing risks that require special coverages or special underwriting techniques. The use of such pools can greatly increase the primary underwriter's capacity to insure extra-hazardous risks. This is because under the pooling arrangement, the association pools all the risks ceded to it and then retrocedes the risks, according to a prearranged proportion, back to the member companies. This process is much like the quota share treaty discussed earlier in this chapter.

The pool, association, or syndicate affords its member companies the opportunity to participate in a line of insurance with a limited amount of capital, with a proportionate share of the administrative costs, and without having to staff the specialists needed for a successful venture.

SALES OR MARKETING TECHNIQUES

Direct or Intermediary

There are two major marketing or selling approaches to reinsurance: direct; or through an intermediary. In the first case, the transaction takes place directly between insurance company underwriters and their counterparts in the reinsurance company. In the latter case, the underwriters of a primary insurer submit their needs to reinsurance brokers (or some managing general agents) who place the business with reinsurers.

Whether dealing directly with a reinsurer or through an intermediary, the primary insurer must offer evidence of its financial strength and the experience of the underwriters submitting the business. The reinsurer looks closely at the insurer's financial statements, stock analyst's reports, insurance department bulletins, trade journals, and other information. Apart from the underwriting merits, some reinsurance submissions are declined either because a poorly financed insurance company is writing the risk or the person submitting the business is of questionable character.[13]

The experience and reputation of the primary insurer's underwriters are of utmost importance to the reinsurer. The concept of "underwriting the underwriter"[14] is referred to in the industry. It concerns itself with an evaluation made by the reinsurer of the knowledge and integrity of the primary underwriters before the risk characteristics are discussed. The insurance principle of "utmost good faith" must exist between the underwriters and reinsurers. Most facultative reinsurance is transacted over the telephone, and, accordingly, the reinsurer must rely on the underwriter to give accurate details on the risk. Utmost good faith requires that the underwriter not withhold detrimental information, underestimate prior losses, or fail to disclose hazardous risk exposures.

Likewise, in selecting a reinsurer, the primary insurer should carefully evaluate the reinsurer's financial condition. This analysis should include the ratio of earned premium income to surplus, total assets and liabilities, and the nature of reserves. In addition, the reinsurer's management, experience, and reputation for prompt claims payment should be determined.

The use of the reinsurance intermediary (broker) extends well back in history and is the prevailing marketing style of European reinsurers. There is also a considerable volume of American reinsurance business transacted through the intermediary or broker. Many American reinsurers operate only with brokers; conversely, many of the branch system reinsurers prefer not to accept offerings from brokers; and finally, some respond to both marketing concepts.

From the reinsurer's point of view, the selection of a basic marketing system depends on the management philosophy, the degree of underwriting control exercised, and the availability of skilled personnel. For reinsurers using both systems, the direct business may be placed with one member company of the group while the brokerage business is handled by an affiliated firm—all to the benefit of a common balance sheet.

The broker is a marketing specialist for the insurer. The technical expertise of a qualified broker can be used to advantage by the underwriter. Such a broker is in a position to place reinsurance on many lines of insurance quickly since he or she is acquainted with prevailing conditions in the various reinsurance markets. Because of this relationship with reinsurers, the broker is able to relieve the underwriter of the time-consuming chore of developing continuing contacts with reinsurers around the world. If reciprocity is the reinsurance vehicle desired by the underwriter to spread risks, the broker can again provide a valuable service. Brokers usually have numerous other clients with whom the proper reciprocal agreements can be obtained.

A primary insurer may elect to deal directly with its reinsurers if it has experienced personnel who are familiar with reinsurance markets and the "ins and outs" of reinsurance contracts, enabling them to negotiate with reinsurers. A lower cost of reinsurance may result through the elimination of a commission to the intermediary.

COST OF REINSURANCE

The cost of reinsurance, like the cost of primary insurance, cannot be exactly determined in advance because covered losses may not be identified and settled for months or years. However, the categories of costs to the primary insurer are known and are common to both treaty and facultative reinsurance transactions although they may vary in significance between the two.

The cost of reinsurance to the primary insurer is the total of

- gross profit to the reinsurer, plus
- loss of investment income, plus
- administrative costs, plus
- profit (or loss) on reciprocal reinsurance accepted (if appropriate).

Gross profit to the reinsurer is estimated by calculating reinsurance premiums earned *less* incurred losses and ceding commissions paid to the primary insurer.

The ceding commission is paid by the reinsurer to the primary insurer and thus reduces the cost of reinsurance. The ceding commission reimburses the primary insurer for producer's commission, inspection fees, policy issuance expenses, and other acquisition and servicing expenses that can be up to 40 percent of the total policy premium. Pro-rata treaties typically pay a ceding commission but not excess treaties. The ceding commission is negotiable and is affected by the actual expenses of the primary insurer, competition in the reinsurance business, and the reinsurer's estimate of the premium volume and loss experience under the treaty.

The commission on facultative reinsurance is usually smaller than that paid under treaty reinsurance because of adverse selection and limited competition. The smaller commission results in less surplus relief under the facultative approach. Some treaties have a retrospective adjustment of the ceding commission based on the actual loss ratio. An example of this arrangement is shown in Exhibit 5-20.

A second type of reinsurance commission is a brokerage commission paid by the reinsurer to the broker-intermediary who brought the primary insurer and reinsurer together. Generally, the rate is higher on excess treaties because they produce lower premiums but still require the same amount of time from the broker.[15]

Loss of investment income on the loss reserves and unearned premium reserves transferred to the reinsurer is greater in pro-rata reinsurance. There is much less investment income associated with excess reinsurance since this method is not used for financing and therefore the reinsurer holds very little cash.[16] In most pro-rata treaties, the loss of investment income is at least partially offset by the amount of the provisional ceding commission paid by the reinsurer and the terms for premium payment to the reinsurer.

Administrative costs include fixed overhead costs, the cost of the time the underwriter expends on calculating a retention level, and the cost of time involved in claim settlements connected with reinsurance coverages. With excess and quota share reinsurance, there are significantly fewer reinsurance transactions to process, requiring less paperwork and resulting in a substantial reduction in these costs.

Exhibit 5-20
Retrospective Ceding Commission (Sliding Commission) Scale—Pro Rata Reinsurance

Actual Loss Ratio	Commission Rate
60% or more	35%
59% but less than 60%	35.5
58% but less than 59%	36
57% but less than 58%	36.5
56% but less than 57%	37
55% but less than 56%	37.5
54% but less than 55%	38
53% but less than 54%	38.5
52% but less than 53%	39
51% but less than 52%	39.5
50% but less than 51%	40
less than 50%	41

The administrative costs of facultative reinsurance are highest because each reinsurance transaction is negotiated individually including telephone calls, letters, and the underwriter's time in deciding whether to accept the submission and in computing the premium. Pro-rata treaties are generally more costly to administer than excess treaties because they cover more frequent and smaller losses.

Profit or loss on reciprocal reinsurance accepted must be included. Under the reciprocal reinsurance arrangement, the primary insurer receives an equal share of a contract previously written by the reinsurer on another insurer in consideration for the cession which the insurer is now making. The policies that are being exchanged are of the same type. The primary objective of reciprocity is to enable the insurer to maintain an amount of premium income approximating the direct premiums written, thereby resulting in more dollars to invest and reducing the net cost of reinsurance to the primary insurer.

SUMMARY

Reinsurance is an underwriting tool that may be used to improve short-term underwriting results on a book of business and to provide the underwriter with a technique for solving problems on an individual risk.

Reinsurance, the "sharing of insurance among insurers," involves one insurer (the reinsurer) arranging with another insurer (the primary insurer) to be responsible for all or some part of a policy or policies written by the primary insurer. Through a reinsurance agreement which stipulates the form of reinsurance and the type of risk to be reinsured, the primary insurer cedes a portion of a risk to a reinsurer, keeping a portion of the risk, called the retention, for its own account. The retention may be expressed either as a dollar amount or as a percentage. The primary insurer pays a reinsurance premium for the protection just as any insured pays for insurance protection.

The two basic types of reinsurance transactions are *facultative* (nonobligatory), under which the primary insurer offers an individual risk to the reinsurer which the latter is under no obligation to accept; and *treaty* (automatic), under which the reinsurer is required to accept all cessions according to the terms of the obligatory contract.

Whether facultative or treaty, reinsurance is provided through pro-rata or excess contracts. In *pro-rata* (proportional) reinsurance, the reinsurer shares losses in the same proportion as it shares premiums and policy amounts. Pro-rata reinsurance can be either on a quota share basis, in which a fixed percentage of every risk included in the treaty is ceded; or on a surplus share basis, in which only those risks where the amount of insurance is greater than the retention are ceded. In the other major type of reinsurance contract, excess (nonproportional), the reinsurer makes loss payments to the insurer only when the latter's losses exceed a predetermined retention level. Excess reinsurance can be written as (1) *excess per occurrence*, (2) *excess per risk*, and (3) *aggregate excess of loss*.

The reinsurance selected for use depends upon the needs of the primary insurer. There are six basic needs (functions) which reinsurance can fulfill: increased capacity, catastrophe protection, stabilization, withdrawal from a territory or class of business, financing (surplus relief), and underwriting guidance.

There are several sources of reinsurance, including the reinsurance departments of primary insurers, professional reinsurers, and reinsurance pools, associations, and syndicates, each source having its own special advantages.

The two major marketing approaches to reinsurance are direct, in which the transaction takes place directly between insurance company underwriters and their counterparts in the reinsurance company; and through an intermediary, who will place a primary insurer's business with reinsurers.

Generally, the cost of reinsurance can be ascertained by the summation of (1) the gross profit to the reinsurer; (2) loss of investment income; (3) administrative costs; and (4) profit (or loss) on reciprocal insurance accepted.

Underwriters often feel that decisions regarding the use of reinsurance are within the realm of top management, but in many companies the primary underwriter is given the authority to use reinsurance. Consequently, the underwriter's knowledge of reinsurance may help in achieving the underwriting objectives of the insurance company.

Chapter Notes

1. Reinsurance Association of America, *Glossary of Reinsurance Terms* (Washington, DC: Reinsurance Association of America, 1972), p. 9.
2. This explanation has been greatly simplified to explain a difficult concept. In this simplification, some of the points made are not necessarily technically correct. To make the explanation technically correct would only confuse the point being made. For a more detailed discussion of unearned premium reserve calculation, see Cormick L. Breslin and Terrie E. Troxel, *Property-Liability Insurance Accounting and Finance* (Malvern, PA: American Institute for Property and Liability Underwriters, 1978), pp. 171-177.
3. Reinsurance Association of America, p. 8.
4. Robert C. Reinarz, *Property and Liability Reinsurance Management* (Fullerton, CA: Mission Publishing Company, 1969), p. 31.
5. Adapted from *Reinsurance and Reassurance* (New York: Munich Reinsurance Company, 1963), p. 38.
6. Reinarz, p. 25.
7. Reinarz, p. 25.
8. Reinsurance Association of America, p. 5.
9. Reinarz, p. 56.
10. Adapted from Edgar C. Werner, *Fundamentals of Reinsurance* (New York: The College of Insurance, 1964), p. 58.
11. Reinsurance Association of America, p. 3.
12. Reinarz, p. 74.
13. Andrew J. Barile, *Reinsurance. Risk Management Manual, Insurance 6, Supplement 19* (Santa Monica, CA: The Merritt Company, 1976), p. 87.
14. Barile, p. 86.
15. Bernard J. Webb, J. J. Launie, Willis Park Rokes, and Norman A. Baglini, *Insurance Company Operations* Vol. I, 3rd ed. (Malvern, PA: American Institute for Property and Liability Underwriters, 1984), p. 370.
16. Webb, Launie, Rokes and Baglini, p. 379.

CHAPTER 6

Numerical Tools for Underwriting

INTRODUCTION

The numerical tools described in this chapter are simply systematic techniques for summarizing quantitative information. Once the important characteristics of a set of data have been summarized, the usefulness of these data in decision making and predicting is greatly increased. In this book, "data" refers to facts, figures, and other information used in making decisions. To be useful, data must be organized and evaluated to become management information. *Thus, throughout this chapter and the next, the term data refers to any set of measured or described characteristics that may be quantitative or qualitative.* Numerical relationships abound in the underwriting environment. Premium rates, loss frequency and severity data, and the resulting loss ratios all represent quantitative relationships. It is difficult to think of anything more familiar to the underwriter than the loss ratio, yet it is seldom considered a statistical measure.

Underwriters use statistics every day, both at work and in leisure activities. In addition to those tools with which underwriters are already familiar, this chapter contains some simple techniques of numerical analysis which can be readily applied in an underwriting setting. Just as the baseball manager uses the batting average and ERA (earned run average) to help determine his batting order, pitching rotation, and pinch hitters, an underwriter can use statistics to help make an informed decision.

Descriptive Statistics

A number describing some feature of a set of data is called a descriptive statistic. It focuses attention on some characteristic of the data, ignoring a great deal of the complexity. The most familiar descriptive statistic is the average. An underwriter reviewing a large workers' compensation risk, for example, might be interested in knowing the average size of losses incurred during the past year. This average, when calculated, is called a descriptive statistic. Descriptive statistics, such as the average, can be calculated to show the central tendency in a collection of data while other descriptive statistics can be computed to indicate the degree of *dispersion. Averages provide indications of the middle or center of a set of data and are therefore referred to as measures of central tendency or central location. Conversely, measures of dispersion indicate the degree of scatter or variability in the data.* Both types of statistics, by summarizing some important characteristic of the data, provide information that is extremely useful for decision making and predicting.

A large number of descriptive statistics can be calculated for any particular collection of data, such as loss frequency and severity figures for a large workers' compensation risk. When all of the applicable descriptive statistics have been calculated, they represent a brief summary of the important characteristics of the loss data, which is much more useful in analyzing the loss history of the account than the mass of raw data itself. The loss history on a large risk may be summarized by the number of losses, the average loss, and the total dollar amount of losses, which are three types of descriptive statistics.

Underwriters have traditionally calculated descriptive statistics and analyzed them to make decisions although they have not considered this activity as statistical. The following brief analysis of the concepts underlying these descriptive statistical techniques will yield valuable insights which will be immediately useful in underwriting.

The Organization of Data

Data can be defined as a set of either measured or described characteristics. *A collection of observations that has not been organized is referred to as raw data.* The first step in a systematic approach to the use of data relating to any subject is to organize it into a form that facilitates further analysis. For example, suppose a property underwriter is considering a submission on a large multiple-location property risk for property coverage. Along with the application, the producer has submitted a premium and loss exhibit for the latest year. This is shown in Exhibit 6-1.

Exhibit 6-1
Premium and Loss Exhibit —
Acme Manufacturing Company

Latest Year Losses		Latest Year Premium
Date	Loss	$12,000
January 10 —	$ 350.	
January 30 —	100.	
February 4 —	150.	
February 26 —	200.	
February 27 —	165.	
March 5 —	200.	
July 4 —	150.	
August 1 —	5,000.	
October 6 —	110.	
October 18 —	200.	
December 9 —	125.	

The Array   One technique for organizing data is to rearrange it into an array. An array is the observed values of the items in a set of data listed in order of size. When there are a small number of observations, as in this case, constructing the array is simple. Exhibit 6-2 shows an array of the loss data on Acme Manufacturing Company.

One immediate use of the array in an underwriting situation is to simplify the analysis of the effect of a deductible. If a $250 per loss deductible had been in effect, what would have been the impact on Acme Manufacturing's loss experience? Nine of the eleven insured losses would have been eliminated completely, and another would have been reduced to $100. The large claim would have been reduced only slightly. By organizing data in an array, this information can be found at a glance.

Quantitative and Qualitative Data   The data on losses shown in the array in Exhibit 6-1 make up, in a technical sense, a set of measured quantitative observations. Observations consisting of quantitative information that can be numerically measured, such as losses or the dollar value of payroll, are defined as quantitative variable. Frequently in underwriting, observations will be made that are qualitative in nature, such as the type of auto or the construction of a building. Data consisting of qualitative observations require a different type of organization and treatment than the data consisting of quantitative variables. In remembering the distinction between qualita-

Exhibit 6-2
An Array of Acme Manufac-
turing Company Losses

Size of Loss
$ 100.
110.
125.
150.
150.
165.
200.
200.
200.
350.
5,000.

tive and quantitative variables, it may be helpful to note that the term "quantitative variable" means that items such as losses or payroll can *vary* and take on different numerical values. A qualitative variable, on the other hand, is an observed characteristic that can be described but not quantified. Therefore, fire protection to buildings and type of business insured are qualitative variables. Exhibit 6-3 shows a frequency distribution of quantitative variables while Exhibit 6-4 shows a frequency distribution of qualitative variables.

Frequency Distributions A frequency distribution is defined as an orderly arrangement of data grouped into classes listed according to magnitude. A *class* is a group of data within two boundary values, a lower and an upper class limit. A *class limit* is a boundary value of a class. A *class interval* is a value indicating the difference between a *lower class limit* and an *upper class limit.* This process of summarizing data by means of dividing the data into classes is known as *grouping* the data. When this process has not been utilized, the data are referred to as *ungrouped.*

MEASURES OF CENTRAL TENDENCY

The array and the frequency distribution represent methods of organizing the information contained in a set of quantitative variables. When data are presented in such a format, many insights can be obtained. However, it is often useful for analytic purposes to summa-

Exhibit 6-3
Latest Year Losses —
Light Manufacturing Classification
(Frequency Distribution of
Quantitative Variables)

Size of Loss	Number of Losses
$ 0.01 — 99.99	262
100. — 199.99	325
200. — 299.99	187
300. — 399.99	118
400. — 499.99	78
500. — 749.99	52
750. — 999.99	31
1,000. — 1,499.99	18
1,500. — 4,999.99	16
5,000. — 9,999.99	10
10,000. — 49,999.99	3

Exhibit 6-4
Construction of Buildings — Light Manufacturing Classification
(Frequency Distribution of Qualitative Variables)

Type of Construction	Number of Buildings
Class #1 — Frame	82
Class #2 — Joisted Masonry	66
Class #3 — Noncombustible	25
Class #4 — Masonry Noncombustible	12
Class #5 — Modified Fire Resistive	9
Class #6 — Fire Resistive	6
	200

rize some of the important characteristics of the entire set of observations under analysis rather than, or in addition to, breaking down the body of data into classes.

Measures of central tendency represent different techniques for describing the "typical" or average value in a set of observations. Three of these measures of central tendency, the arithmetic mean, median, and mode are presented along with the relationship among these measures for a particular set of observations.

Exhibit 6-5
Arithmetic Mean — Acme Manufacturing Company Losses

Size of Loss	
$ 100.	
110.	
125.	
150.	The arithmetic mean ($\overline{X}$) is computed as follows:
150.	$\dfrac{\$6,750}{11} = \$613.64$
165.	
200.	$\$6,750 = $ sum of observation values (total dollar losses)
200.	
200.	$11 = $ number of observations (losses)
350.	
5,000.	
$6,750.	

The Arithmetic Mean

The calculation of the arithmetic mean of a set of quantitative variables is straightforward. Most persons think of the arithmetic mean as the "average." The arithmetic mean is defined as the sum of all of the values in the set of observations divided by the number of observations. (The expression $\overline{X}$ is used to denote the mean in statistical formulas.) That is:

$$\frac{\text{Total of the set of observations}}{\text{Number of observations}} = \text{Arithmetic mean, } \overline{x}$$

Calculation of the arithmetic mean for ungrouped data as in the array of Acme Manufacturing Company losses is shown in Exhibit 6-5.

Characteristics of the Arithmetic Mean The arithmetic mean, or simply the mean, has two advantages. First, it is simple to calculate. Second, the mean uses all the information in the set of data. In ungrouped data, every observation has some effect on the arithmetic mean. However, a disadvantage is that the arithmetic mean is *unduly* affected by extreme values. A single very large or very small value can greatly change the size of the mean. A glance at Exhibit 6-5 shows this to be the case with the Acme Manufacturing loss distribution. If all that was known about losses was that there were eleven losses with a "mean" value of $613.64, an underwriter would not have an accurate synopsis of the information contained in the loss array. The single large loss had a tremendous effect upon the mean. Without this one loss the mean would have been $175.00. In this case, the mean is not representative of most of the values in the distribution. All but one of the variables were much smaller than the mean.

With grouped data, the mean can be calculated as long as both the number of observations (losses) and the total dollar amount of the observations (losses) are known. If the total dollar amount is unknown, it can be estimated using techniques explained in basic statistics texts.

The Median

The median of a set of data is defined as the observation that is halfway through the distribution. Half of the observations in the data set are less than or equal to the median in value, while the other half are greater than or equal to the median. The median observation has half of the observations on one side of it, and the other half on the other side. (The median can be abbreviated as Md.) Thus it is necessary to arrange the data in an array or frequency distribution to determine the median.

Characteristics of the Median   The median does not use all of the information contained in a set of data. (We do not speak of the median of raw data because the data must be ordered in some way in order to find the median.) It is simple to calculate, and this fact frequently compensates for the information loss the calculation of this statistic causes. Since the value of the median is determined by its position in an array it is not affected by the values of the data above and below it. Therefore for arrays with extreme value, it often presents a closer estimate of the "typical" or average value in an array or distribution than the mean.

The Median of an Array   The calculation of the median of an array of quantitative variables is straightforward. If the array consists of an odd number of observations, the median is the value of the observation halfway through the distribution.

Exhibit 6-6 illustrates the selection of the median for an array with an odd number of observations.

In the array shown in Exhibit 6-6, there are five observations that are smaller in value and five observations that are greater in value than $165. Therefore, the sixth observation in this array is the median.

When calculating the median for an array with an even number of observations, first determine the *two* values that lie in the middle of the array. The median is the average of these two values.

Exhibit 6-6
Median — Acme Manufacturing Company
Losses

Size of Loss	Observation Number	
$ 100.	1	
110.	2	
125.	3	
150.	4	
150.	5	*Median is the*
165.	6	*sixth*
200.	7	*observation,*
200.	8	*$165.*
200.	9	
350.	10	
5,000.	11	

The Mode

The mode is defined as the most frequently occurring value in a set of data, an array or frequency distribution. *The value of the most frequently occurring observation is known as the modal value.* (The abbreviation for the mode is Mo.) For most loss distributions encountered by risk managers, the modal value is zero. That is, the most likely outcome is for no losses to occur. For many distributions encountered by underwriters, the same is true. The mode is also useful in that knowing the mode and the median helps to determine the skewness of the distribution (a concept that is described later in this chapter). In looking at the data in Exhibit 6-6, the modal value for Acme Manufacturing is $200 since that value occurs more frequently than any other.

The Relationships Among the Mean, Median, and Mode

The Shape of the Distribution The relationships among the mean, median, and mode of a set of data depend upon the shape of the distribution of that set. The shape of a particular loss or other distribution can be seen by graphing a smooth curve of the distribution.

A distribution is said to be symmetrical if the distribution can be folded along a vertical center line so that the two sides coincide. Exhibit 6-7 illustrates three symmetrical distributions.

If a distribution is not symmetrical, it is said to be *skewed*. If a

Exhibit 6-7
Symmetrical Distributions

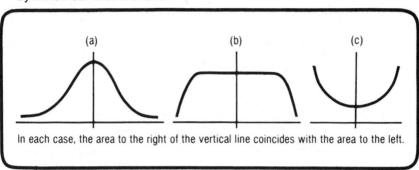

In each case, the area to the right of the vertical line coincides with the area to the left.

Exhibit 6-8
Skewed Distributions

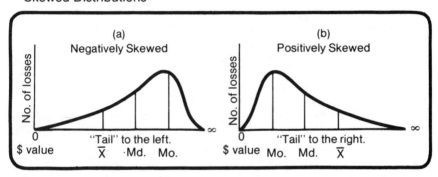

large number of the values in a distribution lie at the right end of the scale (that is, for a loss distribution, most of the losses are large and there are fewer small losses), the distribution is said to be *negatively skewed.* If a large number of the values in a distribution lie at the left end of the scale (near zero) as with most loss distributions, the distribution is said to be *positively skewed.* Exhibit 6-8(a) is negatively skewed, while Exhibit 6-8(b) is positively skewed.

The Mean, Median, Mode, and Skewness In a symmetrical distribution, the mean, median, and mode all have the same value. In Exhibit 6-9, the mean, median, and mode are all $350.

While calculating measures of central tendency for a distribution, the symmetry of the distribution can be inferred from the degree to which the mean, median, and modal values coincide. If they are the same, then the distribution is symmetrical. If the three values are tightly clustered, the distribution, while not perfectly symmetrical, possesses a high degree of symmetry. The farther these values are

Exhibit 6-9
Mean, Median, and Mode — Symmetrical Distribution

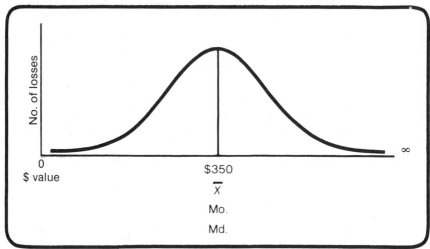

apart, the greater the skewness. The distribution is positively skewed if the $\overline{X}$ is greater than the Md. or Mo. and negatively skewed if the $\overline{X}$ is smaller than the Md. or Mo.

While symmetrical distributions are simple to deal with and have desirable properties, they seldom occur in an underwriting environment. Most loss distributions are not symmetrical, and therefore the underwriter will usually deal with skewed distributions. Most loss distributions are positively skewed. There is a predominance of "small" losses. This type of information can assist the underwriter in determining a course of action such as applying a deductible to eliminate many small losses.

Underwriting Examples of Measures of Central Tendency

Claim Frequency and Severity Two statistical measures that are very familiar to the underwriter are the measures of average claim frequency and average claim severity. Both of these measures are typically calculated as means. Two things should be kept firmly in mind when evaluating average frequency or average severity which have been calculated from some set of observations.

The first consideration is the tendency of the mean to be unduly influenced by extreme values. If the average severity has been calculated to be $614, this figure by itself has limited meaning if the underwriter does not know the other characteristics of the distribution from which it came. Was the distribution highly skewed? In which direction? What were the median and modal values for the same distribution? They will give a good deal of information about the degree and direction of skewness, as has already been pointed out. With knowledge of the mode and median, the mean claim severity of $614 can be evaluated to the extent that it is typical of the distribution.

The second consideration is the *size* of the set of observations from which the average frequency or severity has been calculated. Past claims history has little intrinsic value to the underwriter. Those losses have already occurred, and there is nothing the underwriter can do about past claims at this point. Claims history is studied for the insight it can provide about the likelihood of *future* claims. The claims history of a particular risk, with its average claims frequency and average claims severity, is of interest to the underwriter only to the degree that it provides a means of forecasting the likely future claims pattern of that particular risk.

One way of viewing the relationship between rates and loss distributions is to consider that the actuary who set the rate had in mind a certain loss distribution for the class of business under consideration. If the loss frequency and severity distributions of the particular risk under consideration are the same as the ones the actuary assumed in rate making, then the rate will be adequate for that risk. The only evidence the underwriter has concerning the actual loss frequency distribution of the particular risk is the history of those losses that have occurred. If there are only a few losses for a single risk, it is very difficult to judge if these have occurred in some random fashion from the same type of distribution contemplated by the actuary or if these losses indicate that this risk in fact has a potential for loss (and therefore an overall loss distribution) which is much worse than that contemplated in the rate.

It is very difficult to infer the entire distribution from only a few observations. The loss distribution of Acme Manufacturing in Exhibit 6-2 involving eleven losses is part of the data in the loss distribution for the entire Light Manufacturing Classification in Exhibit 6-3, which involves 1,100 losses. The data on the eleven losses do not tell the underwriter much about the loss distribution of the classification shown by the 1,100 losses. Therefore, calculations of average claim frequency and average claim severity based upon a small number of observations provide very little information that is useful to the underwriter in the process of deciding whether this risk is better or worse than the average in its class. While individual risk information based upon a small number of claims is not worthless, it is perhaps *worth less* than many underwriters perceive it to be. This idea is central to the concept of *credibility*, which will be considered in more detail later in this chapter.

The Loss Ratio as an Average   The loss ratio for a particular risk, class of business, or entire line of business is one of the most familiar statistics in the underwriting environment. The most commonly used loss ratio calculation takes incurred losses, including allocated loss adjustment expenses (those that can be associated with specific claims), and divides this numerator by a denominator of earned premium. This is the "incurred to earned" loss ratio. If incurred losses and loss adjustment expenses were $80,000 and earned premium was $100,000, then:

$$\frac{\$80,000}{\$100,000} = 0.80 \text{ loss ratio}$$

or

$$= 80\% \text{ loss ratio}$$

An important item to consider when analyzing any ratio is that changes in either the numerator or denominator, or both, will change the ratio. One might hear the statement, "Losses have been reduced," referring to a loss ratio which has declined. It may well be that losses have remained constant both in frequency and severity but that earned or written premium has increased, causing the loss ratio to go down. A similar change occurred as the insurance industry began to raise rates in 1985. Because premiums were increasing rapidly and expenses were not rising as quickly, the expense ratio actually declined since the expense ratio is calculated by dividing expenses by written premiums. Analysis of any ratio requires analysis of each of the components separately.

The earned premium figure used as the denominator of the loss ratio is the base of the ratio. Losses are expressed as a percent of that base. The larger the size of the base on which the ratio is calculated, the more stable will be the results over time for any given set of loss experience.

The greatest difficulty in the interpretation of ratios comes from the comparison of those constructed from different bases. There is no simple way that a paid losses to written premiums loss ratio can be compared to an incurred to earned ratio unless the differing bases are carefully recognized and accounted for. Percentage changes are frequently misleading when they come from different bases. For example, a professor once whimsically suggested to his advanced statistics class of three students that one drop out and then re-enroll in order to "increase class size." The student dropping out would cause a 33 percent drop in enrollment based upon the class size of three. Upon re-enrolling, the student would represent a 50 percent increase in enrollment, based upon the new class size of two. If only the percentage changes in enrollment were reported, then the class would have suffered a 33 percent drop in enrollment, which was then more than made up by the subsequent 50 percent increase in enrollment. Considerable lying with statistics, intentional and unintentional, is done by means of the comparison of percentage changes from different bases. In the interpretation of percentage changes, the underwriter should be extremely careful to analyze the base from which the percentage change was calculated.

MEASURES OF DISPERSION

The mean, median, and mode provide some information concerning the characteristics of the set of data and the skewness of the distribution. Another set of measures is required to provide information about the degree of dispersion in the array or frequency distribution. Interpretation of a measure of central tendency in a distribution is affected not only by the skewness of the distribution but also by the degree of dispersion. The less dispersion in the distribution, that is, the tighter the clustering of values, the more reliance that can be placed upon the measures of central tendency, or the more "realistic" the average relative to the distribution. Whether the distribution is symmetrical or skewed, the degree of variability among the differing values in the distribution can be either wide or narrow. This variability in the distribution is of prime importance to underwriters. *Dispersion is defined as the variability or scatter among the values of the observations in a set of data, array, or frequency distribution.*

To illustrate the importance of dispersion in the interpretation of data, consider a distribution where there is no variability whatsoever. In this case, not only would the mean, median, and mode be the same, but every observation would have the same value. Once the underwriter knew the value of one observation, the value of all other observations in this distribution would also be known. However, distributions in the real world do not come in such neat, tight packages. Individual observations, such as losses in a loss distribution, vary a great deal. The extent to which they have varied in the past is an indicator of the degree of variability to be expected in the future. For this reason, measures of dispersion provide very useful information for underwriting purposes.

Exhibit 6-10
Range — Acme Manufacturing
Company Losses

Size of Loss	Range
$ 100.	$5,000—$100 = $4,900
110.	
125.	
150.	
150.	
165.	
200.	
200.	
200.	
350.	
5,000.	

Three measures of dispersion considered here are the range, standard deviation, and coefficient of variation. All three of these measures can be calculated for any array or frequency distribution. Calculation of the standard deviation will not be covered in this course. The student who wishes to learn to calculate this statistic is referred to any standard college statistics text.

The Range

The range is the difference between the lowest and the highest value in a set of data. Exhibit 6-10 shows the calculation of the range from an array.

The range in a frequency distribution is defined as the difference between the lower limit of the lowest class and the upper limit of the upper class. The range is undefined for a frequency distribution that is open-ended at either end. The range in a frequency distribution is not too useful since it depends entirely upon the limits which have been set on the classes rather than upon the data itself. It is extremely difficult to make comparisons, therefore, between the ranges of frequency distributions.

Characteristics of the Range The range is the simplest measure of dispersion, and one that can be easily calculated.

The fact that the range does show the maximum amount of variability in the observations can be useful. If the underwriter wanted to know the difference between the smallest and largest loss which had occurred, the range would provide that information. Statisticians who are studying rainfall data in order to build a flood control channel are interested in the range, since flood control channels must be built with the range in mind rather than any type of average.

The range provides a rough measure of the degree of dispersion. However, since the measure ignores all values except the two extreme ones, the value of the range is limited. Because the range is so simple to determine, it is useful to do so as a check on the other measures of dispersion, if for no other reason.

The Standard Deviation

The standard deviation is a measure of dispersion that indicates the amount of variability between each observation in the distribution and the mean of the distribution. While computation of the standard deviation will not be covered, it is useful to realize that calculation of the standard deviation involves the measurement of the variability of each observation from the mean and then the calculation of an average of these deviations. The fact that the computation of the standard deviation is not covered should not detract from its usefulness. The reason the computation is not shown is that few persons actually compute the standard deviation by hand. In most cases, insurers have large statistical packages (programs) on their computers which make these calculations.

Characteristics of the Standard Deviation An important characteristic of the standard deviation is that it utilizes all of the information in the array or frequency distribution. Since the standard deviation is calculated from the deviations of all the observations from the mean, it provides a powerful indication of the degree of variability in the distribution. When comparing two distributions having the same mean, the one with the larger standard deviation has the larger degree of dispersion. Thus from a predictability standpoint, a distribution with a smaller standard deviation is preferable.

A disadvantage of the standard deviation is its difficulty to calculate (which is why the calculation is usually left to the computer). The focus in this section is not upon the calculation of the standard deviation but upon its interpretation. The abbreviation for the standard deviation is the letter s or the lower-case Greek letter sigma, σ.

Interpretation of the Standard Deviation The standard deviation is easiest to interpret when the distribution from which it has been calculated is a "normal" or bell-shaped distribution. In a normal distribution, slightly more than 68 percent of the observations are

Exhibit 6-11
Areas Under a Normal Curve

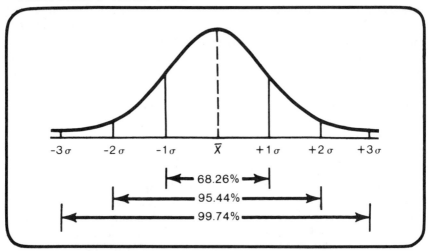

found in the area which is within the area of one standard deviation on either side of the mean. Plus or minus two standard deviations encompasses slightly more than 95 percent of the observations, as shown in Exhibit 6-11.

What does this mean? If insurers were forced to disregard age, sex, and marital status as rating factors for auto insurance and had to turn to total annual mileage as the primary rating factor, they would want to know as much as possible about annual mileage. Knowing that the average annual mileage is 15,000 and that the range is from 1,200 to 85,000 would be helpful. But it would be more helpful to know how "spread out" the mileage among the population is. If the standard deviation of annual mileage was determined to be 3,000 miles (and assuming that the distribution was a "normal" distribution), several conclusions could be made. First, about 68 percent of all persons drive between 12,000 and 18,000 miles per year (plus or minus one standard deviation from the mean—15,000 plus or minus 3,000). About 95 percent of all persons drive between 9,000 and 21,000 miles per year; and 99.74 percent of all persons drive between 6,000 and 24,000 miles per year. This information would be very helpful to the underwriting management as they decide where to make the dividing lines between classifications. Given the number of persons who would be insured and the prices to be charged, the insurer could determine roughly how many persons would be in each new classification and how much premium volume would be developed.

Unfortunately, most distributions the underwriter will encounter

Exhibit 6-12
Standard Deviation, Mean, and Coefficient of Variation —
Acme Manufacturing Company Losses

Size of Loss	Measure of Dispersion	Value
$ 100. 110. 125. 150. 150. 165. 200. 200. 200. 350. 5,000.	Standard deviation (s) Mean $(\overline{X})$ Coefficient of variation (V)	$1,388 $614 $\dfrac{\$1,388}{\$ \ 614} = 2.26$

are not symmetrical or even an approximation of the normal distribution. Interpretation of the standard deviation for a skewed distribution is more difficult. It is possible that 90 percent or more of the observations may lie within the distance of plus and minus one standard deviation from the mean in a skewed distribution.

Both the mean and the standard deviation use all of the information in the distribution; therefore, both of these measures are greatly affected by extreme values. A few very large observations will make the standard deviation quite large, as can be seen in Exhibit 6-12. Finally, the standard deviation assumes the unit of its observations. In loss distributions, for example, both are measured in dollars.

The standard deviation is a measure of relative dispersion and is affected by the size of all values in the distribution. Therefore, when comparing the standard deviations of two distributions to see which has the greater dispersion, direct comparison can be made only if the means of the distributions are the same or approximately the same. If the means are not nearly the same, then another statistic must be calculated to permit comparison.

The Coefficient of Variation

The coefficient of variation is a statistic utilized to permit comparison of the degree of dispersion between two distributions with substantially different means. The coefficient of variation, V, is found by dividing the standard deviation by the mean:

$$V = \frac{s}{\overline{X}}$$

The distribution with the larger coefficient of variation has the larger degree of dispersion.

THE NATURE OF PROBABILITY

The probability of a given event is the long-run relative frequency of that event. One can speak of the probability of rain tomorrow, the probability that a man aged sixty will die within the year, or the probability that a poker player will fill an inside straight on a one-card draw. If the weather forecaster on the 11 P.M. news states that there is a 40 percent chance of rain tomorrow, the forecaster is really stating that the probability of rain is 0.40. The expert poker player takes a dim view of the one-card draw to an inside straight because the *odds* are 11 to 1 against it. (Actually 10 3/4 to 1.)

Probabilities and odds are two different methods of expressing the same information. When the poker expert states that the odds against filling an inside straight are 11 to 1, this means that the probability of not filling the straight is 11 times greater than the probability of obtaining the desired card. The 1980 Commissioner's Standard Ordinary Mortality table states that the mortality rate for males aged sixty is 16.08 per thousand, which means that the probability that a man aged sixty will die within the year is 0.01608. One the other hand, the probability that a man aged sixty will *not* die during the year is 0.98392. This could be roughly expressed in terms of odds by saying that the odds are better than 49 to 1 against a sixty-year-old man dying before his sixty-first birthday.

Numerical Probabilities

If a particular event is certain to occur, it is said to have a probability of 1.00. One could attach a probability of 1.00 to the event of the sun rising in the east tomorrow morning. If a particular event is certain *not* to occur, it is assigned a probability of 0.00. Therefore, the sun rising in the west tomorrow morning can be assigned a probability of 0.00. The number of future events about which we are perfectly certain is relatively small. Any future event, from the turn of a card to the outcome of a sporting event, or even to the incidence of a burglary at a particular location, can be assigned a probability of somewhere between 0.00 and 1.00. The manner in which that probability is determined and the amount of credence that can be placed in it constitute the essence of the study of probability.

Classifications of Probability

The economist Frank Knight, in a classic treatise on the subject, defined three types of probabilities:

1. a priori
2. empirical
3. judgmental[1]

A priori probabilities are those that can be deduced from the nature of a particular situation. The probabilities involved in most gambling situations are of this type. Since there are four kings in a 52-card deck, the probability of drawing a king is 4/52 or 1/13.

A priori probabilities are particularly easy to deal with and understand. Therefore, it is not surprising that the science of probability had its origin among participants in games of chance who were attempting to gain a better insight into their avocation. Particularly with respect to a priori probabilities, it should be easy to see that knowing the probabilities and knowing the future are two different things. The probability of the occurrence of a seven on a single roll of two dice is 1/6. Knowledge of this fact provides little information relative to what the outcome of the *next* roll will be. The probability of 1/6 refers to the long run. The motto, "The dice have no memory," refers to a disturbing characteristic of the short-run, which will be considered in detail later in this chapter.

Empirical probabilities are those that are determined on the basis of historical data. An empirical probability arises from the observation of the relative frequency of the occurrence of the event under consideration in the past. While a priori probabilities by their very nature can be very precisely calculated, empirical probabilities present many more problems. The obvious consideration is that there must be a sufficiently large and accurate body of data from which the probabilities are to be determined. The probability of rainfall in Seattle, Washington, during the month of January, for example, can be determined with a fair degree of accuracy because of the existence of many years of meteorological observations. Similarly, probabilities of death at various ages are based upon a vast store of mortality data. The majority of property and liability insurance rates are based upon empirical probabilities. The accuracy with which an empirical probability will reflect the likelihood of a particular event occurring in the future is dependent upon the precision of available data, amount of data, and degree to which the past circumstances and conditions extend into the future.

Judgmental probabilities are the most difficult of all with which to deal. Knight classified these as events of uncertainty, rather than risk. He classified risk as those events where the probabilities could be calculated, either a priori or empirically. Under conditions of uncertainty, the decision maker has no information about the probabilities of outcomes. *Judgmental probabilities refer to those situations where there is neither the opportunity to deduce the probability of the event, nor sufficient data to calculate a relative frequency on a historical basis.* The probability that a new coffee shop will be successful will most likely be determined judgmentally. Nonetheless, judgmental probabilities are based on experience derived from decisions made in nonidentical, but in some ways similar or analogous, situations. Judgment rating in ocean and inland marine insurance is an example of judgmental probability. There does not exist in these cases sufficient historical data on similar risks from which to calculate rates actuarially.

THE COMPUTATION OF PROBABILITIES[2]

Basic Notation

The notation utilized in probability calculations is a form of mathematical shorthand. This notation includes:

p( ) = probability of the item in parenthesis

n = number of items involved or from which probability is derived

E = expected value (or probabilistic mean); this is derived from the simple formula:

$$E = np$$

p(X|Y) = probability that X will occur given that Y has already occurred. This is called a *conditional probability*.

Computations

Assume that data from California in a given year indicates that there were 80,000 car thefts reported out of 4,000,000 cars registered. The probability that a car would be stolen would be the number of cars stolen divided by the number of cars available to steal. This calculates probability as the relative frequency of the occurrence of an event (car theft). This is shown as:

$$P(\text{car theft}) \; = \; s/n$$

where: s = the number stolen

n = the total number available to steal

or 80,000/4,000,000 = 0.02

The probability that a car will be stolen is therefore .02.

Thus in the above example, the probability that a car will not be stolen is 1 − .02 or .98.

Many probability calculations rest on an assumption which should be made explicit at this point. This assumption is that an event either occurs or does not occur. There are no other possibilities and no middle ground between these two possibilities. Either an auto is stolen, or it is not. Therefore, the probability of any event $p(A)$ occurring and the probability of its not occurring p (not A) add to 1.00. This is expressed as:

$$p(A) \; + \; p(\text{not } A) \; = \; 1.00$$

Of more interest to the underwriter might be the information that 20,000 of the cars in California in a year were Corvettes and that 4,000 of them were stolen. (Do not panic, all this data is hypothetical.)

$$\text{The } p(\text{stolen Corvette}) \; = \; 4,000/20,000 \; = \; .20$$

Assume that the overall probability derived above applies equally to both private and commercial autos. Note that this is assuming that the data from which n, s, and p are derived is homogeneous. The underwriter now has a fleet of 300 commercial autos. The expected number of thefts can be calculated as:

$$\text{Expected thefts} \; = \; \text{number of vehicles} \times \text{probability of theft}$$

or, as shown above,

$$E = np;$$

which is:

$$E = 300(.02)$$

It would be prudent, in this case, to include enough in the physical damage premium to pay for six vehicle thefts.

At the end of the year, the underwriter might find that 2 thefts had occurred, or 10. Does this mean the idea is valueless? No, it indicates that the relatively small n in this fleet is not large enough for sufficient credibility. This concept will be explored more thoroughly later in this chapter.

Joint Probabilities

Calculation of the probability that two or more events will all occur in a given time period is known as a joint or *compound* probability calculation. The first consideration is to determine whether or not the events are independent. The comment that "the dice have no memory" refers to the fact that each roll is independent of the other.

If the events are independent, the formula for joint probability is simply the product of the individual probabilities. That is, the probability of rolling two sevens in a row is:

$$1/6 \times 1/6 \; = \; 1/36$$

Similarly, the probability that an insured's two buildings, one in Santa Monica, California and the other in Carefree, Arizona, will both burn in a given year when their individual probabilities of burning is .01 is:

$$.01 \times .01 \; = \; .0001$$

The equation for joint probability of independent events is therefore:

$$p(A \text{ and } B) \;=\; p(A)p(B)$$

Conditional Probability

Conditional probability comes into play if the multiple events with which one is concerned are *not* independent. For example, consider the case of two stores in a small shopping mall within a common structure with no fire walls. Assume that the probability that either store will have a fire in a given year is exactly .02, [p(F1)] and that historical fire data shows that 40 percent of the time when one store has a fire, it spreads to the second one [p(F2|F1) = .40]. The underwriter wants to know the probability that both stores will be involved in a fire in a given year [p(F1 and F2)].

In this computation, the probability that one store is involved in a fire is multiplied by the conditional probability that the second store will become involved, *given that the first one is already burning.* In notation the equation for conditional probability is:

$$p(F1 \text{ and } F2) \;=\; p(F1)p(F2 \mid F1)$$

In this example,

$$p(F1 \text{ and } F2) \;=\; (.02)(.40) \;=\; .008$$

Alternative Probabilities, Mutually Exclusive Events

An alternative probability is the probability that at least one (and possibly all) of two or more events will occur in a given time period. If the events are mutually exclusive the formula is quite simple. *Two or more events are mutually exclusive if the occurrence of one of them makes the others impossible.* The possibilities that a firm will suffer no embezzlement losses, that embezzlement losses will occur but be less than $10,000, and that embezzlement losses will occur but total $10,000 or more are mutually exclusive events. No single year's embezzlement loss experience can fall into more than one of these categories. For *mutually exclusive events,* to find the probability that one or the other of them will occur, simply add up the individual probabilities.

Assume that the probability that a bank will have no embezzlement losses in a given year is .70 and the probability that embezzlement losses will occur but that they will be less than $10,000 is .25. Therefore the probability that both of these will occur is found by using the following equation for alternative probability, mutually exclusive events which is:

$$p(A \text{ or } B) = p(A) + p(B)$$

In this case,

$$p(A \text{ or } B) = .70 + .25 = .95$$

Alternative Probabilities, not Mutually Exclusive Events

If the events are *not mutually exclusive*, the probability that one or the other will occur is the sum of their separate probabilities minus the joint probability that they will both occur. Assume that the probability of a fire in a store in a given year is .03, the probability of a burglary is .10 and the probability of both occurring is .01. To calculate the probability of having either a fire or a burglary, the equation for alternative probability, not mutually exclusive events, is used:

$$p(A \text{ or } B) = p(A) + p(B) - p(A)p(B)$$

In this case,

$$p(\text{fire or burglary}) = .03 + .10 - .01 = .12$$

It is necessary to deduct the probability of both events happening simultaneously to avoid doublecounting. (Alternative probability calculations involving more than two not mutually exclusive events take on a complexity which is beyond the scope of this introductory analysis.) Exhibit 6-13 summarizes the major equations just described.

PROBABILITY DISTRIBUTIONS

Introduction

A probability distribution is defined as a listing of a possible set of events and their probability of occurrence. A probability distribution

Exhibit 6-13
Probability Equations

Joint (Compound) Probability — Independent Events
  p(A and B) = p(A)p(B)

Conditional Probability
  p(F1 and F2) = p(F1)p(F2|F1)

  [Note: p(F2|F1) means probability of F2 given that F1 has occurred]

Alternative Probability — Mutually Exclusive Events
  p(A or B) = p(A) + p(B)

Alternative Probability — Not Mutually Exclusive Events
  p(A or B) = p(A) + p(B) — p(A)p(B)

can be either discrete or continuous. *A discrete probability distribution will be found whenever the outcomes are whole numbers* (not fractions). *A continuous probability distribution is one where the outcome can take on any value.* For example, a distribution of the heights or weights of individuals is continuous, since these characteristics can assume any value within the relevant range.

Characteristics of Probability Distributions

Probability distributions have characteristics similar to the distributions discussed earlier. They may be either symmetrical or skewed, and have a mean, median, and mode that can be calculated. The mean is most frequently employed when dealing with probability distribution.

The Expected Value The arithmetic mean of a probability distribution is the expected value. Expected values can be calculated for either discrete or continuous distributions, but the calculation of the expected value for a discrete distribution is easier mathematically. Assume a loss distribution for a workers' compensation risk as in Exhibit 6-14. If the underwriter wishes to determine the expected value for this distribution, the procedure involves the computation of a weighted average. Each possible outcome is multiplied by (given a weight of) its probability of occurrence. The summation of these values is the expected value or mean. Exhibit 6-15 shows the calculation of the expected value of the distribution of workers' compensation losses. The expected value is $1,290. What does that indicate? *The proper interpretation of the expected value is that it represents the average result that will be obtained over a large number of trials if the*

Exhibit 6-14
Hypothetical Loss Distribution for a
Workers' Compensation Risk

Total Losses Per Year	Probability
$ 0.	.15
500.	.43
1,000.	.25
2,500.	.10
5,000.	.045
10,000.	.020
25,000.	.004
50,000. or more	.001
	1.000

Exhibit 6-15
Determination of Expected Value of a Hypothetical Loss Distribution

Total Losses per Year (Y)	Probability (p)	Expected Value ($p \times Y$)
$ 0.	.15	$ 0.
500.	.43	215.
1,000.	.25	250.
2,500.	.10	250.
5,000.	.045	225.
10,000.	.020	200.
25,000.	.004	100.
50,000. or more*	.001	50.
	1.000	$1,290

*In an open-ended distribution such as this, the convention is to use the highest value given.

underlying probabilities do not change. The expected value is therefore a long-run concept. In this particular case, it means that given a large number of trials or observations, which could mean many years of experience for one risk or many similar risks observed in the same year, the average result will be $1,290 in losses.

The distribution is graphed in Exhibit 6-16. Note that this distribution is markedly skewed. Most empirical loss distributions exhibit this characteristic.

Exhibit 6-16
Hypothetical Loss Distribution for a Workers'
Compensation Risk Probability

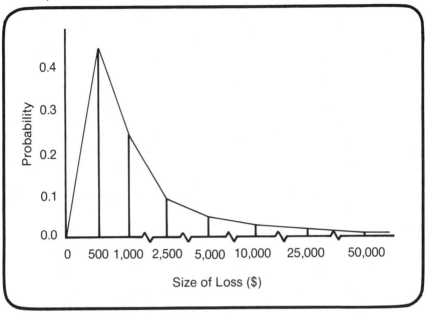

Empirical Distributions in Underwriting

Empirical probability distributions have been developed for loss severities in various lines of insurance. These distributions can be of assistance to the underwriter if properly interpreted. A distribution that shows the probability of the severity of loss, given that a loss has occurred, can indicate the likely impact of a deductible on risks in this class. If the distribution indicates that there is a high probability of relatively small losses, a deductible would eliminate those losses and reduce the amount of premium required for satisfactory results. Exhibit 6-17 indicates a hypothetical severity distribution for auto collision losses. Note that a $250 deductible would likely eliminate 53% of the number of expected losses (not in dollar terms).

The expected value for such a distribution would be calculated by multiplying the probability by the class midpoint, except in the case of the open-ended class, where the highest value given ($5,000 in this case) is used. Exhibit 6-18 indicates the calculation of the expected value that gives the average or expected loss, given that a loss has occurred. Note that with a loss distribution of this type, while a $100 deductible will eliminate a great many claims, a $250 deductible will reduce claims

Exhibit 6-17
Hypothetical Distribution of Auto Collision Severity

Size of Loss	Probability
$ 0.— 100.	.30
101.— 250.	.23
251.— 500.	.17
501.— 750.	.12
751.—1,000.	.08
1,001.—3,000.	.05
3,001.—5,000.	.04
5,001. and over	.01
	1.00

Exhibit 6-18
Expected Value of Hypothetical Auto Collision Severity Distribution

Class Midpoint (Z)	Probability (p)	Expected Value (p x Z)
$ 50.	.30	$ 15.
175.	.23	40.
375.	.17	64.
625.	.12	75.
875.	.08	70.
2,000.	.05	100.
4,000.	.04	160.
5,000.	.01	50.
	1.00	$574.

even more. On the other hand, if the type of insurance is of such a nature that the probability of small losses is relatively low, a deductible would have to be substantial before any significant reduction in covered losses is realized. Nuclear power plant liability and aviation hull insurance are two classes where the probability of small losses is so low that little credit could be given in the rate for deductibles unless they are substantial in dollar amount or on a percentage of value basis.

CREDIBILITY AND THE LAW OF LARGE NUMBERS

Introduction

One of the most important aspects of the use of probability in an insurance underwriting context is deciding when to apply it. The rule is deceptively simple. One can apply probability in those situations when the concept of expected value, or the long-run average, is meaningful. The trick lies in discerning when that condition exists. An interesting, yet fictitious, story may illustrate this point.[3] A statistician in a small nation was approached by a dissident group of army officers and asked to join in a coup to overthrow the government. "Either you're with us or you're against us," he was warned. The statistician carefully calculated that the probability of the coup's success was only 1/10. He declared against the coup. As he ascended the steps to the guillotine, he was heard to remark, "On the average...."

The average was meaningless in this case, since, rather than a long run, the doomed statistician had only one neck to risk. It is worthwhile to note that one may well be sticking one's neck out by applying probability calculations in situations where they are not warranted.

The determination of whether or not an empirical or deduced probability is meaningful in a particular application is the subject matter of credibility analysis. *Credibility may be defined as a measure of the statistical reliability of a given body of data as a representation of past losses for the purpose of loss forecasting.*

The credibility factor may take on a value between 0, no credibility, and 1, full credibility. A typical credibility table is shown in Exhibit 6-19.

If an insured in question had sixty-five workers' compensation losses during the base period, that loss experience would have credibility of .20 (based on the table in Exhibit 6-19). The rating formula would then base the rate for this insured 20 percent upon this experience and 80 percent upon the class experience.

If the insured had 1,400 workers' compensation losses during the base period, the loss experience would be said to be fully credible. In this case the entire rate would be based upon the insured's loss experience.

The concept of credibility means that when the requirements for full credibility are met, the loss experience represents a statistically reliable foundation from which estimates of future premiums can be derived.

The purpose of analyzing loss experience is to determine whether this particular insured is better or worse than the average in its

Exhibit 6-19
Credibility Factors*

Actual Number of Claims	Credibility
0— 10	0
11— 42	.10
43— 97	.20
98— 172	.30
173— 270	.40
271— 389	.50
390— 530	.60
531— 693	.70
694— 877	.80
878—1,083	.90
1,084 and over	1.00

*Adapted from Kulp and Hall, *Casualty Insurance*, 4th ed., 1968, Ronald Press, p. 834.

particular class. If the loss data has no credibility, it indicates that the data cannot be used to determine if this is a good insured with a few random losses or actually an insured that is worse than average in the class.

The substantial number of losses required for even partial credibility should be noted. This number of losses varies from one type of insurance to another. The table used here is shown merely as an example. It may well be that loss history for an individual insured is not as valuable as intuition might indicate.

The direct application of credibility theory in underwriting occurs in the credibility and maximum single loss tables in liability individual risk rating plans. This application will be considered in detail in a subsequent chapter on rating.

In lines of insurance where claim frequency is relatively low, a very large volume of premium (signifying a large number of exposure units) may be required in order to obtain sufficient losses to attach credibility to the loss results. Exhibit 6-20 contains a simulation of premium and losses for a single service office and a national book of business for an insurer for general liability. Note the premium volume, the number of claims, and the variability in the service office results when compared to the national book of business. Larger numbers, both in premiums and claims, lead to national predictability versus unpredictability in the service office.[4]

Exhibit 6-20

Simulated Experience — General Liability Calendar Year — Service Office*

Class	19X0 Premium	19X0 Number of Claims Incurred	19X0 Loss Ratio	19X1 Premium	19X1 Number of Claims Incurred	19X1 Loss Ratio
Service Office						
Contractors	$115,664	6	275.04	$113,748	4	36.19
Service and Mercantile	29,782	1	20.90	35,936	0	1.61
Consumer Goods Manufact.	106,547	7	18.80	87,120	5	889.26
General Manufacturing	98,045	7	108.16	113,452	7	72.95
National Book						
Contractors	$33,556,385	1,016	53.40	$35,529,099	1,112	85.73
Service and Mercantile	6,088,251	289	78.66	7,393,599	233	46.07
Consumer Goods Manufact.	29,002,475	1,143	64.67	26,340,771	765	57.09
General Manufacturing	30,351,179	1,302	102.45	29,734,368	1,043	139.47

*Adapted from J. S. Hammond, E. P. Hollingsworth, Jr., and C. Sadler, "Using a Monte Carlo Simulation as a Part of Training Liability Insurance Underwriters," a paper presented at the ORSA/TIMS Conference, October 1974.

The Law of Large Numbers

The law of large numbers is fundamental to the functioning of the insurance mechanism. Corporate insurance operations involve the pooling of a large number of risks, and the increased predictability of loss results that stem from the pooling are due to this mathematical relationship. The law of large numbers is a mathematical law that states: when the number of similar independent exposure units is increased, the relative accuracy of predictions about future outcomes (losses, in this case) based on these exposure units is also increased. In fact, at least two of the requirements of an insurable risk can be traced to the need to conform to the conditions under which this mathematical law will be applicable. The two requirements are: (1) there must be a large number of independent, homogeneous exposure units; and (2) the loss insured against must be noncatastrophic. That is, it must be unlikely to involve a substantial portion of the exposure units simultaneously. The second condition is merely a strong restatement of the requirement that the units be independent (this often means spread out such as not insuring too many houses within a single city).

It must be stressed that the mathematical properties of the law of large numbers refer to homogeneous, independent, random occurrences. Assume that for a particular class of buildings the probability of a fire in a given year is 1/200. Assume that each year's experience is considered as a separate "trial." Then the *expected* result is that there would be one fire for each 200 buildings in a given year. The *actual* result would be the number of fires divided by the number of buildings in the set under consideration. If the underwriter had only ten buildings in the set under consideration, with a single year's experience or trial, and one building burned, the actual result would be one in ten or 1/10 compared to an expected 1/200. At this point, the underwriters may be tempted to throw up their hands and say that the expected probabilities are meaningless. However, the set of ten is simply too small for the law of large numbers to take effect. An insurer might insure 10,000 buildings. If so, expected probabilities would have more meaning.

The probability of occurrence of an event, such as a fire or an auto accident, is an average concept. In order for the probabilities to be useful for prediction, the law of large numbers must be employed. In the preceding example, the set of ten buildings was too small for the average probability of loss of 1/200 to be actuarially significant. This can be seen even more clearly if the underwriter considers the extreme case of writing one building in this class for one year. Either it will have a fire, multiple fires, or none. In either case, the actual results will vary considerably from the expected. The probability of 1/200 in this case speaks only to the likelihood of the occurrence of the event, but does not predict the actual results.

The law of large numbers, on the other hand, states that when the number of independent, homogeneous exposure units is increased, the relative difference between actual and expected results will decrease. In fact, in the theoretical case, if it were possible to have an infinite number of exposure units and if the occurrence of the event were truly random, the actual results would be exactly the same as the expected results (all other factors remaining unchanged). The significance for underwriting, if the above conditions are met, is that the actual results can be more accurately predicted by probabilities. The further the real-world conditions vary from theoretical ones, the greater will be the variability of actual results.

Causes of Variability

One of the most important causes of variability in results from expectations is the number of exposure units. When the number of exposure units is very small, the difference between the actual and the expected results may be extremely large. This is due to the fact that the law of large numbers requires a large number of exposure units before the actual results either approach or can be used to predict expected results. This can be viewed in several ways.

In a previous section, the average loss for the eleven losses of the Acme Manufacturing Company was determined to be $614. For buildings with the construction occupancy and protection class of Acme Manufacturing Company, there is an underlying probability of loss. From data on only 11 losses, can this expected probability be determined? The answer is, "No." The number of losses is too low; therefore, the law of large numbers is not operative, and it can be said that data based on 11 losses have little credibility. In other words, data on 11 losses are not useful for prediction of expected results.

Another source of variability in results is a lack of homogeneity, which would occur if the data were gathered from exposure units that were not alike. The data on the Light Manufacturing Class in Exhibit 6-3 may be homogeneous, but again it may not be. If part of the class were in frame buildings and a sizable percentage were in highly protected risk construction, the data would lack homogeneity.

Loss of randomness could also cause great variability, particularly if moral hazard were a causal factor in losses. It is frequently quite difficult to judge the degree of homogeneity or the presence of nonrandom bias in a set of loss results. On the other hand, it is easy to determine whether the data are based upon a sufficiently large number of observations for the law of large numbers to take effect.

Insurance and Sampling[5]

The total set of objects of a particular type is known as a population. While the term is popularly used to refer to people, there are populations of dogs, horses, motor vehicles, and single-family dwellings. *A subset of a population is known as a sample. Random sampling can be defined as drawing from a population in which each elementary unit of the population has a known probability of being drawn.* In simple random sampling, the probabilities of drawing each of the elements is the same, and the elements are independent of each other.

There are some significant similarities between sampling theory and the operation of an insurance underwriting scheme. Some of the requirements of an insurable risk are:

1. There should be a large number of homogeneous exposure units. This requirement is met in such lines as auto and single-family dwellings to a higher degree than in some other lines but holds to some degree in any class-rated line.
2. The loss should be definite in time and place.

3. The loss should be fortuitous or outside the control of the insured.
4. There should not be a large probability of a simultaneous loss to a substantial segment of the exposure units. Basically, this is a requirement of independence.

In both insurance and sampling theory, a large number of homogeneous units are required to permit the application of the law of large numbers. The requirement of homogeneity in insurance is similar to the simple random sampling requirements in that each element of the population has the same probability of being part of the sample. The requirement for a loss being definite in time and place is similar to the requirement in sampling that the sampler be able to easily evaluate the results. The requirement that the loss be outside the control of the insured has the effect of reducing losses induced by the existence of the insurance. This is similar in sampling to the requirement that the sampling experiment itself should not alter or disturb the behavior or characteristics of the sample that has been drawn. Finally, in both insurance and sampling, there is a requirement of independence. In sampling, the fact that one element has been drawn should not affect the probability that other elements will be drawn or change the characteristics of other elements of the population. In insurance, independence means that if a loss occurs to one exposure unit, it will not change the probability of loss to other exposure units. Independence in insurance may be seen most clearly when it is not subject to a catastrophic loss.

It can be seen that there are many similarities between insurance and random sampling theory. The fact that the requirements of independence and homogeneity are imperfectly met in insurance merely serves to underline that theoretical conditions are seldom fully realized in actual practice. The significant relationship between sampling theory and underwriting lies in a consideration of the relationship between the population and the sample in simple random sampling. Calculation of the mean, standard deviation, and so on made from a sample serve as an excellent estimate of the those same figures for the population as a whole. For example, rather than interview the population of American voters, it is only necessary to interview a sample of the population and estimate the characteristics of interest from the sample observations.

For underwriting, the development of a book of auto business may be regarded as sampling from a population. But in underwriting there is an important difference. While the sampling theorist strives to avoid the bias where one portion of the population is more likely to be selected than another, the underwriter is actively seeking to obtain a biased sample. Underwriters want the sample (that is, their book of business) to contain more of those elements of the population with the most desirable characteristics. The results on a particular company's book of business then may be considered to reflect the bias which that particular sample contains, provided of course that the sample is large enough for results to be credible.

It has been stated that the underwriter must either select or be selected against. This indicates that if the underwriter is not successful in obtaining a sample that is biased in a favorable manner, the sample of insureds written will reflect adverse selection. It remains for underwriting management to determine whether their underwriting program is achieving results on the book similar to the population as a whole, inducing a favorable bias into the book of business, or if the book reflects the consequences of adverse selection.

SUMMARY

The mean, median, and mode represent measures of central tendency in a distribution. In a perfectly symmetrical distribution, these three measures are equal. Since the underwriter deals primarily with skewed distributions, the relationship between the mean, median, and mode can provide information regarding both the degree and direction of skewness. In selecting one of these measures of central tendency as the most typical value in the distribution, the underwriter must be aware of the primary disadvantage of the mean—susceptibility to distortion by extreme values.

Interpretation of the measure of central tendency in a distribution is affected not only by the skewness of the distribution but also by the degree of dispersion. The less dispersion in the distribution, that is, the tighter the clustering of values, the more reliance that can be placed upon the measures of central tendency, or the more "realistic" the average relative to the distribution.

Measures of dispersion are the range, standard deviation, and coefficient of variation. The range is easiest to calculate but does not use all the information in the original data. Therefore, the standard deviation and coefficient of variation are preferred for purposes of analysis if they are available.

Knowing the average loss or the average claim frequency for a particular risk or class is incomplete information. Interpretation of the average loss severity or average claim frequency can be made only if the underwriter also knows the *number* of observations from which the average was calculated, the degree of *skewness* in the distribution, and the degree of *dispersion* in the distribution. When the underwriter possesses this additional information, it is possible to determine the amount of weight that should be placed upon this loss data in the process of risk evaluation and decision making.

The probability of any given event is the relative frequency with which that event is likely to occur over the long run. Probabilities are classified as a priori, empirical, or judgmental. While a priori probabilities are the easiest to compute and understand, the insurance underwriter will deal chiefly with empirical and judgmental probabilities. A probability distribution is a listing of a possible set of events and their probability of occurrence. These distributions may be either symmetrical or skewed. The mean of a probability distribution is the expected value. The essence of credibility lies in the determination of whether data available have sufficient statistical reliability to be utilized for the determination of the probability of occurrence of the particular events under consideration.

Finally, the insurance mechanism may be considered as a sampling model. There are close parallels between the requirements of an insurable risk and the requirements for random sampling. A particular book of business may be viewed as a sample selected from the population of insureds and analyzed from the standpoint of sampling theory.

Chapter Notes

1. Frank H. Knight, *Risk, Uncertainty and Profit* (Boston: Houghton Mifflin Co., 1921).
2. This section draws heavily from "Fundamentals of Probability Analysis" and "Uses of Probability Analyses in Risk Management," by George L. Head, in *Readings on the Risk Management Function* (Malvern, PA: Insurance Institute of America, 1983), pp. 162-182.
3. From a presentation by James Athearn to the Risk Theory Seminar, April 1971.
4. The author is indebted to E. P. Hollingsworth, CPCU, ARM, of Frank B. Hall & Co., Inc., for the concepts developed in this section.
5. The concept of insurance as a sampling model was developed in the article "Risk, Insurance and Sampling," by David B. Houston, *The Journal of Risk and Insurance*, December 1964, pp. 511-538.

CHAPTER 7

Pricing

INTRODUCTION

The price charged for insurance coverage is critically important to underwriters. As long as the losses occur randomly, a proper price can be determined for virtually any property or liability risk. A fundamental objective of underwriting is to obtain sufficient premium income for the exposures assumed, to cover expected losses and expenses, and earn a reasonable profit. Therefore, underwriters must be aware of what the price should be and how it is developed.

The rate-making process uses historical data on incurred losses. Statistical techniques are applied to these data to develop a forecast of the appropriate rate level necessary to provide sufficient premium income to cover future losses.

The degree of pricing flexibility available to the underwriter varies by type of insurance and size of risk. In personal lines, the pricing task is to select the proper rate for each risk from a rate schedule developed by actuaries. In some commercial lines, an actuarially determined rate is applied without deviation by the underwriter, while in others there is some pricing discretion based on the actuarially determined manual rate. Maximum pricing flexibility is available to the underwriter in those situations where judgment rating is employed. This often occurs in ocean and inland marine insurance where there is not a sufficiently homogeneous body of past loss data to permit the use of actuarial techniques.

Insurance is a pooling device. When a manual rate is developed for a particular class, that rate represents the price that is deemed to be appropriate for the "average" risk in that class. This manual rate is usually developed from a large body of historical data, often representing the combined experience of many insurance companies. Statistically, these data could be considered to represent the population. The book of business written in that class by a particular underwriter, even a particular insurance company, represents a sample from that population in statistical terms.

A rate will be adequate when two conditions occur. First, the actuarial forecast of future losses based on past losses must be accurate for the population. Second, the sample represented by the book of business written by a particular underwriter or insurer must be representative of the population. That is, the sample, on average, should have the same loss results as the population. Some of the risks in the sample may be considerably worse than the population, and some of them may be considerably better. But, it is the average that is compared to the expected losses of the population.

The more accurately the loss causing characteristics are identified, the more accurate the final rate will be. From an actuarial and rate-making standpoint, a high degree of homogeneity within each class will provide more accurate future rate forecasts. From an underwriting standpoint, the risks selected for a particular class should reflect as accurately as possible the risk characteristics of the class from which the data base was constructed. However, the underwriter can still select the "best" insureds possessing those characteristics.

Some terms must be defined at this point. The basic building block of the rate-making process is the exposure unit. An exposure unit is a measure of the susceptibility or vulnerability to loss assumed by an insurer. Examples of exposure units include:

- The auto/year: one auto insured for a period of one year,
- $100 of remuneration in workers' compensation, and
- $100 of property value in property insurance.

A rate is the price per exposure unit. The *premium is the total cost of coverage for a group of exposure units* (that is, the rate times the number of exposure units). *One other term encountered is exposure base which is simply the denomination in which exposure units are expressed.* For example, remuneration is the exposure base in workers' compensation and the exposure unit is each $100 of remuneration.

The term pricing is usually applied, in an underwriting context, to the process of determining that the premium applied to a particular risk is appropriate.

RATE-MAKING CONSIDERATIONS

The regulatory environment within which the insurance industry operates provides a legal framework for the rate-making process. While regulatory systems vary from state to state, three regulatory criteria are found in virtually all of them. These criteria are that a rate must be:

1. adequate,
2. not unfairly discriminatory, and
3. not excessive.

Within this broad framework, insurers establish their own underwriting and pricing rules. One insurer may decide to write only at the manual rates developed by a rating bureau and set its underwriting policy accordingly to develop a book of business for which such rates are adequate. Another insurance company may decide to price its policies below the manual rates. Consequently, it would set a more restrictive underwriting policy in order to develop a book of business with better than average loss results to match the smaller premium income being received.

Adequate

Perhaps the most frequently found regulatory criterion dealing with insurance rates is adequacy. Adequacy implies that the price charged for a particular class should be sufficient to meet all anticipated losses and expenses associated with the item insured.

While the achievement of rate adequacy would appear to be a simple matter, the fact is that adequacy is difficult to achieve. There might be certain exceptions, but it is often impossible for the actuary to guarantee absolute rate adequacy for a single class or for a single insured risk. Therefore, the practical application of adequacy is usually expanded to include an entire line of insurance in a given rating territory, for example, fire insurance rates in a given state. However, this also makes rate adequacy more difficult because insurer experience is combined in developing the rates. For example, if there were only three insurance companies operating in a given line of insurance and if the three respectively computed pure premiums (discussed subsequently) of $1.10, $1.30, and $2.00 per unit of exposure, the unweighted average rate of $1.47 would be highly profitable for the company using a pure premium of $1.10 but highly unprofitable for the company using $2.00. Thus, while a combination of data makes losses more predictable, the use of an average rate will not guarantee rate adequacy for all insurers.

Another factor that can lead to inadequate rates is competition. In some instances, the prices charged consumers may be the major competitive tool available to insurance companies. Some insurers reduce their rates to compete with the rates charged by other insurance companies, but these reduced rates may, in fact, be insufficient to meet actual losses and expenses in the future. Finally, regulatory constraints may come into conflict with the legislated standards for rates. Specifically, insurance commissioners in various states who exercise some control over rates, may cause some insurers to maintain an artificially low rate level.

Not Unfairly Discriminatory

A second regulatory criterion is that insurance rates should not be unfairly discriminatory. This implies that each insured should pay its equitable share of the insurer's losses and expenses. An equitable share generally is based on some measure of the insured's perceived measure of future losses and expenses.

The concept that rates should not be unfairly discriminatory is extremely difficult to apply because if perfect equity were desired, each risk would have to have a rate which reflected that risk's precise loss and expense attributes (which are impossible to predict). The criterion of no unfair discrimination, however, is applied to groups of risks. In these groups of risks, data on losses and expenses are gathered, and the mean or average losses and expenses for that group are applied to each risk on an individual basis. As long as the risks in a particular group are homogeneous, equity is presumed to be achieved. Unfortunately, risks are seldom homogeneous, and the goal of equity requires that provisions be made to modify the rate in line with the probability of loss. The provisions generally include some form of individual rating program.

One important point about this requirement is that rating laws do not prohibit discrimination. They prohibit *unfair* discrimination. Fair and justified discrimination based on loss potential is allowed and is the basis for class rating. The problem which arises (especially recently with respect to rates based on gender) is distinguishing between fair and unfair discrimination. Just because there is a statistical difference in loss costs between males and females, gender as a rating factor is not universally seen as fairly discriminatory. Perhaps there are more accurate measures for which gender is merely an easily obtainable substitute.

Not Excessive

The last regulatory criterion frequently found in statutes is that rates should not be excessive. The rate charged should not cause an unreasonable profit.

Of the three regulatory criteria, this (that rates should not be excessive) probably causes the fewest problems. Some degree of price competition usually exists and serves to keep rate levels for all insurers lower than might be the case without competition. In those states requiring approval of rates, the individual or board charged with approving rates has an influence in limiting the rate level. The test for rate excessiveness is applied on a class-by-class basis.

Social Criteria

An important emerging criterion surrounding proper rates is that of *affordability*. Affordability may mean (1) that a ceiling is to be placed on insurance rates so that most of the population will be able to purchase coverage, (2) that rates will be made in such a manner as to transfer a portion of the costs of coverage from high risk insureds to the remaining insured population, or (3) that a form of subsidy from outside the insurance mechanism will be used to offset the actuarially determined premium when it is deemed to be unaffordable.

Perhaps the most important affordability situation is presented in auto insurance. It is generally believed that a small part of the insured group is responsible for a large portion of auto losses. A market availability and coverage affordability problem has arisen for the insureds believed to be causing disproportionate losses. This stems from an attempt to make the rate adequate and equitable. Affordability problems have been attacked in many jurisdictions by massive subsidization of poor risks by the large numbers of accident-free drivers. In any case, the subsidies have been motivated by the desire of certain groups to maintain low rates that are, by design, affordable.

An additional social criterion for rate-making is *simplicity*. A rate must be reasonably simple to develop and modify. This criterion is a function of the industry's data development and administrative capabilities as well as the need for the industry to be able to explain and defend its system to the public. Many states require that rate changes be accompanied by complete actuarial data before the change may be implemented.

Assume, for example, that an insurer's private passenger auto rating system bases its rate on the number of miles driven per year by each insured in each rating territory in the state. The insurance company would have to determine from each insured not only the number of miles driven, but exactly where the mileage was logged. The data capture and retrieval requirements of such a rating system would make it a statistical nightmare. Such a system is contrary to the criterion of simplicity.

Other Criteria

There are several additional objectives that affect the pricing of insurance. These objectives are generally viewed from the standpoint of the insurance company.

The first additional criterion is that of developing a rating system in such a way that *loss control is encouraged*. Such techniques as auto safe driver plans, experience and retrospective rating in workers' compensation, and sprinklered building fire rates in property insurance all encourage loss control.

A second criterion is that of *responsiveness*. A rate should be responsive to changes in the underlying hazards. This criterion is met if the rate is capable of being modified rapidly to reflect the change. Trend factors are being increasingly employed by actuaries to make insurance rates more responsive. *By the use of trend factors, the actuaries adjust the past losses to reflect more accurately the loss experience that can be expected to develop during the period when the rates will be used.*

If, on the average, loss costs have increased by 10 percent a year over the last six years, an analysis of the trend would indicate that a further 10 percent increase in loss costs each year in the future is likely.

Although trend factors are useful to the underwriter in the prediction of future losses, they do have limitations. Probably the most important limitation is the assumption that past relationships will continue to hold true in the future. That is, losses that have occurred in the past do not necessarily assist in the prediction of future losses because in some situations future losses may be totally independent of losses which have occurred in the past.

A final criterion that might be suggested is *stability*. Stability implies that rate changes should be made only when the experience change is of sufficient impact to warrant the change and that rates should not vary dramatically year-to-year. Stability is important since insureds have come to expect a certain degree of stability in their rates. If windstorm insurance rates were to vary as erratically as the incidence of hurricanes on the east coast of the United States, insureds would sustain premium variations of great magnitude on almost an annual basis. If that were the case, the public relations implications would be quite serious as insureds could not be sure of the price to anticipate for their coverage. Thus, stability is important to maintain the image of the industry's product in the minds of consumers. Insurers try to handle this problem by basing rates over longer periods of time and by using stabilizing factors in their rate making. The years 1985 and 1986 demonstrated that, in commercial lines, stability had yet to be achieved.

THE RATE-MAKING PROCESS

The rate-making process has as its primary goal the development of rates that meet the regulatory, social, and other criteria explained earlier. The regulatory criteria have been legislated by many states in one form or another. The others are not always the subject of state legislation. One other rate-making goal, profitability, should also be mentioned. If insurers are to remain solvent and also expand their abilities to provide greater levels of coverage, adequate profits from underwriting must be forthcoming. The following discussion merely outlines the rate-making process in a general way.

Selection of the Proper Measure of the Exposure

As defined earlier, the exposure base (the term *premium base* is used in the commercial lines manual of ISO) is the denomination in which the exposure unit is expressed. Examples include remuneration and gross sales. The exposure unit is expressed as each $100 of remuneration or $1,000 of sales, for example. The selection of the correct exposure base to measure the susceptibility or vulnerability of the insured to loss is probably one of the most important steps in the initial determination of a rate for a new coverage.

An exposure base may take many different forms, depending on the nature of the risk and the losses to be insured against. Specifically, an attempt is made in the selection of an exposure base to integrate that base or measure with the frequency and severity of losses. For example, if an insurer is attempting to provide liability coverage for a theater owner, possible measures might include (1) the size or capacity of the theater, (2) the number of seats, (3) the number of films shown, and so on. None of these, however, as accurately captures the possible frequency and severity of losses as would the number of customers attending the films. Two measures that could work would be the number of persons entering the premises or the aggregate value of admissions. These two possible exposure bases would best reflect the potential losses.

Different measures are more appropriate in other types of insurance. For example, in fire insurance, the exposure base is the value of the property and the exposure unit is each $100 of property value. In workers' compensation, the exposure base is remuneration. For liability coverage for ambulance services, the exposure base used is the number of attendants, and rates are stated per each attendant.

Number and Nature of Rating Classes

The selection of the number and nature of rating classes is based on the goals previously described. That is, selection of classes is attempted in such a way as to promote adequacy of premiums, equitable treatment of insureds having similar (or dissimilar) loss characteristics, nonexcessive rates, and data collection and analysis that is reasonably efficient and inexpensive.

There are several basic difficulties in developing classes. First, classes must be of sufficient size to obtain a reasonable amount of data so that the law of large numbers can be applied. Small classes do not permit the collection of a sufficient amount of data to provide credibility. Moreover, there are fixed expenses, such as programming and administration, associated with the establishment of the classes, and small classes are excessively expensive because of an inability to spread the expenses over a reasonable number of exposure units.

A second problem which occurs in developing classes is that of establishing a reasonable level of fair discrimination among insureds. As discussed previously, the goal of equity in establishing classes is one that seeks to charge each insured a rate that properly reflects probable loss frequency and severity. The ultimate equity would be that of establishing an individual "class" for each insured and predicating each insured's rate on the basis of anticipated losses during the prospective insurance period. If an insurer does not practice clear and certain classification discrimination, others will enter the market to compete for the business. For example, if an insurance company were to place all youthful drivers in a single category and charge each driver the same price, other insurers, sensing future profits, could enter the market and charge a selected group a lower price than the average developed for the group. An example of this form of competition was the offer of "good student" discounts. "Good students" were clearly perceived to possess better than average loss potentials, and competitive insurers sought them. The result was an increase in the number of classifications.

Ultimate equity should not necessarily be regarded as the most important goal of rate making. The goal of equity must be tempered with reality. Specifically, little credibility can be attached to rates made on classes having a single risk in the class. Consequently, discrimination is probably increased through the development of small classes because the data are inadequate to develop a rate that can be treated as reflective of probable losses. Small classes, moreover, as previously mentioned, are expensive to establish.

Regulations promulgated through the various states often lead to constraints in establishing rating classes. Specifically, insurance commissioners in many jurisdictions have the power to approve or disapprove the numbers and types of classes utilized. Some states appear to be moving toward a reduction in the number of rate classifications and teritories in some lines of insurance (particularly auto liability insurance). This trend has the effect of broadening the classes. In this case, statistical predictability should be enhanced, but the danger of significant and unfair discrimination is increased for insureds whose loss expectations do not cluster around the average for the particular class in which they fall.

Prediction of Losses

Forecasting losses is particularly difficult because of the inherent inability of the predictor to foresee or control all of the factors that may affect losses. For example, the risk itself may change. Additionally, external factors and conditions that affect losses may change. Future external conditions that present unknowns range from financial market conditions to the economic environment and from geographical considerations to socio-political factors. Of course, these factors and conditions represent only the tip of the proverbial "iceberg." Other factors, many of which may be unknowns, exist to frustrate the best of forecasts. Perhaps the most important of the unknowns is the role of people, a significant and constantly changing role. In making risk selection decisions, the underwriter must be aware of the inexact nature of loss prediction. To assist the underwriter in making decisions that reflect appropriate reservations concerning loss predictions, the following section briefly describes several factors that may assist in the development of an understanding of the limits of forecasting.

Data Dependence—Fallacy of Accuracy   The insurance industry is basically dependent on past loss and expense data for establishing future period rates. While the use of past data does lend itself to an objective procedure for setting rates, there are a number of associated problems. For example, one problem that arises is related to the accuracy of the data being used. Large quantities of data are submitted to the statistical organizations operating within the industry. The data are gathered by insurers through their past loss experience as well as through estimates of losses that have occurred but may not be fully paid until many years have elapsed. The ultimate loss when paid some years in the future may be significantly higher or lower than the current estimate of that loss as represented by the loss reserve. As a consequence, there can be no absolute assurances that the estimates are precise.

A second problem concerning the accuracy of data is that of possible errors in processing. All data may contain errors. As a consequence, an error factor is usually assumed. While the errors may be random in origin, the ones that favor the insurance company (such as a rate that is too high) are "caught" by producers or by the insured to the point that they are very nearly self-correcting. The errors against the insurance company have a good chance of going uncorrected.

The accuracy of data used is diminished in a third way by the inclusion of exposure units that will not be included in the forecast set of exposures. That is, exposure units change, are altered over time, or are new. Automobiles may change greatly from one model year to another. Downsizing has gone on in American autos for many years. Smaller, lighter autos save gas but may provide less crash protection for the occupants. Engine enhancements are added which increase the performance capabilities of these small cars, further changing the exposure. Thus, the data used for the forecast may not come from the same units that are to be insured under the forecast rates, and the old data may not reflect future losses.

The Law of Large Numbers   The law of large numbers which was defined in Chapter 6 is at the heart of all insurance rate-making techniques. The mathematical properties of the law of large numbers refer to homogeneous, independent, random occurrences. The application of this law to rate-making is often misunderstood.

If the conditions required for the law of large numbers apply, then the actual result will approach the expected result. This means that the actuary can predict future loss results with much greater accuracy for a pool of many exposure units than would be the case for a pool of a few exposure units.

That is very simple. Except that what is meant by "actual results" and "expected results" might not be immediately apparent. Assume that the actuary is using the law of large numbers to determine auto liability loss frequency. With a large number of insureds in the pool, and all the conditions met, the law of large numbers states that the actual frequency will most likely be quite close to the theoretical "expected" frequency calculated by the actuary. Any rate calculations based upon this would have full credibility. This is shown in Exhibit 7-1.

If, on the other hand, either the number of insureds in the pooling

Exhibit 7-1
Actual and Expected Results, Given a Large Number of Insureds and All Conditions Met

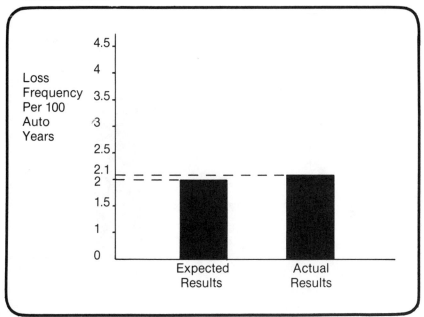

scheme was too small for full credibility, or the three conditions were not met, then the difference between actual and expected results could be very great. This means that any rating calculation based on this would most likely be inaccurate. This is shown in Exhibit 7-2.

The mandatory conditions of homogeneity, randomness, and independence will be examined below in a rate-making context. The difficulty inherent in accurate rate-making can be seen if it is assumed for a moment that all these conditions are met and that the number (n) of insureds in the pool is large enough that the actual result closely approaches the expected one. The ensuing rate should reflect the underlying exposure and result in the proper, calculated underwriting profit. Right? Perhaps. This entire calculation was based on historical data. Even if the actuary knows exactly what losses cost in the base period from which the data were drawn, the ensuing rate will be accurate only if the actuary properly includes amounts for increasing tends in loss costs and changes in the units insured. If new losses cost unexpectedly more than before, or new causes of loss occur which were not present in the base data, the rate will be inadequate.[1]

Homogeneity. The law of large numbers indicates that as the number (n) of risks in a particular pooling scheme increases, the actual

Exhibit 7-2
Actual and Expected Results, Given a Small Number of Insureds or All Conditions Not Met

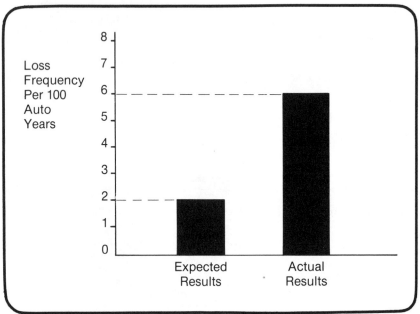

result approaches the expected result and the accuracy of predicted rates improves. It would seem that the goal should be to make each pool as large as possible. That is not the case. The relationship states that the actual result approaches the expected as the square root of the number, n, increases. As n increases into the thousands, further increases in the number of risks provide smaller and smaller improvements in accuracy.

At this point it becomes possible to improve the homogeneity of the pooling scheme by sub-dividing the group into classes. These classes are set up by identifying attributes which can be used to predict the likelihood of future losses. In property insurance, construction is such an attribute. A reinforced concrete building has a different probability of suffering fire damage than does a building of frame construction.

When the pooling scheme contains millions of risks, as is the case in private passenger auto, a large number of classes can be set up without affecting the "large numbers" requirement. The purpose of setting up multiple classes is to improve the homogeneity of the pooling scheme. This improvement in homogeneity improves the accuracy of the resulting rate.

Perfect homogeneity exists only in theoretical models. In a

particular class, individual risks vary in their likelihood of suffering a loss. The goal of the actuary and underwriter when designing a rating system is to make each class as homogeneous as possible. As the degree of homogeneity decreases, so does the accuracy of the rating system.

Independence. Events are independent if the occurrence of one event has no effect on the likelihood of the occurrence of any other event. In an insurance pooling scheme independence is achieved if one risk incurring a loss has no effect on the likelihood of any other risk incurring a loss. In a book of business this concept is applied as a cross-section over the book of business at a particular point in time. A book of dwelling risks are independent if a fire in one dwelling does not increase the chance of a fire occurring in any other dwelling.

Perfect independence, like perfect homogeneity, exists only in theoretical models. It is important that the risks in a pooling scheme be as independent as possible if the developed rates are to be accurate. Loss of independence can result in large differences in results from one time period to another.

If a book of homeowner business consists of dwellings that are separated from each other by a considerable distance, then independence is achieved with respect to fire. If a number of these dwellings are located in a heavily wooded brush area, then independence is lost with respect to fire. A fire in one house in the brush area could quickly spread to others, resulting in simultaneous loss. If thousands of these same dwellings are located in Southern California and are insured for earthquake, independence is also lost with respect to that peril. Underwriters should recognize that whenever independence is lost within a pooling scheme, large catastrophic losses are possible. If insurance is still to be granted when independence has been lost within the pooling scheme, then reinsurance must be purchased. As shown above, independence varies with each peril.

Randomness. The peril or perils insured against in a pooling scheme should result in fortuitous or random losses from the standpoint of the insured. This means that it is a matter of chance which risk within the pooling scheme incurs a loss.

This element of randomness with respect to losses is crucial to the statistical assumptions which underlie insurance rate making. In practice, this fortuitous or random chance aspect of losses is preserved as long as the loss is outside the control of the insured. If the insured can or has reason to cause a loss, randomness is lost. This is why there is no rate for moral hazard. If moral hazard exists, this introduces a nonrandom element into the loss distribution—insured-caused losses.

Much is written in standard statistics texts on random sampling.

As noted in Chapter 6, the purpose of underwriting is not to obtain a random sample from the population of insureds but to obtain a biased sample. The underwriter wants the book of business written to be biased toward those risks that have a smaller than average chance of loss. If the purpose of underwriting were to obtain random samples of business, then the company could fire all the underwriters and simply accept every other submission, or 3 out of 5, or use some other random selection scheme.

Prediction and Allocation of Expenses

While expected loses make up a substantial part of an insurance rate, expenses must also be considered. The expense portion of a rate generally represents between 25 percent and 45 percent or more of the total amount charged insureds. The smaller quantitative importance of expenses should not lead the observer to conclude that expenses are insignificant. On the contrary, there is a need on the part of the underwriter and the actuary to focus extensively on manageable expenses, particularly if those expenses are related to underwriting. Manageable expenses are those outlays that are capable of being varied; that is, this type of expense can be larger or smaller depending on the decision by some responsible person either to incur or not to incur the expense. The control of expenses is very important in a competitive environment since expenses are more controllable than the other components of the rate.

An example of manageable expenses includes the costs of an inspection of a building to decide whether or not to insure it or to charge one rate or a slightly higher rate. The inspection should always be made if it can be demonstrated that, on the average, revenues will increase more than costs, or that losses will decrease more than the increase in cost. If these criteria are always considered objectively and positively, the management of expenses will be beneficial to the insurer and, of course, indirectly to the insureds.

The expense portion of each insurance rate will include a provision for each of the following costs of operation:

1. acquisition costs
2. servicing costs
3. administrative costs
4. taxes

Included in the acquisition component are such costs as commissions paid to producers and other costs of obtaining business, such as inspection or appraisal fees that are purely associated with putting the business on the books of the insurer. Servicing costs include amounts spent for loss control and the costs of follow-up inspections. The component "administrative costs" encompasses the general expenses of operating the insurance company. Salaries, rentals, supplies, and interest cost represent the most important administrative costs. The item "taxes" includes state premium taxes, licenses, and fees.

The allocation of expenses among the various lines of insurance is an exceedingly difficult process. The essential problem is one that arises out of the inexactness of all cost allocations. Specifically, costs can be allocated in various ways, such as by premium amount, by claims amount, by average or marginal cost, or by judgment (arbitrary or informed).

State regulation of insurance companies has tended to reduce arbitrary allocations by requiring substantial uniformity among insurers in reporting expenses. The National Association of Insurance Commissioners has adopted a set of requirements called "Instructions for Uniform Classification of Expenses." That document requires the reporting of expenses through twenty-one basic expense groups.

Aggregate expenses reported by insurers in different states do not appear to be subject to large variation. The data are gathered and reported to the statistical agencies on a countrywide basis even though several states require that any expenses directly attributable to intrastate business be specifically recognized for rate-making purposes. Countrywide expense data will continue to be used until a rational method can be devised to allocate the costs by state. Thus, while expenses may vary by state and by risk, there continues to be a tendency to aggregate costs and to allocate them by type of insurance on a fairly constant basis.

Provision for Profits and Contingencies

The insurance organizations, like other business firms, must obtain a net profit from their operations if they are to survive and grow. Additionally, policyholders in a mutual company, and especially stockholders in a capital stock company, have come to expect dividends. Dividends in the long run can result only from operational profits.

The success of an insurance operation is dependent on a reduction in uncertainty, which is achieved by the technique of pooling and the application of the law of large numbers. However, while predictability is clearly improved by the pooling concept, an insurance company cannot be sure actual losses will equal projected losses. Such differences can arise from greater than expected frequency of losses or from catastrophes. In order that insurance companies be able to meet loss situations in which unanticipated numbers of losses or catastrophes occur, a provision must be made in rates to reflect the possibility of these losses. Therefore, included in the rate calculations for each line of insurance in each company is a provision for profits and *contingencies* (that is, unforeseen and chance variations in losses).

A combined profit and contingencies loading of 5 percent of the gross premium is used in many lines of insurance. However, loadings varying from 1.0 percent to 20 percent have been used, depending upon the actuary's appraisal of the element of uncertainty involved and the amount of investment income attributable to the line of insurance.

For the underwriter, the contingency provision of the premium rate is of particular significance. The underwriter must recognize that the provision is often extremely modest, particularly when compared with the significant water and wind losses that have occurred in certain coastal areas of the United States. Also, there has been a tendency to discount to some extent the loss effects of a single catastrophe occurrence.

In recent years, the profit and contingencies provision for liability insurance (as well as for property insurance) has come under close scrutiny by rate regulators. In a number of states, there have been many discussions and hearings concerning the levels of insurer profits. In each of these states, as well as in others, regulatory efforts have been undertaken to reduce the profit and contingency provisions in rate filings.

The impact of a proper profit and contingency allowance on underwriting capacity should not be underestimated. It is clear that a lack of profitability significantly impacts on the underwriter's decision process. The underwriter must be aware at all times of profit potentials regardless of type of coverage. Where profits appear to be lacking, considerable restraint is indicated.

RATE-MAKING DATA

Rate making is replete with estimates. In fact, it can be argued that rate making is exclusively an estimative process based on the largest amount of accurate data the insurance company or actuary has available. A particularly important aspect of any estimative process concerns how and from whom the data are collected. This section describes the techniques of collection. These techniques are inextricably related to the accuracy and usefulness of the information. If the accuracy and usefulness of the data are below the limits prescribed by the underwriter, any selections of risks using the inappropriate data may cause an unanticipated loss to the insurer.

Loss Data

An optimal system of collecting and reporting loss data must include a method for obtaining a maximum amount of information, processing that information immediately, and reporting the findings to interested parties. The collected data pertaining to losses should include all possible loss exposures and should classify these loss exposures on some defined, systematic basis to assure strict comparability and accuracy. All definitions of losses, types of losses, and amounts of losses should be carefully outlined and followed.

Unfortunately, the optimal system is not in operation at this time because practical circumstances do not permit the absolute definitions required under an optimal system. For example, not all loss exposures are insured, and information for uninsured losses is extremely difficult to obtain and monitor. Secondly, a number of insured losses apparently are unreported. The lack of reporting results from indifference of insureds and from the small size of losses.

The optimal system of collecting data is, moreover, not possible because of the manner in which data are collected. Specifically, many diverse insurers collect and classify loss information on many different forms of coverages, definitions, underwriting, and claims standards. Given the heterogeneous nature of these standards, there is really no way that the loss data collected can be utilized to develop an optimal system.

The data sources used in the insurance industry are primarily the companies themselves. There are several vehicles through which insurer data are reported, including national associations, regional bureaus, single state bureaus, and individual insurers. In addition to insurance companies, there are other gatherers of primary loss data. An example would be the state-administered workers' compensation organizations.

As mentioned in a prior section, perhaps the most significant problem affecting the accuracy of data collected concerns the diverse methods through which the assimilation of information occurs. Some data (for example, most loss data) are collected on a statewide basis while other data (mainly expense data) are collected on a countrywide basis. Secondly, data for nonstandard, standard, and preferred risks may be collected under differing definitions in the various jurisdictions. Finally, certain coverages are packaged in some states or by some insurers, while the same coverages are offered separately in other states. To the extent that such data are combined, inconsistencies will result.

Statistical Periods

A problem of some importance is that of determining the period for which loss data will be collected and analyzed. There are three periods in general use. These three statistics periods—(1) the calendar-year, (2) the policy-year, and (3) the calendar-accident-year—are described in this section.

Calendar-Year Calendar-year is a very common statistical period. Of the three discussed here, this is the simplest to understand and the easiest from the standpoint of data collection. Unfortunately this approach has some serious drawbacks.

The data required for calendar-year statistics are available from the accounting records of the insurer. The accounting records provide the following information:

1. Paid losses,
2. Written premiums,
3. Incurred expenses,
4. Loss reserves, and
5. Unearned premium reserves.

Since statutory accounting requires a calendar year ending on December 31, this time period is used in calendar-year statistics. In workers' compensation and liability lines where there is a significant loss development delay, a loss ratio based on paid losses and written premium has little meaning. An in-depth description of loss ratio is given later in this chapter. A large part of paid losses are on coverage written in past calendar years while much of the written premiums provide protection for future calendar years.[2]

The loss ratio that is meaningful is computed by using incurred losses and earned premiums. To understand these concepts, the operation of the loss reserves and unearned premium reserves must be examined.

An insurance contract agrees to provide a service (insurance coverage) for a time period (the policy period). As the time that the policy is in effect passes, the premium is said to be earned. The concept of earned premium simply means that this premium now rightfully belongs to the insurance company because the promised service has been performed.

For example, assume a one year policy with a premium of $500 is written on 1 July 19X5. This policy term will expire on 1 July 19X6; therefore, this policy will span part of two calendar years. At the end of 19X5, six months have passed from policy inception; therefore, in 19X5

Exhibit 7-3
Written Premium and Earned Premium

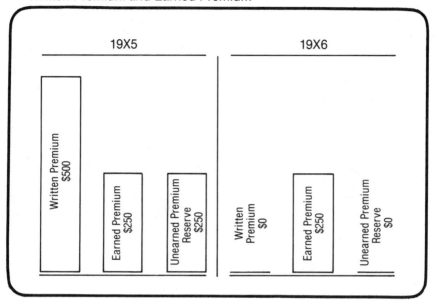

50 percent of the policy premium or $250 has been earned.[3] This is shown in Exhibit 7-3.

At the end of 19X5 half of the premium has been earned, leaving half that is unearned. This unearned premium is reflected in the unearned premium reserve account. This reserve is maintained because, if the policy were canceled pro-rata on 31 December 19X5, the insured would be refunded that $250.

Assuming the policy remains in effect until 1 July 19X6, this remaining $250 is earned during calendar year 19X6. The unearned premium reserve then goes to zero for this policy as of that date.

Earned premium in a given calendar-year refers to policies written in that year and also policies, still in force in that year, written in previous years. To find the amount of earned premium in a given year, one looks at the written premium in that year and then also at the net change in the unearned premium reserve for that year.

This is expressed in the following equation:

$$EP = UPR^1 + WP - UPR^2$$

where:

EP = earned premiums during the calendar year,
WP = written premiums during the calendar year

$UPR^1 =$ unearned premium reserve at the beginning of the calendar year, and

$UPR^2 =$ unearned premium reserve at the end of the calendar year

On the loss side, paid losses provide a very incomplete picture of the actual loss situation. In some lines, losses are paid years after the calendar-year in which they occur. Those that have been reported but not paid are accounted for in the loss reserves. In addition, there are, at any point in time, losses which have occurred but which have not been reported. These are accounted for in the incurred but not reported (IBNR) reserve. The term loss reserves includes both these reserves.

Incurred losses in a given year are defined as including not only losses paid during that year but also the net change in loss reserves during that year. If during a year a large number of serious liability claims were reported, all of which may take five years to litigate, nothing would be shown in paid losses but the loss reserve would go up substantially.

Therefore incurred losses for a given calendar-year may be estimated by the following equation:

$$IL = LR^2 + PL - LR^1$$

where:

IL = incurred losses in a given calendar year
PL = losses paid during the calendar year
LR^1 = loss reserves at the beginning of the calendar year
LR^2 = loss reserves at the end of the calendar year

Note that in the earned premium formula the unearned premium reserve at the *end* of the year is subtracted because it reflects policies with coverage still to run to be earned in future periods. In the incurred loss formula, the loss reserves at the *beginning* of the year are subtracted to show the net build-up (or decrease) in loss reserves during the calendar year in question.

The advantages of calendar-year statistics are that they are available promptly after the close of the calendar year and that they are inexpensive to obtain since they come from accounting records that must be maintained for statutory reporting purposes.

From an underwriting and rate-making standpoint, calendar-year statistics have serious flaws. They lack accuracy and are hard to interpret.

The lack of accuracy in calendar-year statistics comes from the fact that there may be significant differences between the amount for which a loss is reserved and the amount that is ultimately paid. The difficulty in interpretation arises because some of the premiums and losses shown in a particular calendar year actually stem from policies written in earlier time periods. That is, premiums and losses are not matched.

On the premium side, audit premiums and retrospective rate adjustments may be received in a different calendar year than that in which the policy is written. Also much of the earned premium in one calendar year reflects policies written in the previous year.

On the loss side, increases and decreases in loss reserves can make analysis of actual loss results quite difficult. If a reserve set up in a previous year for $100,000 is increased during the calendar year in question to $350,000, it appears that losses during this calendar year have increased by $250,000. Downward reserve adjustments would serve to make loss results look better than was in fact the case.

Policy-Year The policy-year statistical period represents an attempt to remedy the inaccuracies inherent in the calendar-year system. A policy-year is defined as all policies with effective dates within a given calendar year. Therefore, all policies with effective dates in the 19X6 would constitute the 19X6 policy-year. Assuming one year policies, as is the practice with this technique, the last day that a 19X6 effective date policy could provide coverage would be 31 December 19X7. That would be a one year policy written on 31 December 19X6. Sometimes the policy-year is identified by the last date. This would be the policy-year ending 31 December 19X6. Remember that whichever way the policy year is identified, every policy in it has a 19X6 inception date.

The policy-year statistical technique attempts to match up all of the premiums and all of the losses for this particular block of policies. Only in that manner can an accurate analysis be made of the actual underwriting gain or loss from that business.

On the premium side, all written premiums, audited premiums, retrospective adjustments, and endorsements are credited to that particular policy year, regardless of when they were billed or received. This points out one of the drawbacks of the policy year method. It will take at least 24 months to get an initial estimate of the policy-year results, and then audit and retrospective premium adjustments will continue to come in for some time in the future.

On the loss side, all losses whenever paid will be charged to that particular policy-year. Therefore, if a policy were written in 19X5 and a loss that occurred in 19X5 was not closed until 19X9, it would still be charged back to the 19X5 policy year. This provides much greater accuracy with respect to the analysis of loss results because reserve changes only affect the policy-year to which the loss is charged. But the time delay is obvious. Loss reserve changes would continue to occur, possibly well into the next decade for some liability lines with substantial loss development delay.

The second disadvantage of policy-year statistics is the expense involved in setting up a separate statistical gathering system. The data required for policy-year statistics are not available from standard accounting records.

Calendar-Accident-Year The calendar-accident (or exposure-accident) year statistical period was developed as a compromise between calendar-year and policy-year. While the greater accuracy of policy-year is desirable, the greater cost and substantial time delay involved in that system present serious disadvantages.

The calendar-accident-year calculates earned premiums in exactly the same manner as the calendar-year system. Incurred losses are calculated differently. Incurred losses under the calendar-accident year system are defined as the total of all claims arising from insured events that *occurred* during the given calendar year. Whether the claim has been paid during that year or remains as an open reserve, it is charged to that calendar-accident-year. The difference between this and calendar-year is that under calendar-accident-year, future reserve changes, whenever they occur, will be charged back to the calendar-accident-year when the loss occurred.

Under this system, reserve changes do not affect the loss results of any year other than the one in which the loss occurred. This provides more accuracy than the calendar-year but less accuracy than policy-year because policy year also matches the premiums to a given set of policies. All three statistical periods are summarized in Exhibit 7-4.

Loss Ratio

The loss ratio is useful to underwriters in the determination of statewide premium rate changes. This ratio is also used to compare the operations of an insurer from year to year and to compare one insurance company with another.

There are two basic approaches to determine the loss ratio. Both approaches involve the application of a simple equation. The first approach is described only briefly because it is a less used measure of the true loss ratio. The equation for this approach is:

$$\text{Loss Ratio} = \frac{\text{Paid losses}}{\text{Written premiums}}$$

One can readily see the limitations of using this equation to determine the loss ratio. It takes into account only those losses actually paid during a period and compares these losses to the premiums that

Exhibit 7-4
Statistical Periods

Calendar–Year

1. Taken from statutory accounting records
2. Earned premium (EP) = $UPR^1 + WP - UPR^2$
3. Incurred losses (IL) = $LR^2 + PL - LR^1$
4. Neither EP or IL accurately reflect a particular year's results

Policy–Year
1. Requires separate records
2. Defines policy-year as all policies with inception dates in that year
3. All premiums and all losses charged to that year
4. Results available after long time lag

Calendar-Accident-Year
1. Uses same EP data as calendar-year
2. All losses occurring in a particular calendar year charged to that year, regardless of when closed
3. Slightly less accurate than policy-year but quicker and less expensive.

are actually written during the same period. It does not consider the losses that are *incurred,* but not paid, during the present period; moreover it includes all losses that are paid during the present period even if the loss was incurred many years prior to the period under consideration.

The use of written premiums during the period as the denominator is also subject to criticism. Because of situations such as policy cancellations and coverages applicable to other periods, a much better indication of the "income" in a given period is the amount of earned premiums.

Since there are limitations and weaknesses in the equation discussed above, another equation is more often used to determine the loss ratio of a company. This equation is:

$$\text{Loss Ratio} = \frac{\text{Incurred losses}}{\text{Earned premiums}}$$

This equation relates the earned premiums in a designated period to the incurred losses in that same period. Since some of the incurred losses will not be paid until further periods, the amount of losses has to be estimated. Additionally, there is often a lag between the occurrence of a loss and the reporting of that loss. Therefore, there is sometimes added to the known incurred losses an estimate reflecting the amount of losses that have been incurred but not yet reported (IBNR).

For reasons already discussed, the level of premiums earned in a given period has more financial validity than does the amount of premiums written. For these reasons, the loss ratio usually relates the incurred losses to the earned premiums of the same period.

If this ratio is computed and used in a consistent manner from year to year, the relative success of covering current losses out of current premiums can be compared by an insurer to itself and to other insurers from year to year.

As previously mentioned, the loss ratio is also used as a method to determine statewide changes in the premium rate. This is done by comparing the "actual or projected loss ratio" with the state's permissible loss ratio. The actual or projected loss ratio is simply the loss ratio that is anticipated in the succeeding period(s). The permissible (or expected) loss ratio is defined as 100 percent, *less* the expense ratio, *less* an allowance for underwriting profit and contingencies.

To illustrate, assume that future incurred losses are estimated to be $45 million and the amount of premiums that will be earned is estimated to be $70 million. The expected loss ratio is therefore 0.643 (computed: $45,000,000/$70,000,000). If the *permissible* loss ratio in the state is 0.60, then the company needs to raise its premium by 7.2 percent (computed: [0.643—0.600]/0.600) so that only 60 percent of earned premiums will be used to cover incurred losses instead of 64.3 percent, as is currently indicated.

One can conclude from the above discussion that the loss ratio is an important tool in insurance. It is often used to compare the operations of two or more insurance companies (or two or more insureds if they are large enough) or the operations from year to year of one insurer. It is also used as a method to determine rate changes. Even though the loss ratio relies heavily on estimates, these estimates are more accurate than ever before due to more and better information.

TYPES OF RATES

There are three basic types of rates: class or manual rates, individual rates, and judgment rates. In this section, the three types of rates are reviewed briefly, and the importance of each to the underwriter is analyzed.

Class or Manual Rates

Class or manual rates are average rates applied to all members of a group. These rates are developed by grouping together insureds having similar characteristics into a single "class." A commonly cited example of class rate making is private passenger auto liability insurance. While the classes utilized vary among states and insurance companies, drivers generally are classified according to characteristics that are apparent and important. For example, in auto insurance, the following characteristics have been cited as important: (1) the location at which the auto is garaged, (2) the use of the auto—pleasure versus driving to work, (3) the type of auto, (4) the accident and conviction records of the drivers, and (5) the age and sex of the drivers.

Since an essential feature of class rates is rate uniformity within a given class, average anticipated costs are sought. First, data relative to losses are obtained. For example, in auto liability insurance actuaries attempt to ascertain through past experience the losses and loss adjustment expenses that have occurred during a specified period. Then the expenses for the particular class are determined, also from past data. These expenses include provisions for all administrative expenses, acquisition expenses, taxes, contingency margins, and profit. Once this information is determined, the total of the losses and expenses is divided by the number of exposure units for a given class. Exposure units have been defined previously in this chapter. In auto liability insurance the exposure unit is a car-year. A car-year is defined as the insuring of one auto for a period of one year. For example, assume that it was ascertained that the total expected losses plus loss adjustment expenses were $721,346 and that total expenses were $532,621, or a total of $1,253,967, and that the aggregate of car-years was 5,428. The average rate for the class, then, would be $231.02.

Individual Rates

Individual rates have been developed to take into account relative differences in insured risks. If insureds having dissimilar loss characteristics are placed in a class having a single rate, then the insureds having better-than-average loss characteristics will be charged a rate that is too high, while insureds having below average loss characteristics will receive what is, in effect, a subsidy. Individual rates allow insureds to be charged different rates which reflect hazard differences. Differentials in hazards presumably affect loss probabilities, and the rates established reflect the existence and degrees of variation in hazards. In addition to the hazard differentials, individual rates can be based on differences in expected expenses. That is, if the expenses for one insured or a set of insureds are expected to be significantly lower than those of another set of insureds, individual rates can be established to reflect those differences.

Individual rates are found in both liability and property insurance. In many instances, a class rate is utilized with modifications to account for the hazard differentials. In other instances, an entirely new rate must be developed for each individual risk. For example, Kulp and Hall state that unusual or special coverages (example: umbrella liability) and specialty lines (example: airport liability) utilize individual risk rating.

Schedule rates in property insurance have been developed to encourage loss control. In the various schedules that are currently used, considerable attention is paid to building codes, national safety standards, and fire prevention services. Thus, the insured's rate is a direct reflection of loss control devices and programs. Specifically, if the insured takes steps to remove a potential hazard or if a loss control device such as a sprinkler system is installed, the reduction in the insurance rate is immediate and potentially large. This reduction naturally reflects the decrease in hazard.

Judgment Rates

Rates are made by judgment in three situations. First, there are certain types of risks for which there are no distinguishable classes or individual rate systems that can be used. In this situation, the actuary or underwriter must develop a rate based on the available statistical information and an estimate of the probable frequency and severity of the loss exposure. The estimate of the underwriter generally is predicated on information derived from comparable or near-comparable exposures but may be based on purely subjective or nonquantitative estimates.

The second situation in which judgment occupies an important position in developing rates is when an underwriter recognizes important and distinctive hazard differentials among highly distinctive risks. In this situation, the underwriter can evaluate the loss characteristics of the loss exposure by applying various judgment debits and credits to the base rate. An example is the potential "credit" given to a manual-rated jewelry policy when a vault warranty is included.

A third common situation exists when a new coverage is being developed and little, if any, pertinent statistical data are available to establish the initial rates. This would be the case when a brand-new type of insurance is being introduced.

The primary characteristics of all judgment rates is a lack of rating information concerning a particular loss exposure. As a substitute for this information, the subjective judgment or analysis of the underwriter must be used. While the judgment rate may not be precisely representative of the expected value of possible future losses, the underwriter's past experience, training, and knowledge, plus competition in the marketplace, interact to determine the judgment rate. In some cases, however, competition may cloud the judgment of the underwriter.

METHODS OF RATE MAKING

In the previous section, the three general types of rates (class, individual, and judgment) were discussed. These three types of rates are developed and/or adjusted through one or a combination of three methods. Each of the three methods is used currently in one or more lines of insurance. The three methods are: (1) the pure premium method, (2) the loss ratio method, and (3) the judgment method.

The pure premium method can be used to develop new rates or modify existing rates. The loss ratio method is most frequently used to adjust existing rates which may have been developed initially utilizing a pure premium or judgment approach. Judgment rate making can be used to establish rates or modify existing rates.

The Pure Premium Method

The pure premium method requires that substantial amounts of data be gathered and that there be a well-defined unit of exposure to which the data can be related.

The pure premium method can be used for such lines of insurance as private passenger auto, workers' compensation, and other situations where a well-defined exposure unit exists. For auto the exposure unit is a car-year and for workers' compensation it is $100 of remuneration. The data are reported on the specified exposure unit basis to a statistical agency (rating bureau), and the losses and loss adjustment expenses are calculated and expressed as dollars per unit of exposure.

General Development of a Pure Premium The pure premium is an average. This average reflects the losses plus loss adjustment expenses *per exposure unit* for a given period of time, usually one year, which is expressed by the following formula:

$$\text{Indicated Pure Premium for a Specified Classification} = \frac{\text{Incurred Losses } + \text{ Loss Adjustment Expenses}}{\text{Number of Earned Exposure Units}}$$

For example, to develop an indicated pure premium (the pure premium "indicated" by the data) for a class in auto liability insurance, the actuary, upon ascertaining from data collected in the appropriate classification that total losses incurred in the classification were $23,521,073 and that loss adjustment expenses incurred were $4,220, 090, would calculate the indicated pure premium (assuming 400,000 earned exposure units) to be:

$$\text{Indicated Pure Premium} = \frac{\$23,521,073 + \$4,220,090}{400,000} = \$69.35$$

The indicated pure premium is not, of course, the amount that is eventually paid by the insured. A loading for expenses, profit, and contingencies, must be made. The loading can be expressed as a number of dollars or as a percentage of the rate. If the loading is expressed in terms of a dollar amount, the amount will be added to the pure premium to determine the rate. For example, assume that the expenses and profit per exposure unit have been calculated to be $50.22. In this case, the actuary would add $50.22 to the indicated pure premium ($69.35). The result would be:

$$\text{Rate} = \$69.35 + \$50.22 = \$119.57$$

The rate in this instance represents the sum of money per unit that is required to pay losses and expenses (with a profit and contingencies loading) during the experience period.

After calculation of the rate, the losses plus loss adjustment expenses and the expense loading will typically be expressed as ratios—a loss ratio and an expense ratio. These ratios are useful for period-to-period rate change. The loss ratio expresses the relationship between losses plus loss adjustment expenses and earned premiums. The ratio is expressed as:

$$\frac{\text{Loss Ratio in}}{\text{Experience Period}} = \frac{\text{Incurred Losses + Loss Adjustment Expenses in Experience Period}}{\text{Premiums Earned in Experience Period}}$$

The expense ratio exhibits the relationship between expenses and earned premiums. The expense ratio is given as:

$$\frac{\text{Expense Ratio in}}{\text{Experience Period}} = \frac{\text{Total Expenses Incurred in Experience Period}}{\text{Premiums Earned in Experience Period}}$$

If the rate has been properly developed, the sum of the loss and expense ratios equals one, that is:

$$\text{Loss Ratio} + \text{Expense Ratio} = 1.0$$

For example, using the auto liability insurance example cited above, it can be seen that $69.35 represents the indicated pure premium and that $50.22 represents the expense loading (including margins for profit and contingencies). The expected loss ratio is calculated to be:

$$\text{Loss Ratio} = \frac{\$69.35}{\$119.57} = 58\%$$

The expected expense ratio is calculated to be:

$$\text{Expense Ratio} = \frac{\$50.22}{\$119.57} = 42\%$$

There is an alternative way to compute the rate. If the loading for expenses and profit is expressed as a percentage rather than a dollar amount, the rate can be determined from the pure premium as follows:

$$\text{Rate} = \frac{\text{Pure Premium}}{\text{Expected Loss} + \text{Loss Adjustment Expense Ratio}}$$

The expected loss and loss adjustment expense ratio is one minus the provision for expenses and profit. In the example, the provision for expenses and profit is 42 percent or 0.42, and the expected loss and loss adjustment expense ratio is $1.0 - 0.42$, which equals 0.58 or 58 percent. The rate is then determined from the formula as follows:

$$\text{Rate} = \frac{\$69.35}{0.58} = \$119.57$$

Use of the Pure Premium in Rate Modification As has been indicated in the above discussion, the pure premium, when specified as a number of dollars per exposure unit, represents an amount that is expected to be used to pay losses and to meet loss adjustment expenses. The pure premium technique can be used to establish a rate on a new line of insurance where a substantial amount of data exists, or it can be used to modify rates from one year to the next as is done in workers' compensation.

In order to modify an existing rate by using the pure premium technique, the first step is one of determining an indicated pure premium (that is, the pure premium needed). For example, assume that the pure premium data gathered in the state demonstrates that the indicated pure premium rate is $40 based on loss and loss adjustment expenses of $2,000,000 and earned units of exposure numbering 50,000.

$$\text{Indicated Pure Premium} = \frac{\text{Incurred Losses} + \text{Loss Adjustment Expense}}{\text{Number of Earned Exposure Units}}$$

$$\text{Indicated Pure Premium} = \frac{\$2,000,000}{50,000} = \$40$$

The second step is one of determining the current *underlying* pure premium. This is accomplished by multiplying the present rate by the expected loss ratio (including loss adjustment expenses). (The expected loss ratio gives the percentage of each dollar of premium that is expected to be used for the payment of losses and loss adjustment expenses.) If the present rate is $55 and the expected loss ratio is 66.67 percent (or 0.6667), the underlying pure premium is $36.67, as is shown below:

$$\text{Underlying Pure Premium} = \text{Present Rate} \times \text{Expected Loss Ratio}$$

$$\text{Underlying Pure Premium} = \$55.00 \times 0.6667 = \$36.67$$

The third step is one of determining a *rate modification factor* for the rate level. This determination is calculated by dividing the indicated pure premium (based on *actual* loss and expense data) by the underlying pure premium (based on expected loss and expense data).

$$\text{Rate Modification Factor} = \frac{\text{Indicated Pure Premium}}{\text{Underlying Pure Premium}}$$

$$\text{Rate Modification Factor} = \frac{\$40.00}{\$36.67} = 1.09$$

The rate modification factor is then multiplied by the present rate to develop an indicated rate.

$$\text{Indicated Rate} = \text{Present Rate} \times \text{Modification Factor}$$

$$\text{Indicated Rate} = \$55.00 \times 1.09 = \$59.95$$

The indicated rate assumes that the data used for making the modification possess 100 percent credibility. Credibility is a measure of the credence that can be applied to a set of data. High credibility means that the data are presented in such a manner that the actuary believes that the underlying loss potentials are properly and correctly reflected. Low credibility implies that, for some reason (small quantities of data, changed conditions, and so on), there is little reason to believe the accuracy of the data as a reflection of loss potential. If there is low credibility for a pure premium (for example, because of few exposure units within a territory), the pure premium for that area would have a small weight applied to it and a large weight applied to, say, the statewide or the countrywide pure premium. Of course, the sum of the weights would equal one.

The indicated rate may be adjusted as a result of trend analysis. For example, if the average burglary loss has been increasing at a rate of 4 percent per year, the burglary rate should be increased to reflect the probable trend.

Underwriting Utilization of the Pure Premium As previously described, the pure premium can be used for establishing a rate for a new class of business or to adjust a rate for old business. The technique requires a substantial quantity of data, collection of data on an established unit basis, and considerable emphasis on trend and credibility factors.

The underwriter can obtain a considerable amount of information from a pure premium. For example, underwriting management can observe, in the early stages, important aggregate loss trends as well as loss developments in specified lines of insurance. Since the lines of insurance that utilize the pure premium approach (the most important being auto and workers' compensation) are closely regulated by the states, the underwriter can quickly ascertain those lines or classes most favorable to the insurer as well as those lines in which adequate profitability might not be forthcoming. Additionally, the pure premium approach can be used by the underwriter to encourage management to change a particular underwriting policy. For example, an insurance company might conclude that a specific class of auto liability insurance is unprofitable, and restrict its writings in that particular class; but subsequent developments could make the class profitable. If the underwriter were to examine the data and find that there would be a potential for profit, a recommendation could be made to underwriting management that would loosen the underwriting or allow the underwriter to accept an increased level of business in that classification.

The Loss Ratio Method

The loss ratio method is the traditional approach for determining rate level changes. This method seeks to revise rates on the basis of comparing an actual with an expected loss ratio for a particular line of insurance in a defined time period.

Loss Ratio Concept The loss ratio method utilizes a measure termed "the rate modification factor." This factor is a ratio as shown below:

$$\text{Rate Modification Factor} = \frac{\text{Loss Ratio (Actual)}}{\text{Loss Ratio (Expected)}}$$

The *expected* loss ratio is obtained by utilizing the following equation:

$$\text{Expected Loss Ratio} = 1.00 - \text{Expense ratio}$$

The expense ratio is comprised of the following items—commissions, general expenses, other acquisition expenses, taxes, licenses and fees, and profit and contingencies. It is common practice to take an average of three years for expenses. For example, in auto insurance the computation of the expected loss ratio might be as follows:

Commissions	0.150
Other acquisition expenses	0.030
General expenses	0.080
Taxes, licenses, and fees	0.040
Profit and contingencies	0.050
Total expenses	0.350
Expected loss ratio =	1.00 − 0.35
Expected loss ratio =	0.65

The *actual* loss ratio is generated by comparing incurred losses and loss adjustment expenses to earned premiums at *current* rates. Incurred losses are loaded for *loss development* (a factor reflecting the accuracy of loss reserves determined by examining past reserves and the amounts eventually paid) and trends (inflation). Earned premiums at current rates represents the premium that would be earned in the future if all of the exposure units were rerated using the current rate level. This ratio is shown below:

$$\text{Loss Ratio (Actual)} = \frac{\text{Incurred Losses + Loss Adjustment Expenses During the Experience Period}}{\text{Premium Earned at Current Rates During the Experience Period}}$$

If it is determined that actual losses and loss adjustment expenses during the experience period were $21,700,315 and that premiums earned at current rates during the same period were $24,008,721, then:

$$\text{Loss Ratio (Actual)} = \frac{\$21,700,315}{\$24,008,721} = 0.904$$

Using the rate modification factor explained earlier, it can be determined that an increase in the rate is warranted. The specified increase is 39 percent.

$$\text{Rate Modification Factor} = \frac{\text{Loss Ratio (Actual)}}{\text{Loss Ratio (Expected)}} = \frac{0.904}{0.65} = 1.39$$

Assuming a past average rate of $15, the new indicated rate would be determined by multiplying the past average rate by the modification factor (computed: $15 \times 1.39 = $20.85).

Judgment Rate Making

Practically all ocean marine rates and many of the rates for inland marine coverages are made by underwriters according to their judgment. In each line in which a small quantity of data is available (that is, credibility is low), judgment plays an important role. This is particularly true for new insurance coverages. Judgment of an underwriter may constitute a very significant part of the entire selection-pricing process.

The Judgment Rate-Making Process   The first step in the judgment rate-making process is one in which the underwriter makes a thorough examination and evaluation of the actual exposure. This examination may be made through personal inspection of the physical properties and/or through examinations of financial or other data. The examination is designed primarily to ascertain first whether or not the risk might fit into a defined classification having an established rate. If the risk is inappropriate to any of the established classes, the underwriter must proceed with the judgment rate-making process.

The second step is an attempt by the underwriter to forecast loss frequencies and severities attributable to the risk under consideration. The forecast is undertaken through an examination of available past experience of similar exposures, with appropriate attention to the amount and quality of data, and of necessity takes into account proper loss development and trend factors to reflect possible changes in prices (and losses). Past experience data are frequently unavailable. For example, no loss data relative to nuclear ships operating commercially existed prior to the building of the USS Savannah. However, data may be obtained on occasion from applicants insurance industry or insurance company records, through government and association records, or possibly through underwriting files.

A third step in the judgment rate-making process is measurement of the exposure which exists because of operations or events which took place prior to the time when the risk was underwritten. For example, when products liability insurance is written, it is typical to cover previously manufactured or marketed products that are still in use when the risk is assumed. Therefore, the anticipated useful life of existing and future products and the present and future retroactive application of new safety standards must be forecast and analyzed as a part of the exposure.

In the fourth step, the underwriting policy and philosophy of the insurer must be analyzed to determine if the particular risk in question is suitable. An insurer may have an underwriting policy relative to certain classes that may force the underwriter to reject the risk. That is, in certain cases the underwriter may have no leeway because underwriting rules dictate the decision. The fifth and last step requires analysis of market or competitive conditions at the time the risk is underwritten. An underwriter must be cognizant of prices that are likely to be charged by competing insurance companies for a particular risk.

An Illustration Assume that a distinctive products liability risk has been offered to a liability insurance underwriter. The risk is a manufacturing operation that might be classified under the category of "metal goods manufacture."

Following the technique used to make judgment rates, certain investigations are made in order to ascertain the basic nature of the risk.

1. *Products.* What are the products that are produced? Assume that the manufacturer produces various types of blades, including razor blades, saw blades, and propeller blades.

2. *Manual Rate.* An analysis of the rate manual indicates that "metal goods manufacturers" ordinarily develop a rate ranging between $0.05 and $5.00 for basic limits products liability. The rates found in the rate manual are for "basic" limits of liability—usually the lowest limits requested or available. To determine the rate for higher limits, increased limits factors are used.

3. *Severity Potential.* As a practical application, the severity of loss would be expected to be much greater in the propeller blade categories; possible catastrophe exposure may be present if the propeller blades are used for airplane propulsion.

4. *Credibility of Available Data.* Credibility of available statistics would most likely decrease between the first (razor blades) and last (propeller) manufacturing operations; past experience of industry is probably inconclusive, at best, in the last category.

5. *Inflation.* Impact of inflationary trend on anticipated losses is of concern for all three categories, but of course the rate of inflation can vary considerably. There is also the social inflation relating to the increase in the size of verdicts.

6. *Loss Potential of Manufactured Products.* The potential problems associated with existing products are of increasing importance from the first operation to the last.

7. *Underwriting Guidelines and Policies.* It is quite possible that the underwriting attitude of some insurers would almost prohibit writing a manufacturer of propellers, and therefore a higher price may be required if there is an attempt to insure the risk.

8. *Competition.* The competitive market is highly restrictive in that there is little coverage availability and then only at a high rate.

At this point a decision must be made by the underwriter either to accept or reject the risk, and if the decision is to accept, a rate must be set. Given the information listed above, it is likely that the underwriter might view the loss potential as great because of the uncertainties associated with the propeller manufacture. But, in the final instance, it is solely judgment that establishes the products liability rate to be charged.

RATE MAKING IN
DIFFERENT LINES OF INSURANCE

Fire Insurance (and Allied Lines)

There are two types of rates found in fire insurance (including allied lines). These two types are class (manual) and individual (schedule) rates. Class rates, as described in a previous section of this chapter, are used for groups of properties that can be combined into a single, relatively homogeneous class. Briefly, all fire rates are established with reference to the four COPE factors:

1. *Construction.* ISO divides building construction into six classifications which are:

   - frame,
   - joisted masonry,
   - noncombustible,
   - masonry noncombustible,
   - modified fire resistive, and
   - fire resistive.[4]

2. *Occupancy.* There are many occupancy classes which vary by jurisdiction. Generally established classes include (among others):

   - dwelling,
   - multiple occupancy habitational,
   - farm use,
   - manufacturing, and
   - mercantile.[5]

3. *Protection.* A distinction is made between private and public protection. Private protection refers to such items as sprinkler systems amd stand-pipe and hose systems. Public protection

refers to the local fire department. Each fire department is graded based upon the amount and quality of equipment, water supply, training level of personnel, and alarm systems.[6]

4. *External Exposures.* External exposures refer to other buildings, brush, or wooded areas that represent additional hazards to the building under consideration. In a multiple occupancy building, units other than the one being considered for insurance are also considered as external exposures.[7]

The second type of rate used in fire insurance is the individual or schedule rate. The schedule rate applicable in fire insurance is frequently termed a *specific rate.* That is, the schedule rate is one that is specific to a particular risk. Individual rates are developed for large and complex risks as well as for some smaller commercial risks. A schedule is used which, when applied to the individual risk, gives a number of debits and credits which are applied to a base rate to develop a final rate for the specific risk.

Fire insurance rates are made on the basis of experience of insurers in a given state over a period of years. The data of the experience period (frequently five years) are adjusted to the current rate level on the basis of incurred losses and earned premiums. Losses are then trended to adjust for inflation over the experience period and to reflect loss adjustment expenses. The result is a weighted loss ratio on the order of:

Most recent year	30 percent
Preceding year	25 percent
Next preceding year	20 percent
Next preceding year	15 percent
Next preceding year	10 percent

The actual loss ratios (including loss adjustment expenses) are then used to indicate any proposed change in fire insurance rates. For example, if the actual loss ratio was 72.46 percent but the expected loss ratio (the ratio anticipated by the actuary) was 67.36 percent, an increase of 7.57 percent in the rate would be indicated (72.46/67.36 — 1.0).

The increase of 7.57 percent is an indicated increase for all fire insurance classes. However, the increase is not always applied on a uniform basis throughout all of the classes. Inter-class adjustments are frequently made to reflect variations and developments in building materials, types of construction, and levels of fire protection.

Inland Marine Insurance

Inland marine rates, like fire insurance rates, are made on both a class and an individual basis. For example, personal articles floater rates are developed by class. Some of these rates (for example, the camera floater) are applied on a countrywide basis. Other risks are individually rated and the base rates vary by territory. When individual rates are applied, each insurance company has the opportunity to charge rates that satisfy its expectations of losses for the particular risk, and there is often little data that can be used to support the rates. However, competition frequently has a great impact on the development of a final rate level.

One type of inland marine coverage that is individually rated is the contractor's equipment floater. Underwriters, in making decisions on this coverage, typically consider as important factors (1) the type and size of the business being covered, (2) the nature and condition of the equipment, (3) the area in which the operation takes place, (4) the financial experience and business ethics of the insured, and (5) past loss experience. For example, a bulldozer used on a road construction job in the plains states would not take the same rate as that for an identical piece of equipment used in an open-pit mining operation in some mountainous region.

Ocean Marine Insurance

Ocean marine insurance is international in both scope and focus. Traditionally, London markets, particularly Lloyds', have dominated the ocean marine field. Historically, marine underwriters have enjoyed great freedom with respect to coverage form and rate. Most, if not all, ocean marine business is judgment rated. The variables of vessel, master, cargo, and trading area are so diverse as to frustrate any attempt at forming homogeneous classes.

The major categories of ocean marine insurance are hull, protection and indemnity (P and I) which is a liability coverage, and cargo. The ocean marine tradition is one of very broad named perils or "all-risks" coverage, and judgment rating. While an individual ocean marine underwriter enjoys considerable latitude in setting ocean marine rates, most underwriting manuals contain guidelines or ranges for rate acceptability. The major force controlling ocean marine rate levels is the competitive nature of the market.[8]

Burglary and Glass Insurance

Burglary insurance is essentially class rated. In writing commercial burglary coverage, the most important variable is the type of business conducted by the insured. Additionally, territorial multipliers are extremely important in this particular coverage since location appears to influence insurance losses to a significant degree. Glass insurance is also class rated. The most important variables are location of the glass in the building, type of glass, type of business operation, and territory.

For each of these coverages, rate levels are determined and adjusted using the loss ratio approach. This is usually accomplished on a statewide basis.

Auto Insurance

Auto liability insurance is class rated. The rate-making system classifies autos into different groups according to the use of the vehicle such as private passenger, commercial, public, garage, truckers, and miscellaneous. Rates are made on a separate basis for each group.

In auto liability insurance rate making, statistics are collected on a statewide basis for each of the various groups. These statistics are maintained by insurers or reported to a bureau on a calendar-accident year basis. Since exposures are reported for the major classifications, the pure premium approach can be used. However, rate changes are generally based on the loss ratio approach (which will yield the same result as the pure premium method). Physical damage coverages follow the same basic approach using a different classification system, and the statistics are usually compiled on a calendar year basis since there is little delay in claims being reported and settled.

Workers' Compensation

In most states permitting private insurance, workers' compensation insurance is written on a uniform rate basis for all insurance companies. Rates vary by classification. The classifications are based on the work performed by the employee (as in construction), on the product (as in manufacturing), or by type of enterprise (as in retail merchandising).

Earned premium is derived by the application of the class rate to remuneration. Remuneration is initially an unknown figure that is subject to determination at the end of the policy period.

In the loss ratio approach used in workers' compensation, losses are adjusted first to final estimated value and second to reflect any changes which may have taken place in the workers' compensation law in the state under consideration. At the same time, premiums for the same period are adjusted to the current rate level. Adjustments are made by comparing the actual loss ratios with the expected loss ratios.

The indicated change in rate level is then distributed to the individual classifications according to the difference between indicated pure premiums and those pure premiums underlying the current rates. Individual classification change is governed by the credibility of the classification.

Workers' compensation rates for insureds with premiums over stated sizes are subject to modification as a result of individual experience rating. Expense gradation is in the form of premium discount. Premiums for some policyholders may be further modified on an optional basis by the application of retrospective rating. In the 1980s competition has become more evident in workers' compensation through the use of rating deviations from bureau rates, schedule rating, and similar devices. In some cases regulations were the driving force behind the changes.

RATING BUREAUS AND STATISTICAL ORGANIZATIONS

Insurance rate making depends to a great extent on intercompany cooperation. Cooperation is required so that insurance companies can develop rates from data having a reasonable level of credibility.

The form of intercompany cooperation is demonstrated by the development of rate-making organizations. The organizations are termed rating bureaus and statistical agencies.

Rating Bureaus

Rating bureaus are a result of the need for property and liability insurers to obtain and process vast amounts of data in a rapid and efficient manner. The use of rating bureaus depends on the line of insurance, the attitude of a particular insurer toward intercompany rate making, and the regulatory constraints of the states. The fundamental operation of bureaus is one of obtaining information on losses, expenses, and rates charged. They also pool experience obtained from a large number of insurers and develop a set of rates that can be used by them.

The use of a bureau varies by state. In some states, insurers are required to maintain membership in a bureau and use its published rates. In other states, the bureau is advisory only, and individual insurers may join the bureau and use its rates at the insurer's option. Many jurisdictions fall between the two extremes, and insurers may be required to belong to a bureau, but may be allowed, through permission of the insurance department, to charge rates different from those published by the bureau. In some lines, insurers might be able to use the bureau's loss figures but have to use their own expense figures. *Rates that are different from those of the bureau are called deviations.* Deviations can be made for special risk situations or may be given "across the board."

The list which follows is a sample of the bureaus currently operating in the property/liability field:

Fire and Allied Lines.................Insurance Services Office
Workers' Compensation..............National Council on
                                   Compensation Insurance
Auto Insurance—
    Voluntary.........................Insurance Services Office
Auto Insurance—
    Residual..........................Automobile Insurance
                                   Plans
                                   Service Office
Liability Other Than
    Auto..............................Insurance Services Office
Bonding..............................Surety Association of
                                   America

Statistical Organizations

Statistical organizations, like rating bureaus, operate to provide rate-making services to the insurance industry. The statistical organization collects and files statistics on written premiums, losses, and expenses. In some cases, the statistics are compiled by associations that render other services. In other cases, they are supplied by service organizations that are formed for that purpose or that assume the statistical function along with others. However, they do not have the power to make rates. Such organizations are sometimes known as "statistical agents" and, in some states, are recognized and licensed as such.

Current Status of Bureaus

State or regional rating bureaus occupied an important position in the insurance industry in times past. They have, however, become less important in recent years, and all indications point toward a continuation of this trend. This reduced importance may have a rather strong impact on underwriters. However, the reductions in importance may depend on the lines of insurance involved. Some national bureaus have grown significantly in recent years.

The current status of bureaus is one of transition from rate-making authority to an advisory position. In recent years, several jurisdictions have allowed or required insurers to deviate in various lines and to use bureaus solely as advisory organizations. Additionally, some states do not require that data be gathered by insurers in the same manner as that prescribed by the bureaus, and consequently they cannot consistently require insurance companies to use the bureau output in rate making.

With some exceptions (notably the large insurers having substantial premium volume), the underwriter is seriously affected by reduced dependence on the bureaus. Specifically, if there is a lowered reporting to the bureaus on the part of insurers, the data upon which bureaus establish rates will not have as high a credibility as before. Also, if the underwriter's company moves away from using bureau data and rates to using its own data, a reduction in credibility is the result. Thus, the underwriter should be aware of the process through which rate data have been collected and rates developed. The credence which the underwriter attributes to the data used, and the available rates, will, and should, affect the underwriting decisions.

THE UNDERWRITER'S ROLE IN RATE MAKING

This chapter has analyzed the special relationship between underwriting and rate making but has focused primarily on the need for the underwriter to function within constraints of the rate-making process and its extant problems. The previous discussion and analysis should not be construed to mean that the relationship of underwriting to rate making is a one-way street, that is, that the inputs flow from the actuaries to the underwriters, who take those inputs as given facts and then react; such is not the case. Underwriters occupy a positive role in rate making, and there are several critical inputs that underwriters must make.

Development of Data

The first input that the underwriter must extend to the rate-making process is that of collecting, organizing, and disseminating data relative to the losses and expenses of the insurer. The underwriting department is usually responsible for obtaining and allocating those expenses that are related specifically to the business of insuring risks (frequently all expenses other than those associated with investments).

While this job might appear somewhat basic, and even perfunctory, it is extremely difficult to accomplish correctly. The difficulty is in the allocating of losses and expenses to the appropriate lines of insurance. Allocations of this nature are extremely complex and important since the distributions will affect the differential rates among classes over an extended period of time. In order to meet regulatory as well as competitive requirements, the data must be correct and allocated properly.

Development of Certain Rates

There are a number of instances in which underwriters may be called upon to develop the actual rates used by the insurers. Development of rates by underwriters is frequently found in situations where very large risks exist. In the case of such large loss exposures, many complex and interdependent loss probabilities are often found. In this type of situation, the promulgated class or base rates may be inappropriate because independent probabilities are assumed. Additionally, very large risks may present different loss characteristics from those assumed in the rate-making process. Thus, if the average size loss unit assumed in a base rate is, for example, $50,000, but the unit under consideration is homogeneous in every way except that its value is $4,000,000, a different approach to developing its rate might be warranted.

In addition to large exposures, underwriters may be called upon to develop rates for distinctive and/or unique exposures. As is the case in large risks, the distinctive exposure presents a problem in that there may be a lack of relevant data or any data at all. Consequently, judgment of the underwriter may constitute the most appropriate price-setting technique since the underwriter is likely to have greater familiarity with the possible loss characteristics of the risk than has the actuary.

Rate Analysis

Underwriters occupy an important judgmental position in the post-development analysis of rates. When rates are being promulgated by the actuaries, a large number of basic characteristics about risks and factors affecting risks are considered and assumed. However, there is no rate-making system that considers all possible factors that could affect a loss probability. In fact, consideration of all possible factors would, of necessity, require a clairvoyant since there could be unknown factors.

Underwriters are in a position to analyze rates and loss-producing factors over a period of time. They are in a position to view and analyze developments in losses, in economic and financial conditions, and in all other factors that could influence current and near-term losses, and they are in a position to undertake appropriate corrective action. Given the current dynamic conditions surrounding certain types of losses, the underwriter's analysis and actions become an absolutely necessary and critical part of the rate-making process.

SUMMARY

Pricing the insurance product is an important variable in the underwriting decision. Consequently, the techniques or approaches used by insurers in developing rates and premium are of great significance to underwriters.

Important constraints include the regulatory qualifications of adequacy, no unfair discrimination, and nonexcessiveness of rates. Additionally, social and other criteria such as affordability, simplicity, encouragement of loss control, responsiveness and stability affect rates. The law of large numbers is at the heart of all insurance rate-making techniques. This law refers to homogeneous, independent, random occurrences.

Collecting and classifying large amounts of data are integral parts of rate making. However, many problems arise with respect to collecting, developing, and analyzing the data. Dependence on inaccurate data may lead the actuary to promulgate rates that are excessive or not adequate.

One special problem of data collection is the basis on which the collection takes place. The problem is one of matching losses and premiums over an appropriate time period and is compounded by the fact that, while premium collections can be reflected rather quickly, losses may be largely unknown for relatively long periods of time. Various solutions to the problem created by the lag between premium collection and loss payment have been introduced over the years, and there are different methods of collection (calendar-year, policy-year, and calendar-accident year). However, the problem of time continues, and the underwriter must be aware of its existence.

Insurance rates can be grouped into three broad categories: class rates, in which homogeneous insureds are grouped together for rate-making purposes; individual rates, which are used when risks are distinct; and judgment rates, which are used when data are not available.

There are basically three methods of developing rates. These methods are the pure premium method, the loss-ratio method, and the judgment method. The first method (pure premium) is used in situations in which there are substantial amounts of available data and a well-defined unit of exposure. The pure premium method takes losses and loss adjustment costs for a given period and relates those costs to a given number of exposure units. The result is the pure premium that can be adjusted by expenses, profits, and other margins to produce an applicable rate. The loss-ratio approach is one of rate modification. This approach revises or modifies rates in a given jurisdiction by a process of comparing actual loss ratios with expected loss ratios in a defined time frame. The third rate-making approach is that of judgment. Many rates are made by judgment, including almost all ocean marine rates and many of the rates for inland marine. Rates for new insurance coverages and for those lines having small amounts of data are also made by judgment. It is particularly important that an underwriter have some understanding of the relevant implications of making rates by different methods.

The rate-making process is dependent upon a pooling of loss experience from a large number of insurers. Statistical organizations and rating bureaus provide these data as well as rate-making services to the industry. The underwriter's role in rate making consists of collecting and organizing loss and expense data, modifying rates to reflect exposures to loss, and analyzing rates to make certain they are competitive and adequate.

Chapter Notes

1. It is clear from the perspective of the 1980s that liability actuaries during the 1940s under-estimated the loss costs from certain latent diseases such as asbestosis. If one points out that virtually no one knew during the 1940s the loss potential of asbestosis, that certainly provides an explanation.

   This simply demonstrates an unavoidable weakness of rating techniques which are based on historical data. If a new cause of loss surfaces, it is not provided for in the rating technique because there is, by definition, no historical foundation for such funding.

   Marine underwriters have long dealt with this problem in judgment rating for "all-risks" policies. They call it the "X" peril. The unknown cause of loss that is going to surface in the future for the first time is considered in the rating technique and provided with a charge under the "X" peril heading.

   It is unlikely that either regulators or the competitive forces of the market will permit liability rate makers the luxury of an "X" peril charge. Therefore, either future rate inadequacies or disappearing markets for coverage are likely.

2. For a comprehensive analysis of these rate-making principles see Bernard L. Webb, J. J. Launie, Willis Park Rokes, and Norman A. Baglini, *Insurance Company Operations*, 3rd edition, Vol. II (Malvern, PA: American Institute for Property and Liability Underwriters, 1984), pp. 1-65.

3. This example has been simplified for illustrative purposes. A later chapter will show that statutory rules call for only $1/24$ of the premium to be earned in the first month, $1/12$ for the next eleven months, and $1/24$ to be earned the month following expiration.

4. See E. P. Hollingsworth and J. J. Launie, *Commercial Property and Multiple Lines Underwriting*, 2nd edition, (Malvern, PA: Insurance Institute of America, 1984), Chapter 4.

5. See Hollingsworth and Launie, Chapter 5.

6. See Hollingsworth and Launie, Chapter 6.

7. See Hollingsworth and Launie, Chapter 7.

8. For an introduction to ocean marine insurance see Leslie J. Buglass, *Marine Insurance and General Average in the United States*, 2nd edition, (Centreville, Maryland: Cornell Maritime Press, 1981), pp. 3 - 11.

CHAPTER 8

Pricing, Continued

THE RATING PROCESS

Rating means applying rates and rating plans to the exposure units of insureds. The process consists of determining the specific plans under which individuals or groups are eligible, selecting the appropriate classification for those particular risks, and applying the rates to the proper number of exposure units. Also, underwriters must evaluate the nonquantifiable factors which might affect the exposure but which are not a part of the rating process.

The rating process is extremely important in underwriting, and a full understanding of the procedure is vital to underwriting decision making. This chapter begins with a brief overview of the rating process, followed by a discussion of the rating differences in property insurance and liability insurance. Next, description, analysis, and examples of individual risk rating plans are provided, and a section concerning pricing problems concludes the chapter.

Rate Manuals

A rate manual contains the rates for each of the classifications as well as all the necessary rules, factors, and guidelines for the application of those rates. Rate manuals provide a source of information for classifying risks and developing premiums for given loss exposures. Once the classification groupings and the premiums are determined, this information can assist the underwriter in the selection decision by answering the question, "Are we getting enough premium for the potential losses we are insuring?" Additionally, the rate manual provides important information concerning the use of endorsements. Endorsements that broaden coverage or reduce premiums can be a competitive tool to obtain and retain quality business. Restrictive endorsements are often necessary to solve underwriting problems and to make an unacceptable risk acceptable. The rules for use of these endorsements for "tailoring" coverage to individual risks are found in rate manuals.

Some limitations in rate manuals should be noted. First, they may not always contain an appropriate class or rate for each risk. Second, loss exposures change over time, and the rules, procedures, and rates taken from manuals may not always serve the underwriter's requirements in the optimal manner even though the manuals are updated frequently. Finally, there are certain loss exposures for a given risk that may not be covered in the manual. That is, the manuals used by most underwriters contain relatively little discussion of the exposures themselves. Thus, information found in rate manuals must be augmented by the underwriter's practical knowledge.

Classification: A Critical Part of the Process

Generally speaking, the rate that is applied to an individual risk is determined primarily by the classification into which that risk falls. But when a distinctive risk is submitted to the insurance company, the underwriter may use considerable discretion in determining the category or classification into which the risk is placed. This discretion consequently results in some degree of judgment being applied to the application of the rate. As a direct result of the allowed flexibility of classification and thus the rate, underwriters must be familiar with the rate-making system and the classification system and to thoroughly understand the interdependence of the two systems. Additionally, the underwriter must keep in mind that the proper classification of risks is directly related to the accuracy of underwriting information. If information is not verified, a risk may be misclassified, resulting in excess or inadequate premium. For example, incorrect information on the type of product manufactured may result in a rate that is much too low for the exposure. In personal lines, where risk selection is limited, proper classification of insureds is paramount in underwriting a book of business.

While underwriters must possess familiarity with the rating process for individual rating plans, it is also necessary to have a working knowledge of rates and rate levels for specified classes. However, it is probably unnecessary to be familiar with the precise rate applicable to each risk classification. For example, it may not be of utmost importance for the underwriter to be familiar with the rate differentials for private passenger autos for classes 8561 and 8562. Still, there must be an ability to associate an approximate rate with each risk. Since it is the responsibility of the underwriter to develop a rate suitable to the risk, he or she must have a significant degree of familiarity with the loss exposure for which the rate has been prepared. As noted in one underwriting text:

> An underwriter is almost expected to assign the classification or the rate, or both, and must be able to determine at least one of these in order to make his decision on acceptability. Since he (the underwriter) has to determine the classification and rate, he might as well indicate, in the file, the proper one to use. Because an underwriter ordinarily assigns codes and perhaps rate, it may appear that this is a clerical function. Such a conclusion is exactly opposite from the truth; determining classification and rates are essential parts of the underwriting function, and the underwriter must indicate his decision from these items, as on others, in the file for the guidance of other employees.[1]

In many lines of insurance, risk selection is limited and proper classification becomes the most important factor in obtaining the proper premium. A large number of misclassified risks or even a single misclassified risk can cause significant losses. As one analyst has noted:

> Determining the proper rate is an essential part of underwriting. A good risk placed in the wrong classification, or charged the wrong rate, may be a worse risk for the insurer than one on its ineligible list. Rating is even related closely to the social problems underwriters face, particularly with respect to large lines, such as personal automobile insurance[2]

Factors Not Included in Rates

A number of factors are *not* taken into consideration in the insurance rating process. These factors possibly could affect the acceptability of the risk but are not included in the rating process for a number of reasons. For example, some factors are not a part of the rating process because they apply to a limited number of cases or possibly to specific geographical locations. The factors exist, but they are too complex to be included on a generalized basis.

Commercial crime insurance rates, for example, are typically based on four fundamental factors: (1) classification, (2) territorial multipliers, (3) protection, and (4) amount of coverage. Classification distinguishes the trade group, that is, drugstores, dry cleaners, furniture businesses, and banks. Territorial differences are classified to discriminate among the various geographical areas of the country. Type and adequacy of crime protection and the amount of coverage are, of course, two obvious factors in rating. In addition to these factors which *are* used in rating crime coverages, other underwriting factors could be considered but typically are *not* considered in rating: the number of hours the business is open each day, integrity of employees, excess amount of cash held, adequate protection for casual messengers making bank deposits, and the financial stability of the firm and its owners.

Hazard analysis for homeowners insurance includes a number of factors that cannot be used in rating. For example, the number of persons living in the home and the occupations of the residents might significantly affect the possibility of loss. Also, the capacity and state of repair of the heating equipment could be important.

Factors not included in the rating process are nevertheless of great significance to underwriters and may be highly instrumental in determining potential losses. Underwriters must recognize the hazards not included in rates and adjust their decisions accordingly. Additionally, underwriters should be aware of those factors that might exert a *positive* influence on losses, that is, those that might reduce loss frequency and severity.

PROPERTY AND LIABILITY INSURANCE PRICING: THE DIFFERENCES

Introduction

Pricing, as underwriting activity, includes all ratemaking and rating activities that are within the discretion of the underwriter. For example, if an underwriter decides that the applicant should be in a standard rather than a preferred rating structure, or makes a decision on whether the use of a car is for pleasure or nonpleasure, a pricing decision has been made. Also, when a risk is rejected because the underwriter feels that the premium is inadequate, the pricing factor is determinant.

The term "pricing" includes both ratemaking and rating; and implies a greater level of flexibility and discretion than either ratemaking or rating. Ratemaking is often thought to be essentially the province of actuaries, and rating the province of technical personnel. However, the price of the product is most definitely an underwriting variable and is therefore an integral portion of the underwriting function.

The goals of property and liability insurance pricing are the same; that is, each group of risks should develop sufficient premiums to pay for losses and expenses of the group and make some contribution to the insurance company for profits and contingencies. However, the approaches used to develop the final prices charged insureds differ between property and liability lines. This section analyzes some of those differences.

Regulatory Controls

An important difference between property and liability insurance pricing is the distinction between lines that are filed with the departments of insurance in the various states and those lines that are not filed. Taking the nonfiled lines first, the underwriter has considerable discretion in pricing. Examples are found in several commercial inland marine policies (property coverage) and in certain professional liability insurance coverages such as, directors' and officers' liability insurance.

Some inland marine insurance rates are published by rating bureaus and are used by many insurance companies. Some insurance companies deviate from the published rates while others develop their own. Many insurance companies as a general rule use the full rates published by the bureaus since they are unable to internally develop sufficient premium volume in the given classification to obtain a high degree of credibility. On the other hand, some insurers do not hesitate to modify the rate if conditions appear to warrant it: modifications may be upward or downward depending on the circumstances.

The flexibility that exists for the underwriter in pricing many inland marine contracts does not exist to the same degree in the coverage of most fire and allied lines. Fire insurance contracts in many states are written under uniform classifications and rates because of the technical complexity underlying this coverage. There are many different variables reputed to affect loss probabilities; as a consequence, obtaining combined and consistent data is essential for pricing purposes.

Liability rates may be filed or not filed. The most important filed lines (in most jurisdictions) are automobile liability insurance and workers' compensation. In each of those lines of coverage, there are many classifications, and the rate filed with each classification must be used. In the case of filed liability rates and classifications, the underwriter has extremely limited flexibility except on risks developing a large premium. The rating rules are usually specific, and the underwriter must react to the provided information by placing the risk in the designated class and charging the specified rate.

In some liability lines, there is considerably greater flexibility given to the underwriter. The rates for some lines, such as umbrella liability, are not filed, and thus the rate charged is made through the underwriter's evaluation of the potential losses and of competitive prices in the marketplace. In other lines, for example, general liability coverages, the rates and classification may be filed, but the underwriter may have some discretionary power over allocation of the coverage among the various liability classifications. This pricing discretion is discussed in the subsequent section.

Rating in Property Insurance

Property insurance rates may be class rates or individual rates. Class rates are commonly used in crime insurance, dwelling fire and small commercial property risks. Individual rates are used in larger commercial risks that are inspected and rated according to a schedule of debits and credits that reflect its own loss potential.

There are a number of fire insurance rating "schedules" currently being used in various areas of the United States. Each of these different schedules begins with a rate for what is defined as a *standard risk*. Once the rate for the standard risk has been obtained, the rating organization applies to that rate a set of credits and debits based upon various factors that might affect the potential loss frequency and severity of the risk. For example, as noted previously, factors typically analyzed include the COPE factors of (1) construction, (2) occupancy, (3) protection, and (4) external exposures.

Types of Construction Building materials and design greatly affect fire loss frequency and severity and consequently construction types are used to rate property risks. Underwriters have differentiated between a joisted masonry and a frame building for some time and with good reason, because of the smaller hazardous potential for combustion in the former. The rate is adjusted accordingly. Other types of construction have been added in more recent years to expand the number of classes.

Other construction factors taken into consideration in determining fire rates are construction of floors, roofs, walls, and partitions; height and area of the structure; number of unprotected floor and wall openings; and other similar but distinctive features of construction that would have a bearing on potential fire losses. Each of these factors can cause a charge (debit) or a credit to be made in the rate. Knowledge of construction types is necessary to properly classify and rate property risks.

Occupancy (Use) of Structure The use, or occupancy, of a building is generally considered to be one of the most important contributing factors in fire losses. A large percentage of all fires reportedly is caused, to some extent, by the manner in which the building is used or occupied. Two buildings, for example, may be similar in construction, location, and other factors. However, one of the buildings may contain combustible materials, such as oil, or paint, while the other may be used as an office and contain only word processing and office equipment.

In rating fire insurance, underwriters must be aware of the relationship between a building and its contents and usage. Because of possible changes in the use of a structure, it is also important to continually reassess the occupancy and to modify rates when permitted in order to meet changing occupancy conditions within the building. Occupancy factors are not always constant, and equity among insureds requires that insurance companies make allowances for changes in heating, lighting, contents, manufacturing methods, and other changeable situations that can vary with occupancy. The appropriateness of the current occupancy relative to the intended occupancy of the building is also important.

Fire Protection   A third important element in fire insurance rating is the quantity and quality of public and private protection (sprinkler systems, fire extinguishers, and so on) afforded the property to be insured. Public fire protection is a vital factor in determining insurance rates. Depending upon the municipal fire fighting facilities (equipment), the alarm system, and the water supply, a structure may be so inadequately protected that it will very likely be a total loss once a fire has started. Another structure, in a well-protected area, may suffer little damage under similar conditions. For rating and underwriting purposes, towns and cities have been classified according to available fire protection.

External Exposure   Another important contributor to the possibility of fire damage is external exposure. External exposure is defined as the type of environment surrounding the structure that may contribute to a loss. A substantial amount of fire damage may result from a primary fire in one building that travels or expands to other structures nearby.

These four elements—construction, occupancy, protection, and external exposures (COPE)—are the major underwriting and rating factors in property insurance.

Rating in Liability Insurance

Liability insurance rates are generally class rates that are sometimes modified by rating plans that reflect the distinctive characteristics of the individual risk. For example, worker's compensation, general liability, or auto liability class rates are applied to an insured's exposure units and may be modified by experience, schedule, or retrospective rating plans, if the insured is eligible.

There are many variations in hazards presented by different liability risks. The COPE factors in property have no similar counterpart in liability insurance. Because of the wide range of exposures, liability insurance is characterized by a large number of different hazards and rates. It has not been thought possible, over the years, to use individual rating for liability insurance in the same manner as is currently used in property (particularly fire).

There is one more substantial difference between the approaches used for rating property insurance and liability insurance risks. Property insurance debits and credits typically are established on a judgmental basis. However, the manual classification rates used in liability insurance are developed on a statistical basis. It is possible to do this since losses in this line of insurance typically result from a single accident in a given location. As a consequence, the liability losses can easily be assigned to a particular classification, and rates can be made on the basis of those losses within the classification. Property insurance rating, on the other hand, cannot be established on a statistical basis since it is impossible to determine precisely how each of the hazard characteristics of a particular insured contributes to the loss. Since the apportionment is not possible, judgment must enter into the rate-making scheme.[3]

Deductibles

In many property insurance lines, deductibles are mandatory. This is particularly relevant in certain lines of insurance in which the underwriter expects a fairly large number of small losses. In many other lines of insurance, the deductible may be optional. In addition, different deductible amounts may be specified, with the insured having a choice as to which deductible amount to select. Typically, the selection of the deductible amount will depend on the expected losses of the insured.

While the use of the deductibles usually is discussed from the viewpoint of the insured, deductibles are perhaps more important from the viewpoint of the underwriter. Deductibles not only lower the total cost of losses but the expenses of settling numerous small losses are also lowered. These savings may be passed along to insureds through lower premiums.

In addition to the expense savings associated with deductibles, many underwriters utilize such deductibles in order to have better selection of their insureds. For example, it has been suggested by some underwriters that those insureds who are not willing to accept a deductible are the very ones who are most active in presenting small claims to the insurance company.

Additionally, deductibles may control certain types of morale hazards. Specifically, if an insured is required to pay a portion of every loss, there should be a reduction in the degree of carelessness that may contribute to a loss.

Deductibles are not found in liability insurance to the same extent as in property insurance. This is probably due to the need for claims service on all claims—large and small. However, there are some situations in liability insurance in which deductibles are beginning to emerge. For example, directors' and officers' liability contracts typically contain deductible provisions. The deductibles are included as loss control measures.

Expenses

Another element in property and liability pricing is expenses. Insurers require a substantial amount of information from their insureds. In personal lines, the information requirements are standard and can be obtained rather easily from the insured and from motor vehicle records obtained from the Departments of Transportation in the various states. However, for commercial lines the information requirements are much more extensive.

Various types of inspection reports are requested to determine the physical conditions, safety systems and other characteristics of the insured business. These initial inspections and periodic follow-ups increase the expenses associated with commercial property and liability insurance. The engineers or loss control representatives who make these inspections frequently are employees of the insurance company. However, there are firms that provide this service on a fee basis.

While inspection reports may be important in fire insurance pricing, they are of considerably greater importance in liability insurance pricing. This is because the data are more intensively utilized in liability insurance with its large potential exposures. Of course, the more detailed and intensive the reports, the greater the cost.

Another expense differential separating liability insurance from property insurance pricing is claims expense. Property insurance pricing is made more simple in that, generally speaking, the amount of the loss is reasonably certain. However, in liability insurance, the amount of the claim is highly uncertain, and, in addition, the insurance company has agreed to provide for the cost of legal services associated with the claim against their insured. For that reason, the liability insurance policy must contain in its pricing mechanism a charge for the substantial expenses associated with claims.

INDIVIDUAL RATING PLANS

Background

Insurance is designed to reduce uncertainty of financial loss by drawing together (pooling) insureds having similar loss and expense characteristics. These insureds generally are charged the same premium rate, which is termed a "class" rate and which is developed by a rating organization or an insurer based on the aggregate loss experience of the class.

When insureds in a given classification are charged the same class rate, a problem involving inequity may arise. This problem occurs because absolute homogeneity among insureds, even in the same classification, is not achievable. In fact, in certain instances, the potential loss characteristics of an insured in a classification may have greater similarity to insureds in a different classification than to other insureds in the same class. When this type of situation occurs, an inequity may result because of the differences in premium rates charged in the various classes.

These differences can arise from many causes but typically result from an attempt to include too many different insureds in a given class or from a simple lack of understanding about the actual loss or expense characteristics of a particular insured. These inequities may result from price competition among insurers. As an insurer recognizes that certain insureds in a specified class possess better than average loss characteristics, a strong incentive is created for the insurer to use pricing incentives (a reduced rate) to attract those insureds.

There are at least three broad approaches to solving inequities that arise from differential loss and expense characteristics of insureds placed in a given classification. First, it is possible to rearrange the classes. While this solution is conceptually possible, there are practical difficulties.

A second method of increasing equity among different insureds is to create additional classes. If a given class includes insureds who have relatively different loss or expense characteristics, the class can be subdivided. Unfortunately, the creation of additional classes often accentuates credibility problems. Specifically, the reliability of loss and expense predictions is directly related to the amount of data upon which the prediction is based. When new and additional classifications are established, the data upon which future losses and expenses are predicted are spread over more classes and may not be credible from a statistical standpoint. Since credibility is of such great importance to the development of proper rates, the creation of new and additional classifications may not be the best solution to the equity problem.

A third approach is that of developing flexibility within classes, permitting a reflection of individual loss and expense characteristics among different insureds. The system that attempts to accomplish this flexibility is known by various names throughout the insurance industry, but most of the specialized techniques can be grouped under the name of "individual rating plans."

There are many different individual rating plans, each having a set of distinctive characteristics. From an underwriting standpoint, each is important, as some degree of pricing flexibility is given to the underwriter. Each of the individual rating plans is discussed in the following pages: experience rating, schedule rating, retrospective rating, expense modification, and participating plans.

Experience Rating

Experience rating utilizes the loss experience of the insured over a period of time (usually three years) to adjust the class rate either upward (a debit) or downward (a credit). The experience of the individual insured is used to determine if the insured is better or worse than the "average" insured in the same classification. By definition the "average" insured is one whose actual losses during a period are equal to the expected losses during the same period. If the actual losses of an insured are less than expected losses, a credit (a deduction) will be applied to the class rate for that insured. Conversely, if the actual losses of an insured are greater than expected, a debit (an addition) is made to the insured's class rate.

Generally, the experience period used to compute the experience modification is the *latest available three years*. Since the latest loss data may not be available at the time of the computation, the experience period usually ends at least six months prior to the rating date. Oftentimes, underwriters use a two and one-half year experience period which ends six months before the effective date of the rating plan. Once the plan is in effect, each successive experience period will drop the oldest year and add the latest year's experience.

Loss experience reported by other insurers or by the insured under a self-insurance (retention) program may be used. The accuracy and validity of such data must be determined by the underwriter.

A question that must be asked concerning the past experience of a particular insured is "How *valid* is this information?" Validity in this case is measured by a "credibility factor." Generally, the greater the amount of premium, the more confident an underwriter can be that the past loss experience is a good indication of future loss experience. This

Exhibit 8-1
Experience Rating Modification

Experience Rating Modification =

$$\frac{\text{Actual Loss Ratio} - \text{Expected Loss Ratio}}{\text{Expected Loss Ratio}} \times \text{Credibility Factor}$$

is because insureds generating substantial premiums presumably have a larger number of exposure units, and therefore it is less likely that actual losses were a result of "chance" fluctuations. As a consequence, the credibility factor applied to the past experience of an insured having a large premium is greater than the factor applied to a smaller account. This credibility factor is always between 0 percent and 100 percent. The lower credibility factors would give a lower reliance on past experience, while the higher ones would indicate higher reliance.

Experience rating may be used in workers' compensation, auto and general liability, automobile physical damage, burglary, glass, fidelity bonds, and credit insurance. In most jurisdictions, it is optional to use experience rating in any of the above lines of insurance except workers' compensation, in which case it is often mandatory for eligible risks.

Experience rating is essentially the application of an experience rating modification factor to the class or manual rate. This experience modification factor is determined by the equation in Exhibit 8-1. If the resulting modification is negative, a deduction (credit) is made from the class rate. For a positive factor, an addition (debit) is made to the class rate.

To illustrate, assume that an insured's *actual* loss ratio is 48 percent, the *expected* loss ratio is 60 percent, and the insured's credibility factor is 50 percent. Using the equation in Exhibit 8-1, the experience modification would be:

$$\text{Experience Rating Modification} = \frac{0.48 - 0.60}{0.60} \times 0.50 = -0.10$$

Thus, the insured's manual or class rate would be modified by a 10 percent reduction (credit) to reflect its better than average experience. If the actual loss ratio had been 72 percent instead of 48 percent, the modification would have been a 10 percent debit or addition, calculated as follows:

$$\frac{0.72 - 0.60}{0.60} \times 0.50 = +0.10$$

There are minimum requirements (not standard for all jurisdictions) for experience rating. For general liability, an insured might be required to produce a manual premium of $3,000 annually at basic limits. Also, for auto liability, the insured could be required to produce an annual basic limits manual premium of $2,500 for four or more autos to be eligible.

Experience rating has several advantages for the insured: (1) it can be applied by using information that has already been gathered without having to inspect the insured's premises; (2) it is objective in nature because it is based on previous losses; and (3) it is a relatively fair method of modification.

Another advantage of this system of rate modification is that it increases an insured's awareness of the direct relationship between losses and premiums. Therefore, there is an incentive to reduce the frequency and severity of losses as much as possible.

However, there are also limitations to experience rating. First, some eligible insureds are dissatisfied with this method because they expect their loss experience to be given 100 percent credibility for rating purposes. The credibility factor lessens the attractiveness of this approach to those insured with better-than-average loss ratios and may be an incentive to self-insure. Second, some insureds complain that experience rating lacks responsiveness because the experience of the current policy year is not included.

One last limitation of experience rating is that the plan is influenced by average experience. That is, the plan reduces the debits and credits for most insureds "by mixing individual-insured experience with average experience.... It does not dramatize loss-prevention quite as much as retrospective rating, especially because the effect of improved experience is prospective."[4]

Schedule Rating

As previously mentioned, rating by a *schedule* is used in both property and liability insurance. In property insurance, a rating schedule establishes a standard for a type of risk (such as a concrete block building) and credits or debits are applied for conditions that are better or worse than the standard. The result is an individual rate for the risk.

The term "schedule rating" is generally used to refer to a rating plan designed for use in some liability lines to reflect certain risk characteristics not included in experience rating. In some lines of liability insurance, schedule rating is sometimes used in conjunction with experience rating. The resulting debit or credit to the manual or class rate as determined by experience rating may then be increased or decreased by the use of schedule rating. Exhibit 8-2 includes a set of

Exhibit 8-2
Schedule Rating Table*

The manual rates for the risk may also be modified in accordance with the following schedule rating table, subject to a maximum modification of 25%, to reflect such characteristics of the risk as are not reflected in its experience:

	Range of Modifications		
	Credit		Debit
A. Location:			
1. Exposure inside premises	5%	to	5%
2. Exposure outside premises	5	to	5
B. Premises—condition, care	10	to	10
C. Equipment—type, condition, care	10	to	10
D. Classification peculiarities	10	to	10
E. Employees—selection, training, supervision, experience	6	to	6
F. Cooperation:			
1. Medical facilities	2	to	2
2. Safety program	2	to	2

* Insurance Services Office

standards applicable under one widely used general liability plan. The plans for other insurance lines are similar in their approach.

The judgment of the underwriter is of utmost importance in the application of schedule rating plans. This judgment is based on the underwriter's experience in the line of business, the insured's loss experience, the insurer's underwriting policy, and any other relevant factors. Depending on the coverage and type of insured, emphasis can be placed on the physical conditions and hazards of the premises and operations or on management attitude. In some lines, such as general liability illustrated in Exhibit 8-2, substantial emphasis is placed on subjective factors such as the cooperation of management and the training and supervision of employees.

Schedule rating plans have been filed for optional use for some types of auto liability, auto physical damage, general liability, glass, and burglary insurance. Generally, those insureds who are eligible to use experience rating are also eligible to use schedule rating. To become eligible for schedule rating, insureds must meet certain premium levels such as an annual basic limits manual premium of $1,000. Of course, eligibility does not mean that underwriters must use this plan on all eligible risks. On the contrary, schedule rating is usually limited to insureds with premiums well in excess of $1,000 and is used with discretion primarily to meet competition.

One of the most important advantages of schedule rating is that many of the plans utilized are reasonably current. The schedules can be kept up to date and can be easily changed if conditions warrant the alterations. Another advantage of schedule rating is that it attempts to reflect those hazards that are not reflected by the loss experience of the insured. Therefore, schedule rating plans have contributed much to the encouragement of loss control by drawing attention to factors and situations leading to high loss frequency or severity.

One disadvantage of schedule rating is that it is, in some ways, a judgment rating plan. Judgment must be used in setting the standards and in determining the debits and credits to be applied to the class rate. To the extent that the judgment is subjective, it is possible to criticize a plan on the basis of possible inaccuracies.

Retrospective Rating

Retrospective rating utilizes the loss experience of an insured for a *given period* to adjust the premium at the end of *that period*. In other words, unlike experience rating, the final premium is not determined until the end of the policy period. Retrospective rating differs from experience rating in one important way. Experience rating is based on *past* loss experience, and the credit or debit is *guaranteed* for a time period (usually one year). On the other hand, "retro" plans use the loss experience of the *current* year to determine the final premium for the current year. Consequently, the final retro premium cannot be computed until after the policy period.

The premium for the insured may vary between a specified maximum and minimum. The maximum and minimum are established on a percentage basis of the *standard premium*. The standard premium is given by the rate manual but is modified by experience rating and other premium deviations except the premium discount. Normally, at the beginning of the policy year, the insured is charged a *deposit premium* which is adjusted upward or downward within the maximum and minimum limits at the end of the policy year as set forth in the plan.

The retrospective rating method is most often used in workers' compensation insurance. There are four "tabular" (premium factors are listed in a table of values) rating Options, I, II, III, and IV, from which the insured can select. The selection of a particular option will depend on relative stability of premium cost desired by the insured; that is, some of the options have a lower minimum premium but, at the same time, expose the insured to a higher maximum premium. Other options may reduce the possible ranges of prices. In addition, there is another retrospective rating option (Option V) which is particularly flexible and permits an insured to combine premiums for workers' compensation, auto and general liability, auto physical damage, and glass coverages, or any combination of these insurance lines. Two similar retrospective plans are available for boiler and machinery insurance.

Retrospective rating is never mandatory. It is optional for eligible insureds. To be eligible to use Options I, II, III, or IV, for example, the insured generally must produce a standard premium of $1,000 or more. A standard premium of $5,000 or more must be produced by an insured to be eligible to use Option V although a higher minimum is frequently required by underwriting policy.

The minimums and maximums offered vary widely among the four tabular options. Often the prospect of having large premium savings (that is, a low minimum) are offset by the prospect of a fairly high maximum premium. Of course, rates are increased to reflect low minimum and maximum premiums. The more conservative options allow very little fluctuation in the premium relative to the standard premium. In fact, the standard premium might be the maximum premium. (In this case, the insured does stand the chance of "losing" the premium discount if the final premium is the standard premium, since the premium discount does not apply if retrospective rating is used.) Based upon each person's estimate of the future losses, the underwriter and insured must decide just how much fluctuation up and down each is willing to accept.

In addition to the tabular rating options mentioned above, Option V can be applied without the use of tables. When Option V is used, each factor in the retrospective formula is developed and applied on a negotiated basis for *each* individual risk, the only requirement being approval of the appropriate rating organization in the state. Option V is used for large risks only and may be interstate as well as multi-line in nature.

The retrospective premium is calculated by application of a basic formula.[5] This basic formula is:

Retrospective Premium (subject to upper and lower limits) =

[(Basic Premium Factor × Standard Premium) +

(Excess Loss Premium Factor × Standard Premium ×

Loss Conversion Factor) + (Losses ×

Loss Conversion Factor)] × Tax Multiplier

The *basic premium factor* is stated as a percentage of the standard premium. When these two items are multiplied together, the resulting product is called the basic premium. *This basic premium is the amount the insurer needs to charge to cover its fixed expenses other than taxes.* It also includes the actuarial cost of limiting the premium to the prescribed (or, under Option V, selected) minimum and maximum levels.

The loss conversion factor represents those expenses that vary with the losses such as loss adjustment expenses. This factor varies by line of insurance.

The losses are the actual losses that are incurred by the insured during the contract period. After the retro plan is terminated, the final premium is adjusted annually to reflect changes in loss reserves and settlements until all losses are closed or both parties agree to close the plan.

Many insureds do not want all of a large single loss to enter into the retrospective rate calculation because of the resulting wide fluctuation in retrospective premium. Under some retrospective plans it is possible to put a maximum, such as $25,000, on the amount from one claim which will enter the retrospective rating formula. An additional premium is charged for this limitation. The amount of the additional premium is determined by (1) multiplying the standard premium by the excess loss premium factor to find the expected amount of losses eliminated by the maximum limit and (2) multiplying the product from (1) by the loss conversion factor to add adjustment expenses. This section is not shown in the above formula since the limitation of losses is optional.

The tax multiplier is a percent of the premium and covers the state premium tax, license fees, and any other taxes. This factor varies by state.

To illustrate, assume that an insured chooses Option II as the method of determining the premium for workers' compensation insurance. This insured produces a standard premium of $10,000 and incurs losses totaling $5,000 for the policy period. Under Option II, the basic premium factor (illustrated in the manual) is 24.6 percent. The loss conversion factor is 1.14 and the tax multiplier is 1.03. The maximum and minimum premiums as set by Option II for this insured are $16,500 and $6,200, respectively. Using the formula above, this insured's final annual premium is calculated as follows:

$$\text{Retrospective Premium} = [(0.246 \times \$10,000) + (\$5,000 \times 1.14)] \times 1.03$$

$$= \$8,405$$

Since the resulting premium is between the set maximum ($16,500) and minimum ($6,200) limits, $8,405 is the insured's retrospective premium assuming the insured has not chosen to limit the losses. If the formulas had determined that because of higher losses, the retrospective premium would be $23,500, the insured would have been required to pay $16,500. Thus, a savings of $7,000 would accrue to the insured as a result of the maximum premium.

There are significant advantages to both the insured and the insurer in retrospective rating options. The primary advantage to the insured is that the system produces a premium that is determined by the insured's own loss experience *during the term of the contract*. If the insured is able to control losses, an immediate benefit (a reduction in insurance costs) will be available. The insurer, in terms of the retrospective rating system, makes the final premium a direct function of loss experience in the most recent period, and one in which the premium responds quickly to changes in loss experience. As such, the insurer develops a system of positive loss control, and, in effect, any reduction in losses always benefits the insurer in the long run.

The primary disadvantage or weakness of retrospective rating is that insureds can be exposed to substantial fluctuations in annual insurance costs. This possible disadvantage can be mitigated through the use of the more conservative retrospective rating options. However, many insureds appear to prefer an insurance cost that is fixed and known. For these insureds, retrospective rating plans should have relatively little appeal.

Expense Modification

Expense modification, as the name implies, is a plan that modifies the expense portion of an insured's rate to reflect the actual cost of providing coverage to that particular insured. Expense modification may be used in conjunction with schedule and experience rating plans. The expense modification plan allows for the rates to be adjusted upward or downward. A downward modification is frequently used for competitive purposes. That is, it is a form of price competition that can be used by an insurer to attract and retain profitable business. A considerable burden is placed on the underwriter in risk selection decisions because there is less premium income to pay losses. Thus, downward expense modifications must be used with discretion.

Like schedule rating, the expense modification plan must be filed. In addition, the plan depends, to a considerable degree, on the judgment of the underwriter. If the underwriter believes that the expense of handling a particular insured's account is less than the expense of handling the account of the average insured of the same size, that particular insured's premium may be reduced. Often, this reduction is a result of the producer's willingness to take a reduction in commission. For example, if the standard commission rate on a particular line is 15 percent but the producer is willing to accept 10 percent, the insurer will be able to offer insurance to that particular insured at a lower rate than standard rate. This reduction in the producer's commission is *not* rebating, because it is authorized in the filing and is based upon specific expense savings.

The commission rate is not the only expense that can be less than average for a particular insured. For example, inspection costs may be lower in the long run for an insured who cooperates fully with the insurer; any cost savings in this area may be passed along to the insured as a lower premium.

The main advantage of expense modification is that it allows the insured to pay only for the actual expenses of the insurer in providing the coverage. In addition, as previously mentioned, this rating approach can be a very competitive tool for insurers.

The main limitations of expense modification are that it is not available in all states and is available only to insureds with large annual premiums. Also, the problems of determining actual expenses are great. Precision in this area may not be possible. Finally, as in schedule rating, the modifications are based mainly on the judgment of the underwriter, which may be subjective.

Participating Plans

Participating plans, like retrospective rating, utilize the loss experience of an insured for the *current* policy period to "adjust" the premium at the end of the period. This is done, in most cases, by issuing a graded or sliding scale dividend which varies with the size of the premium and loss ratio. The dividend is paid from the surplus premium that remains after all the insured's claims and expenses have been paid. This dividend is somewhat like that paid by mutual insurance companies to their policyholders at the end of a policy period, in that there is no guarantee. However, it is paid *only* to select policyholders who satisfy the requirements of the participating plan. The dividend rate also depends on the size of the insured's premium. All other things being equal (especially the loss ratio), the larger the premium, the larger the dividend. As is true with expense modification, the producer often accepts a lower commission, and this added savings is passed along to the insured as a dividend.

The participating rating plan is used to adjust the class rate after the application of schedule or retrospective rating. It is used by both stock and mutual companies. The dividend is generally expected because insurers allow only "better than average" insureds to participate in this plan. If the losses of an insured ever exceed the premiums, the excess is not charged to the insured. In other words, the standard premium is the maximum amount the insured will ever have to pay in a given year. To be eligible for this plan, the insured generally must produce a standard premium of at least $1,000. Most participating plans are in the area of workers' compensation; the approach, however, can be utilized in any line or combination of lines.

To illustrate a participating plan, assume that an insured produces a standard premium of $5,000. The insured, therefore, remits $5,000 to the insurer at the beginning of the policy year. During the year, the insured incurs losses of only $3,200. Assume further that the expenses (including commissions) of the insurer in providing this coverage total $1,000. By the end of the period, therefore, the insured has paid in $5,000 in premiums and the insured has paid claims and expenses of $4,200. Consequently, the insured receives a portion of the $800 difference as a dividend at the end of the year. Only a portion of the $800 would be returned, since the insurance company must retain some amount of the premium to offset the cases in which the indicated dividend is negative. On the other hand, if the assumptions were the same as above, except that the insured incurred losses of $6,000, the insured would not be charged for the $2,000 difference. The loss above the premium paid would be met by the insurer by a reduction in the dividends of other policyholders.

There are several unique characteristics of the participating plan. First, dividends cannot be guaranteed in advance, but they are often estimated so that the insured is reasonably sure of the results. Second, participating rating plans are available mostly in workers' compensation, but in some states, they are also available in auto and general liability insurance. Third, the participating rating plan is a very competitive and flexible plan. The plan provides an incentive for the insured to practice loss control since the dividend varies directly with the loss ratio. There is one major disadvantage; the insured may come to expect a dividend and therefore may become dissatisfied if one is not received.

COMPOSITE RATING

Composite rating is an optional method by which rates for one or more types of insurance are computed using a single convenient exposure base such as receipts. This is *not* an individual risk rating plan, but merely an administrative convenience. Composite rating neither increases nor decreases premium. It merely substitutes a single exposure base for the various exposure bases found in the individual coverages. It can be used for auto liability and physical damage, general liability, and glass and theft coverages.

Composite rating has three advantages:

1. The single premium base makes for a simpler premium audit.
2. Cost accounting and job cost estimates may be simplified for the insured making allocation of insurance costs to specific products or jobs easier.
3. From the standpoint of the insurer, composite rating makes it difficult for competitors to determine how the premium was calculated.[6]

Choosing the exposure base to be used in determining composite rates is crucial. This exposure unit must properly and accurately measure the hazards to which the insured is exposed. The exposure units most often used are payroll, sales, area, units, and gross receipts. The exposure base that is used for a particular insured usually is determined by the type of business. For example, the composite rate of a retail store usually is based on sales, while payroll is normally used for contractors. Some insurers also believe that it is not a good idea to include auto liability with other lines because the rating base often chosen (for example, sales) does not reflect the true exposure. In these cases, the auto coverage is put into a separate policy with its own composite rating base (if desired). Of course, having two separate rating bases is not quite as desirable as having only one, but the convenience of the plan should not overshadow the need to get an adequate premium.

Not all insureds are eligible for a composite rating plan. For example, a minimum annual premium for basic limits is generally required before an insured is eligible to use this rating method. This minimum annual premium is required to meet the specifications of the rating plan and also to assure the development of sufficient premium.

If the plan applies to auto liability, auto physical damage, and general liability, the annual basic limits premium for all coverages must be at least $70,000. If two of these three are used, the minimum is $50,000. If the plan applies to only glass or theft, the required annual basic limits premium is only $5,000.

To develop a composite rate, the premium is calculated for each individual coverage under the plan using the manual rates, exposure units, and experience and schedule rating plans for that coverage. Next the single rating base is determined. Finally the sum of all the individual premiums is divided by the new rating base to calculate the composite rate.

Assume that the Sticky Wicket Company, a manufacturer, agrees to a composite rate based on sales. The new exposure unit will be $1,000 of sales. Annual sales are $50 million. The calculation of the composite rate is shown in Exhibit 8-3. Total premiums for the three separate coverages are $76,000. When this is divided by 50,000 (there are 50,000 $1,000 exposure units in $50 million), the composite rate is $1.52.[7]

The composite rate is adjusted frequently—it can be recalculated annually or at any other time at the request of either the insurer or the insured. The rate is normally recalculated if there are changes in the classification rates or if the "mix" of the insured's exposures changes significantly.

Ideally, the composite rating plan will produce the same premium figure as the basic rating plans. This will hold true if the special exposure unit is chosen carefully so that it accurately measures the hazards to which the insured is exposed.

RATE-MAKING AND PRICING PROBLEMS AND THEIR IMPACT ON UNDERWRITING

The rate-making process can never be perfect, just as underwriting decisions can never be perfect. For this reason, it is appropriate for underwriters to recognize and understand the problems involved in rate making and to consider these problems while making their decisions.

The Data

As discussed in a previous chapter, one of the most imposing problems in rate making concerns the data used to predict future losses. Specifically, these data are losses that have occurred in the past.

The loss data used often present a fundamental problem in that, with several notable exceptions (for example, private passenger auto liability and homeowners insurance), there are small numbers of losses. This kind of data often does not present the actuary with adequate information. For example, assume that an actuary is considering a set of past data on 100 actual losses in which the aggregate losses have *totaled* $1,000,000, have *averaged* $10,000, and have *ranged* from $25 to $250,000. There is some interesting information contained in this data set. First, the range of losses is large; second, the average loss is high; and finally, the number of losses is small.

Exhibit 8-3
Calculation of Composite Rate for Sticky Wicket, Inc.

Step 1 — Premium

Coverage	Rating Base	Annual Premium
Auto liability	Car-years	$46,000
M&C liability	$100/payroll	25,000
Theft	$100/insurance	5,000
Total		$76,000

Step 2 — Determine number of exposure units — new rating base

Annual sales = $50,000,000   Exposure unit = $1,000 sales

$50,000,000/$1,000 = 50,000

Step 3 — Calculate composite rate

$76,000/50,000 = $1.52 per $1,000 of sales

The relevant question is, "What does the actuary or the under-writer know about this class of business?" The answer must be, "Very little." Regardless of the number of exposures in the class, there is an obvious "low frequency-high severity" character in the data set. The number of losses is small, and the loss severities are apparently quite large except for a few losses. Whenever a situation of low frequency-high severity exists, there is typically inadequate information upon which the actuary can base future loss expectations.

The underwriter faces perhaps an even more difficult task when the low frequency-high severity problem exists. Specifically, while the rate may be adequate and meet the other requirements of an "appropriate" rate, the possibility of a number of severe losses must increase uncertainty for the individual responsible for risk selection, since the possible variations in loss results are large.

A second problem concerns the basic accuracy of data. Many opportunities arise for inaccuracy. For example, data are occasionally reported with errors. Losses that have occurred may go unreported or may be given an erroneous amount through mistakes on the part of the reporter or, through a receiving error on the part of the organization to which the data are given.

Computerization of information has led to the rapid processing of large amounts of data in a very efficient manner. However, this form of processing occasionally permits errors to enter the results through incorrect codings of data, incorrect data entry, and through a myriad of internal programming and associated problems. Those persons who are involved with computers generally assert that the problems are random in nature and errors that do exist should be offset in such a manner that the final product is reasonably accurate. This contention is probably correct in most instances, but underwriters should recognize that, in certain cases, the errors will not balance and an inaccurate final rate may result.

Inflation

The fundamental problem brought about by inflation is that prices change substantially between the periods of data collection and future loss occurrences. The data used for forecasting future losses are inappropriate for future periods because prices can change. *Trend factors* are used to mitigate the basic problem. For example, if an actuary is attempting to project auto physical damage insurance losses for a given period, data that is three or four years old must be used. The actuary must go back to the data and adjust for the differences in price levels of autos, auto parts, and labor costs. This is accomplished by reviewing precisely how much change has occurred and by multiplying the raw data by the amount of price level changes over the period of time being used. This review is generally undertaken by referring to a particular index. Indices of price changes are published by various sources, the most important being the U.S. Bureau of Labor Statistics.

For example, assume that in 19X6 an underwriter is trying to determine future auto glass breakage and collision rates, using 19X5 data. Assume the average auto glass breakage loss in 19X5 is $195, broken down as follows:

Average labor	$120
Average automobile parts	75
Total average automobile loss (19X5)	$195

If the unadjusted figure was used as a basis for developing 19X6 rates, it would be below the appropriate rate. Now assume that the price for labor and parts has increased 3 percent and 5 percent, respectively. The underwriter is now able to "bring the old data up" to the present. This is done by simply multiplying the raw data by 1 plus the inflation rate, i, as illustrated in Exhibit 8-4.

Price inflation can cause important differences over relatively short periods of time when the inflation rate is high. For example, the crash-parts index shown in Exhibit 8-5 indicates that an auto part which cost

Exhibit 8-4
Data Adjustment Example

	19X5 Raw Data	×	(1 + i)	=	19X6 Dollars
Labor	$120	×	1.03	=	$124
Parts	75	×	1.05	=	79
Total	$195				$203

$176.60 in 1975 would cost $341.50 in 1984, a compound annual increase of 7.60 percent.

A great deal of effort has been undertaken by certain auto insurers, bureaus, and regulators to ascertain the actual changes in price levels that have occurred in recent years. The auto parts index was the first index designed solely to reflect "parts" of an auto and has been of great assistance in the attempt to adjust loss data for changes in the prices of auto parts. In Exhibit 8-5 the crash-parts index, along with a number of other indices, are presented for comparison purposes.

Underwriters should be able to recognize the areas in which inflation might have the greatest impact on the company's loss results, and the various methods through which to adjust for the effects. For instance, the types of insurance that are underwritten can cause considerably different loss results than would occur if other types of insurance are underwritten.

There are several methods by which an underwriter can mitigate the effects of inflation. First, the term of the policy can be shortened; for example, a one-year or a six-month policy can be issued instead of longer-term policies. The shorter the policy term, the less time inflation will have to erode the value of the premium dollar before a revision of the premium can be undertaken. Second, deductibles can also be used by the underwriter to somewhat offset the effects of inflation.

Third, trend factors can be used to predict future loss costs. A trend factor operates to produce a number that represents an "average" change in prices over a given period of time, specifically, the experience period. There are several statistical techniques that can be utilized to produce different averages, for example, weighted averages, moving averages, geometric averages, and others. The problem, however, is in being able to select the correct average and being able to apply that average to the data in such a manner that an accurate picture of past losses in current (and near-future) dollars is presented.

Exhibit 8-5
Price Indices for Auto Insurance and Related Items and Annual Rates of Change, 1975-1984 — (Base: Except as Indicated, 1967 = 100) *

Year	Cost of Living (all items) Index	% Change
1975	161.2	
1976	170.5	+ 5.8%
1977	181.5	+ 6.5
1978	195.4	+ 7.7
1979	217.4	+ 11.3
1980	246.8	+ 13.5
1981	272.4	+ 10.4
1982	289.1	+ 6.1
1983	298.4	+ 3.2
1984	311.1	+ 4.3
% Change. 1975-1984		+ 93.8

Year	Medical Care Items Index	% Change	Hospital Rooms Index	% Change	Physicians' Fees Index	% Change	Auto Repairs and Maintenance † Index	% Change
1975	168.6		236.1		169.4		176.6	
1976	184.7	+ 9.5%	268.6	+ 13.8%	188.5	+ 11.3%	189.7	+ 7.4%
1977	202.4	+ 9.6	299.5	+ 11.5	206.0	+ 9.3	203.7	+ 7.4
1978	219.4	+ 8.4	332.4	+ 11.0	223.1	+ 8.3	220.6	+ 8.3
1979	239.7	+ 9.3	370.3	+ 11.4	243.6	+ 9.2	242.6	+ 10.0
1980	265.9	+ 10.9	418.9	+ 13.1	269.3	+ 10.6	268.3	+ 10.6
1981	294.5	+ 10.8	481.1	+ 14.8	299.0	+ 11.0	293.6	+ 9.4
1982	328.7	+ 11.6	556.7	+ 15.7	327.1	+ 9.4	315.8	+ 7.6
1983	357.3	+ 8.7	619.7	+ 11.3	352.3	+ 7.7	330.0	+ 4.5
1984	379.5	+ 6.2	670.9	+ 8.3	376.8	+ 7.0	341.5	+ 3.5
% Change 1975-1984	+ 125.1		+ 184.2		+ 122.4		+ 93.4	

Year	Auto Crash Parts Prices†† Index	% Change	Labor Rates Auto Repairs††† Average Rate	% Change	Auto Insurance Index	% Change
1975			$10.71		145.9	
1976	100.0		11.45	+ 6.9%	187.9	+ 28.8%
1977	109.3	+ 9.3%	12.13	+ 5.9	210.5	+ 12.0
1978	120.6	+ 10.3	13.33	+ 9.9	216.6	+ 2.9
1979	133.0	+ 10.3	14.63	+ 9.8	228.7	+ 5.6
1980	148.1	+ 11.4	16.45	+ 12.4	247.4	+ 8.2
1981	168.8	+ 14.0	17.39	+ 5.7	259.0	+ 4.7
1982	188.0	+ 11.4	17.82	+ 2.5	275.7	+ 6.4
1983	193.6	+ 3.0	18.15	+ 1.9	302.7	+ 9.8
1984	194.9	+ 0.7	18.97	+ 4.5	326.3	+ 7.8
1985	190.0	- 2.5	20.07	+ 5.8		
% Change 1975-1984	+ 90.0#		+ 87.4##		+ 123.6	

† The cost of auto crash replacement is not reflected in this index, which includes prices for water pump replacement, motor tune-up, automatic transmission repair, front end alignment and chassis lubrication. The trend in the cost of parts commonly used to repair auto crash damage is reflected in the index of auto crash parts prices developed by State Farm Mutual Automobile Insurance Company.
†† Base: Jan. 1, 1976 = 100. Index figure for each year is as of Jan. 1.
††† Not computed as an index. Dollar figure for each year is as of Jan. 1.
# Percent change 1976-1985.
Percent change 1975-1985.

Sources: Auto Crash Parts Prices. State Farm Mutual Automobile Insurance Company. Labor Rates, Auto Repairs, Allstate Insurance Company: other data, U.S. Department of Labor, Bureau of Labor Statistics.

*Reprinted, with permission, from *Insurance Facts 1985-86*, (New York: Insurance Information Institute, 1985), pp. 49-50

A problem concerning trending is that only *linear* techniques or factors are used in projecting loss data forward. Linear models are simpler to construct than nonlinear models but are generally less accurate since changes in price levels may not be constant.[8]

In a severe inflationary period trend factors are not welcomed by many regulators since large rate increases result from their use. This is especially true if the period is one of significant consumer education and interest in prices, particularly the prices charged by regulated industries such as electric and other power utilities, transportation, and, of course, insurance. The practice of using high trend factors occasioned by past inflation was anathema to some regulators and consumer groups in the mid-seventies. These groups contended that the trend factors were exaggerated or simply a method to develop excess prices and profits. As a consequence, trend factors were, on occasion, not allowed in rate filings or were reduced during this period.

Territorial Imbalances

The distribution of risks by territory in a given classification may create serious ratemaking problems. These problems are a result of territorial imbalances which can lead to (1) nonindependent loss frequencies and severities and (2) possible catastrophic loss situations.

Territorial imbalances are of small consequence in many lines of insurance, such as products liability and boiler and machinery insurance. These coverages are characterized by independence of individual losses, and countrywide schedules are used in both lines. However, a number of insurance lines, most notably auto, are greatly affected by territorial imbalance. The basic problem stems from a concentration of risks in particular areas or zones. For example, factors that produce substantial differences in loss experience in auto insurance include topography, climate, quality of highways and driver education programs, and density of population. While there is available information concerning loss probabilities in given locations, this information is often imperfect because of gaps in data, and changing geographical and demographic conditions.

Additionally, for any insurer or group of insurers, territorial imbalances are increased by the distribution of business in given classes. The desired balance of above-average risks over all territories is impossible, simply because an insurer cannot place producers having precisely homogeneous business methods in each territory.

Presumably, actuaries develop some appropriate measures to offset the problems of territorial imbalance. However, it would appear that because of the problems that do exist, the underwriter may be subject to even greater difficulties than the actuary. These difficulties arise because the underwriter is ultimately responsible for accepting risks and has knowledge of their primary locations. Some appreciation of the exposure problems presented by territorial imbalance is required of the underwriter since he or she may increase or mitigate the problem through selection.

Improper Classification Systems

Classification systems may cause serious difficulties for actuaries as well as for underwriters. A classification system is based on the premise that insureds having similar loss and expense characteristics can be grouped together for rating purposes. Then, once this grouping ("pooling") has occurred, a rate can be developed that will meet the regulatory requirements of the various states while continuing to promote an acceptable level of competition.

The classification systems that have been developed have been subject to several criticisms. First, the judgments that have produced the classes have not always produced rates that have met rate regulatory criteria. In certain instances, the rates produced by the classification systems have not been adequate, nondiscriminatory, or nonexcessive. Second, classes have been produced in which an extremely small number of exposure units comprised a single class. Other classes have been developed which included a large number of exposures but which have had a considerable range of loss probabilities in a single class. Classes having small numbers of risks have little loss predictability; the data upon which losses are forecasted are simply too skimpy to allow the operation of the law of large numbers. The quality of loss predictability is also minimal in classes in which there is a wide range of loss probabilities; it is not possible statistically to forecast precisely when large variations exist since the probability distributions cannot be strictly measured. Third, in an attempt to make rates more equitable and to promote certain elements of price competition, a proliferation of classes occurred in certain lines of insurance. An example of class proliferation is the 260 Plan which has been used as a base plan in a number of jurisdictions for classifying private passenger auto insurance. Given all of the possible classes and permutations inherent in the 260 Plan, it is alleged that, in some territories, *no* drivers qualify for certain of the classifications.

Perhaps the most important allegation against the classification system is that it does not accomplish what is intended—the system does not discriminate properly or fairly among insureds. In such a case, the obvious implication for the underwriter is one of conservatism in accepting risks. If the classification system does not assist or assists only to a limited extent in predicting loss frequency, restraint must be exercised; otherwise, rates can be charged that are inadequate for the loss exposure.

A number of jurisdictions have proscribed the use of certain classification attributes. In his monograph on discrimination in property and liability insurance pricing, Daniel J. McNamara, President of Insurance Services Office, noted the following restrictions as of May 1984:[9]

1. Michigan legislation prohibits the use of sex and marital status as rating criteria. In addition, territorial rate differentials are restricted but not eliminated.
2. New York legislation stipulates that, "Unless supported by the reflective of actuarially sound data," classification factors based on age, sex, or marital status applicable to insurance for loss of or damage to a motor vehicle by other than collision or upset are forbidden.
3. Massachusetts prohibits the use of age, sex, and marital status as rating criteria. One exception is a special class for operators aged sixty-five or over.
4. Hawaii legislation prohibits basing any standard or rating plan, in whole or in part, directly or indirectly, upon race, creed, ethnic extraction, age, sex, length of driving experience, credit bureau rating, or marital status.
5. North Carolina legislation prohibits basing any standard or rating plan for private passenger automobiles or motorcycles in whole or in part, directly or indirectly, upon the age or sex of the persons insured.
6. Montana legislation, effective 1 October 1985, prohibits discrimination in rates solely on the basis of sex and marital status.

Sex as a rating attribute is also discussed in Chapter 12 of this text. That discussion considers the economic implications of regulations that prohibit the use of this classification attribute.

The Long Tail Problem

An important pricing problem primarily related to liability insurance is that of uncertainty in the *amount* of the loss and the *time* when the claim will be settled. For liability insurance, the traditional language has been on an "occurrence" or "accident" basis. This meant that if an incident, for example a physician's negligence during an operation, occurred on 7 July 19X0, and the claim of the injured patient was filed on 5 January 19X5, and finally settled on 1 November 19X9, that claim would be allocated to the policy year in which the incident occurred, not to the years in which the claim was filed or settled. Because of some rather recent developments in the pattern of frequency and severity of losses, insurance companies have adopted an alternative method of determining in which policy year certain types of liability losses are to be placed. This is the claims-made form which was described earlier in this text.

In 1967, Lloyd's of London changed its medical professional liability insurance policies from an "occurrence" basis to a "claims made" basis, and in 1975 some of the medical professional liability and attorney's professional liability insurance companies in the United States made the same switch. Under the claims-made basis, the claim is allocated to the year in which the claim is made, not the year in which the incident that caused the claim occurred. Using the same fact situation as in the previous paragraph, the loss under the claims-made contract would be allocated to the policy year which included 5 January 19X5, not to the policy year that included 7 July 19X0, when the incident giving rise to the claim occurred.

The insurance companies that underwrote medical professional liability insurance felt that, for several reasons, the occurrence basis contract was not manageable. First, on an occurrence basis, the premiums are based on the expected frequency and severity of future incidents that would occur during that policy year. Therefore, under this system there is a time lag between the incident that caused the claim (for example, rendering professional services) and the filing of a claim, because in most cases the alleged damages are not detected under several years after the service is performed. Indeed, in a small percentage of incidents, the filing of a claim may occur eight or ten years after the service that allegedly caused the damages is performed. This situation has been referred to as the "long tail" (of the claims frequency distribution). Although characteristic of the medical professional liability and products liability risks, the long tail problem exists, to a lesser degree, in other liability lines.

Because of the long tail, the insurance company has to project the frequency, severity, attitudes of society and juries toward negligence, and possible changes in negligence law in order to determine the premium. Additionally, the underwriter must also forecast the same variables well into the future in order to make a decision concerning acceptance of the risk. In the early 1970s in the United States, the insurance companies that were underwriting medical professional liability and products liability risks felt that in the future: (1) the frequency and severity of claims would continue to increase substantially and (2) society and juries would become more liberal (from the viewpoint of the person who suffered a loss) in their attitudes toward negligence. Because of these factors, these insurers contemplated higher premiums, and because of the uncertainty in predicting future claims, the insurers also required an additional uncertainty premium which further increased premiums. However, under an occurrence basis contract, there is still no way to ascertain the adequacy of the additional premium.

A second basic problem of the occurrence basis contract is that from the viewpoint of the insured, currently acceptable limits of liability may not be adequate when the claims are settled. The problem is that these limits may be adequate for claims filed and settled shortly after the policy year but inadequate for claims filed many years later. Thus, for these later claims, the *occurrence* or *aggregate per year* limit could possibly be exceeded if a substantial increase in the size of awards occurs between the year of coverage and the time when the claim is settled.

Hence, because of the difficulty in predicting claims that will be filed many years in the future, and the potentially inadequate limits, some insurers decided to adopt a different method of allocating claims to policy years. The *claims-made basis contract* was introduced as a replacement to the occurrence basis contract. The claims-made contract allocates the loss to the policy year when the claim was filed. From the ratemaking standpoint, the advantage is that the insurer only has to project a few months into the future rather than project many years to determine the adequate premium. So, relative to the occurrence basis contract, premiums for a claims-made basis contract are determined using much shorter projections for expected claims frequency and severity. For the insured, there is more confidence that the limits of liability purchased under a claims-made basis contract will be adequate than if the same limits were purchased under an occurrence basis contract. Starting in 1986, ISO is offering a new commercial general liability policy on a claims-made basis for all types of commercial risks. This proposal has not been received enthusiastically by insurance buyers who view it as a reduction in coverage.

The long tail in liability claims demonstrates again how distinctive the insurance contract has to be for certain liability exposures. In property insurance, losses occur and are paid relatively quickly; additionally, the amounts to be paid are seldom in question as the values are known to be within a fairly narrow range. In liability insurance, however, the liabilities (reserves) of the insurer possess two very distinguishing features. The first feature is that the liabilities are deferred; they are not to be paid until some unknown point in the future. Second, the liabilities are indefinite; the amounts to be paid out in the future are uncertain.[10] These two features are certainly present in the medical professional liability and products liability lines. Latent disease losses that represent an extreme instance of the long-tail problem are considered in Chapter 12.

Regulatory Constraints

Regulation constitutes a constraint on many insurance rate systems. There are many rules and regulations that have been promulgated by insurance departments in the various states that may restrict flexibility.

The constraints that affect the actuary are of major concern to the underwriter. Because rates may be improperly made, may be inadequate, or may reflect a political or other bias, the underwriter must take these circumstances into consideration in risk selection.

In a majority of states, rate filings with the department of insurance are required. Generally, for each line of insurance where a rate filing is required, every insurer must file (1) a manual of classifications, (2) the rates applicable thereto, (3) a description of the coverages, (4) the underwriting rules to be followed in classifying and rating risks in accordance with the classification schedules and rates, (5) the unit of exposure or premium base applicable, and (6) all rating plans for adjusting classification rates in recognition of variations in hazard for individual insureds (individual-insured rating plans).[11] In addition, for each territory that requires a rate change, necessary supporting information is usually provided, including (1) the loss experience of the insurer making the filing, (2) an interpretation of any statistical data that it relies upon, (3) the loss experience of other insurers or organizations, and (4) any other relevant factors.

In some states for some lines of insurance, a rating bureau will file for rate changes on behalf of insurance companies that are members of the bureau. On the other hand, in some states one or several insurance companies may file rate changes individually. Furthermore, in several states, insurance companies can calculate rate changes and implement them without getting approval from the state insurance department.

After the information has been submitted to the Department of Insurance, the burden is on the insurer or bureau to prove that alterations are necessary and will meet the basic regulatory criteria. Unfortunately, the regulatory criteria are not always interpreted in a consistent manner across state lines and, indeed, may be subject to fluctuation in a single jurisdiction. The difficulty of making a case for a rate increase varies with the line of insurance and, most importantly, with the publicity and attendant emotional environment surrounding the rate filing.

The organization that seeks changes in rates often finds itself in a position of attempting to defend ratemaking judgment where no statistical proof is readily obtainable. A regulator may require the submission of various sets of data. Then, after analyzing and studying the submitted data, the regulator may deny the filing on any one of many bases. As a consequence, redress to the courts may constitute the only remedy for the insurance company or bureau.

A final regulatory-associated and rate-associated constraint applicable to the underwriter deals with the residual market. Most states have passed legislation that requires insurers to provide certain insurance coverage, often at rates controlled in such a way as to cause underwriting loss. These requirements influence the insurer's composite book of business and should particularly concern underwriters.

Credibility of Loss Data

Once the actuary has obtained data for a particular period or periods, it becomes necessary to interpret the data in order to make rates for a future period. Interpretation of the data ultimately must focus on a basic issue, that is, whether or not the data as obtained represent a fair and reasonable picture of the losses in the experience period and thus can be used to forecast losses in future periods.

The actuary's interpretation of loss data must look to the data's inherent "credibility." Credibility reflects the actuary's belief in the data as a sufficiently accurate representation of reasonable past losses for the purpose of loss forecasting. High credibility implies a strong reliance on the data; low credibility implies little or no reliance on the data.

Generally speaking, the level of credibility is dependent upon the amount of available data, considerations of alternative data, and judgments based on past experience, training, and education. The degree of credibility is represented as a numerical factor which may range from the level of zero to one (or 100 percent). The zero level is frequently used when data are so limited that the actuary has no confidence in the results. Credibility of one is used only when there is a sizable amount of data and the actuary's experiences give no reason to doubt either the accuracy of the data or the relevance of the data as a predictor of future losses.

Credibility is used both within and across property and liability lines. In simple arithmetic terms, credibility alterations are based upon recent loss experience and give different weights to data from different time periods. This credibility adjustment is represented by the equation:

$$NR = (C)(A) + (1 - C)B$$

where:

NR = the new rate or the modification of the former rate
C = the credibility factor, expressed as a percentage from 0.00 to 1.00
A = the most recent experience
B = the long-term experience norm of the lines of insurance under consideration, including the actuaries' judgment, experience, and training

Use of the credibility factor, C, combines data from the latest experience period with the long-term experience. For example, reference to the equation will illustrate that when the actuary has a considerable amount of recent experience that is deemed representative of future losses, a high credibility factor may be assigned to that data. If the factor assigned is equal to 1.00, then only the data from the most recent experience period would be used to formulate a rate for the next period; the long-term normalized data would be accorded no recognition. Alternatively, if the data from the most recent period were sparse and incomplete, the credibility factor would be near zero and those data would be accorded low impact on the new rate or rate modification. The position that the data occupy between zero and full credibility determines the relative weights of recent and long-term data for the forecast of future losses. In some lines of insurance, this recent/long-term breakdown might be combined with a local/national breakdown. That is, a separate credibility factor applies to the experience from the "local" territory and its complement applies to the national loss experience.

SUMMARY

The rating process—applying rates and rating plans to given risks—is very important in underwriting.

Although little flexibility is permitted the underwriter in the actual choice of a rate, he or she has a considerable say in rating through classification, a critical procedure. In many insurance lines, risk selection is limited, and proper classification becomes the most important factor in helping the insurance company to obtain the proper premium. Conversely, improper classification can result in significant losses to the insurance company.

Pricing includes all rate-making and rating activities within the discretion of the underwriter and is the only term in the insurance world that defines both the ratemaking and the rating functions of the underwriter. Ratemaking itself is often thought to be the province of actuaries and rating that of technical personnel, but the price of the product is most definitely an underwriting consideration.

Pricing in property and liability insurance, while sharing similar goals, is full of contrasts. A major area of contrast occurs because regulatory controls for the lines differ, thus affecting the underwriter's pricing activities.

Individual rating plans are another major aspect of the rating process. These plans are designed to correct inequities that can arise from placing an insured in a given rate classification and charging that insured the average rate for the class.

There are a number of different individual rating plans: experience rating (a technique that utilizes an insured's experience over a given period of time), schedule rating (which reflects subjective underwriting factors not included in other rating plans), retrospective rating (an individual rating system that utilizes the loss experience of an insured for a given period of time to determine the premium for *that* period of time), expense modification (an approach that allows an underwriter to modify premiums to reflect differentials in expenses), and participating plans (adjusting premiums by the use of a dividend). There is also composite rating (a rating plan which calculates premiums for several lines using a single exposure base).

Several ratemaking and pricing problems have an impact on underwriting. Among these problems are the difficulty of obtaining data, receiving data which is of questionable quality, inflation, improper classification systems, the long tail problem, and regulatory constraints.

Chapter Notes

1. Robert B. Holtom, *Underwriting* (Cincinnati: The National Underwriter, 1973), p. 167.
2. Holtom, p. 168.
3. Jeffrey T. Lange, "General Liability Insurance Ratemaking," in *Insurance Insights* (Cincinnati: South-Western Publishing Co., 1974), pp. 454-455.
4. C. A. Kulp and John W. Hall, *Casualty Insurance*, 4th ed. (New York: The Ronald Press, 1968), p. 926.
5. C. Arthur Williams and Richard M. Heins, *Risk Management and Insurance*, 3rd ed. (New York: McGraw-Hill, 1976), p. 498.
6. Bernard L. Webb, J. J. Launie, Willis Park Rokes, and Norman A. Baglini, *Insurance Company Operations*, 3rd ed., Vol. II (Malvern, PA: American Institute for Property and Liability Underwriters, 1984), pp. 150-151.
7. Webb, Launie, Rokes, and Baglini, p. 150.
8. That is, if the average change from year 1 to year 10 is equal to 3.57 percent, the use of a linear model will use that factor (3.57 percent) to forecast losses for years 12 and 13. In fact, however, there may have been elements operating during years 7-10 which would tend to understate linear forecasts for years 12 and 13. Such elements can be reflected properly through use of a nonlinear model.
9. Daniel J. McNamara, "Discrimination in Property-Liability Insurance Pricing," in John D. Long and Everett D. Randall, eds., *Issues in Insurance*, 3rd ed., Vol. I (Malvern, PA: American Institute for Property and Liability Underwriters, 1984), pp. 39-40.
10. Kulp and Hall, p. 999.
11. Generally, insurers issuing participating contracts are not required to file dividend schedules for regulatory approval, although dividend practices may be reviewed by insurance examiners at the home office.

CHAPTER 9

Analysis of Underwriting Information/Financial Analysis

Information is vital to underwriters. Without accurate and reasonably low-cost information, it is impossible for underwriters to make prompt and sound decisions. This chapter will analyze the usefulness of underwriting information generally and provide an in-depth study of financial analysis.

INFORMATION NEEDS

An underwriter must have an organized procedure to determine the type and amount of information required to make a particular decision. Without an organized plan, the underwriter may overlook the need for vital information or rely on irrelevant information. In either case, inefficiency results. There are three basic steps that should be taken when determining information needs. These steps are:

1. identify the crucial risk characteristics or hazards
2. determine how the risk characteristics can be measured
3. acquire only the information necessary to measure (evaluate) the risk characteristics[1]

Underwriting decisions in some lines of insurance (especially personal lines) must be made with only the information provided on the application and producer's report. The low unit price precludes the collection of substantial amounts of information for economic reasons. Moreover, the homogeneity or similarity of most personal lines and small commercial risks makes it possible to include almost all crucial information on one document—the application. Notwithstanding the comprehensiveness of the application, it is essential that underwriters who discover a questionable item (such as a swimming pool that may not be fenced in) complete the three steps before making the final decision.

Chapter 2 introduced the concept of *information efficiency*. This term means that before allocating time and money to the development of additional information, the underwriter should consider how much of an improvement in the decision the new information is likely to make possible. Gathering and analyzing information costs money and takes time. The desire for additional information may conflict with the need to make decisions promptly and keep backlogs to a minimum.

To aid in developing information efficiency, the underwriter should classify all information into the following categories:

1. *essential information*—information that is *absolutely necessary* to arrive at a decision
2. *desirable information*—information that is not absolutely necessary, but would be *helpful* in evaluating the risk if it can be obtained at an acceptable cost and without undue delay
3. *available information*—information that may or may not be helpful and not worth any special effort to obtain

Examples of essential information are the names and driving records of all drivers on a submission for private passenger auto insurance. Underwriting manuals of insurers generally state what is essential information on each risk.

Judgment is necessary in determining what is desirable information because of the time and costs involved. For example, a replacement cost evaluation may be desirable in a commercial property submission if there is some concern about the amount of insurance requested. An engineering report is another desirable piece of information for many commercial risks.

As the words imply, available information is simply "available" and may not assist the underwriter at all in the evaluation of the risk. This information must be sorted to separate the *useful* data from the *useless* data.

Each commercial account may be thought of as a "cluster" of various types of loss exposures (property and liability), and the magnitude or seriousness of the exposure varies from risk to risk. Thus, certain items of information are crucial to one risk but less important to another. The factors that determine this are the type of business, loss history by line, present operations, plans for future operations, and many others. When underwriting these large commercial accounts, the steps in analyzing information needs are the starting points in effective decision making.

Identification of Crucial Risk Characteristics or Hazards

The underwriter has three possible decisions for all applications: (1) accept the application as submitted, (2) accept the application with modification, or (3) decline the application. The ultimate outcome, that is, the decision, will be based primarily on the risk characteristics. Crucial risk characteristics or hazards are those aspects and elements of a risk that can be directly related to potential losses. These are the factors underwriters must evaluate before they can properly analyze a risk.

There is a multitude of different risk characteristics for each line of insurance. For example, in private passenger auto insurance lines, the following factors can be directly related to the frequency and/or severity of losses: (1) the age of all drivers, (2) the type of car, (3) driving experience of all drivers (number of years), (4) the principal operator, (5) miles driven per year, (6) purpose of vehicle use, (7) distance to work, (8) where the car is located, (9) accidents and violations, and many other factors. None of these factors would be considered crucial in fire insurance since entirely different underwriting factors exist which have a bearing on potential fire losses. These factors generally include (1) the construction of the building, (2) the occupancy and use of the building, (3) the existence and quality of fire protection, and (4) the exposure of the structure to other buildings or to hazards that could cause a loss.

Determination of Possible Measurements

Information must be collected in order to measure or evaluate risk characteristics. To obtain the appropriate information, there must be an organized methodology dealing with how these factors might be capable of being measured. The measurement techniques vary significantly from one type of insurance to another. Some hazards are more objectively measured than others, depending upon the strength of the relationship between the existence of hazards and their resulting losses. In addition to the amount and credibility of loss experience, there is a significant difference between measuring hazards on a private passenger auto application and an application for products liability insurance on a new type of product. In the first case, the relative seriousness of hazards associated with frequency and severity of loss has been clearly identified and measured through many years of accident records. In the second case, the hazards have not been clearly identified because there has been no prior loss experience from this unique risk. Some original research by the underwriter is necessary to determine how these factors can be measured.

Despite these line-by-line differences, two elements are always useful when measuring crucial risk characteristics. These elements are:

1. insurance company guidelines
2. the judgment of the underwriter

For example, the private passenger auto underwriter can obtain the age of the applicant from the application. The underwriter must then decide on the significance of this set of data. The crucial question is: How much more or less of a hazard is an applicant who is twenty-five years old compared to one who is sixteen or sixty-five years old? Sometimes the significance of the driver's age is specified in strict underwriting guidelines established by the insurer. For example, an insurance company may consider the age of a driver to be a more significant factor until age twenty-five, with the significance decreasing substantially thereafter. In this situation, the crucial risk characteristics are measured to some degree by reference to the insurance company guidelines.

In other situations, the hazards are not so easily measured. For example, in all lines of insurance, the attitude of the applicant toward loss control is considered critical. However, this is a very difficult factor to measure. The underwriter must rely on the loss control department, training, education, experience, and personal judgment to measure this factor. In some cases, correspondence with the insured and an evaluation of existing loss control efforts may add objectivity to this measurement process. If the underwriter inaccurately measures the loss control attitude factor, a poor decision may result. This poor decision may end in a loss of profits to the insurer through rejection of a high-quality risk or acceptance of a low-quality risk.

Acquisition of the Necessary Information

Once the underwriter has identified the crucial risk characteristics and develops a plan to measure these factors, a sufficient amount of information must be gathered to measure them.

There are many ways in which information can be secured. Some of the most often used methods of obtaining information were previously introduced in Chapter 2. These methods will not be discussed again in this section, but they include:

1. analyzing the questions and omissions on the application,
2. evaluating reports (such as financial reports, MVRs, and so on),
3. inspecting the premises or analyzing an inspection report,
4. reviewing the underwriting and claim files,
5. asking questions of the applicant or producer, and

6. consulting underwriting manuals.

Once the information has been gathered, the decision-making process can begin.

DATA REQUIREMENTS: PERSONAL LINES VERSUS COMMERCIAL LINES

The underwriter utilizes data in different ways, depending on the specific risk being analyzed. For example, the data required for personal lines underwriting are quite different from those required in underwriting commercial lines.

The personal lines underwriter uses data that are appropriate to that type of risk. Much of the data are highly qualitative and are generally obtained through inspection reports and consumer investigation. Underwriters of both personal and commercial lines can avail themselves of several types of reports, including those specifically directed toward:

1. the physical characteristics of the insured property (physical inspection reports),
2. moral and morale characteristics of the insured (moral reports),
3. rating factors (rating reports), and
4. financial reports regarding the financial strength and managerial expertise of the insured.

Physical Inspection Reports

Physical inspection reports vary greatly between personal and commercial lines insureds. Underwriters require a greater amount of detailed information on physical characteristics when underwriting a commercial risk than is required in personal lines underwriting. For example, when homeowners policy is written on a dwelling, the underwriter may require some knowledge of the construction, maintenance, and external protection (fire hydrants) of the property. Perhaps a physical inspection report will be required; however, in many cases, a photograph and a producer's report will be sufficient. In commercial property underwriting, however, the individuality of each risk requires more detailed information on the existence and seriousness of physical hazards such as occupancy, internal protection, loss control programs and devices, and other factors.

Physical inspection reports are useful only to the extent that the physical attributes of the risk are identified and evaluated.

Moral Reports

Moral reports were at one time used fairly extensively in personal and commercial lines of insurance. These reports provided the underwriter with data on the reputation, habits, ethics, and morals of prospective insureds. The information was obtained from interviews with persons who lived close to the applicant or who knew the applicant. The type of information derived included characteristics such as reputation, stability, associates, use of drugs and alcohol, and housekeeping.

Because of the subjectiveness of the information, many insurers stopped using these reports. In addition, states began to enact legislation that prohibited the use of many of the factors or characteristics as a reason for rejecting a risk. Finally, the possibility of unfair discrimination and invasion of privacy suits made many insurers hesitant to use the information even if they were legally allowed to do so.

Rating Reports

Rating reports generally are used to develop or confirm data for classification purposes. Rating is, in most cases, a simpler process than hazard analysis. Usually, the underwriter has a list of the qualifications the applicant must possess in order to be placed in a particular classification. Therefore, the underwriter knows what and how much information should be secured.

A typical use of a rating report is in the field of private passenger auto liability insurance. The classification into which an insured is placed depends heavily on certain factors, such as (1) age, (2) driving record, (3) driving distance, (4) use of auto, and (5) geographical location. While each of these factors may be given in the application, the rating report is used for confirmation purposes.

Financial Reports

Financial reports provide information on the financial strength of the insured. In personal lines underwriting, this information is rarely sought. In commercial lines underwriting, however, the financial report may be the single most important variable in the underwriting process. Financial reports can be an indicator of the insured's attitude toward encouraging or allowing losses to occur. In addition, financial reports will enable the underwriter to determine the ability of the insured to comply with loss control recommendations and to sustain the business during downturns in the economy or adverse business cycles. Most financial reports are based on accounting data. Accounting principles provide the framework for the recordkeeping of businesses. The analysis of these accounting records is the province of the field of finance. Thus when reference is made to accounting data, the reference is primarily to the business records and when reference is made to the presentation of these records for analysis, the reference is to financial report analysis. This distinction between accounting and finance is important since the words or terms are often used in a very similar context.

EVALUATION OF INFORMATION

The underwriter can normally secure a greater amount of information concerning an applicant than can possibly be used while staying within time and budget constraints (that is, "available information"). Often, the underwriter is inundated with information from many different sources and must be selective so that only the best information is used. On occasion, conflicting information may be received. For example, the applicant for auto insurance may claim that there have been no citations within the last three years. However, information received from the State Department of Motor Vehicles may show that the applicant has had two citations.

The need to be selective and to resolve conflicting information makes it necessary to develop some bases by which information can be evaluated. Two criteria that can be used when evaluating information are (1) the usefulness of the information and (2) the cost of obtaining the information. Utility analysis is used to determine the usefulness of the information, and cost-benefit analysis is used to determine whether the benefit potential from the information justifies the cost of obtaining that information.

Utility Analysis

Several standards can be applied to any piece of information to determine its relative usefulness. The application of these standards is known as utility analysis. Five specific standards that can be used to determine the usefulness of information are:[2]

1. accuracy
2. relevancy
3. timeliness
4. completeness
5. understandability

Accuracy In the previously described example of conflicting information concerning a motor vehicle report, it is clear that at least one of the two sources supplied inaccurate information. Obviously, the accurate information is more valuable. The problem for the underwriter is to determine which version is, in fact, accurate. In some cases, if the conflicting facts seem reasonable, it may be difficult to determine which are accurate. However, as previously discussed in Chapter 2, experience will often enable the underwriter to get "a feel" for accuracy. By knowing the reliability of the source of the information and the situation in which the evidence was gathered, the experienced underwriter can often deduce accuracy of information.

Facts may be inaccurately reported for several reasons. For example, there may be a simple typographical error, or the reporting source may have processed the data inefficiently. Incompetence in reporting the facts may also be a factor. Regardless of what causes inaccuracy, the impact is the same and the underwriter therefore must resolve the discrepancies. Information is as reliable as its sources. The degree of reliance an underwriter can place on the accuracy of information depends directly on the reliability of the source. Information that comes from an unreliable source must, of necessity, be viewed with suspicion and carefully verified.

Many factors determine how much an underwriter can trust sources of information. Previous experience with the various sources is one important factor. For example, an underwriter is more likely to rely on a source that has been reliable in the past than on one that frequently has been inaccurate. A well-known source is more reliable to an underwriter than a new, unknown source, other things being equal. In judging the reliability of a source, the underwriter must consider previously demonstrated competence and motivating factors that might cause the source to report biased or even inaccurate information. In the previously described example of the conflicting information concerning a motor vehicle report, the underwriter would probably rely more on the Department of Motor Vehicle's report than on the information contained in the application, because the Department would have no motivation to report false information, whereas the applicant might feel that supplying truthful information could lead to a declination.

Relevancy Information that is accurate is useless if it is not also relevant. The use of irrelevant information increases the cost of information and the time necessary to make a decision, and may possibly confuse the underwriter and lead to an unwise or unsound decision. The underwriter should make every effort to assure that irrelevant information is not collected or used in the decision-making process. This is best achieved by continually analyzing the precise decisions that must be made and requesting only the *essential* information needed to make those decisions. For example, the commercial auto underwriter who is trying to decide the proper classification of a risk does not need to know the age or the construction of the applicant's garage.

Timeliness Accurate information that is relevant is still less useful if it is not received in time to aid in decision making. Underwriters are under considerable time pressure. The applicant and producer usually want a prompt response from the insurance company. Frequently coverage is bound even before the underwriter receives the application. In this situation, there is a need to make an early decision in order to avoid lengthy coverage of a risk that does not meet the insurer's basic requirements.

In some states, laws make certain types of insurance noncancelable by the insurance company after a "discovery period" has elapsed. Typically, this discovery period is forty-five to sixty days after the effective date. Any information received by the underwriter after this period may be useless for the initial decision. In addition, it would be a waste of money to order information that could not possibly be received in time to aid in the decision. Therefore, timeliness is an important standard to consider when evaluating the utility of information.

Completeness Sources that supply incomplete information are of questionable use. For example, a producer's report that does not answer all the questions is obviously less useful than a report upon which all questions have been properly answered. The underwriter should insist that all missing information be completed if at all possible, and suspicion should be aroused if a question is avoided. In fact, certain omitted data should be utilized as a possible barometer of potential problems. For example, an application for products liability that omits information regarding "batch control" (a quality control program where batches are recorded and can be traced and recalled) should cause the underwriter to contact the producer for this information. The omission of this information may indicate that a batch control program is nonexistent or does not meet acceptable standards. Likewise, when underwriting accounts receivable insurance, the failure to provide specific information concerning the type of safe or fireproof file cabinet is crucial not only to rating but also to acceptability.

Incomplete information may be misleading. Without proper explanations and recommendations, the underwriter may make incorrect assumptions and therefore make an unwise decision.

Understandability To make full use of information, the underwriter should understand the nature, limitations, and meaning of the information, and the conditions under which the facts were gathered.

There should be an understanding of what the information implies and what it does not imply. For example, in order to get full use of accounting data, the underwriter should have a basic understanding of the accounting principles and procedures followed in obtaining these data. It will be demonstrated subsequently in this chapter how a lack of understanding of accounting principles can cause the underwriter, using this form of data as a basis, to come to an unsound decision.

Utility Analysis Summary In summary, there are five basic standards by which the usefulness of information can be determined. The most useful information will be accurate, relevant, timely, complete, and understandable. No one characteristic is always more important than the others, and the most useful information should meet all the standards. For example, a computer data run that is accurate, relevant, timely, and complete is almost useless if the underwriter does not understand the information. It is likely that the information will be disregarded altogether. Likewise, information that meets all the other standards but which is not relevant is also useless.

Utility analysis is a vital process by which underwriters determine the usefulness of information. This process is important because of the overabundance of information available and because, at times, pieces of information conflict with one another.

Cost-Benefit Analysis

The cost of information is a very real and important factor that must be considered when evaluating information. Most insurance companies establish budgets and guidelines which limit the amounts that should be spent to secure information. Because of the need to remain competitive, insurers expect their underwriters to operate within these limits and to establish procedures to justify any exceptions to these limits. For these reasons, underwriters must always consider the question of whether the benefits emanating from the information justify the cost. Of course, methods and techniques should be employed on a continuous basis to keep information-associated expenses to a minimum.

The question of the exact cost limit that should be imposed for information gathering is very complex and probably is not subject to generalization. It is clear that sufficient funds should be expended in order to optimize decisions. However, it is the responsibility of the individual underwriter and of the underwriting department to continually seek out alternative methods of obtaining information *and* alternative pieces of underwriting information. Decisions among the alternatives should take cost into account.

Often, there is little correlation between the cost of information and the usefulness of that information. For example, an inspection report is much more expensive than a report or file from a previous underwriter, which is furnished at no charge. Also, the information contained in the previous underwriter's report may be much more valuable than the information in the inspection report.

Two practices should be followed as a method of keeping costs to a minimum. First, underwriters should know exactly what information is needed, and when, so that they will not request irrelevant material. Underwriters should also know when enough information has been received so that they will not order unnecessary data.

The second practice underwriters should follow to reduce the cost of information is to consider all the possible sources for the same information and to use the least expensive source possible, assuming equal quality. A previous underwriter's report, for example, is obtained at almost no cost; yet it may be of significant quality.

FINANCIAL DATA
AS AN UNDERWRITING VARIABLE

Financial data is an important source of information for the underwriter in determining the desirability of a risk. Financial analysis involves the comparison, interpretation, and evaluation of this particular form of data. Major sources of financial data are the financial statements of business firms, and consumer investigation reports on individuals. Through the use of financial and credit analysis, the experienced underwriter can use various types of data as indicators of important factors considered in the underwriting decision.

Indicator of Potential Moral and Morale Hazard

Moral hazard is a subjective characteristic of the insured that tends to increase the probable frequency or severity of an insured loss. It is generally believed that moral hazard arises from a combination of ethical weakness, financial difficulty, and undesirable associates. Often, financial statements are the sole sources of information available in detecting financial difficulty and providing an indication of possible moral hazard. This factor in itself makes financial records a vital source of underwriting information.

There are three financial situations that should alert the underwriter to possible moral hazard. *The first situation exists when the firm experiences a liquidity problem, which is defined as insufficient cash to meet present obligations.* Liquidity problems can occur in an otherwise strong and growing firm. If attempts to borrow cash or convert assets into cash fail, the firm may be tempted to intentionally create an insured loss as a means to obtain the much-needed cash.

Another financial situation that should alert the underwriter to possible moral hazard is *lack of profitability*. If a firm continually fails to make a profit, it will not be able to remain in business over the long run. In this situation, there may be an advantage to the owners of such a firm to destroy the entire business by some insured peril rather than to continue operating. No premium is adequate if an underwriter suspects that the owners are likely to cause a loss to their own property.

The third basic financial situation that may indicate possible moral hazard is an *unused or overvalued asset*. This situation is often difficult to detect; however, careful financial analysis may alert the underwriter to such a condition. For example, if part of a firm's inventory is obsolete, it is not useful to the firm and "ties up" funds that could be used more profitably. However, it may still be on the accounting records at "cost," which implies that its value is overstated. Under these circumstances, it may be advantageous for the owners to intentionally destroy this overvalued inventory or allow it to be destroyed or damaged by an insured peril, and then file an insurance claim for the loss. Another example of this type of situation is a firm that owns an unused building which has been or will be condemned by building safety authorities. Instead of paying a demolishing company to raze the building, the owners may arrange to have the building destroyed and then collect from the insurer.

Morale hazard is an attitude problem closely related to the moral hazard. Essentially morale hazard is the absence of a desire to safeguard assets because of the presence of insurance. In the example of the unused building, the insured may not actually destroy the building but may choose to do little to prevent a fire or to stop a fire from spreading once it has started.

Indicator of Ability to Pay Premiums

Financial records are the best source of information to determine if an insured will be able to pay premiums. Often it may appear at first glance that a firm does not have a liquidity problem (insufficient cash to meet present obligations) when, in fact, a severe problem exists. The underwriter must analyze the financial statements, using the techniques described later in this chapter to elicit this information. If an insured may be unable to meet premium payments, the underwriter may require advance payment in cases when advance payment would not otherwise be required. Likewise, the producer or the accounts department may be alerted to the situation so that the insured will not be allowed to fall behind in premium payments.

Determining whether an insured will be able to pay premiums may also save needless expense for the insurer. The underwriting process costs time and money in determining if a risk is insurable and in establishing a proper rate for the risk. If the insured is unable to pay the premium, the time and money are wasted. If large underwriting expenses are involved, the underwriter should try to determine not only if the risk will be able to pay the current premium but also if it will be able to afford future premiums (including additional premiums developed by audits) that are projected to increase due to rate changes and/or growth in the insured's business. In such a situation, the underwriter should be concerned with the profitability of the firm as well as its liquidity position.

The ability to pay premiums may even affect the type of rating plan used. Under a retrospective rating plan, the final adjusted premium may not be determined until two or three years after the expiration of coverage (this delay comes about through adjustments in loss reserves caused by settling claims after the expiration of the policy or retro plan). Thus, an insured who is in financial difficulty may be unable to pay a substantial additional retro premium, and the insurer must absorb this additional cost. In this situation, an underwriter may choose to write the risk only on a guaranteed cost (non-retro) basis solely because of the financial condition of the insured.

Indicator of Financial Strength and Sound Management

Financial records are the best source of information for the underwriter to get an indication of the financial strengths or weaknesses of a firm.

Financial analysis also can indicate to the underwriter the quality of a firm's management. The analysis can demonstrate how well major management decisions have fared compared to management decisions in other firms. The underwriter can also determine by financial analysis how efficiently the business is being run. A firm that is not managed well is generally a poorer risk than a firm that *is* managed well.

The establishment of deductibles can also be facilitated by examining the financial strength of a risk. Setting the deductible amount at such a high level that the insured would not be able to cover the amount is clearly improper. On the other hand, a financially strong firm should not pay for insurance that is not needed. Such a firm may enjoy substantial cost savings by being self-insured to a greater extent through higher deductible levels.

Indicator of Potential Growth and Possible Future Desirability from an Underwriting Standpoint

The underwriter should be interested in whether a firm is growing or deteriorating. A firm that is currently in fair financial condition may be in severe financial trouble in future years. Such a firm may not be a moral hazard during the year in which it requested insurance coverage. However, if the firm is deteriorating, decay may occur to a point at which moral hazard arises. What is important is the degree to which the financial condition of the firm will affect moral and morale hazard. A firm that has liquidity problems may defer necessary maintenance, cut down on safety efforts, and allow poor housekeeping to occur.

These physical hazards are directly related to losses and often are the results of a deteriorating financial position. Maintenance of equipment, employee safety programs, security measures, and other factors involve costs to the firm. When financial difficulties arise, these risk improvement programs may be eliminated, thus increasing hazards.

The underwriter who fails to consider the *growth* of a firm may reject applications that should not be turned down. For example, consider a relatively small, but rapidly growing company. The firm's cash position may not be as good as another company's, but it may have greater profit potential. Also, a rapidly growing company generally is less of a potential moral hazard than a declining one. The financial records are often the only source of data available to underwriters in their search for indicators of the potential growth or decline of a firm. This is another example of why financial records are vital sources of information.

FINANCIAL STATEMENTS

The Use of Financial Statements

Four basic financial statements usually are available to the underwriter: (1) the balance sheet, (2) income statement, (3) the statement of sources and uses of funds, and (4) the statement of retained earnings. An example and detailed description of the balance sheet and the income statement is presented later in this section. The other two financial statements are more infrequently used in underwriting. For a description of them, see any basic finance text.[3]

The Balance Sheet

The balance sheet, often called the statement of financial position, shows what is "owned" and "owed" by a firm as of a given time. The statement is composed of three basic classifications: assets, liabilities, and owners' equity (or stockholders' equity) in the well-known equation:

Assets = Liabilities + Owners' Equity (or stockholders' equity)

Assets are the properties and property rights owned by the business. These items are arranged on the balance sheet in descending order by their degree of liquidity. *Liabilities are the creditors' interests in the assets or, put more simply, what is owed by the firm.* These liabilities are arranged in order of when they become due. Owners' equity (or stockholders' equity in a corporation) is also referred to as *net worth. Owners' equity is the value of the interest of the owners in the assets of the firm.* In essence, it is the difference between the total assets and total liabilities of the firm.

The assets listed on the balance sheet are on the left-hand side of the page, and the liabilities and stockholders' equity are on the right-hand side. This format is called the *accounting form.* Often the liabilities and stockholders' equity sections are listed below the asset section in what is known as the *report form.* Both forms are widely used, and each has its own advantages. The accounting form aids the reader when comparing assets and liabilities, whereas the report form is easier to prepare.

Any analysis of the balance sheet items should take one inherent limitation of the statement into account. Because the statement of financial position contained in the balance sheet represents only one moment in the life of a firm, it can be deceiving. For example, seasonal fluctuations may be misleading. Also, the position of a firm at one point in time may be enhanced to some extent by management manipulation of the accounts.

For example, it is possible to "improve" a firm's current ratio (current assets/current liabilities) through repaying short-term debt just prior to the date of the statement. The current ratio is increased by the repayment of short-term debt. If a firm has (prior to repayment) current assets of $100,000 and current liabilities of $75,000, its current ratio is 1.33. If the firm has $10,000 in cash available for repayment and actually does repay $10,000 of its debt, its current ratio is increased to 1.39 (calculated: $90,000/$65,000). Though such practices (often termed "window dressing") are legal, they can be very deceiving, and many consider the techniques unethical. The underwriter should always be aware of these inherent limitations.

The financial position of ABC Company, as illustrated by the balance sheet in Exhibit 9-1, can be compared between two points in time. This analysis is accomplished through what is called a *comparative balance sheet*. A comparative balance sheet is more valuable to an analyst than a single balance sheet because of the ability to look at the firm's position at two points in time and compare the sets of data.

Comparative financial statements are created by placing two balance sheets or income statements from two different time periods side by side. Analysis of the changes from one to the other show whether the firm is gaining or losing financial strength.

Assets Assets usually are divided into two major classifications: current assets and fixed assets. *Current assets* include cash and other assets that are expected to be converted into cash or used in the operation of the business within the *normal operating cycle* of the firm. The normal operating cycle is the average time between the acquisition of an asset and the conversion of that asset into cash. For simplicity, an asset is often considered to be current if it is expected to be converted into cash within one year. Current assets are usually listed in the order of their liquidity and commonly consist of the following items:

1. cash
2. marketable securities
3. receivables (notes and accounts)
4. inventories
5. prepaid expenses

Cash is always listed first and includes coins, currency, checks, bank drafts, money orders, and demand deposits in commercial banks. If cash is held for some designated purpose such as that held in a fund for the eventual retirement of a bond issue, it is not included as a cash item but is placed in an account designated for the specific purpose.

Marketable securities are temporary investments that can easily be converted into cash. Usually a firm will invest in marketable securities when there are excess funds not immediately needed in operations. Marketable securities normally consist of short-term notes such as U.S. Treasury notes.

Receivables consist of the amounts owed to the firm by customers and other outsiders. Receivables are often subdivided into notes receivable and accounts receivable.

Inventories consist of goods available for sale to customers. For a manufacturing firm, the inventory item is enlarged to include two other

Exhibit 9-1
ABC Company
Comparative Balance Sheet (Thousands of dollars)

Assets	Dec. 31, 19X4	Dec. 31, 19X5
Current Assets		
Cash	$ 50	$ 40
Marketable Securities	142	90
Prepaid Expenses	8	10
Receivables (net)	200	215
Inventories	350	300
Total Current Assets	$ 750	$ 655
Fixed Assets		
Gross Plant and Equipment	$2,000	$2,500
Less Depreciation	400	650
Net Plant and Equipment	1,600	1,850
Total Assets	$2,350	$2,505

Liabilities and Stockholders' Equity	Dec. 31, 19X4	Dec. 31, 19X5
Current Liabilities		
Accounts Payable	$ 65	$ 80
Notes Payable	100	120
Accruals	10	12
Provision for Federal Income Taxes	130	135
Total Current Liabilities	$ 305	$ 347
Long-Term Liabilities		
Mortgage Payable	$ 650	$ 625
Total Liabilities	955	972
Stockholders' Equity		
Capital Stock (100,000 shares)	1,000	1,000
Retained Earnings	395	533
Total Stockholders' Equity	1,395	1,533
Total Liabilities and Stockholders' Equity	$2,350	$2,505

types of inventories: raw materials, and products that are in the process of being completed.

Prepaid expenses represent the amount that has already been paid for services that have not been received or used. A common example of a prepaid item is *prepaid insurance*. The ABC Company, on November 1, 19X5, paid $12,000 for an annual policy (or an annual installment on a three-year policy), and "expensed" only $2,000 by December 31, 19X5 ($1,000 for each month of coverage). The remaining $10,000 is classified as prepaid insurance.

The other major asset classification on the ABC Company's balance sheet is *fixed assets*. These are the assets that are not expected to be sold and converted into cash. Examples of fixed assets are land, buildings, and equipment. Land is carried "on the books" at its original cost and is never depreciated because it will never be worn out or become obsolete. Buildings, machinery, and equipment, however, are valued at their original cost less an amount for *accumulated depreciation*. Instead of charging the entire cost of such an asset to any one year as expense, the cost is spread over the years on some basis via the use of depreciation charges. The total amount that has been expensed up to the financial statement date is known as *accumulated depreciation*. It should be noted that the financial statements reflect "accounting" depreciation rather than "physical" depreciation. Accumulated *physical* depreciation is considered in determining the actual cash value of the asset for insurance purposes. The "accounting" depreciation has no relationship to "physical" depreciation.

There are three other major classifications of assets that might be found in balance sheets. One other such classification is *investments*. The investments of a firm are listed between the current assets and fixed assets. These are the investments that are held for an *indefinite* period of time or for some designated purpose (marketable securities are temporary investments). Investment in the stocks and bonds of another company, real estate held for income-producing purposes, and investments held for a special fund such as a pension fund are all items that would be classified as "investment."

Intangible assets is another major asset classification often found in balance sheets. These are assets that lack physical substance but have a real value to the firm. The more common examples of intangible assets are patents, copyrights, franchises, and goodwill. Goodwill normally is reported only when a firm is purchased. In essence, it is the excess of the price paid for the business over the book value or agreed value of all *tangible* net assets purchased.

The last major classification of assets is known as *other assets*. These are simply those assets that cannot be otherwise classified. Items commonly found in this category are the cash surrender value of life insurance owned by the firm on its officers, receivables from officers, and miscellaneous funds held for special purposes.

Liabilities Liabilities of the firm generally are found on the right-hand side of the statement and are divided into two major classifications—current liabilities and long-term liabilities.

Current liabilities are those obligations whose payment is reasonably expected to require the use of cash or the creation of other current liabilities during the ordinary operating cycle of the business. All liabilities to be paid within one year are classified as current. Current liabilities are usually listed in the probable order in which they will become due.

Examples of current liabilities include accounts payable, notes payable, the estimated amount for income taxes, and accruals. Accruals are those obligations that are owed because of the passage of time, but that will be paid in the future. A common example of an accrual is accrued wages payable. Assume that the ABC Company, on December 31, 19X6, owes its employees $10,000 for wages already earned but not payable until the following week. This $10,000 must be set up as a current liability because it is an obligation of the firm.

Long-term liabilities are obligations not due for more than a year from the balance sheet date. Notes, bonds, and mortgages are often listed under this heading.

Owners' Equity The owners' equity, or net worth, represents the difference between the total assets and total liabilities as of the date of the balance sheet. It represents the value of the interest of the owners in the business. The owners' equity is reported differently for the different forms of business organization. The three common forms of business organizations are: (1) corporations, (2) proprietorships, and (3) partnerships.

The ABC Company used in the examples is a corporation. Because the stockholders own the corporation, the net worth of ABC Company is referred to as *stockholders' equity*. Two items—capital stock and retained earnings—usually make up the stockholders' equity section.

Capital stock is the amount of funds that have been contributed by the stockholders through the purchase of stock. Assume that the ABC Company sold 100,000 shares of stock with a par value of $10 per share. This would account for the $1,000,000 capital stock figure. Frequently, stock will sell for more than par value. In a situation such as this, any excess over par value is reported as *additional contributed capital*. If the stock of ABC Company (having a par value of $10) sold for $12, it would report capital stock as being $1,000,000 and additional contributed capital as being $200,000 (computed: [$12−$10] × 100,000).

Retained earnings are a part of the total stockholders' equity that represent the accumulated *undistributed* earnings of the corporation. That is, this item represents the total profits of the firm less total dividends paid and losses sustained from the date of organization.

A proprietorship reports the owners' equity in a slightly different manner. The statement simply reports the firm's net worth as capital of the owner. A partnership reports owners' equity in a similar manner. The only difference is that the capital for each partner is disclosed to arrive at the total partners' equity.

Once familiar with the format and various classifications of the balance sheet, the underwriter may begin to interpret the data and develop answers to a number of underwriting questions. There are various tools available to the underwriter to facilitate analysis of the balance sheet. For example, the raw data in the statements may be converted to indexes with a base year when comparing two or more years (trend analysis), or common-size statements can be developed. These tools are explained and analyzed in a subsequent section of this chapter.

The Income Statement

The income statement, also known as the profit and loss statement, summarizes the results obtained from business operations over a period of time (usually one year). This is in contrast to the balance sheet, which represents the financial position of a firm at one particular time.

The income statement details the revenue and the various types of expenses incurred during the year. The excess of total revenue over total expenditures during this period constitutes the profits to the firm. If expenses exceed revenue, a loss is incurred.

The underwriter must understand and appreciate the relationship between the income statement and the balance sheet. If a net profit is realized during a year, the net worth of the firm has been increased by the amount of the profit (assuming no dividends). This increase in net worth is shown on the balance sheet as an increase to the owners' equity (retained earnings specifically). Conversely, if the firm experiences a net loss during the year, the owners' equity in the firm has decreased.

Because the income statement normally summarizes the operation of a firm over one year, care should be exercised by the underwriter when analyzing this statement if one year does not properly reflect the full operating cycle of the business. When such a situation exists, the income statement may be misleading because revenues and expenses are not properly matched. The matching of revenues and expenses is a basic accounting principle. In essence, this principle requires that the earned revenue of a period should be related to the actual expense incurred in realizing that revenue.

The income statement has, as its entry item, net sales. *Net sales* represents the gross sales of the period less all returns and allowances. It does not include any sales tax revenue.

The *cost of goods sold* is the second item found on the income statement. This item represents the cost to the ABC Company of merchandise sold during the year. Cost of goods sold is developed from the inventory at the beginning of the period adjusted for all purchases made during the period, less those goods on hand at the end of the period. When the cost of goods sold is subtracted from net sales, the resulting figure is the *gross margin on sales*, often known as the *gross profit.*

Operating expenses are then subtracted from gross profit. Operating expenses generally are reported in two categories: (1) selling expenses and (2) general and administrative expenses. Selling expenses include those items that can be related directly to the sales of the goods. Examples of sales expenses include such accounts as sales commissions, advertising displays, delivery expenses, and depreciation on store furniture and equipment. General and administrative expenses are those expenses that cannot be related directly to the selling of the goods, but which are necessary in the operation of the business. Examples include officers' and clerical salaries, office supplies used, postage, telephone, business licenses and fees, and depreciation of office furniture and fixtures. After operating expenses are deducted from the gross margin on sales, the *operating income* for the year is derived. This is the income that resulted from the normal operations of the firm during the time period covered by the statement.

Other revenue and expense items are listed below the operating income figure. These items are miscellaneous, usually nonrecurring, and unrelated to the primary operations of the firm. For example, if the firm earns revenue in the form of interest and dividends, or from rentals, royalties, and service fees, it would be reported as other revenue. These items are then added (revenues) or subtracted (expenses) from operating income to determine the *net income before taxes.* After taxes have been deducted, the resulting figure is the *net income (or loss) after taxes.* It is important that the underwriter be certain in which manner "net income" is being used—before or after taxes.

The final item on most income statements is *earnings per share* (EPS). In a simple capital structure, EPS is calculated by dividing income after taxes by the total number of shares of common stock

Exhibit 9-2
ABC Company
Comparative Statement of Income for the Years
Ended December 31, 19X4, and 19X5

		19X4		19X5
Sales (Net)		$3,000,000		$3,075,000
Cost of Goods Sold		2,550,000		2,650,000
Gross Margin on Sales (Gross Profit)		450,000		425,000
Operating Expenses				
Selling	25,000		28,000	
General and Administrative	43,000		40,000	
Other	25,000		20,000	
Total Operating Expenses		93,000		88,000
Operating Income		357,000		337,000
Other Expenses				
Interest		55,000		45,000
Net Income Before Taxes		302,000		292,000
Tax (45%)		135,900		131,400
Net Income After Taxes		$166,100		$160,600
EPS (earnings per share)		$1.66		$1.61

outstanding. For a complex capital structure, EPS is a very complicated area and is beyond the scope of this discussion.

The format of the ABC Company's income statement is known as the *multiple-step form* (see Exhibit 9-2). This is by far the most widely used format. However, the underwriter should be acquainted with the single-step format as well. In this latter format, total expenses are deducted from total revenues to derive net income after taxes. There is no distinction between operating income and other income, or between operating expenses and other expenses.

Once the underwriter is familiar with the format and items found on the income statement, underwriting information can be obtained. The same fundamental techniques used to analyze the balance sheet are also used to analyze the income statement. These techniques, described in the following section, include trend analysis, common-size statements, and ratio analysis. It should also be noted that any one statement should never be used independently from other financial statements. Only by analyzing all the statements in conjunction with one another (and with any other information available) will any one statement be of value.

The balance sheet and income statement together form the

backbone of financial analysis. They are the best means yet devised for measuring the solvency, stability, and performance of a firm.

Financial Statement Analysis

The underwriter examines the financial records of a firm in the search for underwriting information pertaining to the financial health of the firm. The financial statements in and of themselves are of limited usefulness. However, there are several tools available to the underwriter that transform these statements into useful information sources. These tools include (1) comparative statements; (2) percentage analysis, which includes trend percentages, and vertical statement analysis; and (3) ratio analysis. These tools enable the underwriter to evaluate the financial data of a business by comparing it to some standard. These standards include the company's past performance (trend analysis) and the performance of other companies in the same industry (industry analysis).

The most basic financial analysis tool is in *comparative financial statements*. Referring to the comparative financial statements of the ABC Company (Exhibits 9-1 and 9-2), imagine that only information as of December 31, 19X5, was presented. In this case, it would be very difficult to draw valid conclusions from such data unless the firm was exceptionally weak or strong. For example, the ABC Company had a net income of $160,600 in 19X5. This fact in itself is not very useful. However, if the underwriter knew that the firm had been earning an annual net income exceeding $500,000 for the previous five years, the current net income figure might signify a possible moral or morale hazard and/or financial weakness and deterioration. Conversely, if the firm had never earned over $50,000 previously, the current income figure might indicate (1) a stronger and growing company, (2) a reduced likelihood of moral hazard, or (3) some nonrecurring transaction having an impact on income only in the single year.

Individual account classifications on all the statements can be compared in this manner as a means of obtaining useful underwriting information. A good example is the conclusions that can be drawn by comparing inventory data of the past few years found in the balance sheet. The fact that the inventory of a firm is currently valued at $1,000,000 is somewhat useful to the underwriter. However, it is much more beneficial when the figure is compared with several previous years' inventory levels, which, for example, might reveal that inventories are increasing. Such a discovery might indicate obsolete or damaged inventory, which may, in turn, indicate a possible moral hazard. It may also indicate that a portion of the inventory will never be sold and converted into cash. One word of warning must be made concerning comparative statements. The underwriter must make certain that accounting principles have been consistently applied over the period of time covered by the comparison. A change in the method of inventory valuation, for example, can create false impressions, either of change or stability.

Comparative financial statement analysis may be made easier by the use of *trend percentages*. This technique converts the dollar amounts to percentage increase or decrease from one year to another, with the first year serving as the base year. All dollar amounts in the base year are assigned a weight of 100 percent. The amounts in subsequent years are then expressed as percentages of the figures for the base year. By substituting percentages for large dollar amounts, readability and brevity are achieved. Trend percentages are extremely useful in singling out unfavorable developments which may appear over a period of time.

Common-size statements (or vertical analysis) is another financial analysis tool. It is very useful when comparing the statements of two or more businesses, especially those of different size. Common-size statements are constructed by converting total assets, total liabilities, stockholders' equity, and net sales of each firm to a base of 100 percent. Each item within each classification is then expressed as a percentage of the base. Since these lines represent 100 percent in all the statements being compared, there is a common basis for analysis. Thus, the statements are known as "common-size statements." A comparative common-size balance sheet for the ABC Company is shown in Exhibit 9-3.

The underwriter should be careful not to confuse vertical analysis with trend percentage. For example, inventories did *not* decrease by 2.91 percent from 19X4 to 19X5 (14.89 percent less 11.98 percent). However, the *percentage* of inventories to total assets *did* decrease by that amount.

Such information can be particularly useful if compared to industry averages. Assume that the industry average for inventories is only 5.0 percent of total assets. This information may alert the underwriter to obsolete inventory and to a potential moral hazard. If the industry average for net plant and equipment for firms with the same level of sales is only 55 percent (compared to the 74 percent level for the ABC Company), the ABC Company may be operating very inefficiently.

Financial tools such as comparative statements, trend percentages, and common-size statements are useful when interpreting accounting records. They allow the underwriter to compare the current operations of a firm against some standard of performance. Using the firm's past performance and industry averages as standards, the underwriter can

Exhibit 9-3
ABC Company Common-Size Balance Sheet

Assets	Dec. 31, 19X4	Dec. 31, 19X5
Current assets		
Cash	2.13%	1.60%
Marketable securities	6.38%	3.99%
Receivables (net)	8.51%	8.58%
Inventories	14.89%	11.98%
Total current assets	31.91%	26.15%
Fixed assets		
Net plant & equipment	68.09%	73.85%
Total assets	100%	100%
Liabilities and Stockholders' Equity		
Current liabilities		
Accounts payable	6.81%	8.23%
Notes payable	10.47%	12.35%
Accruals	1.05%	1.23%
Provision for federal income taxes	13.61%	13.89%
Total current liabilities	31.94%	35.70%
Long-term liabilities		
Mortgage payable	68.06%	64.30%
Total liabilities	100%	100%
Stockholders' equity		
Capital stock	71.68%	60.17%
Retained earnings	28.32%	39.83%
Total stockholders' equity	100%	100%

obtain much underwriting information and draw conclusions from these statements.

Accounting Information from Alternative Sources

The underwriter should be aware that sources of accounting data other than financial statements exist. Though these sources are possibly less important than the financial statements, they can be used to supplement the statements and aid the underwriter in gaining a greater understanding of a particular risk.

The Annual Report One such source of information can be the annual report of a firm. There are various types of information included in an annual report that go beyond the financial statements themselves. Generally, the annual report provides a brief description of the company's background and growth. Usually, there is also a summary and analysis of the previous year's operation. Commonly, future plans of the firm are discussed by management; and charts, graphs, and ratios are often included in the report to aid the reader in understanding the financial data.

The underwriter should be cognizant of the fact that the annual report is prepared by the management of the firm. As a result, this information may be somewhat biased in favor of the company. For example, managerial statements may present a more optimistic prediction of the future than is actually reasonable. Nevertheless, the underwriter can gain some insight into the financial condition of a firm by reviewing its annual report.

The Prospectus Another source of financial information concerning a firm is its prospectus. A prospectus is a registration statement issued by the firm for the purpose of describing a new security (stock or bond) issue. It must be filed with the Securities and Exchange Commission at least twenty days before the new securities are publicly offered. A prospectus provides high-quality financial, legal, and technical information about the company. The major disadvantage of the prospectus is that it is prepared only if a new security issue is offered by a firm.

The 10-K The Securities and Exchange Commission (SEC) requires all publicly traded companies to file an annual report updating their registration statement. This report is Form 10-K. It contains financial statistics and supplementary statements. A significant supplementary statement from an underwriting standpoint is Item 5, Part I of the 10-K, legal proceedings. Major libraries often have 10-Ks of large companies on microfiche. The 10-K is also available at a fee from Disclosure, Inc., which contracts with the SEC to provide copies of material from the SEC public files.

Other Sources of Information There are several other sources of information. For example, in addition to the annual report, most firms also issue quarterly reports. These reports are not as detailed and often are not certified by a public (outside) accounting firm, but they can give the underwriter up-to-date information and help to determine the seasonal fluctuations of the business, especially inventory values. The underwriter can also obtain financial information about a firm from sources that gather and report such information. As will be discussed later, one well-known outside source of information is Dun & Bradstreet, Inc. Additionally, Robert Morris Associates and the credit departments of individual firms are also sources of financial information on business firms and individuals.

Shortcomings of Accounting Data

Before the underwriter can make use of financial statements, the accounting data from which the statements are derived must be understood. Financial statements are of greatest value when they are compared either with the firm's past financial statements, financial statements of similar firms, or with applicable industry averages.

The cost method of valuing assets is a major factor that makes comparability between statements difficult. Land, buildings, equipment, investments, intangible assets, and most inventory usually are carried on the books at the original purchase price or at a depreciated value based on original purchase price. The different cost methods in use can cause financial statements to include dollars that do not have the same value. For example, assume that Company X bought a truck for $12,000. Company Y bought the same type of truck six months later, after the cost had risen by 12 percent. Company Y would then carry the same type of truck on its books at $1,440 more than Company X carries on its books. Such a situation can easily distort relationships, because dollars with more current purchasing power are being compared with dollars having some other purchasing power.

Variations in accounting methods make comparisons between financial statements difficult. Two firms of similar size may handle the same product lines and yet have entirely different items and amounts on their financial statements. These differences do not necessarily indicate that one firm is financially stronger than the other. Observe in the following example how different inventory methods result in different values for ending inventory, costs of goods sold, and gross profit, even though the same events took place during the same year.

Assume two firms started business on January 1, 19X6. On that date, both purchased 10,000 widgets at $1.00 apiece. On July 1, 19X6, they each purchased 10,000 additional widgets at $1.20 each. Assume further that each firm sold 15,000 widgets during the year at $1.25 apiece. The only difference is that Company X used the first-in first-out (FIFO) method of valuing inventory, and Company Y used the last-in first-out (LIFO) method.

The value of the ending inventory is derived by multiplying the number of units purchased by their purchase price and adding the result to the beginning inventory balance. The number of units taken out of inventory (sold) is multiplied by the assumed cost of the particular units taken out. The first-in first-out method assumes that the first items purchased are the first items sold. The last-in first-out method assumes that the last items brought into inventory are the first items taken out. *In a period of rising prices, the LIFO method produces a higher cost of goods sold figure, and therefore a smaller net income amount.* For this reason, LIFO is being used more frequently as a means of minimizing income taxes. The computation of the ending inventory, the cost of goods sold, and the gross profit for both firms is illustrated in Exhibit 9-4.

The accounting methods, procedures, and estimates that a particular firm uses can be found either on the face of the statements or in a section of the statements normally entitled "Notes to the Financial Statements." These notes are an integral part of the financial statements, and the underwriter should not attempt to analyze the statements without studying them. The notes normally explain the accounting methods and estimates the firm uses for (1) notes payable, (2) income taxes, (3) long-term debt, (4) common stock, (5) stock options, (6) pension plans, (7) inventories, (8) retained earnings, (9) research and development costs, and (10) contingencies. Underwriters must remember that the notes are an important part of the financial statements and that the information contained in them is vital when interpreting accounting data.

Qualified versus Unqualified Statements

Financial statements that are audited are more credible than unaudited statements. Audited statements are accompanied by an *audit report* prepared by an independent certified public accountant (CPA), who expresses a professional opinion as to the fairness of the company's statements. The underwriter should always review the auditor's report for the type of opinion rendered. There are three types of opinions that an auditor may render: (1) unqualified, (2) qualified, and (3) adverse. The auditor may also disclaim an opinion.

An unqualified opinion indicates that the financial statements have been examined and that they fairly present the financial position, the results of operations, and the changes in the financial position of a firm. This suggests that the statements are free from bias and dishonesty and that information contained in the statements is complete. Such an opinion denotes that the firm is applying "generally accepted accounting principles," (GAAP) and that these principles are applied on a consistent basis. An unqualified opinion does not contend that the

Exhibit 9-4
Computation of the Ending Inventory,
the Cost of Goods Sold, and the Gross Profit

Company X—FIFO

Ending Inventory

	Quantity	Unit Cost	Total Cost
Purchase 1/1/X6	10,000	$1.00	$10,000
Purchase 7/1/X6	10,000	1.20	12,000
Sales for 19X6	(10,000)	1.00	(10,000)
	(5,000)	1.20	(6,000)
	5,000		$ 6,000

Cost of Goods Sold
Beginning Balance+Purchases−Ending Balance
   (0+$22,000−$6,000=$16,000)

Gross Profit

Sales (15,000 × $1.25)	$18,750
Less Cost of Goods Sold	16,000
	$ 2,750

Company Y—LIFO

Ending Inventory

	Quantity	Unit Cost	Total Cost
Purchase 1/1/X6	10,000	$1.00	$10,000
Purchase 7/1/X6	10,000	1.20	12,000
Sales for 19X6	(10,000)	1.20	(12,000)
	(5,000)	1.00	(5,000)
	5,000		$ 5,000

Cost of Goods Sold
Beginning Balance+Purchases−Ending Balance
   (0+$22,000−$5,000=$17,000)

Gross Profit

Sales (15,000 × $1.25)	$18,750
Less Cost of Goods Sold	17,000
	$ 1,750

statements are "exactly correct," and it does not imply that there is no possibility of fraud. However, fraud is occasionally uncovered in the course of an audit made by the accounting firm prior to its expression of opinion.

If, in the auditor's opinion, the financial statements fairly present the financial condition of a firm with only minor exceptions, a qualified opinion will be issued. The auditor will commonly issue a qualified opinion when a firm has changed its inventory valuation method from the preceding year.

The auditor will issue an *adverse* opinion if it is found that the financial statements do *not* fairly present the financial position of a firm. The reasons the auditor has come to this conclusion are also explained.

If an auditor cannot formulate an opinion for any reason, such as auditing restrictions imposed by the client, or lack of auditor's independence, a *disclaimer* will be issued with the financial statements. It should be recognized by the underwriter that the auditor expresses an opinion only on the financial statements, not on the entire annual report.

RATIO ANALYSIS

Ratio analysis is an important tool for the underwriter in the study of the financial condition of a risk. Ratio analysis uses data items found in the accounting records of a firm and relates these items to one another in a meaningful and useful manner.

The first step in the use of ratios is to decide what information is needed in reference to a particular risk and then to choose which ratios will provide this information in the most efficient manner. Literally hundreds of ratios can be produced from the data in the accounting records, but only a few are useful. To assure that only meaningful and useful ratios will be used, the underwriter should never lose sight of the objective of financial analysis—the search for any information that will aid an underwriting decision. As discussed previously, the underwriter is using financial analysis as (1) an indicator of potential moral and morale hazards, (2) an indicator of the risk's ability to pay premiums, (3) an indicator of financial strength and sound management, and (4) an indicator of potential growth and possible future desirability from an underwriting standpoint.

While there are twelve ratios covered here, the underwriter might only examine three or four when analyzing a particular firm. The particular ratios employed depend on the underwriter's area of concern.

A suspected liquidity problem would call for one group of ratios while a suspicion of high indebtedness would call for another.

A ratio is a meaningless number in and of itself. Before becoming useful, it must be compared in a logical manner with some base or guidelines. Normally, ratios are compared with (1) the same ratios of the firm for past years to determine if the firm is improving or deteriorating (trend analysis); or (2) other firms in the same industry to determine how the firm compares with similar firms; or (3) the applicable industry average. Key business ratios are available from some financial reporting firms, such as Dun & Bradstreet.

Before continuing further with a description of the various ratios, a forewarning is essential. Ratios *must* be used with caution. Specifically, ratios are constructed from accounting data, and these data are subject to different interpretations and even to manipulation. Important factors to consider include inventory valuation methods, depreciation methods, and the accounting for leases. Depending on which method is used, net income can be substantially modified.

Ratios generally can be classified into four basic groups:[4]

1. *liquidity ratios*, which measure the risk's ability to pay short-term obligations.
2. *leverage ratios*, which measure the extent to which the firm is financed with debt.
3. *activity ratios*, which measure how well the risk is using its assets.
4. *profitability ratios*, which measure the degree to which the firm is meeting its goal of profit for its owners.

In the ratio examples that follow, the data are taken from the previously given financial statements of ABC Company.

Liquidity Ratios

Liquidity ratios measure the firm's ability to pay its current maturing obligations. The ABC Company has $347,000 of obligations that must be paid within the next year (see Exhibit 9-1). Can this debt be paid? Is a strain on cash probable? Liquidity ratios can help answer these types of questions. A firm with a low ratio is not in a good position to satisfy obligations (including insurance premiums) as they become due. Low and high are relative terms, of course. Remember, a ratio is useless unless compared to other ratios—either in trend analysis or industry analysis. A high ratio indicates that the firm is in a better position to pay its current premiums. Liquidity ratios can also help indicate a potential moral and morale hazard. A risk with lower liquidity ratios may be more of a moral hazard because of the temptation to intentionally cause a loss in order to receive badly needed cash. The two most commonly used liquidity ratios are the *current ratio* and the *quick ratio* (sometimes known as the *acid test*).

Current Ratio The data used to determine the current ratio are found in the balance sheet. The ratio is computed by dividing current assets by current liabilities. Current assets typically include cash, marketable securities, accounts receivables, notes receivables, and inventories. Current liabilities normally include accounts and notes payable, the currently due portion of long-term debt, and accruals. The current ratio indicates the extent to which assets that are expected to be converted to cash in the next year will cover the claims of short-term creditors. For example, a current ratio of 2:1 indicates that for every dollar of current debt, the firm has two dollars of current assets. A current ratio of 2:1 has traditionally been considered satisfactory, but this is not a hard and fast rule.

The current ratio is calculated:

$$\text{Current ratio} = \frac{\text{Current assets}}{\text{Current liabilities}}$$

Application of this ratio, using the data in Exhibit 9-1 for the ABC Company, yields:

$$\text{19X4 Current ratio} = \frac{\$750,000}{\$305,000} = 2.5$$

and

$$\text{19X5 Current ratio} = \frac{\$655,000}{\$347,000} = 1.9$$

The decrease in the current ratio results from the fact that the ABC Company had fewer current assets to cover more current liabilities in 19X5 than in 19X4. If the average current ratio for the industry is 2.0, the ABC Company appears to be more in line with that average. Industry averages are useful for comparison; however, they are not magic numbers that all firms should attempt to maintain. What is crucial is the extent to which the firm is representative of the industry from which the average is calculated. In some industries, the average is greatly influenced by a few large firms, in which case the average is less meaningful for the smaller firms in the industry. In the case of ABC Company, even though the current ratio has decreased by 0.6, it is still very close to the industry average. Furthermore, with $1.90 of current assets for every $1.00 of current liabilities, the ABC Company should not have a liquidity problem, barring some dramatic adverse development in the near future.

Quick or Acid Test Ratio The quick ratio is similar to the current ratio. It is calculated by dividing the quick assets by the current liabilities. *Quick assets include cash, readily marketable securities, and receivables.* In other words, the *only difference between quick assets and current assets is that the quick assets do not include inventory.* The term "quick" is used to describe those assets that either exist in the form of cash, or can quickly be converted into cash in order to pay current obligations.

The quick ratio is calculated:

$$\text{Quick ratio} = \frac{\text{Current assets less inventory}}{\text{Current liabilities}}$$

Using the data in Exhibit 9-1 for the ABC Company:

$$\text{19X4 Quick ratio} = \frac{\$400,000}{\$305,000} = 1.31$$

and

$$\text{19X5 Quick ratio} = \frac{\$355,000}{\$347,000} = 1.02$$

In this illustration, it is apparent that every $1.00 of current debt was backed by $1.31 of cash or near-cash assets in 19X4, and by $1.02 of cash or near-cash assets in 19X5. Assume the industry average is 1:1 (1:1 is the traditionally favorable level). Even though the quick ratio decreased in 19X5, it is still above the industry average. The firm should be able to satisfy all current liabilities by liquidating its quick assets.

The quick ratio shows the extent to which the firm could meet its obligations if it were to shut down or be liquidated immediately. A quick ratio of less than 1:1 is usually interpreted as a danger signal. Both quick and current ratios are widely utilized by short-term creditors, such as banks, and can be used by an underwriter as clear indicators of the financial well-being of a firm.

Leverage Ratios

Leverage ratios indicate the relationship between the amount of funds supplied by creditors and the funds supplied by the owners of the firm. Leverage ratios can give the underwriter a "feel" of how the firm is utilizing borrowed funds, and they may be good indicators of the financial strength of the firm and the soundness of management.

Leverage ratios are indicators of soundness—the greater the amount of debt, the greater the chance that the firm will be unable to meet its interest payment requirements. The industry average ratios are particularly important for analytical purposes, since the "normal or standard" leverage amount varies greatly from industry to industry. For example, industries with large amounts of fixed assets and fairly stable earnings can generally carry large amounts of debt. The public utility industry is a prime illustration of a highly leveraged industry.

The three most commonly used leverage ratios are:

1. the total debt to total assets ratio,
2. the times interest earned ratio, and
3. the fixed charge coverage ratio.

Total Debt to Total Assets Ratio The data used to calculate the total debt to total assets ratio are found in the balance sheet. It is calculated by dividing total debt by total assets. The higher the ratio, the more funds creditors have supplied to the firm's total financing. An exceptionally high ratio may indicate to the underwriter that the firm has been financed too much by debt, and it may indicate financial weakness and doubtful growth. Under these circumstances, the underwriter must be aware of possible moral and morale hazards.

The total debt to total assets ratio is calculated:

$$\text{Total debt to total assets ratio} = \frac{\text{Total debt}}{\text{Total assets}}$$

Using the data in Exhibit 9-1 for the ABC Company:

$$\text{19X4 Total debt to total assets ratio} = \frac{\$955,000}{\$2,350,000} = 0.41$$

and

$$\text{19X5 Total debt to total assets ratio} = \frac{\$972,000}{\$2,525,000} = 0.39$$

This ratio informs the underwriter that for every dollar of the firm's assets in 19X5, creditors financed $.39. If the industry average for this ratio is 0.35, the ABC Company is slightly above the average but probably not high enough to cause concern.

Times Interest Earned To calculate the number of times interest on borrowed funds is earned in a year, divide earnings before interest payments and taxes (EBIT) by the interest charges. These data items are found in the income statement (see Exhibit 9-2). The times interest earned ratio is a good indicator of the financial strength of a firm because it measures the extent to which earnings can decline before the firm is unable to pay annual interest costs. The times interest earned ratio is calculated:

$$\text{Times interest earned} = \frac{\text{EBIT}}{\text{Interest charges}}$$

Using the data in Exhibit 9-2 for the ABC Company:

$$19\text{X}4 \text{ Times interest earned} = \frac{\$357,000}{\$55,000} = 6.5 \text{ times}$$

and

$$19\text{X}5 \text{ Times interest earned} = \frac{\$337,000}{\$45,000} = 7.5 \text{ times}$$

In 19X5, the ABC Company incurred interest charges of $45,000, and had an operating income of $337,000. In other words, the ABC Company earned enough to pay its interest charges 7.5 times. This is an improvement over 19X4. If the industry average was 8.0 times, the ABC Company would be below the average in 19X5, but somewhat improved over its previous year. The important relationship here is the vitality of earnings. If the firm is in an industry where earnings fluctuate widely from year to year, then this interest earned multiple should be large. Stable earnings permit a smaller multiple.

Fixed Charge Coverage The sole difference between the times interest earned ratio and the fixed charge coverage ratio is that the latter includes lease and other fixed obligations. Lease obligations have very similar characteristics to interest on debt obligations in that both *must* be paid. Therefore, the fixed charge coverage ratio is more inclusive and perhaps more important than the times interest earned ratio. The reason for the importance of this ratio is that a firm can lease a facility rather than borrow to purchase the same facility. Thus, rather than incurring an interest obligation, the firm accepts the obligation to meet lease payments. Missing a lease payment can place the firm in just as severe financial difficulty as missing an interest payment. Any analysis of a firm should thus include a measure for all fixed charges rather than just interest charges. The data for this calculation are also found in the income statement (Exhibit 9-2). Notice that the ABC Company had no lease obligations. Therefore, this ratio is the same as the times interest earned ratio.[5] The fixed charge coverage ratio is calculated:

$$\text{Fixed charge coverage} = \frac{\text{EBIT} + \text{Other fixed charges}}{\text{Interest charges} + \text{Other fixed charges}}$$

Using the data in Exhibit 9-2 for the ABC Company:

$$\text{19X4 Fixed charge coverage} = \frac{\$357,000 + \$0}{\$55,000 + \$0} = 6.5 \text{ times}$$

and

$$\text{19X5 Fixed charge coverage} = \frac{\$337,000 + \$0}{\$45,000 + \$0} = 7.5 \text{ times}$$

Activity Ratios

Activity ratios compare the level of sales with the various asset accounts. Therefore, data from both the balance sheet and income statement (Exhibits 9-1 and 9-2) are needed to compute these ratios which measure how effectively management employs the resources at its command to produce sales.

Using these ratios with other types of ratios, other information, and good judgment, the underwriter can deduce many indications of possible moral and morale hazards, and future desirability from an underwriting standpoint. There are four common activity ratios: (1) inventory turnover, (2) receivables turnover, (3) fixed assets turnover, and (4) total assets turnover.

Inventory Turnover The inventory turnover ratio indicates the number of times the inventory was replaced during the year. This ratio is calculated by dividing the cost of goods sold by the average inventory. The cost of goods sold is found in the income statement. The average inventory is the sum of the beginning and ending inventory (found in the comparative balance sheets) for the year, divided by two. The ABC Company, for the year 19X5, had a beginning inventory balance of $350,000, and an ending balance of $300,000. The average inventory for 19X5 was $325,000 (computed: [$350,000 + $300,000]/2). The inventory turnover is calculated:

$$\text{Inventory turnover} = \frac{\text{Cost of goods sold}}{\text{Average inventory}}$$

Using the data above and in Exhibit 9-2 for the ABC Company:

$$\text{19X5 Inventory turnover} = \frac{\$2,650,000}{\$325,000} = 8.1 \text{ times}$$

If the industry average is 10 times, it is clear that this firm's inventory does not move quite as fast as the average inventory. This could indicate obsolete merchandise, over-buying, or increases in prices over the year. The underwriter should be certain that the firm did not change inventory policies during the year, which might result in incomparable beginning and ending inventory balances. The ABC Company's inventory turnover is probably not enough below the average to cause concern. However, if the turnover is well below the average, the underwriter should consider if the risk is holding damaged or obsolete materials which are carried on the books at a cost much higher than the actual value. The firm may be tempted to intentionally destroy the overvalued inventory in order to collect on an insured loss.

Receivables Turnover The receivables turnover, sometimes referred to as the *collection ratio,* measures the relationship between credit sales made during the year and the average amount of accounts receivable over the same period. The underwriter may encounter some difficulty obtaining the correct numerator for the ratio by simply examining the income statement. Specifically, the ratio's numerator calls for credit sales, but the income statement generally does not break down sales between credit and cash sales. The underwriter may check other financial records to determine the amount of credit sales.

In 19X5, let us assume that the ABC Company had $2,000,000 in credit sales and $1,075,000 in cash sales. The numerator for the ratio, then, is $2,000,000. The calculation of the average accounts receivable is similar to the calculation of the average inventory previously described. The sum of the beginning and ending accounts receivable balance for the year is divided by two. The receivables turnover is calculated:

$$\text{Receivables turnover} = \frac{\text{Credit sales}}{\text{Average accounts receivable}}$$

Using the data above and in Exhibit 9-1 for the ABC Company:

$$\text{19X5 Receivables turnover} = \frac{\$2,000,000}{(\$200,000 + \$215,000)/2}$$

$$= \frac{\$2,000,000}{\$207,500} = 9.6$$

This ratio can then be used to determine the average number of days an accounts receivable remains outstanding. This is found simply by dividing 365 by the receivables turnover as follows:

$$\text{Average collection period} = \frac{365}{9.6} = 38 \text{ days}$$

The underwriter, by using these ratios, is looking for indications of poor collection policies on the part of management. The longer an account remains unpaid, the lower the likelihood of collection. However, if the firm has an average collection period that significantly exceeds the industry average, an early warning of financial problems may exist. That is, a firm that has excess funds tied up in receivables may have difficulties in financing its other operations. Slow collections may indicate unsound management and possible financial weakness.

A firm may appear to have improved its average collection period when, in fact, the problem still exists. This is done by "writing off" the bad debts and thus improving the collection ratio. A review of the balance sheet and other records will show the underwriter if this has been done.

Fixed Assets Turnover   The fixed assets turnover ratio measures the number of times that sales of the year cover net fixed assets. This ratio is calculated:

$$\text{Fixed assets turnover} = \frac{\text{Sales}}{\text{Net fixed assets}}$$

Using the data in Exhibits 9-1 and 9-2 for the ABC Company:

$$\text{19X4 Fixed assets turnover} = \frac{\$3,000,000}{\$1,600,000} = 1.9 \text{ times}$$

and

$$\text{19X5 Fixed assets turnover} = \frac{\$3,075,000}{\$1,850,000} = 1.7 \text{ times}$$

This ratio shows the utilization level of plant and equipment. Low fixed asset turnover may indicate excess capacity. It is acceptable if this is a temporary condition due to a seasonal business cycle slowdown in sales. However, persistent excess capacity leads to possible moral hazard, since a major fire is one way to quickly reduce capacity.

Total Assets Turnover   The last activity ratio is also used by the underwriter to get a better idea of the financial strength and soundness of management. This ratio measures the turnover of the risk's total assets instead of only the fixed assets. It is calculated using the following formula:

$$\text{Total assets turnover} = \frac{\text{Sales}}{\text{Total assets}}$$

Using data in Exhibits 9-1 and 9-2 for the ABC Company:

$$\text{19X4 Total assets turnover} = \frac{\$3,000,000}{\$2,350,000} = 1.3 \text{ times}$$

and

$$\text{19X5 Total assets turnover} = \frac{\$3,075,000}{\$2,505,000} = 1.2 \text{ times}$$

As with other ratios, the total assets turnover ratio should be used in trend and industry analysis in order for it to be meaningful.

Profitability Ratios

The ratios discussed thus far furnish useful information as to how well a firm is operating in certain specific areas. Profitability ratios, on the other hand, yield final answers about the efficiency of a firm as a whole.

There are three common profitability ratios. Each can be used to compare net profit after taxes to some other item on the balance sheet or income statement. Since a major goal of virtually all firms is to produce a large net profit after taxes, profitability ratios are good indicators of how well the firm is achieving its goal. Even nonprofit organizations strive to operate efficiently, which is an indicator of sound management.

The three common profitability ratios are (1) the profit margin on sales ratio, (2) the return on total assets ratio, and (3) the return on net worth ratio.

Profit Margin on Sales Ratio The profit margin on sales ratio, sometimes known as the *net profit ratio*, measures the net profit realized per dollar of sales. It is computed by dividing net income after taxes by sales. Both of these figures are found in the income statement. The net profit ratio is calculated:

$$\text{Profit margin} = \frac{\text{Net profit after taxes}}{\text{Sales}}$$

Using data in Exhibit 9-2 for the ABC Company:

$$\text{19X4 Profit margin} = \frac{\$166,100}{\$3,000,000} = 0.055 \text{ or } 5.5\%$$

and

$$\text{19X5 Profit margin} = \frac{\$160,600}{\$3,075,000} = 0.052 \text{ or } 5.2\%$$

In 19X5, the ABC Company realized a 5.2 percent net profit after taxes. This is a slight decrease compared to 19X4. Of course, two years is not an adequate number to develop a trend analysis. Normally, a minimum of five years should be used in trend analysis.

Assume that the average profit margin ratio for the industry is 5.0

percent. The ABC Company is slightly above this average, which is a good indication. Of course, if the industry average is 10.0 percent, the underwriter should be concerned and attempt to determine why the firm's ratio is substantially below the average.

As a final note, this ratio is sometimes expressed as a before-tax figure because of changing tax laws. In such cases, trend analysis is very difficult due to the unavailability of comparable data.

Return on Total Assets Ratio This ratio is computed by dividing net profit after taxes by total assets. It measures the return on the total investment in the firm. Net profit is found in the income statement, and total assets is found in the balance sheet. Return on total assets is computed:

$$\text{Return on total assets} = \frac{\text{Net profit after taxes}}{\text{Total assets}}$$

Using data in Exhibits 9-1 and 9-2 for the ABC Company:

$$\text{19X4 Return on total assets} = \frac{\$166,100}{\$2,350,000} = 0.071 \text{ or } 7.1\%$$

and

$$\text{19X5 Return on total assets} = \frac{\$160,600}{\$2,505,000} = 0.064 \text{ or } 6.4\%$$

The reason for the decline from 19X4 to 19X5 is that ABC Company purchased more assets, and net profit after taxes decreased. This may indicate to the underwriter that management made a poor decision in purchasing the assets. Again, two years is not enough time to develop a trend analysis, and this ratio, like all ratios, should be used in conjunction with other measures of financial strength.

Return on Net Worth Ratio This ratio measures the rate of return on net worth, which is found in the balance sheet. Net profit after taxes is used as the numerator. Return on the net worth is calculated:

$$\text{Return on net worth} = \frac{\text{Net profit after taxes}}{\text{Net worth}}$$

Using data in Exhibits 9-1 and 9-2 for the ABC Company:

$$\text{19X4 Return on net worth} = \frac{\$166,100}{\$1,395,000} = 0.119 \text{ or } 11.9\%$$

and

$$\text{19X5 Return on net worth} = \frac{\$160,600}{\$1,533,000} = 0.105 \text{ or } 10.5\%$$

In many respects, this is the most important ratio since it is the "bottom line." This ratio measures the profitability of the firm to its owners, which in the last analysis is of fundamental importance. If this ratio is lower than the industry average, the other ratios can be used to diagnose where the problem or problems are. It may be that there is too much money tied up in capital due to poor inventory management and a poor credit collection policy. The firm may be operating at a too-low percentage of capacity, which would surface in the total asset turnover and the fixed asset turnover. Finally, the firm may have too much debt or be paying too high an interest rate for it. These problems would be diagnosed by the leverage ratios. Consideration of the entire set of the firm's ratios in comparison with the industry average may provide an indication of the trouble areas and the areas of outstanding performance. These ratios are summarized in Exhibit 9-5.

INFORMATIONAL REPORTS

As previously mentioned, several organizations collect, analyze, and disseminate financial and operational data on business firms. One such concern is Dun & Bradstreet, Inc., and this section is devoted to reviewing that organization's activities and its two principal products in detail—the *Business Information Report* and the *D&B Reference Book*. These products are representative of the types of external information available to the underwriter for financial analysis. In addition, several more specialized reports are briefly examined.

There are several other sources for much of the information provided by Dun & Bradstreet. These include, among others, TRW, Equifax, and Robert Morris Associates. In some cases, D&B might be "the only ball game in town," since D&B is the world's largest credit reporting organization. Various D&B reports are discussed here in order to give the underwriter an idea of the type of reports that are available and the information found in each.

One aspect of the reports described that is not mentioned is their cost. In some cases, the more detailed reports can become quite expensive. As with any underwriting information, they must be used with discretion and only when necessary. One underwriting training manager put it very appropriately when he said, "Why should I pay for D&B to analyze the insured's financial status when I have spent quite a bit of money on training my underwriters how to read and analyze financial reports?" A D&B report may be necessary to get some basic

Exhibit 9-5
Ratio Summary

Liquidity Ratios

Current ratio $= \dfrac{\text{Current assets}}{\text{Current liabilities}}$

Quick ratio $= \dfrac{\text{Current assets} - \text{Inventory}}{\text{Current liabilities}}$

Leverage Ratios

Total debt to
total assets ratio $= \dfrac{\text{Total debt}}{\text{Total assets}}$

Times interest earned $= \dfrac{\text{EBIT}}{\text{Interest charges}}$

Fixed charge coverage $= \dfrac{\text{EBIT} + \text{Other fixed charges}}{\text{Interest} + \text{Other fixed charges}}$

Activity Ratios

Inventory turnover $= \dfrac{\text{Cost of goods sold}}{\text{Average inventory}}$

Receivables turnover $= \dfrac{\text{Credit sales}}{\text{Average accounts receivable}}$

Fixed assets turnover $= \dfrac{\text{Sales}}{\text{Net fixed assets}}$

Total assets turnover $= \dfrac{\text{Sales}}{\text{Total assets}}$

Profitability Ratios

Profit margin $= \dfrac{\text{Net profit after taxes}}{\text{Sales}}$

Return on total assets $= \dfrac{\text{Net profit after taxes}}{\text{Total assets}}$

Return on net worth $= \dfrac{\text{Net profit after taxes}}{\text{Net worth}}$

information; on the other hand, more detailed or specialized reports may be unnecessary if underwriters can make the calculations performed by and charged for by D&B. Insurers select the reports they wish to purchase based on costs and the expertise of their underwriters in financial analysis.

Introduction

The business of D&B and many of the similar organizations is gathering and maintaining information on *commercial* enterprises and supplying those data to legitimately interested subscribers, including underwriters. The latter group, faced with the continuing task of measuring the risk's financial stability, can benefit considerably by using these organizations. Sometimes, a "D&B" report is the only source necessary for such analyses. Accordingly, underwriters need to be thoroughly familiar with the services available from the various sources and able to interpret the many types of information provided.

One of the major reasons for the widespread use of financial reporting firms among underwriters is the scope of their activities. These firms investigate and analyze literally *millions* of commercial enterprises and, importantly, do so on a continuing basis.

For example, D&B (1) reports on the history of the company and the background of its owners and managers; (2) describes, in detail, the method of operation; (3) outlines the firm's paying record; (4) analyzes financial status, operating results, and trends; and (5) assigns composite credit ratings for the bulk of these concerns.

The analytical information thus provided substantially reduces the effort necessary to analyze risks. And since underwriting costs are largely determined by the time factor, these outside services help underwriters investigate applications as completely and rapidly as possible. Information from outside reporting organizations also has the advantage of being prepared by a neutral third party unrelated to either the applicant or the insurer. This fact tends to make the information less subject to bias. It should be noted, however, that reporting agencies must sometimes rely on data provided directly by owners of the firm. While much of this information can then be confirmed by other sources, a manager's financial estimates, for instance, will obviously be less precise than an accountant's audited balance sheet. Underwriters should thus appreciate the need for somewhat closer attention to reports and analyses based largely upon the owner's verbal statements.

Dun & Bradstreet Reference Book

The *Dun & Bradstreet Reference Book,* published and updated every sixty days, carries information on nearly three million businesses throughout the United States and Canada. Arranged in five volumes, the *Reference Book* presents these businesses alphabetically, by city and town within the state or province. The names listed in the *Reference Book* are *commercial* enterprises—manufacturers, wholesalers, and retailers—regularly purchasing goods and services on credit. Professional activities such as accounting or law and service operations such as real estate brokers and barber shops are *not* shown in the *Reference Book*—since their credit purchases are relatively small and intended for internal use rather than resale. However, while these and other non-commercial operations are *not* listed in the *Reference Book, Business Information Reports* on such concerns are compiled and available from Dun & Bradstreet.

For businesses that are carried in the *Reference Book,* the listing includes (1) the exact business name used for buying; (2) a four-digit Standard Industrial Classification number identifying function and product line; (3) a year-date code indicating when the business started or came under present control; and (4) for most concerns, a Dun & Bradstreet rating reflecting both financial worth and the composite credit appraisal. In addition, some listings will be prefaced by the letters A or C—both are important to the underwriter. "A" signifies that the listing has been *added* since the previous *Reference Book* edition; "C" means the rating has been *changed* since that edition.

The Key to Ratings illustrates the range of the D&B evaluation system. Most ratings are of the capital-and-credit variety, a letter and number combination. For example, in the rating code BB1, the letters BB identify financial strength (net worth) as being between $200,000 and $300,000, and the number "1" indicates a "high" composite credit appraisal. In sum, a business so rated would be regarded as financially strong. A concern somewhat less strong, but still satisfactory from the standpoint of credit, would likely be rated BB2. But then, as the degree of financial strength decreases because of less favorably balanced finances or slow paying record (or both), "fair" and "limited" credit appraisals (BB3 and BB4) would come into play.

In some instances, generally when net worth cannot be precisely pinpointed, the usual capital and credit rating will not be assigned. Instead, other rating symbols—"1," "2," or "INV"—will be used. The single digit "1" or "2" ratings, while providing a wider dollar range for the net worth figure, still imply that the composite credit appraisal is judged as being either "high" or "good." An INV rating means only that a pending investigation of the business was incomplete at the time that issue of the *Reference Book* went to press.

Finally, some *Reference Book* names will lack any of the above rating symbols. This absence of rating, expressed by two hyphens (--) is *not* to be construed as unfavorable. It simply (1) indicates the existence of circumstances difficult to classify within the condensed rating codes and (2) suggests that, for details, the *Business Information Report* be obtained.

To fully utilize the information so concisely presented in the *Reference Book*, it is essential to develop complete familiarity with Dun & Bradstreet's rating system. In this regard, the Key to Ratings provides practical benchmarks that expand the value of *Reference Book* listings for underwriters. Sometimes, (depending upon the insurer's established procedures) underwriters may not be required to make a further check on concerns rated "high" or "good"—if other underwriting information tends to confirm the *Reference Book* rating. More often, however, data beyond that supplied by the *Reference Book* listing is required. In these situations, underwriters should order a *Business Information* or similar report.

The Business Information Report (BIR)

A sample (but fictional) BIR, Drexel Men's Wear, is shown in Exhibit 9-6 to illustrate the considerable amount of data available to aid the underwriter's decision making.

In the BIR's heading, starting at the top left, is an identifying number. Then, immediately below this number appears the business name used for buying; the full headquarters address complete with phone number and zip code; and the identity of the proprietor, partners or, in a corporation, the chief executive officer.

In addition, when appropriate, this heading will also indicate the existence of branches or multiple locations. This item of information alone may well influence the underwriting decision. It is easily appreciated that in a multi-unit operation, insured property may be transferred from one outlet to another and the physical hazard may vary widely among the several locations. Beyond those obvious considerations, however, branch activities sometimes contribute to serious financial problems, particularly if the business has expanded too rapidly. Without sufficient capital to maintain all normal activities, housekeeping or safety factors may be curtailed and, in time, a moral hazard could develop.

At the top right of the BIR is SUMMARY—in effect, a "headline" for the story covered in the body of the BIR. But it should be realized that SUMMARY can only highlight certain financial or operating

Exhibit 9-6
Dun & Bradstreet Business Information Report

		This report has been prepared for:	
Dun & Bradstreet, Inc.			
BE SURE NAME, BUSINESS AND ADDRESS MATCH YOUR FILE	ANSWERING INQUIRY	SUBSCRIBER: 006-881342	

			FULL REVISION

DUNS: 00-647-3261 DREXEL MEN'S WEAR	SEPT 27 19X6 MEN'S & BOY'S CLO & FURNGS	SUMMARY RATING BB3 STARTED 19X3	
1209 LEMOYNE AVE AND BRANCH(ES) AUGUSTA, GA. 30901 TEL 404 872-9664	SIC NO. 5611	PAYMENTS PPT-SLO 40 SALES 750,000 WORTH 250,000 HISTORY CLEAR CONDITION FAIR	
ROBERT A. MORTON, OWNER		TREND UP	

PAYMENTS REPORTED	PAYING RECORD	HIGH CREDIT	NOW OWES	PAST DUE	SELLING TERMS
	Prompt	16000	8000	0	2 10 30 Sold 4 yrs
JUL X6	Prompt	29000	14000	0	30 Sold 3 yrs
	Prompt	9000	6000	300	2 10 30 Old acct
	Slow 30	61000	22000	10000	Special Satis acct
	Slow 30	45000	27000	2000	2 10 30 Good
	Slow 40	15000	6000	6000	2 10 30 Over 3 yrs

FINANCE   Fiscal statement dated August 31, 19X6

Cash	$	50,000	Accts Payable	$ 140,000
Accts Receivable		40,000	Due Bank	50,000
Inventory		280,000	Accruals	10,000
Current		370,000	Current	200,000
Fixtures (net)		80,000	NET WORTH	250,000
Total		450,000	Total	450,000

SALES 76: $750,000. Net Profit $40,000. Withdrawals $15,000. Mo. rent $5,000. Fire ins. on mdse & fixts: $340,000. Accountant: T. M. Lewis, CPA.

--0--

Tho sales, profits and worth have advanced annually, finances now strained after $70,000 inventory and fixtures investment for new branch plus opening own charge accounts. Interviewed 9/23/X6 Morton reports branch sales on pace. Expects minimum volume $900,000 this year. Says trade slowness will be corrected by retained profits, return of 'X6 withdrawals, closer collection control and year-end reduction in merchandise levels from present seasonal peak.

BANKING   Balances average middle five. Renewable note in similar amount now open. Loan granted for working capital to assist branch opening.

HISTORY   Morton born 1930, married. Started as employee of father's Army-Navy store 1962. At father's death 1966 he inherited unit. Later opened additional outlet before selling to others 1972 for $55,000. Same year started Morton's Junior Wear here and 1975 opened branch, Children's House. In 1982 sold both units to national chain for $135,000. Used those proceeds to start this business late 19X3.

OPERATION   Retails men's (60%) and boy's (40%) clothing and furnishings for cash (75%) and house credit terms. Previously accepted only national credit cards, cashed weekly. Carries moderate to high priced name brands. Sells shoppers, office workers at main store, nearby residents at branch. Employs 14. LOCATION: Rents 8000 sq ft, ground floor of modern downtown office bldg; 2500 sq ft at branch, 2130 Van Horn Rd, Augusta opened 9/1/X6
08-19 (400.10) 0754/0409632142

features and may not provide all details necessary for understanding. Underwriters, therefore, must make it a habit to review the total BIR before reaching decisions.

For ease of reading, the BIR is sectionalized according to information content. In the Payments section of Drexel Men's Wear, for example, is noted good-sized high credits, established relationships with suppliers but, in addition, a mixed pattern of debt retirement—some trade bills paid promptly, some on a past-due basis with discounts missed. Such a situation may result from a temporary cash flow problem, chronic under-capitalization, poor marketing programs, inept management—or a combination of these factors. In this BIR, Payments has raised a warning flag but it has not provided a full answer.

The point is that all areas of the BIR are interrelated and interdependent. Payments, like all other BIR sections, is only part of the business story, and with but rare exception, no single item is sufficient, on its own, to serve as the basis for decision.

To understand Drexel Men's Wear, it will be necessary to evaluate Payments in conjunction with all other areas of the BIR. And when that process is followed it is found (from Finance, Banking, and Operation) that present delinquency in retiring trade bills is due to recent changes within the business. The owner has opened a second outlet requiring expenditures for fixtures, credit selling has been expanded, and the inventory investment, prior to start of the selling season, has been increased well above normal. These moves have brought about a heavier debt position, reduced working capital, and slowness in paying. However, we also learn that the owner anticipates a faster movement of goods and increased profits which should, in time, begin to remedy the situation.

The success of the Drexel operation, however, depends (as it always does) upon the owner's management talent and business acumen. But how does the underwriter determine whether the stated objectives can be attained and the business condition improved? There are no guarantees in business. But there is the previous record of the owner to provide some guidelines. In this respect a review of History shows the owner with an unbroken record of success over a period of seventeen years. Further, in earlier enterprises, the owner twice built up single outlet businesses into multi-unit operations.

As a result of studying *all* areas of the Drexel report, the underwriter obtains a clearer picture and a different perspective of the venture than if the decision had been hastily reached solely on the basis of payment record or from the data provided by the summary. There can be no substitute for the full story.

Specialized Reports

There are several more specialized or detailed reports available from D&B and others. For example, D&B offers what is called its *Duns Underwriting Guide* (DUG) to be used as a screening device to see if more detailed reports are required. The DUG is similar to a BIR, but provides financial analysis based on four key ratios, commentary on the firm, and more detailed information on the firm's operations. This latter category might include any special events which have occurred or are about to occur (for example, fires, burglaries, change in control, bankruptcy petitions, and so on). Additionally, the operations section covers public filings (suits, liens, and so on) and a detailed history of the firm. D&B has also developed a two-digit rating called PAYDEX which is shown on the DUG. PAYDEX is an indicator of the payment trends for the firm and can be a good indicator of potential financial pressure. Finally, the DUG has an overall classification for the firm which is one of three options:

- Does not require review of detailed D&B reports,
- Requires careful review of this D&B report, or
- Careful analysis of this and other detailed reports is essential.

Another more specialized report is the *Payment Analysis Report* (PAR) which details a company's payment habits with 24-month PAYDEX trends and industry comparisons. The PAR also includes industry norm scores for comparison and trend evaluation.

Finally, *Duns Financial Profile Report*, (DFP) is a detailed financial spreadsheet report. It features fourteen key financial performance ratios for up to three years on each firm. It also includes comparisons with norms for the industry.

When to Order a Report Although it is not necessary for the underwriter to order a BIR for every applicant, there are three situations when a BIR or other report should be considered (underwriters should consult their company's underwriting manual for instructions on ordering financial reports). These are (1) when the *Reference Book* does not list a rating (Business Information Reports are available on some, but not all, businesses not rated in the *Reference Book)*; (2) when the credit rating is "fair" or "limited" regardless of financial strength; or (3) when the rating has dropped from that previously assigned.

There are also occasions when the underwriter should order a BIR for midterm reunderwriting: situations in which the underwriter should not renew coverage without a premium adjustment or when policy cancellation is required. BIRs are helpful when making these midterm decisions. They should also be ordered when any of the following situations exist:

- declining sales
- indebtedness in excess of net worth
- new management
- operations at a loss
- large buildup of inventory
- slow payment record
- insufficient working capital
- rating has dropped from previous listing

SUMMARY

This chapter provides the underwriter with insight into various methods of information analysis, and describes in considerable depth *one* form of information, that is, financial data. The chapter begins with an analysis of three steps an underwriter should perform in developing information needs. The first step is an identification of the crucial risk factors; the second step deals with the techniques of developing quantitative or qualitative measures that can be used to determine the potential impact of a crucial risk factor; and the final step is an acquisition of the information necessary to perform the measurements.

The various forms of information required by underwriters are evaluated through the use of two criteria: (1) the *usefulness* of the information to be developed (utility analysis) and (2) the *cost* and resulting benefit of obtaining that information (cost-benefit analysis). The standards used to determine the usefulness of information are (1) accuracy, (2) relevancy, (3) timeliness, (4) completeness, and (5) understandability.

A major segment of this chapter deals with an analysis of financial information, which is a critical source of data for underwriters. A great deal can be learned about a firm through the analysis, comparison, interpretation, and evaluation of financial data. Financial data can provide a good indication of potential moral and morale hazards and can also be an indicator of an ability of the firm to pay premiums. Finally, financial data can be an indicator of potential growth and possible future desirability from an underwriting standpoint.

The information that can be developed by an underwriter is found in the firm's financial statements, including the balance sheet, the profit and loss statement, the statement of sources and uses of funds, and the statement of retained earnings. In addition, there are other sources of financial information. For example, the underwriter can obtain information from the annual report. Also, there are prospectuses and reports that are undertaken by external firms such as Dun & Bradstreet, Inc., which can provide the underwriter with a considerable amount of information.

The study of accounting information and financial statements can be highly advantageous to an underwriter, but any analysis that uses such information is subject to certain shortcomings. For example, accounting records are not always consistent, due to differing accounting methods. The major financial statements are the balance sheet and the income statement. All things being equal, a highly profitable firm is vastly superior from an underwriting standpoint to one in which earnings are marginal.

Ratios of financial data are frequently the most important tool through which an underwriter can develop an understanding of the character of a particular firm. Ratios, in and of themselves, are meaningless. However, ratios in a single company can be analyzed over time, can be compared with the ratios of other firms in the industry, or can be compared to an industry standard or average. Ratios are commonly divided into four basic groups: (1) liquidity ratios, which measure a risk's ability to pay its short-term obligations; (2) leverage ratios, which measure the extent to whcih the firm is financed with debt; (3) activity ratios, which measure how well the risk is using its assets; and (4) profitability ratios, which measure the degree to which profit goals are met.

The final section of this chapter deals with one particular source of financial information, Dun & Bradstreet, Inc. (D&B). Dun & Bradstreet services include:

1. D & B Reference Book,
2. Business Information Report (BIR),
3. Duns Underwriting Guide,
4. Payment Analysis Report, and
5. Duns Financial Profile Reports.

These reports and those of similar organizations provide perhaps the quickest and simplest way to investigate a firm's financial condition. While the reports are not always sufficient for the underwriter, they can provide information that is usually objective and reliable.

Chapter Notes

1. Donald H. Sanders, *Computers in Business—An Introduction,* 2nd Ed. (New York: McGraw-Hill, 1972), p. 14.
2. Sanders, pp. 15-18.
3. For example, Glenn V. Henderson; Gary L. Trennepohl and James E. Wert, *An Introduction to Financial Management* (Reading, MA: Addison-Wesley Publishing Co., 1984), Chapter 2.
4. Henderson, et al., pp. 24-32.
5. In some cases, payments made toward the principal of a loan are also included since many firms consider repayment of principal to be close to mandatory. If added, the payments have to be converted to a before tax basis since they are not deductible.

CHAPTER 10

Decision Making and Monitoring

THE APPLICATION OF DECISION-MAKING TECHNIQUES TO UNDERWRITING

Problems and procedures involved in the *application* of the decision-making process to underwriting decisions are considered in this chapter. As the experienced underwriter is well aware, a particular procedure, like the decision-making process developed in Chapter 2, may seem reasonable as an abstract concept, but the real test is the implementation of the procedure.

A frequently heard cliché is "all right in theory, but no good in practice." This is a misconception: if a theory does not stand the test of practice, it is not a good theory.

An Underwriting Flow Chart

The underwriting process involves a *series* of decisions that lead to the final underwriting decision on a risk or book of business. Thus, the barriers to effective decision making can affect the process at any of several points.

Exhibit 10-1 is a presentation of the underwriting decision process in a flow chart format.[1] When the offer or submission is received, the underwriter ascertains whether it includes sufficient information for proper analysis. If the information is at hand, the process moves directly to the next step—analysis and evaluation. If the information is not at hand, the underwriter collects and organizes information until the file is complete and then moves on to analysis and evaluation. During the evaluation process, the physical characteristics of the risk, the coverage, price, and producer in some cases are evaluated relative to the "average" risk in the class. If the submission is clearly good, the flow moves directly to accept. If the submission is clearly poor, the process moves directly to decline. For the intermediate cases, it is necessary to generate alternatives such as acceptance on the basis of modification of the risk, product, price, or compensation of the producer. The trade-off matrix indicates the procedure by which the underwriter *weighs* the relative strong and weak points of the submission. The next step is the decision to either accept, implementing the best alternative, or to reject, which would indicate that declination was determined to be the best alternative.

One important facet of the flow chart is the explicit indication that the underwriting decision process does not end with acceptance. Implementation and monitoring of the decision remain. Implementation of the decision requires communication with the producer; careful monitoring of the decision is important to assure continued acceptability of the risk. Finally, when conditions warrant it, reunderwriting is called for, which involves another complete cycle of the process.

Sorting of Decisions

During the course of a working day, an underwriter makes many decisions, some difficult and complex, and others simple and routine. Establishment of a priority order may be essential to effective utilization of decision-making skills and available time. Assignment of lower and higher priority categories between routine and nonroutine decisions can be helpful in maximizing an underwriter's operational efficiency which in turn can lead to even more effective decision making.

Routine Decisions Decision theorists refer to routine decisions as "programmed decisions." These decisions are so numerous and are made so often that they rank in a low-priority decision category and can be moved rapidly into their "task" implementation, which is really work processing. Often underwriters can delegate this processing to underwriting assistants, clerical personnel, or the computer. A broad form homeowners application containing a very large jewelry schedule and indicating that the client travels abroad and is away from home frequently for extended time periods may be clearly set forth in the underwriting manual as unacceptable. The underwriter or delegated assistant may quickly implement the declination with a phone call or letter to the producer or insured. Likewise, the homeowners application that meets all criteria satisfactorily can be quickly routed to rating, coding, and policy-issue processing while confirmation of acceptance is

Exhibit 10-1
Underwriting Flow Chart

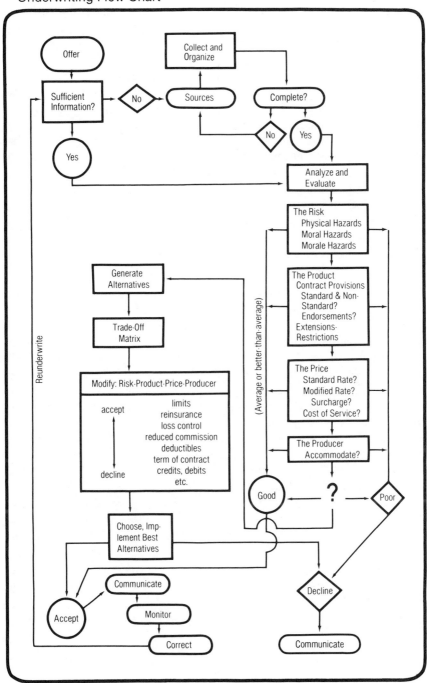

communicated to the producer or insured. Many times mere lack of declination may serve as an acceptance.

A slightly higher priority category may evolve as the result of a need for more information on an incomplete application. Again, a quick phone call or note to the producer about the dwelling alarm protection question left unanswered in the initial submission may change the decision. Receipt of further information may, in fact, move this risk to a higher priority, nonroutine decision level. This repetitive, automatic type of decision making is often referred to as "screening." Much as the gravel quarry operator filters diggings through a succession of screens to obtain the finest grade of sand, so the underwriter "filters" decisions through priority "programmed screens" and moves the routine risks quickly to activity processing. Effective decision making requires that these programmed decisions be handled efficiently and with dispatch in order to leave the underwriter time to deal with the more complex nonroutine decisions. Underwriters who devote a sizable part of the day to routine matters that could be delegated to clerical and other less technically trained (and less well paid) personnel are not allocating their time efficiently.

Nonroutine Decisions The full scope of the underwriting decision-making process comes into play with respect to higher priority, nonroutine decisions. Rather than decline the homeowners because the jewelry schedule may involve substantial values, facultative reinsurance might be used. Special off-premises limitations might help alleviate the seemingly excessive travel exposure; or more information regarding the handling, use, and protection of the jewelry during travel may modify the decision. Even with all of the additional information, referral to the home office may be required by the underwriting manual. Finally, there may be a submission that is unacceptable as it stands but where the premium volume and profit of the producer or the existence of collateral business requires that the underwriter attempt to find some alternative means of rendering the risk acceptable.

Dealing with nonroutine decisions requires judgment and creativity. In decisions of this type, the gathering of information, development of alternative courses of action, and the careful evaluation of the various alternatives to select the best solution to the problem are areas where a structured approach will yield the best results. The underwriting decision-making process will be most helpful with respect to these nonroutine decisions.

The ratio of routine to nonroutine decisions will differ according to a number of variables, including the type of business being underwritten. An underwriter dealing with private passenger auto, homeowners, and small commercial risks may have a relatively high proportion of routine decisions. On the other hand, an ocean marine underwriter responsible for open ocean cargo policies and commercial hulls may have a high proportion of nonroutine decisions. As a general rule, there are more nonroutine decisions to be dealt with in commercial lines than in personal lines. In both cases, the effectiveness with which the nonroutine decisions are handled will have an important effect upon the overall underwriting results of the insurer.

CONSIDERATIONS IN THE EVALUATION OF ALTERNATIVES

The major considerations in the evaluation of alternatives while making an underwriting decision can be classified under five major headings:

1. the hazards inherent in the risk,
2. the underwriting authority applicable to the risk,
3. the underwriting manual and insurer attitude toward the risk,
4. the insurer's relationship with the producer of the business, and
5. the existence of regulatory constraints on the decision.

Hazards Inherent in the Risk

In the evaluation of the hazards inherent in a particular risk, the underwriter must first identify the various physical, moral, and morale hazards and then make some estimation of the severity of these hazards. One approach is to make a list of the hazards and to indicate next to each hazard the underwriter's estimate of its severity, that is, whether it is low, average, or high. A fourth classification—unacceptable—may be included to deal with those hazards that are so severe that the hazard, by itself, is cause for declination.

One approach to listing and evaluating the various hazards systematically is shown in Exhibit 10-2. This is an account analysis slip utilized in the commercial lines department of a major insurer. It has been modified by adding the unacceptable column.

Purpose of the Account Analysis Slip The purpose of the account analysis slip is to provide underwriters with a simple checklist for compiling their evaluations of the major considerations in a particular risk. These major elements include the underwriter's evaluation of:

1. major characteristics of the account in terms of likelihood of loss and probable maximum loss,
2. rate adequacy,

Exhibit 10-2
Account Analysis Slip

INSPECTED ☐   NOT INSPECTED ☐

INSURED/APPLICANT	ANALYST	OFFICE	DIST

ADDRESS OR LOCATION NO. AND BUILDING NO.

	GOOD	AVERAGE	POOR	UNACCEPTABLE
GENERAL • Management-Moral Hazard and Performance Including Experience, Finances, Attitude, Adequate Records, Employee Selection and Training.	☐	☐	☐	☐
• Location-Neighborhood, Public Protection, Unusual Area Exposure.	☐	☐	☐	☐
• Building & Premises—Age, Maintenance, Housekeeping, Hazardous Exposures.	☐	☐	☐	☐
• Loss Record & Future Potential-Consider Past Record, Deductibles or Restrictions of Coverage, Improvements.	☐	☐	☐	☐
• Concentrated Exposure-Coverage Overlap or Exposing Accounts in This Company	☐	☐	☐	☐

	LOW	INTERMEDIATE	HIGH	UNACCEPTABLE
FIRE & INLAND MARINE • Fire-Likelihood of Loss-Common and Special Hazards, Internal and External Exposures.	☐			☐
Probable Maximum Loss-Building	0-25% ☐	26-60% ☐	61-100% ☐	
-Contents	0-40% ☐	41-85% ☐	86-100% ☐	
-Time Element-Months to Repair: Bldg._____; Mach._____; Stock_____	**TOTAL PML $**_____			
• Water Damage-Likelihood of Loss-Processes, Condition of Pipes, Packaging. Probable Maximum Loss-Damageability, Pumps, Drains, Storage Areas, Concentration.	☐	☐	☐	☐
• Inland Marine: Coverages-_____				
Likelihood of Loss- Probable Maximum Loss-	☐	☐	☐	☐
• Burglary of Contents-See Crime.				

GENERAL LIABILITY • Premises-Operations-Likelihood of Loss-Public Access, Kind of Business and Operations Hazard. Number of Persons Exposed or Value of Property Damageable.	☐	☐	☐	☐
• Products/Completed Operations-Likelihood of Loss-Type of Product, Operations Completed, Controls. Underwriter Judgement Considering Degree of Hazard.	☐	☐	☐	☐

AUTO • Likelihood of Loss-Consider Selection and Control of Drivers, Maintenance of Equipment, Commodity, Scheduling and Routing Including Intensity of Use and Traffic Conditions.	☐	☐	☐	☐
Heavy Loads, Flammables or Explosives, Passenger Exposure, Express Schedules.				
Amount of Driver Turnover (Non-Seasonal)	0-10% ☐	11-20% ☐	21%+ ☐	

CRIME • Fidelity/Forgery-Likelihood of Loss-Consider Security Controls. Probable Maximum Loss-Consider Fidelity Minimum Limits Formula	☐	☐	☐	☐
• Burglary-Money & Securities-Likelihood of Loss-Consider Physical Security Relative To Target Attraction Value. Probable Maximum Loss-100% of Exposure	☐	☐	☐	☐
• Burglary-Other than Money & Securities-Likelihood of Loss-Consider Physical Security Relative to Target Attraction Value (Trade Group No.). Probable Maximum Loss-Consider Unit Value and Portability (Coinsurance Limit).	☐	☐	☐	☐

WORKERS' COMP. • Likelihood of Loss-Work Injury Hazards, Occupational Disease, Exposure, Work Environment, Safety Programs.	☐	☐	☐	☐
• Severe Occupational Hazards, Explosion, Fire, Fumes, Height or Cave-in.				

RATE ADEQUACY—Are Rates or Premiums Adequate for Each Coverage Yes ☐ No ☐ If 'No'—Comment Below.
Fire Rates (For Home Office Submissions): Enter adjusted 80% Coins. Building_____, Contents_____.

	GRADE WITHIN CLASS					CLASS DESIRABILITY			PRICING			
	ABOVE AVG.	AVG.	MARG. INAL.	NON- STD.	UNAC- CEPT.	DESIR- ABLE	AVG.	LESS DESIRE.	DIS- COUNT	STANDARD	SUR- CHARGE	OTHER OR MODIFICATION %
FIRE & I.M.	☐	☐	☐	☐	☐	☐	☐	☐	☐	☐	☐	_____
GENL. LIAB.	☐	☐	☐	☐	☐	☐	☐	☐	☐	☐	☐	_____
AUTO	☐	☐	☐	☐	☐	☐	☐	☐	☐	☐	☐	_____
CRIME	☐	☐	☐	☐	☐	☐	☐	☐	☐	☐	☐	_____
COMP.	☐	☐	☐	☐	☐	☐	☐	☐	☐	☐	☐	_____

COMMENTS:

3. grade of risk within its class, and
4. class desirability.

In addition, the slip provides a record of whether the risk has been priced on a discount, standard, or surcharged basis. This enables the underwriter to establish a written record for the file which will provide a history of the underwriting and pricing of the risk. This also provides a means for management to review and evaluate the quality of underwriting and pricing. This slip provides an excellent summary which can be employed when it is necessary to submit exposure analysis and pricing data to a higher authority level or to the home office for approval.

Quantification of Hazards and Exposures It is normal procedure in most property lines for the underwriter to estimate the probable maximum loss (PML). *Probable maximum loss is defined as the largest loss that the underwriter considers likely to occur, based upon experience and judgment.* The account analysis slip differentiates on fire risks between low, intermediate, and high, based on the relationship between the limit of liability and the PML. On the building item, if the PML is 25 percent or less of the limit of liability, it is classified as low; 26 to 60 percent is the intermediate range; while 61 percent or greater is considered high. On contents, less than 40 percent is considered low, 41 to 85 percent intermediate, and 86 percent or greater high. Liability insurance lines such as general liability, auto liability, or workers' compensation cannot generally be quantified by estimating probable maximum loss. Rather future loss payments are estimated from past loss experience. Thus, in making a decision about acceptability of a package policy application, the underwriter *must* separate consideration of the PML for property lines and the expected loss ratio for liability lines and weigh the significance of each in relationship to the overall account. Assume that on a package risk the underwriter sets a PML for building fire at $500,000, for contents at $800,000, business interruption for $1,000,000, and transportation exposure at $200,000. If the probable loss figures are all set forth, with no additional data, the implication is that these maximum losses are all equally probable. This may not be the case. The underwriter may reason that if the insured's main building were to become fully involved in a fire, the $500,000 building loss and the $800,000 contents loss would almost certainly be realized. On the other hand, the business interruption PML might be based on a simultaneous loss of two buildings at the same site, the likelihood of which is much more remote. Similarly, the transportation PML might be based upon a major terminal fire, which might be even more unlikely, while still within the definition of "probable."

Exhibit 10-3
Probable Maximum Loss and Estimated Probabilities

Coverage	Probable Maximum Loss	Estimated Probability
Fire: Building	$ 500,000	0.05
Fire: Contents	800,000	0.05
Business Interruption	1,000,000	0.02
Transportation	200,000	0.01

Next, the underwriter might consider that a major fire could occur once in 20 years, while a major business interruption occurrence might happen only once in 50 years, and the plant explosion only once in 100 years. From these subjective estimates, it is possible to give relative weights to maximum losses and their estimated "probabilities" (see Exhibit 10-3).

It should be exphasized that these are not actuarial probabilities. They are not and should not be used for rate-making purposes, except possibly as an input into an inland marine judgment rating computation. These estimated probabilities merely represent an attempt on the part of the underwriter to quantify the estimate of the indicated PML. In the case above, the indicated absolute level of the probabilities is less important than the relative differences between the probabilities. That is, the fire loss reaching the PML is considered to be more than twice as likely as the business interruption occurrence and five times as likely as the transportation catastrophe. If desired, it would also be possible to estimate the probability of a catastrophic loss, such as a major plant explosion which would cause simultaneous fire, business interruption, and transportation exposure losses, together with a combined PML for all affected lines.

A Hazard Scale Rather than simply categorizing hazards as low, intermediate, high, and unacceptable, the underwriter might want to express each hazard numerically. A scale of 0 to 10 could be employed, with 0 meaning that the hazard was not present at all and 10 standing for unacceptable. Once again, precision is not possible in this type of estimation, but a scale lets the underwriter express in brief and simple form his or her subjective evaluation of the seriousness of the hazard, based upon the information presently available. Rather than stating that the physical hazard of construction is extremely low, it can simply be noted on the form as a 1. Similarly, if there are no environmental or external exposures, that would be a 0. If the occupancy is average in hazard, that could be expressed as a 5, while slightly better than average would rate a 4.

One of the advantages of the utilization of a scale of 0 to 10 to express the underwriter's judgment of the seriousness of the various hazards is that it enables the underwriter to pick up the file at a later date and quickly recall the entire previous hazard analysis. This advantage is even more pronounced if a different underwriter or an underwriting manager reviews the file at some later date.

A Composite Risk Picture A form similar to the account analysis slip in Exhibit 10-2, with the various hazards listed and their severity estimated in a scalar form, greatly simplifies the task of the underwriter in pulling together a composite evaluation of the overall risk. While it would not be meaningful to add up the scalar values and make a decision based on the total, a risk with a preponderance of 8s and 9s would certainly indicate a rather unfavorable picture.

Underwriting Authority

When evaluating the alternatives on a particular submission or renewal, a major consideration is the underwriting authority applicable to that particular decision. In many insurance companies, the underwriting authority for a particular class of business is detailed in the *line guide* (an older term referring to the number of "lines" an underwriter could write without referral to a higher authority) or *underwriting manual* (guide). This underwriting manual generally represents the present state of accumulated knowledge and experience on a given line of insurance and must be considered an important information source for the underwriter. Reference to the manual whenever a question of authority arises can readily indicate action required of the underwriter. It may be necessary to refer a particular risk to the regional or home office for decision because the underwriter lacks the authority to make the decision at this level.

The underwriter must ascertain that he or she has authority to make the decision on this risk by giving consideration to two governing characteristics:

1. The underwriting manual will indicate the acceptability of the particular class of business by a limitation on binding authority or an outright prohibition of the class.
2. Even if authority has been given to underwrite a particular class, most underwriting manuals set upper limits of liability beyond which the underwriter cannot act without submission to higher underwriting authority. Special coverages or rating plans may also require approval.

Exhibit 10-4 is a selection from an underwriting manual. While the format of these manuals varies from line to line and company to company, the nature of the content is generally the same.

Underwriting Manual and Insurer Attitude

In addition to the underwriting authority applicable to individual classes of business, the underwriting manual contains information about the relative desirability of the class. Because the manual reflects what the insurer does not want to write, the manuals of different insurers will reflect different ways of looking at hazards of the same type of risk. If the insurer does not want to write a certain kind of business, the negative aspects of the business will be emphasized in the manual. If the insurer does want to write the business, the manual will emphasize the positive aspects of such business. The information in the manual is based upon the insurer's previous experience with that particular class of business, the desired market niche of the insurer, together with restrictions based upon filings, capacity, and reinsurance treaties. In property insurance, for example, bars and restaurants of frame construction located in densely populated and deteriorating areas or unprotected fire districts have had notoriously poor experience. The underwriting manual contains this information. In property lines, the underwriting manual sets down the retention limits, usually based on construction, occupancy, and protection classes.

In general liability, the underwriting manual contains information regarding the relative desirability of a particular class and also special hazards or exposures to be analyzed with respect to a particular risk within that class. Exhibit 10-4 includes information that would be found in an underwriting manual.

In addition to data regarding desirability and special hazards or exposures, the underwriting manual usually contains information regarding eligibility for special rating plans, rules regarding the use of reinsurance where applicable, and data pertaining to the forms and endorsements to be utilized in the class. The underwriting manual assists the underwriter in decision making, particularly with respect to an unfamiliar class of business. Since the manual indicates the insurer's attitude toward various classes of business, it is important that it be periodically reviewed and updated by underwriting management. In this review, management must consider not only the changing charac-teristics of the risk or class but also many interrelated factors. Changes in physical hazards merit consideration, for example, a paid fire company replacing a volunteer company in a town. Recent rate changes authorized by regulators or a milestone court decision may affect the review. The influences of the changing economic, social, or legal environment must be considered.

Producer Considerations

The Marketing System The type of marketing system utilized by an insurance company bears directly upon the relationship between the underwriter and the producer. This relationship affects underwriting decisions. There are three major types of marketing systems employed in the property and liability industry. These are:

1. the independent agency system,
2. the exclusive agency system, and
3. the direct-writing system.

The effect of the marketing system on the decision falls into three general categories. First, the overall quality of the producer's prior submissions has an important effect. Second, the producer may present or already have in force supporting business on the same account which must be taken into consideration on a marginal risk. Third, even in the absence of supporting business, a marginal risk is occasionally accepted as an accommodation to a profitable producer.

In the independent agency system, the underwriter must be aware that the producer can place business in another of the insurance companies that the producer represents. It may be necessary to accept an occasional piece of marginal business as a favor to a producer for competitive reasons in order to continue the flow of good business from that producer.

In the exclusive agency system, the competitive pressure of alternative markets within the producer's agency is not present, but accommodation risks must still be considered. Since the insurance company, by definition, is the producer's only market, there frequently are pressures placed upon the underwriter to accept marginal business out of loyalty and support to the producer in order to enable that producer to compete effectively in the marketplace and retain profitable accounts.

In the direct-writing system, the producer is an employee of the insurance company and has no other markets or outlets for placing business. The producer's goals under this system are fundamentally those of the insurer. Producers write what and where the insurance company wants them to write. Therefore, if a marginal piece of business is important in acquiring a profitable account or in entering a certain area, both the producer and the company will exert pressure to accept that business. Additionally, the underwriter may be aware that the producer's continued employment depends upon meeting certain

Exhibit 10-4
Underwriting Manual

Section I

AUTHORITY LEGEND:

(P) Prohibited
(H) Refer to Home Office
(R) Refer to Region
(B) Refer to Branch Mgt.
    SOME CLASSIFICATIONS ARE PROHIBITED
(C) CRITICAL CLASS FOR FIRE—REFER TO SECTION II

UNDERWRITING AUTHORITIES (INCLUDING MULTI-PERIL)

1 - AUTO & GARAGE LIABILITY—ALL AUTO PHYS. DAMAGE
2 - GENERAL LIABILITY & OCP
3 - PRODUCTS & COMPLETED OPERATIONS
4 - WORKERS' COMPENSATION & EMPLOYERS' LIABILITY
5 - PLATE GLASS
6 - BURGLARY & THEFT
7 - INLAND MARINE
8 - FIRE & ALLIED LINES—MULTI-PERIL (SECTION I)

HAZARD, RISK, OR EXPOSURE	AUTO - 1	GEN. LIAB. - 2	PROD. - 3	W.C. - 4	GLASS - 5	BURG. - 6	I.M. - 7	FIRE - 8
Credit or insolvency insurance								
Crop dusting		B					P	B
Dance halls (c)		B		B				H
Deductibles—other than manually rated (see also excess of loss)			R					
Deductibles—risks where deductibles of $100,000 or more apply (see also excess insurance)			R					
Deferred payment plans, installment plans and finance accounts (dual or single interest)	R							
Detective or patrol agencies		R		R			H	H
Difference in conditions		R		R			H	H
Directors and officers, errors and omissions (refer to Excess Department)		P						

Risk	1	2	3	4	5	6	7	8	9	10
Discount houses (c)	B						B		B	B
Drive away or haul away contractors										
Drive-in movies (c)	B						B		B	B
Driving schools—commercial and student instruction										
Drug, cosmetics, pharmaceutical, surgical, or hospital equipment or supplies—equipment intended for therapeutic or cosmetic use, manufacturer or dealer			P			R		P	B	B
Earthquake, explosion, windstorm or riot and civil commotion on risks without fire insurance in proportionate amount on the same Risk									P	P
Electric or electronic equipment manufacturer			R			R				
Elevator or escalator-manufacturer, erection, installation, repairs service	B	R	R	R		R				R
Emergency vehicles				B		B				
Errors and omissions-malpractice or professional liability for abstractors, accountants, architects, broadcasters, engineers, lawyers, surveyors, insurance or real estate agents										
Errors and omissions coverage in installation floaters		P								
Excelsior mills (c)							H	H	H	H
Excess insurance liability lines (other than personal umbrella policies) refer to excess dp.	R	R	R	R		R	H	H		B
Excess insurance liability lines (personal umbrella) policies	R	R	R	R		R				
Excess insurance or risks (property lines) where deductibles of $10,000 or more apply									R	R
Excess of loss reinsurance—assumption of									R	R
Excess of loss reinsurance where it is needed to reduce company limits of insurance									P	P
Excess of loss-uninsured or franchise deductibles or deductibles insured elsewhere which exceed $2,000,000:policies written on a layered basis-whether primary or excess	H	H	H	H		H	H			R
Exhibitions—more than 2,000 attendees	B									
Explosion or collapse or underground damage—for limits in excess of 100/100 PD	R									
Explosives or incendiary devices, assembling, dismantling, storage, transportation, handling or destruction of any loaded device intended for use as a weapon of war (except risks engaged in the manufacturing of small arms ammunition)	P	P				P	P			

Section II—Limits of Liability Referral List (Including Multi-Peril)

Underwriting Authorities

A. Automobile physical damage and dealers physical damage
   1. If excess of $2,000,000 .... R
   2. If excess of $750,000 .... B

B. Automobile physical damage and dealers physical damage
   1. Limits in excess of $1,500,000 concentration at one location .... R
   2. Limits in excess of $500,000 concentration at one location .... B

C. Fidelity Authorities:
   1. Refer *all* fidelity coverages to regional bond personnel for their approval.
   2. Also refer the following coverages to regional bond personnel:
     a. Bank burglary and robbery policies
     b. Comprehensive dishonesty, disappearance and destruction policies written on fidelity forms
     c. Blanket crime policies

D. Fire:
   1. Any single property risk where after the application of surplus share our net liability exceeds $10,000,000 and/or probable maximum loss (PML) exposure exceeds $3,000,000 .... H
   2. Aggregate property and business interruption values in excess of $12,000,000. Any one location of PML in excess of $3,500,000. Both on a net protected by excess basis. .... P
   3. Any risk where the total insured value for all interests exceeds $75,000,000. .... H
   4. Policies written on risks covered in whole or in part by pools and associations (except underwriters service association) .... H
   5. Refer for approval all fire risks when company net retention (protected by excess) at any one location equals or exceeds $750,000 PML and/or $750,000 total insurance at any one location. Report by letter to home office any risk written with PML of $1,600,000 or higher (company name, policy number, insured, type and location of risk, expiration date, amount PML and amount of company's total liability at location required). .... R
   6. Risks in critical classes designated by (c) include a disproportionate number of undesirable risks and are to be handled by senior underwriting personnel. Consideration must also be given to according them accommodation treatment. Refer to the home office risks in these critical classes on which limits in .... R

Underwriting Authorities

   excess of $50,000 are desired. . . . . .R

E. General liability products and completed operations*

   1. Limits in excess of $2,000,000 combined occurrence or aggregate limit* . . . . .R

   2. Limits in excess of $750,000 combined occurrence or aggregate limit* . . . . .B

   3. Contractual Liability**:

     a. Limits in excess of $2,000,000 combined aggregate limit* . . . . .R

     b. Limits in excess of $750,000 combined aggregate limit* . . . . .B

F. Glass:

   1. Glass valued at $50,000 or more at one location . . . . .H

   2. Glass valued at $10,000 or more for one plate . . . . .H

G. Inland Marine:

   1. Filed classes—Loss limits exceeding $400,000 (exclusive of agency reinsurance) . . . . .R

   2. Unfiled classes—Loss limits exceeding $100,000 (exclusive of agency reinsurance) . . . . .R

   3. Any single property risk where after the application of surplus share our net liability exceeds $10,000,000 and/or probable maximum loss (PML) exposure exceeds $3,000,000 . . . . .P

   4. Any risk where total insured value for all interests exceeds $75,000,000 . . . . .H

   5. Policies written on risks covered in whole or in part by pools and associations (except underwriters service associations) . . . . .H

   6. Refer for approval all fire risks when company net retention (protected by excess) at any one location equals or exceeds $750,000 PML and/or $750,000 total insurance at any one location. Report by letter to home office any risk written with PML of $1,600,000 or higher (company name, policy number, insured, type and location of risk, expiration date, amount PML and amount of company's total liability at location required) . . . . .R

Combined occurrence or aggregate limit or combined aggregate limit means the sum of bodily injury occurrence limit of liability and property damage occurrence limit of liability or the sum of bodily injury aggregate limit of liability and property damage aggregate limit of liability on the policy declaration or endorsed to the policy.

**Refer for limits of liability when contractual and operations exposure are combined and exceed office authority aggregate limit (E1).*

sales goals and objectives, a different kind of pressure on the underwriting decision.

The Producer as an Underwriting Factor

The Producer as a Factor on Individual Submissions The extent to which the producer is a factor in the underwriting of an individual submission will vary by insurer. However, it can generally be said that the producer is usually not a factor when a submission is otherwise clearly unacceptable or clearly acceptable. The producer may become a factor in the wide range of submissions between these two groups. These submissions are often called "marginal."

For marginal submissions, underwriters may be instructed (perhaps through their underwriting manuals) to consider the producer submitting the business. In such a case, underwriters may want to consider a number of factors, including:

1. Is the producer newly appointed and trying to get established in the area? Perhaps the insurer has made a commitment to help the producer get established.
2. Is the producer an established, profitable, large volume producer for the insurer that seldom submits marginal business?
3. Is the producer an independent agent who favors a different insurer with the agency's best business? In such a case, perhaps the submission has already been rejected by the other insurer.
4. Is the producer one who frequently promises certain actions (for example, a larger volume of more profitable business) in return for a favor, but seldom delivers on such promises?
5. Does the producer specialize in the class of business to which the submission belongs? Perhaps the underwriter, knowing less about the class than the producer, can rely on the producer to have used his or her knowledge to "preunderwrite" the submission.
6. Has this specific producer received any instructions from the insurer regarding this class of business? This might include instructions to either increase or decrease writings for this class if the producer's book is "out of balance" with the desired book of business.

In some cases, the underwriter may accept a submission as an "accommodation" to a producer. *An accommodation is an acceptance of a submission which, without consideration of the producer, would have been rejected.* The actions underwriters should take when accepting a submission as an accommodation are described later in this chapter.

Regulatory Constraints

In the process of identifying and evaluating alternatives, underwriters must consider any possible regulations that might limit the available alternatives. Regulatory constraints generally affect an underwriter's flexibility to accept, modify, or decline a risk in the areas of coverage, pricing, and classification.

The majority of state insurance codes contain requirements for specific policy wording of the insuring agreements and no forms or endorsements that restrict this coverage may be allowed. Particular attention has been focused on cancellation and renewal provisions in auto policies. Restriction of flexibility regarding the conditions and timing of cancellation or nonrenewal can be a serious consideration in making decisions about new or existing business.

Restrictions of flexibility in the use of rating plans or classifications exist in auto and workers' compensation insurance codes in most states. Several states promulgate the rates and classifications which must be used by all insurance companies desiring to underwrite auto business in that state. Compensation boards or bureaus set forth rates, rating plans, and classifications with specified rules for modification outside the plans.

Each of these situations, when it exists, must be carefully evaluated by the underwriter. In rating, for example, the state insurance code may eliminate flexibility by establishing mandatory classification or setting a mandated rating policy.

Particularly in auto insurance, many states have cancellation laws which dictate the conditions and timing of cancellations. This lack of flexibility must be taken into account, not only when considering the appropriate action for a marginal or substandard risk already on the books, but also when making decisions on new business. If cancellation is difficult, acceptance of business in the first place must be carefully evaluated.

IMPLEMENTING THE DECISIONS

There are three aspects to implementing an underwriting decision. The first is the communication of the decision to the producer and to other company personnel affected by the decision. The second is the creation and maintenance of a claims information system to aid in the monitoring of the decision. The third is the execution of the appropriate documentation to carry out the decision.

Communication

Communication in an underwriting setting is such an important subject that it is covered in depth in the following chapter. Its importance cannot be overemphasized. Many of the complaints against insurers are the result of miscommunication.

The Claims Information System

The purpose of a claims information system is to alert the underwriter to claims activity during the period the coverage is in force. This type of ongoing file review is essential to monitoring the results of the decision to accept the risk in the first place. A well-planned and implemented referral procedure will make it possible for the underwriter to stay alert for developing claims problems and thereby take corrective action more effectively.

A typical claims information referral procedure usually includes a set of instructions to the claims department stating the circumstances which require referral of the file to the underwriter. An example in auto insurance might be:

1. any claim involving bodily injury,
2. any property damage claim estimated at more than $5,000, or
3. any claim, regardless of type or size, if there are two previous claims reported during the policy period,
4. any claim that, in the opinion of the claims adjuster, suggests moral or morale hazard.

Additional special instructions may also be set forth. These are sometimes referred to as "red flag" referral indicators. Claims of a suspicious nature arising from an unusual hazard might fall into this category. Also, where policies in several different lines of insurance have been written for an individual risk, instructions to make a cross reference to check the entire account should be set up.

Documentation

An important aspect in implementing decisions is the execution of the appropriate documentation. There are three major categories of documentation: filings, endorsements, and binders.

Filings   Filings are evidence of insurance coverage in force required by various public agencies. Motor truck carrier liability risks require Interstate Commerce Commission (ICC) filings and often Public Utility Commission (PUC) filings as well. (These two commissions are federal and state, respectively.) Automobile insurance or assigned risk plan filings have to be made on private passenger risks with the state regulatory authority where required. Auto risks require special financial responsibility filings in some states. Completion of the appropriate filings for the risk being underwritten in an accurate and timely fashion is an important part of the underwriting process. Usually, the underwriting manual or similar manual will indicate the necessary filings for each class of business. It is extremely important for the underwriter also to remember to cancel these filings when the insured's coverage is canceled or nonrenewed.

Endorsements   Often a particular policy will require one or more endorsements to provide the proper coverage, conditions, and identification of interests insured. There are routine endorsements such as those which modify payment plans, but occasionally a manuscript endorsement is required to modify coverage or conditions. These must be drafted with great care and in some cases require review by higher underwriting authority.

Binders   At the time coverage is bound, there should be some form of written binder executed as a confirmation of coverage. The oral binder can be a great source of difficulty for all concerned. Since the binder is legally a temporary evidence of policy coverage, failure to reduce the terms to writing can create serious problems for the insured, the producer, and the underwriter. The written binder should include a brief description of the property or interests insured, the conditions of coverage, and, where possible, the rate.

One aspect of the implementation of the underwriting decision is the creation of a binder control procedure to assure the timely issuance of the policy and to minimize the possibility of "free" insurance. Virtually every underwriter is familiar with the problem of Friday afternoon telephone calls requesting "weekend binders." Often, these are oral and never reduced to writing. While no solution to this problem is readily available, a log of "weekend binders" indicating the producer, the class and type of business, and the ultimate disposition of the submission will help to keep the problem under control. Requiring that all such binders be put into writing would also help. A second log, containing all binders carefully entered by date, will permit periodic review to assure that either policies are issues or coverage terminated in a timely fashion.

MONITORING

The concept of monitoring was introduced in Chapter 2. The monitoring activity applies to individual risks, both personal and commercial, as well as to a book of business.

The monitoring activities on an individual risk may be initiated in the following types of situations:

1. A request for an endorsement is received.
2. A claim report is received.
3. Information is received (or a diary file comes up for review) which indicates that the risk has changed or is about to change.
4. The risk is approaching renewal.

As an example of the first instance, a package policy on a shopping center located in an unprotected area was originally written for $180,000 on the building. A request for endorsement increasing coverage to $300,000 brings the file to the underwriter. If the underwriting manual restricts the amount of coverage on buildings in unprotected areas to $250,000, handling this endorsement will call for more than a routine decision. If feasible, it may be necessary to ask the producer to split this line (ask other insurers to insure part of the total amount of insurance), or facultative reinsurance might be obtained to bring the amount retained down to $250,000.

Monitoring claims activity is usually initiated by the automatic claim referral system described earlier. Claims that meet certain criteria are automatically routed to the underwriter for possible underwriting action.

Two examples are necessary to illustrate the monitoring activity associated with changes (present or future) in the risk itself. First, an underwriter might note that at the time a private passenger auto application was approved, the insured had a fourteen-year-old son. The underwriter flags this file to be reviewed when the son reaches driving age to determine whether or not the son will be driving the car.

Second, a workers' compensation audit report may indicate a sharp increase in machine shop remuneration in a wholesaling business that previously maintained a small job shop for repairs to merchandise being sold. This increase in shop remuneration may indicate an expansion in that facet of the operation and a substantial change in the risk. A new inspection by a loss control representative might be warranted to determine the nature and extent of this change in the operation.

Finally, monitoring activities include renewal underwriting. In some lines, renewal is automatic unless some undesirable change in the risk or unfavorable loss experience warrants reunderwriting. In large commercial lines, individual risk monitoring at renewal time is more prevalent.

Since it is difficult to distinguish between good decisions with poor outcomes, and poor decisions, the loss ratio alone does not provide an adequate measure of performance. Underwriting efficiency can be evaluated by utilization of *standards of performance.* Standards of performance are activities that can be specifically defined, observed, and recorded, and that, collectively, constitute evidence that the actions taken were of the quality, quantity, and timeliness that—*in the long run*—should produce the desired objective, such as profit or increased sales. If standards of performance are met, the probability of success is greatly increased although there is no guarantee that the intended result will be achieved. The difficulty in attempting to evaluate insurance company performance by a review of loss and expense ratios alone can be demonstrated by a consideration of the various elements that affect these ratios.

If an insurance company sets as an annual objective the earning of a statutory profit of, say, $1,000,000, it could evoke much unwanted behavior if only the desired dollar profit were to be used as a criterion for rewarding behavior of the sales force, underwriters, and claims departments. For example, assuming a steady and sufficient flow of potentially profitable sales were made the year before, a *decrease* in sales this year could increase the earned premium in relation to underwriting expenses and thus enhance profit. Underwriters could fail to write either new or renewal business that was not of superior quality and cancel good or average business. The claims department could attempt to underpay claims or postpone a review and update of files, or even take down the IBNR (incurred but not reported) reserves, thus understating true current liabilities. All of these measures would conceivably contribute toward the goal of $1,000,000 in statutory profit this year. But the overall effects on the company for the following years would be most undesirable.

Examples of standards of performance include those with regard to file documentation, following underwriting guidelines, turnaround time for new business and endorsements, and the new business written compared to quotes given. These are described in more detail later in this chapter.

Accounting Systems for Presenting Loss Data

Effective underwriting results, besides being obscured by chance (good decisions with poor outcomes), are also somewhat affected by the accounting system employed. Underwriting results are reported on a calendar-year basis under statutory accounting rules. In Chapter 7 the differences between calendar-year, calendar-accident-year, and policy-year accounting were defined in a rate-making context. Underwriting results are similarly affected by the accounting method used. Losses or changes in loss reserves on losses which occurred in a previous period can obscure the underwriting results in the current year on a calendar-year basis.

Careful examination of the data in Exhibit 10-5 indicates that the results for the garage liability policy issued in 1977 are very different, depending on the year in which the results are reviewed and the accounting system employed. Utilizing this case as an example, the implications of calendar-year, policy-year, and calendar-accident-year accounting systems for the evaluation of underwriting results will be shown.

Calendar-Year   Calendar-year accounting views each policy individually but records only events that occur in that calendar year. In Exhibit 10-5 the policy was issued to Sorensen Motors, an automobile dealer, in November 1977.

The written premium (the total premium for the contract period) was $2,400. The earned premium for 1977 was only $300. (The statutory formula provides that only 1/24 of the annual written premium is earned in the first month; thereafter, 1/12 of the annual written premium is earned each month; the last 1/24 is earned in the month following expiration or renewal.) The loss ratio (incurred losses divided by earned premium) is a "favorable" 0 percent.

The decision continues to look good at year end in 1978. The policy expired in November and no losses were reported. In addition, the remaining written premium was fully earned. To conclude that the decision on Sorensen based on these results was a good one would still be premature. Exhibit 10-5 clearly shows that ultimately in 1985, a loss of $300,000 was paid. To examine calendar-year results, even at year end, is frequently "premature." It is not unlike deciding the winner of a baseball game after the third inning.

While a loss did occur in October 1978, neither the insured nor the insurance company knew of the seriousness of the event until October 1980, two years later. The time lag might have been greater were it not for a statute setting time limitations for the filing of suits. In this instance, it can only be surmised why Sorensen's customer waited until just before the deadline stipulated in the statute of limitations. First, the claimant had been severely injured in the accident, and sufficient time was required for recovery or partial recovery in order that the extent of physical damage and bodily injury could be determined. Second, as the plaintiff (Sorensen's customer) began preparing the suit with an attorney, it was clearly to the customer's advantage to gather evidence, depositions, and affidavits while memories were fresh and witnesses more easily identified and located. In other words, the customer fully built a case while it was fresh, and only after that was done notified Sorensen. Finally, during an era of ever-increasing jury awards and inflation, every month of delay may substantially affect the outcome in the plaintiff's favor and to the disadvantage of Sorensen, the underwriter, and the insurance company.

The Sorensen policy was one of many garage liability policies written in 1977 by the insurer. The outcome of that book of business can be severely distorted by a single large loss such as the Sorensen claim.

Furthermore, in calendar year 1980, the other garage liability policies in the book may or may not be of good quality. The 1980 calendar-year results include a $10,000 loss, although there is no premium from that particular policy against which it can be charged. The Sorensen premium was fully earned in 1977-78. Therefore, the $10,000 loss affects the loss ratio and statutory profit of 1980, not 1977-78. The underwriter who originally wrote the Sorensen policy may have been promoted, transferred, or terminated by 1980. If this is the case, the underwriters on the book in 1980 are charged with a loss from a policy underwritten by their predecessors. Note that in April 1982, four years and five months after policy issuance and three years and six months after the accident, there is a $40,000 increase in the loss reserve. This loss must also be charged to the garage liability results and premiums earned in 1982. The effect is even more disastrous in January and February of 1984. If the underwriters were to be evaluated purely on the basis of calendar year loss results, they would look very bad in 1984. Conversely, the same criteria would indicate that they merited bonuses in February 1985 when the final settlement occurs and the incurred loss shows a decrease of $200,000 (the reserve "take down" has the same effect as earning that amount in loss-free premiums).

The Sorensen chronology viewed in *calendar-year* terms clearly shows the distortions in underwriting results produced by loss lags and reserve changes over the several years from policy inception to final claim settlement. In any one of the eight years it takes for the events to unfold, the results in that one year do not indicate the final outcome. One year the results are good, in another they are poor, and in each they are unrepresentative of the total.

The length of time for the total picture to be known varies by insured and product line. In third-party lines the distortion is greatest. For example, medical professional liability cases may stretch over twenty or twenty-five years. The time problem can be highlighted by an incident that occurred in 1968 during a review of current loss data on a protection and indemnity (ocean marine) policy. The file, originally

Exhibit 10-5
Evaluation of Loss Data

	Nov. 1977	Dec. 31, 1977	Oct. 1978	Oct. 1980 *	Nov. 1980	April 1982
Chronology of Events	Garage Liab. Pol. issued Limit $500,000 An. Prem. $2,400		Accident: insured's customer hits another auto on interstate highway. Insured's customer severely injured.	Customer initiates suit vs. Sorensen. Alleges "faulty operation" via work on customer's auto as prob. cause Suit: $1,633,000 *(Three days prior to expiration of statute of limitations.)	Insurer establishes $10,000 reserve based on first notice from Sorensen's agent. Little data for setting reserve.	Reserve increased to $50,000 as result of investigation and initial contacts with plaintiff's attorney.
Calendar Year	W.P.:$2,400 E.P.:$100 L/R: -0-	W.P.:$-0- E.P.:$300 (YTD) L/R: -0-	W.P.:$-0- E.P.:$2,000 (YTD) L/R: -0-		W.P.: -0- E.P.: -0- Loss: $10,000 L/R: XXXX	W.P.: -0- E.P.: -0- Loss: $40,000 L/R: XXXX
Policy Year		W.P.:$2,400 E.P.:$2,400 Loss:$300,000 (developed in 1985) L/R: 12,500%				
Calendar-Accident Year			W.P.:$-0- E.P.:$2,000 Loss:$300,000 (developed in 1985) L/R: 15,000%			

Continued on next page

	Dec. 1982	Dec. 1983	Jan. 1984	Feb. 1984	Feb. 1985
Chronology of Events.	Insurance Co. wins summary judgment in lower court; no legal basis for a trial.	Appellate court reverses summary judgment.	Reserve increased from $50,000 to $300,000.	Reserve increased to total of $500,000.	Settled out of court for $300,000...few days prior to scheduled trial.
Calendar Year			W.P.:$-0- E.P.:$-0- Loss: $250,000 L/R: XXXX	W.P.:$-0- E.P.:$-0- Loss: $200,000 L/R: XXXX	W.P.:$-0- E.P.:$-0- Loss: minus $200,000 (reserve take down) L/R: XXXX
Policy Year					
Calendar Accident Year					

established for an accident occurring in 1917, was under review because a reserve increase of $100,000 was necessary in 1968. A seaman had been injured in the course of employment in 1917. The liability of the vessel owner was uncontested and by law was established as "wages, maintenance, and cure" for the rest of the seaman's life. The original reserve was based on the extent of injuries, projected medical costs, and the life expectancy of the seaman. The seaman outlived the original projections, and the original reserve proved insufficient. Therefore, in 1968 the underwriter was faced with a loss to the book of protection and indemnity business when, in fact, the accident had occurred *five decades earlier*. The original underwriter had long since retired.

Such gaps or time lags in the histories of individual accounts are examples of loss development delay. These lags or "tails" are particularly bothersome in calendar-year accounting. Exhibit 10-6 illustrates some typical loss development delays for two lines of business. Note the contrast between direct damage fire and allied lines and general liability. Even in fire, however, there is some delay; but almost all insurer liability is clearly known within twelve months after the close of the calendar year.

Policy-Year Policy-year accounting as described earlier is based wholly on the year of policy issuance. All losses, loss payments, and adjustments, whenever they occur, are charged back to the block of policies issued during the policy year being analyzed, and to the premium earned on them.

In the Sorensen Motors chronology, events were scattered over eight years. Yet, in Exhibit 10-5 it can be seen that for the final "developed" policy year, 1977, the reserve transactions and final settlement are all "totaled" and represent the final product of the several intervening events.

Obviously, the final policy-year figures were not available as of December 31, 1977, but developed over an eight-year period. Nevertheless, the losses from 1980, 1982, 1984, and 1985 were all charged to 1977 against the premium for that year. Therefore, records for ensuing years 1978 through 1985 were not cluttered and clouded by the subsequent events that properly were attributable to a 1977 underwriting decision.

Policy-year data are incomplete while any claims remain open. As time goes by, the changes affecting that policy year have no effect on other years' results. Each year is independent. The loss development delay factors still cause distortion in a policy year until that policy year is fully developed, but distortion of subsequent years' results by these developments does not occur. This is an obvious disadvantage.

Exhibit 10-6

Example of Loss Development Delay*

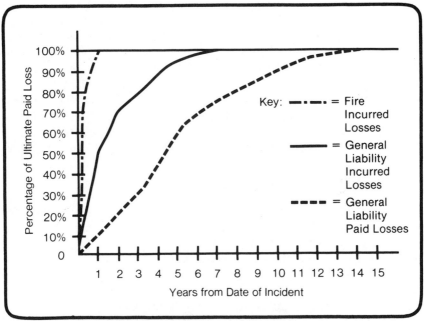

* Sample from countrywide book of business of a multiline insurer.

Calendar-Accident-Year As explained earlier, calendar-accident-year data and policy-year data are quite similar. The major difference is that accident-year records are based on the year of the loss event. In the Sorensen chronology, therefore, the records reflect a running tabulation for only the year 1978, rather than the policy year of 1977.

Summary of Calendar-, Policy-, and Calendar-Accident-Year Accounting While calendar-year accounting is the most predominant method for property and liability insurers, it is the least reliable of the three for use in measuring and monitoring the performance of underwriting. The primacy of the calendar-year system lies in the fact that it is required in all states by statutory regulations. Insurance regulation, in turn, has as its foremost aim the overseeing of the solvency of insurers. The calendar-year method makes results available shortly after the end of the year and is sufficiently accurate for regulatory purposes.

On the other hand, calendar-year accounting obscures and clouds the monitoring and measurement of underwriting decisions because unfolding events frequently appear in the data for a year that is quite different from the year and circumstances under which the underwriting decisions were actually made.

Policy-year accounting is, conversely, the best of the three for monitoring underwriting decision making. The unfolding events are aggregated and maintained for the year in which the decision was made. Unfortunately, there is a severe lag problem with policy-year accounting since it takes a minimum of thirty months to get reasonably complete loss data, and in many lines, much longer.

Calendar-accident-year accounting is similar to policy-year in that unfolding events are registered to the one year being recorded, that is, the year of the claim against the policy. Unfortunately, the accident may or may not occur in the year the underwriting decision is made.

Use of Ratios in Monitoring

Loss Ratios Loss ratios are frequently used as measures for monitoring underwriting performance. The most common of these is the incurred losses to earned premium loss ratio. Note that the phrase "incurred loss" is construed to mean incurred loss and loss adjustment expenses unless otherwise stated. Loss ratios all too frequently are quoted when IBNR (incurred but not reported) is or is not included, and confusion naturally results. Accurately used, it is stated: "loss ratio, excluding IBNR" or "loss ratio, including IBNR." Failure to so designate these components can dramatically change the meaning, since in third-party lines the IBNR may add as much as 10 to 40 additional percentage points.

A loss ratio is merely an index of underwriting results. Assume that Company A has an annual earned premium of $1,400,000 and a loss ratio of 74 percent (incurred loss of $1,036,000). Assume further that Company B has an annual earned premium of $1,100,000 and a loss ratio of 69 percent (incurred losses of $759,000). Which company had the better year? In fact, the question cannot be answered from the data thus far presented. Clearly, Company B had the lower loss ratio, but Company A could have had a larger statutory profit. The relative expense of doing business by each would have to be established. If, for example, Company A had underwriting expenses of $100,000, its statutory profit would have been $264,000; if Company B had the same expenses ($100,000), its profit would have been $241,000.

A further compounding of this example would result from the knowledge that Company A wrote only property insurance while Company B was concerned solely with writing general liability insurance. It was illustrated earlier that general liability would have a much greater loss development delay. Therefore, one must know whether or not this IBNR factor had been included in the loss ratio. If these are both statutory results, then the IBNR is included in both since that is a requirement of statutory accounting. If not, it is questionable whether Company B has made a profit at all. Even if the IBNR were included, over time Company B's IBNR could prove to be woefully inadequate.

Loss ratios cannot be compared accurately from one insurance company to another because of possible variances in underwriting expenses. The same reasoning holds for comparisons between lines in the same insurance company and from one year to the next.

As stated previously, a loss ratio is an index to underwriting and, at best, is a rough gauge of the results being obtained. It can never answer the question whether or not the decisions symbolized by the ratio were good or poor.

Expense Ratios As previously discussed, another component of statutory accounting is underwriting expense. *On a trade basis, the expense ratio is calculated by dividing underwriting expense incurred by written rather than earned premium.* This method presumes that all expenses other than loss and loss adjustment expense are incurred at the time of policy issuance.

Since the expense ratio is an expression of the costs of doing business, and since these costs are essentially under the direct control of management, insurance companies quite properly give great weight to them as a key index of efficiency.

When written premiums are decreasing the expense ratio tends to go up, presuming everything else remains equal. This is because reduced written premium will cause certain business expense items to be reduced but others will remain the same. Certain costs of doing business, such as office leases and salaries, are fixed, at least temporarily, and cannot be reduced. In addition, even if all expenses remain stable, the decrease in written premiums causes the ratio to go up.

In Exhibit 10-7, the premium volume declines in 19X6 from the previous year by $10,000,000, but expenses are reduced by only $1,000,000. While commissions were reduced in this hypothetical example by $2,000,000, there were increases in salaries and other expenses by $1,000,000 caused by inflation. Similarly, in 19X7 a written premium increase of $30,000,000 (33.33 percent) reduced the expense ratio by only 2.7 percent. Again, certain "fixed" costs presumably were subject to continued inflation, and commission expense was dramatically increased.

Combined Ratio The combined ratio was defined earlier as the sum of the loss ratio and expense ratio. It is considered to be favorable when it is less than 100 percent and unfavorable above this figure.

Exhibit 10-7
Trade Basis Expense Ratios

	19X5	19X6	19X7
Written Premium	$100,000,000	$90,000,000	$120,000,000
Commission Expense (Average 20%)	$20,000,000	$18,000,000	$24,000,000
Salaries of Employees	10,000,000	10,500,000	11,000,000
Rent, telephone, travel, and all other expenses	2,000,000	2,500,000	3,000,000
Total Underwriting Expenses	$ 32,000,000	$31,000,000	$38,000,000
Trade Basis Expense Ratio	32.0%	34.4%	31.7%

Exhibit 10-8
Combined Ratios

Year-End Figures	19X5	19X6	19X7
Written Premium	$100,000,000	$90,000,000	$120,000,000
Earned Premium	98,000,000	91,000,000	92,000,000
Underwriting Expense	32,000,000	31,000,000	38,000,000
Loss Expense	58,800,000	54,600,000	55,200,000
Trade Basis			
Loss Ratio	60.0%	60.0%	60.0%
Trade Basis Expense Ratio	32.0%	34.4%	31.7%
Trade Basis Combined Ratio	92.0%	94.4%	91.7%
Statutory Basis			
Loss Ratio	60.0%	60.0%	60.0%
Statutory Expense Ratio	32.6%	34.1%	41.3%
Statutory Combined Ratio	92.6%	94.1%	101.3%
Statutory Profit or (Loss)	$7,200,000	$5,400,000	($1,200,000)

Exhibit 10-8 illustrates that a trade basis combined ratio considerably under 100 percent does not necessarily mean that the insurance company made a statutory profit.

A trade basis expense ratio divides expenses by written premium rather than earned premium. Since most expenses are incurred in putting premium on the books, it is felt that relating expenses to written premium rather than earned premium is most accurate. A *trade basis* combined ratio adds the trade basis expense ratio to the loss ratio.

The *statutory* combined ratio includes the statutory expense ratio with expenses divided by *earned* premium. *The statutory profit is defined as the amount by which the statutory combined ratio is less than 100 percent. Conversely, the statutory loss is defined as the amount by which the statutory combined ratio is more than 100 percent.* In Exhibit 10-8 there was considerable growth in 19X7, the written premium jumped 33.33 percent from 19X6. But the earned premium was only $1,000,000 greater than a year earlier. The quality of business, on the other hand, remained relatively stable, as witnessed by the 60 percent loss ratio that held for all three years. (Actually, it appears that the quality was improved. Assume average premium size of $1,000. Thus, there were 100,000 policies in 19X5, 90,000 in 19X6, and 120,000 in 19X7. The 120,000 policies produced proportionately fewer losses than the other two years.) Yet, in 19X7 the company had a statutory loss. The negative impact was primarily produced by the great increase in underwriting expense, which was approximately 22.6 percent more than in 19X6. Thus, it can be seen that if all else remains equal (quality of units, size of units, commission, percentage), a company experiencing a significant growth in written premium will concomitantly experience a deterioration in its statutory profit.

To this point, this analysis has centered on statutory and trade basis profit and their components as measures or monitoring devices for underwriting. These are measures primarily emphasizing results of overall underwriting activity. They fail to measure those items over which underwriters have some modicum of control.

The Small Loss Ratio Loss ratios are subject to fortuitous events. Good risks (well underwritten) can have losses; poor risks may be loss free. Large fortuitous losses will dramatically affect the loss ratio. Even sound selection, pricing, and loss control will not necessarily preclude a series of unfortunate large losses. In short, the underwriter may experience some bad luck.

To offset the dramatic effects of large losses for the branch office, or even for an individual risk underwriter writing a fairly large volume of business, some insurance companies have adopted the small loss ratio concept. It is based on the belief that no individual underwriter will control a book of business of sufficient size to withstand shock losses; therefore, large losses will frequently produce statutory losses. Large losses are statistically predictable over the insurance company's entire book of business, but not for a given underwriter or even for a given branch office territory. Therefore, large losses should not be taken at face value in analyzing the underwriter's performance. The concept of the small loss ratio holds that a given permissible loss ratio consists primarily of frequent small losses. For example, assume that for a given line, 80 percent of all losses are less than $25,000. The remaining larger losses are significantly *less frequent in occurrence* and therefore are *less predictable.* These large losses often are less easily managed by loss control, by use of coverage restrictions and deductibles, and by other underwriting tools. The *small loss ratio* is defined as the ratio to earned premium of all incurred losses of less than a selected dollar severity limit. The appropriate severity limit must be determined for each line. A small loss ratio as a standard of performance presumes:

1. an identifiable product line.
2. a statistically derived "large loss" or severity limit. A "large loss" is defined as a loss that in magnitude generally produces about 25 percent of the dollars of loss for the entire product line but in frequency may constitute 2 to 10 percent of all occurrences. Losses of this size and greater are excluded from all calculations.
3. an information system that permits the individual underwriter to have the available data to calculate the actual small loss ratio and compare it to the permissible small loss ratio that has been promulgated as the benchmark.

As an illustration, the total loss ratio objective may be 64.77 percent for the commercial package class in a national book of business. This consists of small loss ratio of 28 percent and a large loss ratio of 26.31 percent, with miscellaneous additional components such as bulk reserves (IBNR) and paid unallocated loss adjustment expenses of 10.46 percent. The objective small loss ratio for a branch office may be further modified from the national objective of 28 percent because of territorial differences and the differences in their product mix within that product line compared to the national book.

The small loss ratio is then calculated, preferably on a *rolling twelve-month basis.* (One method to establish and maintain a "rolling twelve" [which is a moving average] is to start with the last calendar year, subtracting the January figures from that year and adding the new January figures for this year. During each ensuing month, the previous February, March, April figures and so forth are subtracted and the new month added from this year.) The larger time span plus the larger premium and loss information via the "rolling twelve" basis tends to minimize fluctuations and increase credibility.

Exhibit 10-9 graphically illustrates a small loss ratio plotted over a ten-month period. It clearly reveals, in this instance, an upward trend.

Exhibit 10-9
Small Loss Ratio

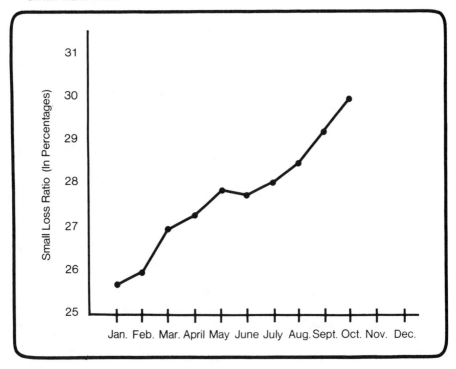

Such a trend indicates a deteriorating performance and appears to call for corrective action. Just what action is called for may require some fact-finding such as a sampling of in-force policies and review of underwriting files for such things as:

1. possible abuses in providing scheduled credits or failure to debit certain accounts properly,
2. poor use of judgment rates for transportation exposures or liability exposures requiring Guide "a" rates or similar exposures,
3. failure to use current, appropriate property values that are rising especially during times of inflation, and
4. frequencies of small losses that should perhaps be borne by insureds via deductibles.

If fact-finding indicates that one or more of the above problems exist, files can be marked for corrective action at renewal or immediately (mid-term corrections), if deemed necessary. New business, in turn, can be closely watched to avoid repeating earlier mistakes.

Standards of Performance

Selection Standards If underwriters are given well-defined bounds within which to make selection decisions, these decisions can be monitored. The selection standard of performance presumes that the insurance company, in its underwriting manual, has set up certain selection rules. The selection standard of performance measures the extent to which a particular underwriter or branch office has adhered to these selection rules. For example, assume that a particular company's commercial package strategy includes the following:

Apartment Class - highly desirable: Masonry or better construction; or garden-type apartments, not exceeding three floors, not more than ten years in age, having public protection of I.S.O. class six or better, with no more than twenty-five units within the same fire division.

Average: Apartments not included within *all* the criteria under "highly desirable" but of no greater than twenty years in age, having public protection of not less than class eight, with no more than forty units within the same fire division. In addition, the electrical wiring, plumbing, and heating systems have been certified within the past twelve months by a licensed electrician or plumber as meeting current applicable fire, building, and/or safety codes applicable in that jurisdiction.

Below Average: All apartments not qualifying under "highly desirable" or "average" and, in addition, all apartments having the following:
1. Swimming pools without clear markings of depths, proper supervision, and fencing at least to four feet in height fully enclosing the pool with locked gate(s) when not supervised.
2. Restaurants exceeding 1,600 square feet. Restaurants less than this size must meet all criteria for at least "Average" under the restaurant classification. (These selection criteria are merely illustrative and in no way are to be construed as criteria for actual use in underwriting. Indeed, they are not complete enough and are contained herein only to emphasize that *minimal* selection standards are required if underwriters are not to make decisions in a vacuum.)

Underwriters can then be measured on whether or not they wrote primarily "highly desirable" and "average" risks in a class or in the "below average" category. If the strategy was wisely created, the former two categories will more than likely produce the desired result, which is a profit in the apartment subline. If there is no profit and the underwriter wrote only "highly desirable" and "average" risks, then the loss either was the result of fortuitous events (good selection decisions but poor outcomes) or there was substandard performance in some other area of underwriting such as pricing or risk improvement. But, the underwriter did what was expected.

Conversely, if the underwriters had selected a large number of "below average" risks *and* had made a profit, they were merely lucky (poor decisions with favorable outcomes). Their performance failed to meet selection standards since continued selection on this basis eventually and inevitably will lead to unprofitable results.

Product Mix Standards A reasonable underwriting strategy may be to avoid placing all eggs in one basket. In addition, marketing strategy may dictate that in order to write many of some classes, it will be necessary to write a few of some other less desirable classes.

During the late 1960s it became increasingly clear, for example, that social, economic, and political values were shifting in a manner that was making general liability insurance unprofitable. Due to loss development delay, the effects of these shifting attitudes were not fully felt by most insurers until 1974 and 1975. By then, enormous losses made the shifts all too obvious. Insurance companies were suddenly faced with extremely difficult choices especially those who had traditionally written the larger general manufacturing classes where the deterioration was most severe. To withdraw entirely from general liability lines would adversely affect writings in other commercial lines, such as fire, commercial packages, and workers' compensation. Some companies further hypothesized that rate adequacy and juridical restraint were not possible in the foreseeable future. Strategies required that these contingencies be faced squarely. The result was a strategy aimed at drastically altering the makeup of the existing book of business; in short, a shift in the product mix.

Changing a product mix within a $15, $20, $50, or $100 million book of business is not accomplished easily. Branch offices and individual underwriters have been known to drag their feet over such issues. But measuring the underwriters' performances, not on profit or loss results (which were plainly going to continue in a negative vein for some time anyway) but on quotas of classes within the product line, will usually bring about the required change.

A product mix standard of performance for general liability underwriting may look, in part, like this:

Product Mix Standard for Performance

A. At least 80 percent of the *new* experience-rated and/or schedule-rated units (policies) of the total branch office general liability book shall come from the following classes:
   Contractors

> Service and Mercantile

B. At least 70 percent of the *new* experience-rated and/or schedule-rated premium writings of the total branch office general liability book shall come from the following classes:
> Contractors
> Service and Mercantile

C. No more than 8 percent of the *new* and *renewal* experience-rated and/or schedule-rated written premium of the total branch office general liability book shall come from the following class(es):
> General Manufacturing

Product mix standards of performance are similar to an old fire insurance concept called "the balanced book." Certain undesirable classes of risk were numerically weighted, and the underwriter was charged with writing enough unweighted premium to offset the premium generated by the weighted categories. Hence, a frame, unprotected metal-working firm with a negative weighting of 50 and producing $1,000 in premium would have to be offset or balanced by $50,000 of premium from nonweighted risks, such as brick protected churches.

Pricing Standards Both underwriters and actuaries go to great expense and to great lengths to develop large data bases for the promulgation of rates. Because the resulting manual rates are mathematically determined, they measure the exposures of a given risk only by accident. Rather, the manual rate is for the "average" risk in class. The rate, therefore, assumes some risks to be better than average and some that are poorer than average, with the bulk of the risks hovering closely on either side of the mean. But when underwriters are given the additional tools of experience-rating plans and schedule-rating plans, the mathematical precision can be quickly lost. Reasons for this include:

1. Underwriters believe implicitly that their own expertise and experience enable them to select risks more precisely than the arithmetic mean, and to price the risks accordingly.
2. Experience rating loss data all too frequently are more favorable on applications for new business than subsequent experience tends to bear out.
3. Risks suffering losses are frequently remarketed, and loss data tend to be skewed in the insured's favor (see 2 above).
4. Competition frequently focuses on rate cutting rather than on the underwriter's skill, the quality of the insurance company's engineering or claims settling abilities, and the other services the insurer may have as assets.

Whether the above reasons are really the root cause is immaterial; some estimates in general liability and commercial auto rating during the early 1980s clearly show a propensity to charge for the total book at 70 percent or less of manual rate levels. Therefore, for whatever reasons, manual rates were clearly being ignored. If the manual rate is proper, charging 30 percent less than the manual rate on an entire book of business can hardly be expected to produce favorable results.

In reaction to such behavior, some insurance companies measure underwriters' performance on their pricing. Rather than second-guess the underwriter's discretion on any one single risk, these insurance companies simply insist that competent pricing performance presumes that over an entire branch office book of business for a line such as commercial auto, the charge will be not less than 100 percent of manual.

In practice, this means that any one individual risk may have experience credits and scheduled credits, justifiable according to the filed rate plan, to the full limit allowed. At the same time, another risk (or several other risks) must be rated with enough experience and/or scheduled debits to equalize the credits previously given.

In order to measure such a standard, certain steps must be taken, and data must be captured at the individual risk underwriter or branch office level:

1. Monthly and cumulative experience- and schedule-rated risk records must be maintained. The records must display units (policies), dollar amounts, percentages of manual for each line, such as auto liability (BI/PD) or products liability (BI/PD), for example.
2. Each exposure must be correctly classified and rated according to ISO, other bureau, or company manuals.
3. The underwriter must request prior insurer experience on all new experience-rated submissions directly from the prior insurer.
4. The underwriter must log the number and size of accounts outside the ranges of 95 to 105 percent of manual and their impact (current and estimate on renewal).
5. Each underwriting unit must develop and maintain a "bank account register" of premium over 100 percent of manual and a strategy for its use. (The bank account register is a log in which all premium volume generated at over 100 percent of manual is cumulated. If there is $50,000 "in the bank," then $50,000 of discounts from manual could be given with the overall book still at 100 percent of manual.)

"Accommodated Risks" Standards Frequently, an underwriter is faced with a submission or a renewal where pricing and risk improvement can in no way be adjusted to make the risk acceptable. However, because of other reasons, the underwriter is inclined to write that risk as a "favor" for a good producer.

In most cases, the underwriter is making the accommodation because of past performance of the producer, or promises of future performance. If the accommodation is made because of past performance, then there is no special monitoring associated with that decision. The accommodation should still be recorded in case the producer attempts to trade too heavily on the basis of past performance. It should also be confirmed by memo in order to establish in the file a record that an accommodation was made in this case. Otherwise, the producer might consider that acceptance as a change in underwriting standards or policy. It should be made clear that this is an exception.

When the accommodation is made on the basis of a representation of future performance on the part of the producer, special monitoring of that performance is in order. An example of future performance by the producer would be an increased flow of higher quality submissions. If a personal line underwriter accepts an otherwise unacceptable personal auto risk as an accommodation, for instance, the standard may call for the producer to lower the percentage of young driver submissions during the next year.

The problems for the underwriter in these business transactions are essentially that:

1. the producer has less incentive to remember his or her obligations acquired in such a situation than does the underwriter. As a result, the burden for remembering an accommodation falls on the underwriter.
2. follow-up is inevitably required in order to collect the "increased flow" previously promised.

Therefore, when an accommodation is made, the underwriter should:

1. log the facts in an "accommodation diary";
2. immediately confirm the accommodation by written memo specifying all particulars; and
3. follow up each accommodation for "payment" on not less than a quarterly basis, if the accommodation is based on future performance.

Accommodation logs, in turn, should be reviewed at least semiannually by underwriting management to insure that the procedure is followed and that accommodations are the exception rather than the rule.

The Retention Ratio Standards To fill a barrel with water when it leaks at a rate faster than it can be filled is a futile exercise. To attempt to increase policies and written premium when the failure-to-renew rate exceeds new business is equally as futile. More importantly, a failure in the renewal rate (or *retention rate*) is invariably linked to significant deficiencies in several possible areas of underwriting. These include service to the producers, pricing contrary to the market, and unfavorable claims service.

After a careful analysis of prior performance, such as the past three years, a retention ratio can be established. Considerations should include the strong possibility that a certain amount of renewal business will be unacceptable one year or so from original acceptance. For example, a suspicious loss history may develop; characteristics of the insured itself may alter due to expanded or new operations; or the values at risk may now exceed insurer policy on line limits. Furthermore, retention ratios must be defined. Are risks not renewed due to termination of the producer to be included or excluded? Are risks to be differentiated as not renewed at insurance company initiation from those not renewed at insured or producer initiation? The answers to these questions obviously play an important role in establishing a worthwhile standard.

Data must be gathered to provide information necessary to calculate the retention ratio. This can be done via a diary system based on records of renewal quotes or by means of computer programs where renewal billings are so handled.

Ratios kept on a rolling twelve-month basis (see the earlier discussion of the small loss ratio) will indicate favorable and unfavorable trends. Trends, in turn, warrant fact-finding to discover root causes of change. Finally, the retention ratio is a valid device for monitoring expenses. Renewal business is invariably less expensive to book than a new submission.

The Success Ratio Standards Success ratios or written-to-quoted ratios indicate the efficiency and economy of activity in acquiring new business. A ratio deemed inordinately high may suggest:

1. lessening of competition for various reasons,
2. rate inadequacy or poor pricing (too low),
3. unduly broad covering or form, or
4. general deterioration in the quality of underwriting.

Conversely, a ratio suspiciously low might suggest:

1. increasing severity of competition,
2. rates or prices that are too high, or
3. coverages or forms that are too restrictive.

In establishing a success ratio, it is necessary to anticipate planned activity that may impact on it. A production campaign, for example, probably will cause the ratio to jump dramatically. Furthermore, a "successful" campaign may cause a counter-balancing drop in the retention ratio the following year if an independent agency marketing system is faced with another insurer's current campaign for similar business.

On the other hand, the success ratio should also reflect stricter underwriting selection, pricing, or coverage policy than is planned during the monitoring cycle.

Both retention and success ratios benefit from comparison at the local level with national or company-wide experience. Insights into territorial variations are highlighted and may indicate opportunities awaiting a vigorous marketing action or potential problems that can be corrected before they exact serious tolls on allied underwriting activities and functions.

The Service to Producers Standards For the past two decades, producers have invariably ranked insurance companies and branch offices on their services to them and their customers. This is possibly the most important single criterion by which their placement decisions are made. Superior service satisfies producers and presumably influences the quality of business they place with their insurers. Some insurers categorize their producers, in turn, and provide services based on these ratings.

Following is a standard of performance used by one company to monitor its service to producers:

Category	*Minimum Acceptable Standard*
1. Quotations	6 working days
2. New policies	6 working days
3. Risks subject to reinsurance	12 working days
4. Cancellations, endorsements, certificates	5 working days
5. Direct cancellation notices	Same day service
6. Renewals	No later than 30 days prior to expiration

SUMMARY

A major characteristic of underwriting decision making is the repetitive nature of the decisions.

Underwriting decisions are of many types—from difficult and complex to simple and routine. Decisions can be sorted into routine and nonroutine categories. Decisions theorists refer to routine decisions as "programmed decisions." Routine decisions can often be quickly and easily disposed of, and frequently their implementation can be delegated to clerical personnel. Nonroutine decisions require the use of the full underwriting decision-making model. In decisions of this type, the gathering of information, development of alternative courses of action, and the careful evaluation of the various alternatives to select the best course of action can best be done in a structured manner.

The major considerations in the evaluation of alternatives can be classified under five major headings. These are:

1. the hazards inherent in the risk,
2. the underwriting authority applicable to the risk,
3. the underwriting manual and insurer attitude toward the risk,
4. the insurer's relationship with the producer of the business, and
5. the existence of regulatory constraints on the decisions.

The next step in the process is the selection of the best alternative, the decision itself. At this point, the decision must be implemented. There are three aspects to implementing an underwriting decision. These are communication of the decision to those affected by it, creation and maintenance of a claims information system to assist in monitoring, and execution of the appropriate documentation.

The results of underwriting decisions are poor guides to the quality of the underwriting function because:

1. underwriting decisions are subject to fortuitous outcomes, and these may be good or poor regardless of the quality of the decisions,
2. underwriting results are subject to a variety of external factors over which the underwriter has little control, and
3. the current, most prevalent or pervasive method of aggregating results is via statutory accounting methods. These are subject to distortions. A shrinking volume, all else being equal, will show improvement, while a growing volume, all else being equal, will show deterioration. Also, the calendar-year method (which is widely used) is greatly distorted by the loss development delay.

The best method for measuring performance requires the clear definition of objectives (desired results) and a specified series of activities the achievement of which cannot *guarantee* the results but will materially enhance the probability that the desired results will be attained.

Standards of performance for underwriters may be based on, but are not limited to, such things as (1) selection; (2) product mix; (3) pricing, including specified percentages of manual rates; (4) accommodated risks; (5) retention ratio; (6) success ratio; and (7) service to producers.

Measurement of underwriting activity is most efficiently and productively accomplished by frequent and periodic monitoring of standards of performance rather than by examination of the actual results of individual underwriting decisions.

Chapter Note

1. Flow chart developed by E. P. Hollingsworth, CPCU, ARM, Vice President, Frank B. Hall & Co.

CHAPTER 11

Communications and Underwriting in a Changing Environment

COMMUNICATIONS AND UNDERWRITING

Introduction

Every interaction between an underwriter and others involves communication. Whether formal or informal, written or verbal, the process of communication is an integral and frequently overlooked part of underwriting. The efficiency with which the underwriter gathers information prior to a decision is heavily influenced by the underwriter's skill as a communicator. A verbose, poorly organized letter requesting additional information from a producer usually requires a further exchange of letters or phone calls and wastes time and money for both parties. It also leaves an unfavorable impression with the producer. Similarly, a message of declination that is handled with diplomacy and tact is preferred to a snarled, "We don't write that junk!" punctuated by a slam of the receiver. In any technical activity such as underwriting, there is a natural tendency for the communicator to become preoccupied with the information being sought or provided by the communicator, ignoring the technique of the communication process itself. This frequently leads to miscommunication or ineffective and inefficient communication.

Internal and External Communications

Internal communications consists of conversations, letters, memos, and reports used to contact other members of the organization

411

(insurance company, agency, and so on) in the performance of the underwriting task. External communications encompass all contacts between the underwriter and persons outside the same organization. Providing or obtaining information underlies all internal or external communications. Both internal and external communications can be evaluated by considering the effectiveness of the communication—that is, the extent to which the goal of the communication is achieved relative to the cost of the communication.

Increased proficiency in external communications can improve the relationship between the underwriter and the producers and insureds, while reducing costs. An improvement in the techniques or channels of internal communications can expedite and improve decision making, provide speedier service, and reduce costs.

The Functions of Communication

There are three primary functions of communication:

1. The information function,
2. The command or instruction function, and
3. The influence or persuasion function.

Before initiating a particular message, it is useful to consider the purpose or purposes intended. Is the message intended to inform, command, or influence?

The Information Function The primary function of all communication is the transmission of information. For analytic purposes any particular communication can be subdivided into three major parts: the originator, the message, and the receiver. A clear distinction should be made between the concept of a message and the concept of information. Information is data that increases the knowledge or decreases the uncertainty of the receiver. For example, assume that an underwriter sends a letter to a producer stating that the liability risk submitted cannot be written due to "lack of business background." This will lead to a phone call from the producer asking "what business background?" From the letter it is not clear if the underwriter found a deficiency in the business experience of the insured, or financial history, or education and training. The letter did not increase the knowledge of the receiver and increased rather than decreased his or her uncertainty.

The Nature of Information.[1] The amount of useful information a particular message will contain depends upon the manner in which that message is perceived by the receiver. The following conditions must be present for a message to be informative. The message must be:

1. physically attainable by the receiver,

2. comprehensible to *that* receiver,
3. credible from the viewpoint of the receiver, and
4. relevant to the receiver.

Attainability of the Message.   Before a message can convey any information to the receiver, it must be delivered to that receiver in some form. It is obvious that a letter must be received before it can be read. Quite frequently, however, messages are left with one party and never received by the right person. It is essential, therefore, to assure that the message has been physically received by the person for whom it is intended.

For example, let us assume that a workers' compensation under-writer writes a letter to a large industrial insured suggesting that a certain safety procedure be followed in one of its large plants. The message should be received by the plant manager. If the letter ends up in the files of the financial vice president, the plant manager may never become aware of it. It might be necessary for the underwriter to follow up to determine that the desired recipient "got the message." The requirement that a particular message be received by the appropriate individual is even more vital with internal communications such as those between claims and underwriting.

Comprehensibility of the Message.   Virtually all texts on business writing contain the exhortation, "Be clear." Unfortunately, clarity is seldom defined. A message will contain information only to the extent that it is phrased or written in terms that can be understood by the person for whom the message is intended. A message on the estimation of IBNR (incurred but not reported) reserves written by an actuary might be easily understood and comprehended by another actuary. It would contain no information whatsoever for a newspaper reporter gathering data for a story on medical professional liability insurance. While a message may be perfectly clear to the originator, it will convey information only to the extent that it is clear to the receiver. When writing a letter or report, or conducting a conversation, underwriters should orient the level and content of the communication to the audience for whom it is intended. Technical terms and phrases that are easily understood by another underwriter may be both inappropriate for and incomprehensible to a layperson.

A message is fully comprehensible only if the information obtained by the receiver corresponds to the information that the originator intended to convey.

The utilization of terms and phrases that are incomprehensible to the receiver is only one facet of the problem of miscommunication. The originator of a message should be careful to avoid ambiguity. A message that conveys misinformation is worse than one that contains no information whatsoever. The sources of ambiguity are numerous and will be considered in detail later in this chapter, but the following example illustrates the difficulties that ambiguities can create.

A property underwriter might write a letter to a producer asking for current building values on a large schedule of industrial property. The underwriter wants the values stated on an actual cash value basis. The producer, not understanding the intent of the request, provides the values based upon accounting book values. The message from the underwriter is not comprehended by the receiver, and the miscommunication results in misinformation being supplied to the underwriter.

Credibility of the Message. A message may contain information for the receiver because it is comprehensible and yet be disregarded because it lacks credibility. If the receiver does not believe the information contained in the message, then little useful communication has taken place. Suppose a commercial liability underwriter writes a letter to a producer stating that a hazardous situation exists at the manufacturing location of one of her commercial accounts. If the information in the letter runs counter to the producer's beliefs about the situation, then the letter may well lack credibility unless the information in the letter is substantiated in a convincing manner. When the underwriter is the originator of a message, the degree to which information in the message is likely to be credible to the receiver should be considered.

The underwriter is the receiver of a great many messages. The validity of information contained in these messages hinges on the amount of credibility that can be placed in them. In the analysis of this problem, the phrase "consider the source" is frequently employed. To a large degree the credibility of any particular piece of information depends upon the veracity and reliability of the originator. Some information may have to be "taken with a grain of salt" and regarded with suspicion. Other information merits no consideration because of its lack of validity. Evaluating the credibility of information is one of the most challenging aspects of underwriting. Therefore, an awareness of the problem is important, and past experience with producers, insureds, and fellow employees can be of considerable help.

Relevance of the Message. A message may be both clear and credible and yet constitute a waste of everyone's time because it is not relevant to the matter under consideration. The rambling letter or report filled with data that has little or no relevance to the subject can effectively obscure those bits of pertinent information that it does contain. It is both time-consuming and irritating to be forced to sift the residue of five pages of verbiage in order to obtain a few nuggets of information. It seems at times that some messages have been designed to confuse and obscure the subject matter, rather than to clarify it.

The underwriter should strive to confine messages to the data that is relevant and avoid verbosity. The overly long communication contains the implication that the receiver's time is not valuable. It might also be found that the receiver of the message totally disregards it because the underwriter failed to demonstrate the relevance of the information contained within. Messages that are clear, concise, and relevant bring about a mutual understanding of the information being requested: that is, the message is informative.

Underwriting Information. There are two major components of the information function in underwriting communications. These are the gathering of information prior to a decision (and in monitoring decisions) and the dissemination of information about decisions which have been made.

Information Gathering. Only a portion of the information required for the typical underwriting decision is tendered with the submission itself. It is usually necessary to develop additional information from internal and external sources. When drafting inquiries, the underwriter should be particularly careful to determine that the person or agency to whom the questions are directed can clearly perceive what information is being sought. Messages originated by the underwriter seeking information should be comprehensible, credible, and relevant from the viewpoint of the particular receiver to whom they are addressed.

Information Dissemination. After a decision has been reached, the underwriter must inform the producer or insured of that fact, together with the rationale behind the decision if it is a negative one. First, consider exactly what information is to be conveyed and then determine the manner in which it can best be accomplished. Assume that upon the renewal of a large contractor's equipment floater the inland marine underwriter decides to increase the theft deductible from $100 to $1,000 because of the frequency of theft losses. The information to be communicated to the producer or insured includes not only the deductible change but also the reasons this change is deemed necessary. In addition, this information should be disseminated to those other departments of the firm, such as claims and inspection, that would be affected by the change. Clear, accurate, and timely communication of information of this type to all parties affected by the decision is an essential part of underwriting.

The Command or Instruction Function Within any organization, including an insurance company or agency, many messages are sent with the purpose of giving orders or instructions rather than merely of providing information. The command function of communications includes messages designed to shape, modify, or control the behavior of the individual or individuals to whom they are sent. Messages of command or instruction are sent throughout both the formal and informal organizations of the firm. Whether a particular communication is a command or an instruction depends upon the authority relationships between the sender and receiver.

The Formal Organization. The organization chart for a firm shows the structure of the formal organization. Exhibit 11-1 indicates a typical organization chart for a branch office of a multiple-lines insurer. The lines of authority indicate the chain of command within the firm. To an important degree, the organization chart represents a model for the communications system within the formal organization. The organization chart indicates the channels through which the command and instruction functions of communication are implemented. A directive from the home office dictating a change in a specific aspect of underwriting policy would be an example of a message in which the command function is dominant.

Good communication is essential for the efficient management of any underwriting department. Underwriters can follow the policies of management only to the extent that those dictates are comprehended. An order or instruction must be perceived to be authoritative before it will be followed. Chester I. Barnard states in his classic work:

> The necessity of the assent of the individual to establish authority *for him* is inescapable. A person can and will accept a communication as authoritative only when four conditions simultaneously obtain: (a) he can and does understand the communication; (b) *at the time of his decision* he believes that it is not inconsistent with the purpose of the organization; (c) *at the time of his decision* he believes it to be compatible with his personal interest as a whole; and (d) he is able, mentally and physically, to comply with it.[2]

Underwriting manuals, policy statements, and other underwriting communications transmitted through the formal organization should meet Barnard's requirements. One of the most frequent types of miscommunication that occurs in this setting is the issuance of orders that are in apparent or actual conflict with one another. In such a case, the individual receiving the instruction does not understand what is being communicated, resulting in confusion rather than being instructed by the communication.

The Informal Organization. Lines of communication and authority set forth in the organization chart describe only the formal structure of the firm. Within any formal organization, whether it is a business organization, governmental agency, or military unit, there exists an informal organization. The informal organization consists of the

Exhibit 11-1
A Simple Formal Organization

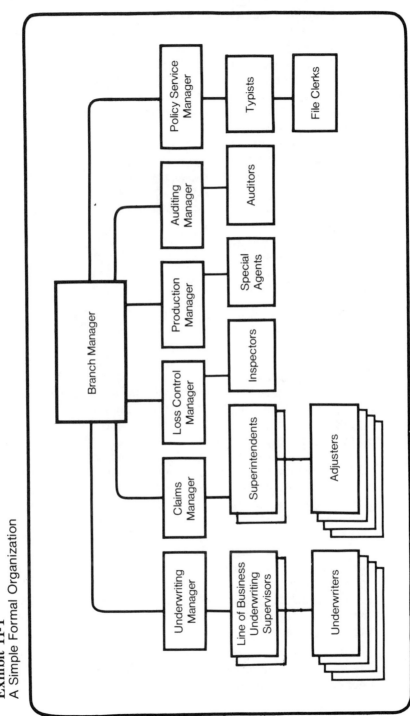

network of interpersonal relationships that develop within the organization. One of the most pervasive aspects of the informal organization is communication. An interesting item of information swiftly moves through the firm in a nebulous "grapevine." The speed of the "grapevine" provides ample evidence of the efficiency of the informal organization as a communications medium.

Management experts regard the informal organization as a useful and necessary part of the firm. In addition to the communications aspect, the informal organization serves to humanize the impersonal firm and to provide individuals with a feeling of group acceptance and self-respect. It can frequently be utilized to help implement the command function of communications. "The word" often filters down through the informal organization with more dispatch, and perhaps with more authority, than would have been possible through use of a more formal communications medium. The perceptive underwriting manager is aware of and utilizes the informal organization as a means of communicating commands and instructions which are to be implemented.

The Influence or Persuasion Function The purpose of many communications is to influence or persuade. The function of persuasion is to move the receiver to some specific action or behavior. The influence function is intended to have a more general effect. The underwriter might *persuade* a producer to accept a modification of the form with respect to a particular risk while *influencing* the producer to be favorably disposed toward the insurance company. Basically the two have the same objective that they are trying to get someone to do something without doing so through a command.

The influence function pervades all communications. The impression the underwriter makes on those producers and insureds contacted will reflect either favorably or unfavorably on the insurance company. In a very real sense, this is a public relations aspect of underwriting. This does not mean that the underwriter should depart from sound underwriting principles in order to curry favor with a producer or insured. It does mean that the underwriter should be aware that the *manner* in which underwriting decisions are communicated to producers or insureds is important. A conscious attempt to create the most favorable possible impression, within the constraints imposed by sound underwriting, will contribute to the performance of the influence function of communication.

Selling the Decision. Once the underwriter has made a decision regarding a particular risk, the task of selling that decision to the producer or insured remains. If the decision is to write the business at the rate and on the terms requested, little persuasion is needed. If the underwriter's decision is to modify the submission in some way, considerable persuasive skill may be required in order to obtain the business. The most straightforward approach is to explain, clearly and succinctly, the rationale behind the suggested modifications and the resulting long-term benefits.

For example, assume that an underwriter has received a submission for contractor's equipment to be utilized in hazardous terrain. The producer requested an "all-risks" form, and the underwriter is willing to write it only on a named-perils basis. A statement by the underwriter that the "all-risks" form is not available "due to underwriting policy" is not very informative and even less persuasive. On the other hand, if the underwriter analyzes the difference between the perils covered under the two forms and indicates the specific aspect of the "all-risks" form that is not acceptable at the quoted rate, the message to the producer will be much more persuasive. Specific facts tend to persuade more effectively than vague generalizations.

Declinations. One of the most difficult messages to phrase and deliver is the "bad news" letter or phone call. The communications task in this case is to sell a negative result. If the underwriter can convince the producer of the validity of the reasoning behind the declination, a certain amount of education will have taken place. The producer would then be better able to "pre-underwrite" future submissions. The challenge is to persuade the producer or insured to accept the underwriter's viewpoint by explaining the specific reasons for the declination.

Behavior Aspects of Communication

Communication consists of interactions between individuals. Any serious study of communications should go beyond the analysis of the messages being communicated to consider the psychological makeup of the persons who are parties to the process. An in-depth study of psychology is beyond the scope of this book, but certain behavioral aspects of communication will be considered. If communication took the form of electronic exchanges between computers, no consideration of behavior would be necessary. However, in communications between individuals, the behavioral or human element is too important to ignore.

The Role of Perception An individual makes contact with the real world primarily through the senses. Even when a physical inspection is made, a property underwriter's knowledge of a commercial risk consists only of that information which the underwriter can assimilate from what has been seen, heard, or read concerning the risk. (It is also possible for the senses of touch and smell to convey useful underwriting information, such as grease on a kitchen vent and odor from flammable liquids.) Therefore, it is not what the risk *is* that is important, but what the risk is as the underwriter *perceives* it. If perception is accurate in every detail, no problem will arise, but any distortion or omission in perception may lead to difficulty.

A Model of Perception. Perception involves the interaction of the individual with the environment. It has been defined as "imputing meaning to experience."[3] That is, through the process of perception, the individual gathers the data received through the senses and sorts, evaluates, and analyzes the data based upon inherent knowledge, beliefs, and value systems. This constitutes the individual's mental "set" or attitude. The model of perception considers the manner in which a particular individual, with a particular mental set, interacts with the environment which the individual perceives through the senses. Information theorists state that the human eye can process about 5 million bits per second, while the brain can handle about 500 bits per second.[4] A process of selection must take place. *Psychologists refer to the data that are absorbed by the brain as the stimuli while those that are unabsorbed are called the unnoticed remainder.*

The mental set of an individual will determine what is absorbed and what is ignored. An experienced marine surveyor will glance at a yacht and notice the condition of the hull, the size of the rigging, the size and type of winches, and the material of the spars. A layperson with the same glance will see a sailboat. The mental set of the marine surveyor, developed over many years of experience, enables the surveyor to perceive many things unnoticed by the layperson. Since the experience, backgrounds, and interests of no two people are alike, it then follows that perception is an individual matter. That is why no two people in a crowd viewing the same scene can obtain exactly the same *perception* of that scene. Their difficulty in communicating what they "saw" can be understood.

In a simple model of perception, the individual's mental set can be considered as a "filter" which sorts out certain bits of data which are retained as stimuli and rejects other bits of data which are the unnoticed remainder. Exhibit 11-2 illustrates the model. The stimuli that have been perceived then become part of the individual's experience, which makes up the next mental set.

Defensive Behavior Defined. An important aspect of communication is the exhibition of defensive behavior on the part of individuals. A basic tenet of the model of perception is that the individual does not

Exhibit 11-2
A Model of Perception

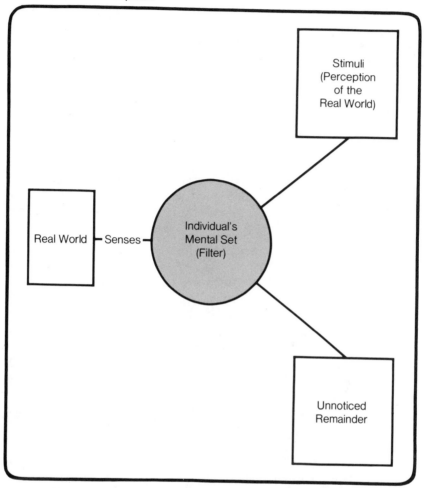

experience the real world but a perception of the real world. Defensive behavior results from a refusal to acknowledge that there is a difference between the perception and actuality on the one hand and the differing perceptions of others on the other hand. Defensive behavior is an attempt to protect an individual's values, beliefs, or perceptions from real or imagined attacks from others.

An example may clarify the concept of defensive behavior. A commercial property underwriter considers a particular building to be a poor risk because it contains a "hazardous occupany." A second underwriter reviews the same submission and states, "This is a good piece of business." The reply of the first underwriter may well be, "You are off your rocker." The reason for this outburst is that the first underwriter considers this different perception of the submission to be a threat to the underwriter's view of the world. The reaction is that anyone holding such a widely divergent viewpoint must be crazy. It is the personal belief of the first underwriter that his or her competent judgment of the desirability of this risk is being threatened. The "attack" triggers the defensive behavior.

Attitudes of Insureds The mental set of an individual, which is made up of that individual's beliefs, values, and experience, has been shown to be the vital determinant of perception. For this reason, an understanding of the attitude of the insured is a necessary precondition to effective communication with the insured. Communications based upon what the insured's attitude *should be,* as viewed by the underwriter, rather than on what the insured's attitude *actually is,* are doomed from the outset.

Claims Consciousness. A term frequently employed in claims reports is claims consciousness. This term is generally used to refer to an insured who aggressively attempts to maximize recovery under the policy. Although this attitude primarily affects adjusters, underwriters should be aware of its existence. Claims consciousness has many manifestations. Some insureds continually file small claims under the homeowners policy for "losses" that are really maintenance expenses. Other insureds attempt to increase their recovery on an actual loss by artificially inflating values. Claims consciousness is a characteristic of insureds that is subject to a wide degree of variation.

Claims consciousness plays an important part in communications. It is part of the mental set of the claimant. Depending on the degree of influence claims consciousness has on the claimant's total mental set, it could be an important factor in settling the claim. It follows that any communication about the claim must include a recognition of claims consciousness of the claimant.

The motives that cause claims conscious behavior are numerous, complex, and frequently intermingled; this is the case with most facets of human activity. One common motive is greed. While greed is not to be condoned, it certainly should be recognized. Another recurrent motive stems from a lack of understanding of the insurance mechanism. To the average person, the concept that the insurance premium represents a payment for the transfer of the possibility of a loss for a particular time period is too abstract to comprehend. Therefore, if the insured has paid a $300 auto premium for one claim-free year, the insured may feel that no value was received for the dollars spent. This may lead to the attitude that the insurance company "owes" a payment to the insured for past premiums when a claim does occur. Since the purchase of property and liability insurance is virtually or actually mandated in many situations, insureds frequently harbor resentment toward insurance companies under any circumstances.

Cultural and Moral Value Systems. Other important determinants of the attitude of the insured are the cultural and moral value systems the insured holds. These value systems or beliefs greatly influence a person's mental set. Religious beliefs and personal convictions mold an individual's moral value system. The cultural value system is a product of the influence of the segment of society to which the individual belongs. A value system can be defined as a set of rules or precepts of conduct defining acceptable and unacceptable behavior. Many writers have stated that American moral values are on the decline. Without being drawn into the debate, it can be said that moral and cultural values do appear to be changing rapidly. What is of concern to the underwriter is not what the insured's moral and cultural values should be but what they are.

Value Systems and Veracity. A most important aspect of the impact of value systems of the insured on underwriting is their influence on the *truthfulness of statements* made by the insured. One of the most difficult tasks in communications is the validating of information contained in a particular message. One source of misinformation arises from misperceptions on the part of the insured. More difficult to deal with is the misinformation that results from deliberate distortion, omission, or fabrication of data by the insureds. The degree to which this occurs will depend, in large measure, upon their value systems.

If an insured's peer group condones a certain type of behavior, that behavior is "right" in the eyes of the insured, no matter how others outside the group might view it. If it is accepted behavior among the insured's peer group to smash windows of their houses with a tree branch prior to the onset of a hurricane in order to have the subsequent water damage covered, that behavior is "right" in the eyes of the insured. The statement, "Everybody's doing it," is simply an expression of a particular cultural value system. Therefore, it is necessary for underwriters to determine what the value system of the insured is (to the degree that is possible) and to evaluate statements of the insured in the light of that value system. This is not an easy task.

Territorial Variations. An underwriter who is moving to a new territory must recognize that there are significant territorial variations in value systems. The value systems that predominant in a small, rural

Exhibit 11-3
A Communication Process Model

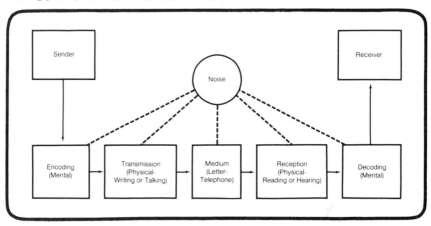

town may be quite different from those in the heart of a major metropolis. The differences spring from many causes which would require a major sociological study to unravel. From an underwriting standpoint, what is important is that territorial differences do exist, not why they exist. Equally important is objectivity on the part of the underwriter in the evaluation of the value systems of a new territory.

It is essential for the underwriter to be completely familiar with the territory or territories being underwritten, not only with respect to specific individual risks, but also with respect to the general cultural and moral environment. Just as a particular insured's moral character is of importance to the underwriter, so are the general moral tone and cultural standards of the neighborhood and community.

The Process of Communication In order to understand the importance of the behavior aspects of communication, it is useful to consider a model of the process of communication itself. A simple model of the communications process will be developed and then applied to underwriting situations.

A Communication Process Model. Communication can be viewed as a five-step process:

1. encoding
2. transmission
3. medium
4. reception
5. decoding

Exhibit 11-3 indicates the operation of the model. A breakdown occurring in any one step of the process will result in miscommunication. Each of the steps will be considered in detail.

Encoding.   Encoding is the mental process whereby the message is composed and the communicator decides on the transmission technique. When writing a business letter, for example, the encoding step encompasses: (1) deciding what to say, (2) determining the manner in which the thoughts will be expressed, and (3) deciding when the letter will be written. Although there is a temptation to focus upon the physical aspects of communication, such as writing style and telephone personality, the mental aspects are more important. The phrase, "I did not get my point across in my letter ...," means that during the encoding process the information the sender was attempting to send was improperly expressed.

Transmission.   The transmission of a communication refers to the physical act of writing, dictating, or speaking. This step is obviously necessary and is essentially a routine, mechanical part of the underwriter's daily activities. The concern in written communications is with the content of the letter since the physical production of the letter is usually a matter of office management rather than underwriting.

Vocal emotion in the transmission step can affect the information transmitted. In a telephone conversation, for example, the listener obtains information not only from what is said but also from the manner in which it is said. The human voice, by variations in tone, is capable of indicating the entire gamut of human emotion. The phrase, "I believe you," can register meanings ranging from deep conviction to indecision or outright skepticism, depending upon the inflection. While time and space limitations preclude an in-depth discussion of the complex subject of "telephone personality," underwriters should be concerned with the *impression* being communicated along with the words. During face-to-face conversations, many more facets of nonverbal communication come into play. Mannerisms, facial expressions, and even physical distance affect what is being communicated. Entire volumes have been devoted to this subject, but a detailed treatment of body language is beyond the scope of this book.

Medium.   The medium of communication is the physical instrumentality employed. This would be the letter or telephone by which information is sent. An important consideration is that the medium should be appropriate from the standpoint of speed, cost, and the possible need for a permanent record. A short telephone call may clear up a matter that would otherwise require several letters. However, the decision to use the telephone must consider not only this method's speed but also its cost and its lack of documentation.

Reception.   Reception is the physical process of reading the letter or listening to the conversation. There are several aspects of this process that can lead to miscommunication. People may scan a letter rather than read it carefully. Responding to what the reader thought the letter said rather than what it actually said can be embarrassing and sometimes costly. Similarly, not all people are good listeners. Some people are more concerned about what they are going to say next than with paying attention to what the other person is saying. Obviously, it is impossible to comprehend what has not been heard or, more accurately, what has been heard but not listened to.

Decoding. The final step in the process involves the mind of the receiver. Decoding takes place when the receiver deciphers information originally encoded by the sender. The accuracy of decoding depends upon both parties. If the information received by the recipient has been stated in a clear, unambiguous manner, it can be easily decoded, unless the recipient has a mental block or some perceptive difficulty in interpreting the message. Encoding and decoding (both mental activities) are the two most important steps in the process because most miscommunication is mental in nature.

An analogy can be found in military communications. A message is encoded using the code for the day. If the person receiving the message has the proper code book, that person can unlock the cipher and receive the information. A great deal of miscommunication stems from the fact that the mental set of the receiver may not be attuned to the same "code book" as that of the sender; therefore, misinformation results. The exasperated lament, "I don't think you understand what I am trying to say," indicates some difficulty in communication. Very likely the area of difficulty is a result of the sender's being unable to properly *encode* the thoughts or the receiver's lacking the ability or perception to properly *decode* the information. Specific examples of mental attitude that constitute a barrier to proper decoding of communications are considered in the following pages.

The Communication Process Model in Underwriting. The communication process model provides a framework for analysis of any underwriting communication. The most troublesome portions of the model are encoding and decoding. When an underwriter is writing a letter to a producer, for example, it would be useful to consider the degree to which the written word corresponds to those thoughts the underwriter attempted to encode. Similarly, when receiving a communication, the underwriter should be alert to the importance of proper decoding. While breakdowns are possible in transmission, the medium or reception problems in these areas are usually obvious. Most difficulties in communication stem from either faulty encoding of the message or misperceptions in decoding.

When writing an underwriting report, it is important to analyze the purpose of the report before preparing it. Proper encoding in this case means not only conveying the information in the report clearly and concisely but also arranging and organizing information in such a manner that important facts and insights are evident. A recognition of the problems in perception which may be present during the decoding stage will lead the underwriter to focus on the technical level, wording, and structure of the report in a manner consistent with the recipient's mental set. While communications problems cannot be eliminated, a sensitivity to the need to frame every message in a manner that can be decoded by the receiver easily and accurately should minimize miscommunication.

Communication Barriers

A communications system, human or electronic, contains a certain amount of *noise* or interference. Noise is a term used to describe the mental or physical obstacles to effective communications. Thus, any form of noise is a potential communication barrier.

The most difficult source of noise to deal with is the human mind itself. The attitudes, perceptions, and beliefs of the individual, which constitute the mental set, may obscure and hinder effective communications. Some of the most common barriers to communication are described below.

Confusion of Inferences and Observations[5]   When an individual observes something, it is common to infer a great deal beyond what is actually witnessed. The problem arises when one fails to distinguish properly between *facts* that are known and *assumptions* that have been inferred. For example, V. M. Jones, an underwriter, is driving back to the office after lunch and notices an oncoming car with its left turn signal blinking. From this observation Jones infers that the car is going to turn left, a realistic inference. If the information that the other car is going to turn left is treated as an assumption and not as a fact, there is no problem. However, if Jones fails to distinguish between observed fact and inferred assumption, and turns left, a collision is likely if the oncoming car does not turn. (See Exhibit 11-4). A left turn in front of a car that was expected to turn left is an example of observation-inference confusion with which the auto adjuster is only too familiar.

Assume that an auto underwriter receives a submission for a single auto where the wife is listed as the principal operator. The

Exhibit 11-4
Inference-Observation Confusion

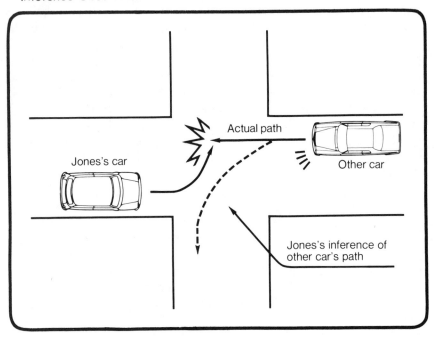

occupation of the wife is listed as housewife, and the husband's occupation is given as salesman. The wife has had no accidents or tickets. The husband has had three tickets in the last three years and one accident. The underwriter calls the producer and says, "This insured is trying to put something over on us. I know that the salesman is the principal operator." This is likely to lead to an acrimonious exchange, particularly when the producer reveals that the husband's company supplies him with a car, which he drives exclusively. The underwriter had inferred something from the submission beyond the actual facts presented. An immediate reaction of the experienced underwriter to this is, "An underwriter must make inferences all the time!" It is true that an underwriter continually makes inferences. The problem is that sometimes an underwriter forgets that a certain piece of information was inferred, rather than being an observed or verified fact. If the underwriter acts on the inference as if it were a fact, it may lead to bruised feelings and misunderstandings.

The Semantic Jungle Too frequently, one has difficulty in finding the word that adequately expresses the intended meaning. Even more difficult is the situation in which a particular word has two or more different meanings. It has been stated that the 500 most frequently used words in English have over 14,000 meanings.

When a single word is taken to mean two different things to the two parties in a conversation, *bypassing* may occur. Bypassing is the term used to refer to those situations in which there is no meeting of the minds of the people conversing or communicating. Their thoughts literally bypass each other. For example, a producer calls a workers' compensation underwriter to discuss an account which had been submitted. "Did you personally survey this risk?" asks the underwriter. "I certainly did," is the reply. "It took me two days." Unfortunately, the underwriter's use of the term "survey" meant physical inspection of the premises of the insured, while the producer meant a careful review of all of the policies and exposures of the firm under consideration. If, after the risk is written, a dangerous situation is found on the insured's premises, the following exchange may well take place. "You told me that you made a physical inspection of the premises; how could you have missed that hazardous process?" asks the underwriter. "I never said that I made a physical inspection," retorts the producer. The relationship between underwriter and producer is hardly harmonious at this point and is likely to deteriorate rapidly. The problem is that bypassing has taken place with respect to the word "survey." It meant one thing to the producer and another to the underwriter.

The important consideration in semantics is to attempt to determine, as nearly as possible, that both parties involved in any communication understand not only the words in the message but the meanings of those words. If not, bypassing can take place and lead to further misunderstandings. Miscommunication of this type can have tragic consequences. The relations between the United States and Japan prior to World War II may have been worsened by the misunderstandings that stemmed from Cordell Hull, who was meeting with representatives of the Japanese government. Hull spoke with a Boston accent made more difficult to understand by his poorly fitting false teeth. He also could not understand the heavily accented English spoken by the Japanese. Both sides were too proud to ask the other to repeat. Therefore, both parties nodded sagely and politely, while understanding hardly a word that was said.

The Closed Mind and Stereotyping Another important barrier to communication occurs when one of the persons communicating has a closed mind. The attitude of, "Don't bother me with facts, my mind's made up," while unacceptable anywhere in business, is particularly dangerous in an underwriting setting. The underwriter with a closed mind, while apparently listening to the argument of the producer or insured, is merely waiting for the conversation to end. This characteristic is quite easily diagnosed in others, while our own "blind spots" are exceedingly hard to recognize.

Underwriting with an open mind does not mean discarding past knowledge and experience. It does mean a willingness to listen to the other side in a discussion and see if perhaps some evidence is being offered that was not previously considered.

One of the prime causes of a closed mind is the use of stereotypes. The term "stereotype" comes from the printing industry, where it referred to a plate used to print the same picture over and over again. Frequently, when dealing with either individuals or applications for insurance, there is a tendency to place each new contact in a previously established pigeonhole or category. This seems to reduce both the mental effort involved and the uncertainty as well. Prejudice, in all of its many manifestations, is nothing more than the use of particular stereotypes or labels to apply to all members of an ethnic or other group. It is obvious that these have no place in underwriting.

Another common stereotype occurs in commercial property underwriting with respect to a class such as restaurants. The underwriter looking at a submission in this class may actually be reacting to a stereotype of a restaurant, which has been unconsciously developed, rather than to the particular risk which has been submitted. Since the stereotype is not acceptable from the view of the underwriter, the fate of the submission is hardly in doubt. The stereotyping of risks is a special case of the closed mind. Putting labels on things and placing them in separate, tight little compartments is extremely easy to do, particularly since it reduces apparent uncertainty and limits the number of decisions which have to be made, but it is not good underwriting.

The role of the stereotype in creating miscommunication can best be seen with respect to a particular case. A producer calls the auto underwriter about a twenty-two-year old, single male with a sports car. In the underwriter's mind this triggers the stereotype of a reckless driver and a poor auto risk. The producer describes this particular risk as an individual with no accidents, no tickets, and a spotless record in every regard. The potential insured purchased a sports car because of its appearance rather than its speed or handling potential. The producer, who has known the individual for many years, knows him to be a thoughtful, introspective individual who drives carefully and is presently studying nuclear physics which takes up so much of his time that the auto is seldom driven. The underwriter, however, is not reacting to the particular risk which has been submitted but instead is reacting to the stereotype which flashed into the underwriter's mind when a single male under twenty-five, with sports car, was mentioned. No productive communication will take place from this point forward because while the producer is describing the particular risk the underwriter is reacting to (and declining) the stereotype.

The use of stereotypes is a bad habit which is easy to acquire. Underwriters should consider whether, in a particular decision, they are reacting to the actual risk submitted or to a stereotype based on preconceived notions about the general *type* of risk.

A careful distinction must be made between stereotyping and the practice of not writing a particular risk category or classification. If a particular class is listed as unacceptable in the underwriting manual, that does not mean that all members of that class have been stereotyped as unacceptable and therefore placed in the unacceptable pigeonhole. What it could mean is that an underwriting management decision has been made that the task of individually evaluating the members of that particular class to determine their acceptability has been deemed uneconomical. That is, while some members of the class might well represent profitable business, the time and effort that would be necessary to identify them outweighs the possible gain. Other reasons for a prohibited classification are reinsurance treaty requirements or the view, on the part of management, that the insurance company lacks the necessary expertise to deal with the specialized hazards present in the classification. An insurance company may refuse to write underground mining for workers' compensation, for example, not because all underground mining risks are bad, but because it does not have the trained personnel to service them.

Polarization   One of the most difficult areas of philosophy is the search for the distinction between good and evil, and the search for absolutes is usually a futile one. Very few things are either wholly and irrefutably good or evil. Most lie somewhere in between the two extremes. Likewise, few barriers to communication are as formidable as the one that occurs when one of the parties to the communication holds rigidly to the dichotomy of good and bad.

In underwriting, it is as unlikely that there is a risk which is excellent in every respect as it is that there is a risk which is undesirable in every detail. There is a very large middle ground, or gray area, with many degrees and shadings along a continuum from excellent to undesirable. If the underwriter approaches a submission from the standpoint that either it is good, and therefore clearly acceptable, or it is bad, and therefore clearly unacceptable, great difficulty will be encountered with those cases that have both good and bad aspects. Remember, rates are based on "average" risks—that large middle ground.

There are many underwriting examples of polarization. Underwriters view particular producers as either good or poor. What has happened in this case is that all producers have been placed into one of two absolute categories. The tendency that follows from this polarized view is that the "good" producer's submissions will be expected to be "clean" and merit a cursory review, while the poor producer's submissions will be suspect and will be minutely analyzed for the "catch" which is expected to be there. The truth is that producers fall along a continuum, and their submissions do the same. If the middle ground is recognized, then the opportunity for meaningful communication is improved.

A similar problem occurs with respect to "account selling." In this case, an industrial risk may be submitted on a "complete account" basis. The risk may be good from the standpoint of fire and allied lines but mediocre from a general liability viewpoint. The workers' compensation may be excellent but the auto fleet poor. The underwriter who attempts to pigeonhole an account of this type into one of two slots labeled "good" and "bad" is in for a good deal of frustration. While it is a simple matter to recognize the need for the middle ground, it is quite easy to unconsciously slip into the habit of viewing things in terms of a dichotomy. Polarization and stereotyping are similar. The primary difference is that stereotyping usually refers to groups or classes of risks while polarization is more of an individual risk barrier.

UNDERWRITING IN A CHANGING ENVIRONMENT

The environment within which underwriting decisions are made is not a static one. It is important that the underwriter be able to recognize and react to change when it occurs.

The Pervasiveness of Change

Our modern civilization is characterized by the bewildering speed and complexity of changes which take place. This rapid rate of change requires mental flexibility and adaptability on the part of those who would cope with it. It affects all facets of our society.

Examples of Change During the period prior to World War II, railroad mortgage bonds were a gilt-edged investment. These bonds were held to be so safe and to offer such a good yield that they were frequently included in the "widow's and orphan's" portfolios managed by large investment trust managers. Particularly favored were railroad first mortgage bonds on the right-of-way which were characterized as "next to the rail." These were the safest bonds of all, the reasoning went, because holders of the bonds could literally stop the trains in the event of default.

After World War II, trucking and air freight made large inroads into the business of the railroads. Much of the mail began to travel by air instead of rail. The railroads found themselves in increasing difficulty. The distress of the railroads was matched by the deterioration of the investment quality of those "next to the rail" railroad first mortgage bonds. When the railroads defaulted, as many of them did, it was because profitable operation simply was not possible. Unprofitable commuter service continued to operate as a result of the dictates of public regulatory officials. The bondholders were helpless as the bonds went into default, since there was no useful foreclosure remedy. The gilt-edged investment of the past had become the highly speculative, and often worthless, investment of the present.

Technological advances have been responsible for a host of changes since the industrial revolution. The rate of technological advance appears to be increasing rather than slackening. In the area of electronics and the applications of physics, change is so rapid as to be almost revolutionary. Inexpensive pocket calculators are available today that match in some applications the performance of large computers of less than two decades ago. Progress in medical technology has been equally dramatic.

Underwriting Examples of Change   Rapid change can result in the class of business that was highly desirable and profitable in the past becoming the problem class of today. Perhaps the most significant change has occurred in the area of medical professional liability. A combination of factors including changes caused by court decisions, attorneys' fees, increased expectations on the part of patients, and a growing willingness on the part of juries to make large awards have markedly changed the hazards facing the medical professional liability underwriter.

Similar changes have taken place with respect to other areas of professional liability such as directors' and officers' liability and lawyers' professional liability. Changes in the law and in the attitude of society in these areas have significantly changed the hazards in these classes of business. Every commercial liability underwriter is only too familiar with the changes that have taken place in the area of products liability. Changes in the legal environment have led to the shift from occurrence to claims made forms in commercial and professional liability. Other changes include the growth in no-fault auto plans, starting in 1970 in Massachusetts and spreading to over twenty other states. However, some states have now repealed their no-fault laws, demonstrating the difficulty in trying to predict change.

While the changes listed may include many of the most visible changes affecting underwriting today, they are by no means exhaustive. Many changes that significantly affect underwriting are more subtle and difficult to detect. The emergence of new construction techniques is relatively easy to detect, but the existence of a shift in cultural values or public attitudes, while much more difficult to discern, may have an even greater effect upon underwriting results.

The Major Arenas of Change

Since change is such a pervasive part of our modern society, it can be overwhelming unless it is systematically analyzed. For the underwriter, the major changes are taking place in the cultural, physical, and legal environment. These may be considered the three major arenas within which the drama of our rapidly changing society unfolds.

Changes in the Cultural Environment All business activities, including insurance underwriting, are greatly affected by the cultural environs within which they take place. Social attitudes and value systems will dictate types of behavior that are favored or condoned, together with those that are censured. The underwriter is concerned with cultural changes to the extent that they may alter the underlying hazards, change the frequency of losses, or affect the severity of losses that occur. To take an extreme example, in a society where wrongs, real or imagined, could be settled legally by a gunfight, a life underwriter would have a harried existence. Yet, during the settling of the American West, it was both legally and socially acceptable to settle disputes with revolvers, as long as the gunfight was "fair" according to the unwritten but acknowledged code of the times. In other times and other places, dueling was both legal and honorable, provided the code governing the matter was strictly adhered to.

Changing Value Systems. Among the most heatedly debated issues in modern sociology are, first, the extent to which American value systems have changed in recent years and, second, the effect of these changes. It would not be appropriate in this text to enter that debate. From an underwriting standpoint, what is important is a sensitivity to the possibility that changing cultural values could have an effect upon underwriting results. Whether the changes take the form of an erosion in moral values or a variation from territory to territory, their effect on underwriting results in the paramount consideration.

In Oriental cultures, respect for the dictates of elders results in strong family control of behavior. Police officials in some large

American cities have cited the growing Americanization of Oriental youth, and a resulting weakening of familial control, as a possible reason for growing crime rates. Without attempting to assess the merit of this argument, it is evident that cultural value changes do significantly affect behavior.

Territorial differences in value systems are often subtle but nonetheless important. There is a vast difference between the small, rural community where people know and are concerned about their neighbors and the impersonal New York City neighborhood where the screams of Kitty Genovese brought no response. In some rural communities, the neighborhood is a closely knit social group, with each member familiar with the activities and proclivities of the others. In a large city and even in neighborhoods of large, single-family dwellings, one might not even know the name of the next-door neighbor. It is pointless to argue the merits of one cultural lifestyle over another, but the underwriter should be aware of the implications of the differences that do exist. In an impersonal community, for example, it is not unknown for burglars to back up a moving van to a single-family house whose members are away on vacation, or even merely away to work, and strip the house to the bare walls. This could not occur in a closely knit community where a family moving in or out of the neighborhood is major news.

Increasing Permissiveness. Many social critics state that one major development in recent American society has been an increase in permissiveness. As evidence, they cite the youth ethic that people should be allowed to "do their own thing," whatever that may be. The increasing pressure on police departments to decrease their prosecution of "victimless crimes" is also noted as evidence of this same trend. If society continues to condone behavior it once condemned, the effect upon underwriting results could be considerable. Cheating a little on one's taxes and artificially inflating the extent of an insured loss are examples of the type of behavior that could result from an increase in permissiveness.

On the other hand, some argue that the only change that has taken place is a reduction in hypocrisy, in that actions that were formerly hidden because of social taboos are now in the open. In some groups, people living together out of wedlock are accepted as a matter of course. The difficult task facing the underwriter during times of rapidly changing value systems is to identify those characteristics associated with the average and better-than-average risk in the class, recognizing those facets of change that are significant from a standpoint of underwriting results, and those that, while they may be at variance with the underwriter's value system, are of no underwriting significance.

Changes in the Physical Environment The status quo assumption, or the assumption that nothing has changed, is particularly inappropriate with respect to the physical environment. New materials and processes may drastically change the hazards in a familiar risk category.

The Utilization of New Materials. The search for lighter weight autos has caused manufacturers to substitute aluminum or plastic for steel. An aluminum hood or trunk lid is much more easily damaged and more expensive to repair than its steel counterpart.

The use of aluminum wiring in homes and businesses was a development that resulted in some increase in hazard. In the case of the homeowners submission, it is very difficult for the underwriter to determine the exposure since the insured seldom knows what type of wiring is in the home and it is not feasible to undertake an inspection by removing a fixture to determine the type of wiring actually employed.

In commercial property risks, some newer types of insulation and office wall material made of plastic are highly flammable. In modern construction, the use of movable partitions rather than full interior walls has increased the likelihood of a major fire spreading quickly through an entire floor. Both are examples of changes in the utilization of materials and changes in design which have substantially modified the hazards from a property standpoint. The underwriter should ascertain that current submissions are being underwritten based upon the materials and design presently being utilized rather than upon the underwriter's experience with what was formerly used.

New Processes and Techniques. Change in the physical environment does not confine itself to development in construction materials. Particularly with respect to commercial risks, there is constant change in industrial processes. A manufacturing plant with an extremely dusty environment may develop a filtering system which improves the workers' compensation risk. The introduction of automated and computer-controlled manufacturing techniques may greatly reduce the probability of disabling injuries to the work force. The use of the exact fare system for cabs after a certain hour may drastically reduce the incidence of robbery, greatly altering the risk from the standpoint of crime insurance.

Another change recently implemented in building codes for the construction of new single family dwellings and apartments is the requiring of smoke detectors connected to the dwelling or apartments' electrical unit. This has reduced the loss of life and property through early warnings as well as eliminated the maintenance that was required for the old battery operated smoke detectors (a maintenance that was often ignored).

The underwriter who is sensitive to changes in the physical makeup of risks will be able to respond quickly to both improvements and impairments in risks which are submitted.

Changes in the Legal Environment The legal environment within which the insurance industry operates can have a substantial effect upon underwriting results. The framework of laws is not constant but is in a continual state of evolutionary change. These changes may be considered under two headings: court decisions and legislative changes.

The Effect of Court Decisions. Frequently a court decision will alter the manner in which contract wording is interpreted. Often the effect of the ruling is to broaden the coverage of the contract and to increase the exposure to loss. While the underwriter is hardly expected to be an attorney, the legal department of the insurer will often inform underwriting management of a recent legal development. The underwriter is then notified of the change as it affects the risks being written.

A California Supreme Court decision had the effect of changing California from a contributory to a comparative negligence state for example. A possible reaction of the underwriter may be that such a change is a problem for the claims department, not underwriting. However, the change may well affect underwriting results in a subtle way. Under the old system, in an intersection auto accident in which one of the parties was 10 percent at fault and the other party was 90 percent at fault, there would result only one claim under the third-party section of the auto insurance contract. Under the comparative negligence doctrine, the same accident would result in two claims. Therefore, in a state that changes from one system to the other, the underwriter might well encounter a marked change in claims frequency, even though the underlying characteristics of the book of business remain the same. The frequency would indicate a deterioration in the book of business that did not, in fact, exist.[6]

The Effect of Legislative Changes. The passage of legislation, both on the state and federal level, can significantly alter the underwriting of particular lines. One of the most sweeping changes in recent years has been the enactment of no-fault auto insurance laws. Depending upon the particular no-fault law, underwriting may be materially influenced by no-fault legislation. If the law includes unlimited medical, for example, it may greatly increase the severity of a one-car accident in which the driver hits a tree or telephone pole. Formerly this type of accident would have resulted in a moderate payment under the medical coverage and a total loss under collision if those coverages had been purchased. Under no-fault with unlimited medical coverage, the entire medical bill would be covered in *every* one-car accident. If the driver became a paraplegic, the medical costs could run into hundreds of thousands of dollars.

More recently, state laws requiring persons to wear seat belts will likely reduce injuries over time, even if only a small part of the population obeys the law. Similarly, federal standards for a third, high mounted brake light and passive restraints, decrease injuries. In workers' compensation, legislative changes in benefits and in the definition of covered employment may also significantly affect loss costs. Presumably, the increase in benefits should be allowed for in the rate, but the underwriter should be aware that an increase in loss severity may stem from the change in legislation, rather than from a deterioration in the risk itself. This change in the legal environment complicates the comparison of loss severity experience on a particular risk before and after the benefit level change.

The effect of other legislative changes on underwriting may be more subtle and difficult to detect. Changes in the building code may alter the materials utilized in construction, affecting the physical hazards for property fire risks. Changes in the law in the area of medical professional liability may appreciably alter the exposure to risk in that area.

A Checklist for Evaluating Legislation. When underwriting management becomes aware of a change in the law that may have a marked impact upon the risks being underwritten, the following legislative checklist will provide a framework for analysis. Does the new law or regulation

1. increase frequency by making claims easier to file?
2. increase severity by increasing the size of awards?
3. increase the hazard by altering the physical environment?
4. increase expenses, such as a requirement of mandatory inspections?

Of course, it is also possible for the legal environment to be improved as a result of new legislation, in which case the above variables would decrease. The legislative changes of concern to underwriting management are those that affect underwriting results. The checklist details the types of impact that could affect either losses or expenses.

Changes in the Regulatory Environment. One of the most important aspects of the insurance underwriting environment is regulation. In order to discern the trend of future changes in insurance regulation, it will be useful to briefly consider the present structure.

Changes in both state and federal regulation of insurance will have a more immediate impact on underwriting than any other environmental sector.

Objectives of Regulation. Professor Spencer L. Kimball, probably this country's best-known authority on insurance regulation, has listed two major objectives or purposes of regulation.[7] The first he calls *solidity* of the insurance enterprise, the financial ability to properly perform its duties in the community. Professor Kimball has given a Latin title to the second purpose: *aequum et bonum*—those things that are equitable and good, and equal and fair. Much of the philosophy behind the regulation of insurance rests on the belief, expressed by Professor Kimball, that insurance companies must have financial strengths necessary to meet the contractual obligations contained in insurance policies, and that they must also fulfill those obligations in ways that are fair and equitable and in the best interests of their policyholders and the public in general.

Rate Regulation. The regulation of insurance rates is probably the form of insurance regulation that affects underwriting most directly. Insurance rates must be adequate, fair, and not excessive.

The prior approval method of rate regulation has been used in the property and liability insurance industry for many decades. Basically, the system involves the prior approval, by the office of the state insurance commissioner, of any property or liability insurance rate used in the state. Insurance companies send draft copies of rate manual pages to the offices of state insurance commissioners for the approval of their staffs, and approval is required before those rates can be used.

File and use rate regulation is a more recent system under which insurance companies may change rates simply by filing a copy of new rates with the office of the insurance commissioner at the time the new rates are first used. Many of the delays inherent in the prior approval system are thereby eliminated, and the action of free competition in the insurance marketplace is expected to prevent the use of excessive rates. A variation of the file-and-use law referred to as *use-and-file* does not require filing prior to use. Rates must be filed within a short time period following use, usually 15 days.

Within these two major categories there exist variations deserving at least a brief mention here. In two states, insurance rates are set by an agency of the state government although in one of these they permit rate deviations. Several states require the use of bureau rates for fire coverages, and/or auto insurance. Under laws that require the use of state-made rates or the use of a standard bureau rate, rate competition does not exist. Essentially, every insurance company must charge the same premium for the same coverage. Under these systems, political factors, rather than economic ones, tend to determine rate levels.

The majority of states use a prior approval or modified system of rate regulation, most of them for both fire and casualty coverages. (Though this text uses the property and liability division, some states regulate rates along fire and casualty lines.)

California is the largest of three states that allow an insurance company to set its own rates, completely independent, without even the requirement that rates be filed with the state insurance commissioner (open competition). Finally, about a dozen states have laws which are some slight variation from those described.

Solvency Regulation. If the regulation of insurance rates affects the present relationship between policyholders and insurance companies, the regulation of solvency affects the future of that relationship. (Rate regulation also has an obvious impact on solvency, too.) Policyholders buy insurance so that insurance companies can offer financial help in times of policyholder financial crisis. Solvency regulation is designed to assure the policy-buying public that insurance companies will be able to fulfill their future financial obligations.

In the main, such regulation is accomplished in three ways: (1) surplus requirements needed to write particular lines of coverage, (2) annual reports to insurance commissioners, and (3) periodic audits of insurance company home and regional offices. Though none of the three *directly* affect the underwriting function, their impact on insurance company operations is widespread, and the underwriter needs to be aware that this type of regulation exists and that it has an *indirect* effect on all company operations, including underwriting.

Underwriting Response to a Changing Environment

In a period of rapid change, such as the present, a sensitivity to and an awareness of change is essential. But detection of change is only the first step. The likely impact of the change on the book of business must be evaluated and then an underwriting response must be developed.

Product Design An important response to perceived change is to modify the policy form to deal with the new conditions. As loss experience steadily deteriorated in medical professional liability because of changes in the cultural and legal environment, the "claims made" policy was developed. The claims-made form of the medical professional liability policy eliminated the need to estimate and reserve for a long IBNR tail which was subject to inflation.

Legislative requests for clearer language generated changes in policy forms to clarify and simplify the wording. As a result of a change in the statutes, homeowners policies in some states have been modified to add workers' compensation coverage for domestic employees. The doctrine of concurrent causation caused modification of homeowners policy language. In short, alterations in the policy form represent a major area of response to a changing environment.

Pricing the Product   The second major area of response to a changing environment lies in the area of pricing. If the rate structure is not responsive to change, results may be adversely affected. In those lines of business that are manual rated, the response to changing conditions is primarily an actuarial rather than an underwriting function. The underwriter needs to be aware of the reasons for the rate changes in a general manner in order to be able to interpret the rate level changes for producers and insureds. In addition, selection standards for certain classifications may have to change if rates are not responsive enough.

In those lines such as commercial liability, where the underwriter has a certain degree of rate discretion, response to a changing environment is a responsibility shared by the underwriting and actuarial departments. The actuaries will modify the basic rates as conditions change. The underwriter has the task of evaluating the risks based upon the present and forecast future conditions and pricing the business accordingly.

Assume that a large commercial liability risk has been submitted for consideration. The underwriter has determined that this is desirable business, provided it is properly priced. When considering what rate discounts to apply, the underwriter should take into account the effect of possible changes in the risk environment. From the standpoint of loss history alone, the submission might merit a 20 percent discount. If the risk environment for this particular class of business has recently deteriorated, a 10 percent discount, no discount, or even a debit might be the appropriate pricing response.

In those lines such as inland marine, where judgment rating is employed, responsiveness to changing conditions when pricing the product is of paramount importance. For example, assume that a large contractor's equipment floater has been submitted. The loss history for the risk indicates a rate of 0.90 would be sufficient based upon a five-year loss history. If the cost of repairing contractors' equipment has recently exhibited a large increase, then historical loss costs may not be a good indication of future losses. If the average claim in the past cost $1,000, it might now take $1,200 to repair the same damage. If the underwriter prices the risk strictly on the basis of historical loss costs, this is the same as making the assumption that the loss environment that existed in the past will persist in the future. This assumption of no change is inappropriate if the underwriter is aware of changes due to inflation, changes in the legal environment, or changes in the cultural environment.

Monitoring and Implementing Decisions One important underwriting duty is the monitoring of decisions to ascertain that objectives are being met. While reviewing loss and other information on present insureds, the possibility of a change in the conditions of the risk should be continually considered. These changes should be classified as either *particular* changes, in that they affect only the individual risk, or *general* changes as a result that affects an entire class or line of business.

Another response to change lies in the review and updating of line guides and underwriting manuals. This should be a continuous process designed to keep the acceptability rules current in the midst of changing market conditions. Change is not limited to the cultural, legal, and physical environment; it also affects the industry itself. An increase or decrease in capacity on an industry-wide basis can dramatically affect the competitiveness of the market. The entry and exit of firms from particular classes of business, or from entire territories, also shifts the competitive picture.

Current Trends in Underwriting

The underwriting task itself is subject to substantial change as new techniques and processes are introduced. Computer technology has probably had greater impact upon insurance company procedures than any other scientific advance. The following is an indication of the way in which one insurance company is adopting computer technology in the underwriting area.

***The Mechanical Underwriter*[8]** Many companies have utilized the computer to make major changes in the performance of underwriting. The concept of the mechanical underwriter calls for the underwriter working with data processing specialists to create a computer system providing an expanded information base and enhanced flexibility. In addition, this computer system can be used to reduce human error on policy production.

In auto lines, the computer can be given the full vehicle identification number (VIN) and, through appropriate programming, create the vehicle description and properly rate the vehicle. In personal lines, computer ZIP code rating or city name rating can be used to increase accuracy and save time.

Another aspect of the mechanical underwriter is the maintenance of the file information on computer disk media and the elimination of the need to always refer to a paper underwriting file. Access to the file by the underwriter is provided by means of cathode ray tube displays (CRTs). The computer can contain underwriting, claims, and billing information as well. The file information is current as of the evening of the previous day. One important advantage of this system is that the file can never be "out of file," something that frequently occurs when there is a serious claim and both the claims and underwriting departments are reviewing the file.

Perhaps, in the future, the paper underwriting file (other than the retention of those documents required by law) may become obsolete, going the way of the green eyeshade and the Sanborn Maps of an earlier day. Whether computerized or in a paper file, the basic task of underwriting decision making remains unchanged.

Underwriting in the Year 2000   By the end of this century, there will have been many substantial changes in underwriting, insurance company operations, and the business world in general. Based upon the trends over the last quarter-century, the following represents some *speculations* about underwriting in the year 2000.

The Underwriting Labor Force.   Since the beginning of the industrial revolution, the prediction has been made that machines will replace humans, but that has not happened yet and will not have occurred by the year 2000. Many changes will have occurred in the labor force by that time, however. People will be in the labor force for a shorter time period as one of the effects of greater productivity. Highly skilled employees will enter the labor force at age twenty-five after schooling, which will include a college education and two or three years of specialized training, such as in underwriting. Increased productivity per employee will mean that fewer workers can produce more, freeing many members of the labor force for education, in one age group, and retirement in the other. A large part of the increased productivity will be the result of the automation of many underwriting activities.

By the year 2000, there will be many more women in underwriting and underwriting management positions. Many predict that the work week will be four days, leading to obsolescence of the phrase, "Thank goodness it's Friday!" and its replacement with the slogan, "Thank goodness it's Thursday!"

The Insurance Product.   Insurance policies may consist of only two policies, one for all property and liability coverages and one for life insurance. It is possible that the various lines of property and liability insurance will have disappeared, and underwriters will have been trained to deal with all types of loss exposure. Insurance contracts will be greatly simplified in language and much shorter than at present.

The Underwriting Function. The underwriter probably will not have paper files but will have a computer work station with a keyboard through which the underwriter may interact with the computer. The insurance company's computer will be linked to other computers containing various types of data. The underwriter will be able to obtain MVR data simply by querying the company computer, which will then obtain the information from the Motor Vehicle Department computer. Autos, although much smaller, lighter, and more efficient, will still be the dominant mode of transportation.

Physical information on property risks may be available from the property rating bureau computer, which will maintain an up-to-the-minute data bank on property construction, occupancy, protection, external exposures, and state of repair. Financial information will also be available from a financial data bank. One casualty of the changing world will be the paycheck. In the employer's environment of the future, a credit will be made by the employer's computer in the bank account of the employee. Loss drafts will also have disappeared, with similar credits being made to a payee's account when the payment of a loss is authorized.

Underwriting will be somewhat different from today in that the role of the insurer will change slightly. In the year 2000, the underwriter will scrutinize the particular risk submitted by the producer. The underwriter may perform a risk analysis, using a computer to determine the optimum insurance program for the business or individual, setting retention levels, and determining those areas where retention is appropriate. After the risk analysis has been completed, the computer will determine the areas of coverage that are to be provided, produce the contract, and determine the premium. The insurance company computer will determine the premium by linking up with the rating bureau data banks, where loss and premium information is stored on a realtime basis. The rate and the policy premium could therefore be based upon data no more than twenty-four hours old.

The underwriter will still be required to analyze the risk based upon the information developed by the computer and based upon the premium which the computer has also developed. The underwriter will then determine whether or not the risk is desirable. The information revolution which may have taken place by the year 2000 will make available all pertinent *historical* information. The business of insurance will remain the taking of calculated risks, and in the year 2000 it will be more possible to predict the future than it is today.

SUMMARY

Every interaction between the underwriter and the persons with whom the underwriter comes in contact involves communication. Effective and efficient communication on the part of the underwriter will greatly improve underwriting performance.

There are three major functions of communication:

1. information
2. command or instruction
3. influence or persuasion

The information function encompasses the transmission of information that is defined as data that increase the knowledge or decrease the uncertainty of the receiver. The command function of communication includes those messages designed to shape, modify, or control the behavior of the individual or individuals to whom they are sent. The command function utilizes both the formal and informal organizations of the firm as channels of communication. The purpose of many communications is to influence or persuade. The term influence is used to describe those communications designed to have a general effect upon the receiver, while the term persuasion is applied to communications intended to sway the receiver with regard to some specific action.

Since communication consists of interactions between individuals, it is useful to consider the psychological makeup of the persons communicating. The first behavioral element considered is the role of perception. Perception, which involves the interaction of the individual with the environment, has been defined as "imputing meaning to experience." In a simple model of perception, the individual's knowledge, beliefs, and value systems act as filters, sorting out certain bits of data that are retained as stimuli and rejecting all other data.

An understanding of the attitudes of various insureds is a necessary precondition to effective communication, either with insureds or with others in reference to them. The claims-conscious insured is characterized as having a mental attitude that attempts to maximize recovery under the insurance policy. Another important determinant of the attitude of the insured is the cultural and moral value system the insured holds. An understanding of the territorial and other variations in these value systems is an aid to improved communications.

Communications can be viewed as a serial process consisting of the following steps:

1. encoding
2. transmission

3. medium
4. reception
5. decoding

While all steps are important, the most troublesome communications problems occur in the mental stages of encoding and decoding. Accurate information will be transmitted only if the receiver is able to determine from the message the exact idea the originator had in mind.

There are many barriers to communication. These include the confusion of inferences and observations, semantic confusion, having a closed mind likely caused by the use of stereotypes, and polarization. These factors can lead to serious misperceptions and often create "noise," which impedes effective communication.

One of the most significant characteristics of our modern civilization is the bewildering speed and complexity of change within it. Change is all-pervasive within the cultural, legal, and physical environment. Changing value systems and increasing permissiveness are important in the cultural area. In the physical environment, there is the utilization of new materials and the development of new processes and techniques with which to contend. Changes in the legal environment are the result of both court decisions and legislation.

In a look at one company's approach to underwriting, the mechanical underwriter is seen as a technique whereby a computer provides assistance in the daily underwriting routine. A goal of this firm is to provide a paperless environment in which the cathode-ray tube replaces the traditional paper underwriting file. A crystal ball look at underwriting in the year 2000 sees an even larger role for the computer as an aid in underwriting decision making.

Chapter Notes

1. Adapted from Lee Thayer, *Communication and Communication Systems: In Organization, Management, and Interpersonal Relations* (Homewood, IL: Richard D. Irwin, 1968), p. 187.
2. Chester I. Barnard, *The Functions of the Executive* (Cambridge: Harvard University Press, 1938), p. 165.
3. W. V. Haney, *Communication and Organizational Behavior*, 3rd. Ed. (Homewood, IL: Richard D. Irwin, 1969), p. 56.
4. Haney, p. 57.
5. Haney, pp. 179-193.
6. The author is indebted to Robert B. Holtom, Asst. Vice President, Farmers Insurance Group, for this insight.
7. Spencer L. Kimball and Herbert S. Denenberg, *Insurance, Government, and Social Policy*, pp. 5-6.
8. Erwin F. Fromm, "The Mechanical Underwriter," *Best's Review*, Property/Liability Insurance Edition, Vol. 76, No. 2, June 1975, p. 16.

CHAPTER 12

Underwriting Trends and Issues

INTRODUCTION

Underwriters should be aware of changes in the environment in which underwriting takes place. Some of the most significant changes occur in the legal environment. Court decisions may have a profound effect upon the coverage provided by current and future insurance policies. Court interpretations of insurance contracts may surprise the underwriters who wrote the policies. Several of the sections in this chapter examine the changing legal environment in such areas as concurrent causation, punitive damages, environmental impairment liability, and latent injury diseases.

Social movements may also alter the underwriting environment. The current women's rights movement has caused changes in underwriting practices through both court decisions and by means of legislation. This subject is considered below under the heading of unisex and social pricing.

CONCURRENT CAUSATION

The doctrine of concurrent causation requires that all potential concurrent proximate causes of a loss must be identified and if any of these causes is not specifically excluded under an "all-risks" contract, coverage may be provided. This doctrine has its genesis in third-party liability principles. An early case in which it was applied was an auto case, State Farm Mutual Automobile Co. v. Partridge.[1] This theory was recently expanded to apply to first-party property insurance cases.

First-Party Concurrent Causation

An important case applying this doctrine in a first-party situation was Safeco Insurance Co. of America v. Guyton.[2] In this case, the Ninth United States District Court of Appeals decided that coverage applied under a homeowners policy for flood damage despite a specific exclusion for flood.

In the Palm Desert area of California where the Guyton loss occurred, the annual rainfall is quite low. When rainstorms do occur they can be severe, often causing flash flooding. In September 1976 there were heavy rains which overtaxed the capacity of a network of flood control channels, levees, and dikes. It was determined that this flood control system was negligently maintained by the flood control district.

Additionally, it was determined that the negligently maintained flood control system was a concurrent proximate cause of the loss along with the flood. While one concurrent proximate cause, the flood, was excluded, the other concurrent cause, negligent maintenance of the flood control system, was not excluded under the "all-risks" section of the homeowners policy in question. Since negligence had not been considered by most insurers to be a first-party property peril, there was no specific exclusion for it in the "all-risks" homeowners insurance policy.

The doctrine of concurrent causation also provided coverage under an "all-risks" homeowners policy when a hillside gave way damaging the insured's house, in spite of the earth movement exclusion in the policy. This case was Premier Insurance Co. v. Welch.[3]

During a period of heavy rains, a subdrainage system was unable to adequately carry off the water, resulting in a landslide which damaged the house. The court held that the drainage system had been negligently constructed by a third party and that this negligence was a concurrent proximate cause of the loss along with the excluded earth movement.

The earthquake exclusion in many homeowners policies was effectively negated by the doctrine of concurrent causation following the earthquake in Coalinga, California. The name Coalinga stems from the fact that originally the town was a coaling station for the railroad. It was, in fact, coaling station "A." Many of the dwellings dated from those company town days and it was found that they were negligently constructed in that they were not properly tied to their foundations. This negligent construction was held to be a concurrent proximate cause of loss along with the earthquake which was excluded.

The three concurrent causation cases cited above provided coverage for flood, landslide, and earthquake in the face of specific exclusions for these perils.

Dealing with the Doctrine of Concurrent Causation

Many insurance companies changed their policy language to deal with the theory of concurrent causation. For example, the HO-84 policy states that the general exclusions apply "regardless of any other cause or event contributing concurrently or in any sequence to the loss."

The same policy responds to the requirement that concurrent causes must be specifically excluded in an "all-risks" policy by adding the following three exclusions for coverages A and B:

1. Weather conditions that contribute to the loss in any way with one of the eight General Exclusions.
2. Acts or decisions (including the failure to act or decide) of any person, group, organization, or governmental body.
3. Faulty, inadequate, or defective (a) planning, zoning, development, surveying, or siting; (b) design, specifications, workmanship, repair, construction, renovation, remodeling, grading or compaction; (c) materials used in repair, construction, renovation, or remodeling; or (d) maintenance of any property on or off the residence premises.[4]

Note that the doctrine of concurrent causation was extended by the courts to apply to first party coverages, effectively eliminating the effect of several important exclusions. This left the insurance industry vulnerable to potentially crippling losses from catastrophic natural disasters. The new policy language is intended to restore the original exclusions.

In California, legislation was passed which permits the use of this new policy language. Legislators wanted homeowners to be aware that earthquake coverage was available through the earthquake coverage endorsement, which enables the insured to eliminate the earthquake exclusion. The legislature therefore required insurance companies in California to formally notify all their insureds that this earthquake coverage was available. This was done, completing the industry's response to the doctrine of concurrent causation.[5]

Concurrent causation illustrates the dynamics of the underwriting environment. The interpretation of policy language, well established over the years, can be changed overnight by a court decision or legislative act. When this occurs, prompt response must be made to assure insurance company solvency and equity to all insureds.

Underwriters must stay abreast of changes in the legal, regulatory, social, technological, and economic environments in order to respond to these changes. This can be accomplished by reading the trade press, business journals, and newspapers; attending seminars and workshops; and exchanging information informally with other underwriters.

THE INSURABILITY OF PUNITIVE DAMAGES

The practice of asking for punitive damages in addition to compensatory damages has become increasingly common. When they are awarded in a civil proceeding, punitive damages are designed to punish wrongdoing and deter certain types of behavior. Frequently a punitive damages award greatly exceeds the amount awarded for compensatory damages.

Punitive damages have been awarded in professional liability, municipal liability, and auto cases where the insured was guilty of gross negligence such as driving under the influence of alcohol. The sizes of these awards in product liability cases have made headlines in newspapers across the country.

If an insurance policy is interpreted to cover punitive damages in addition to compensatory damages, the size of potential losses is greatly increased. This has implications for both rate-making and underwriting.

Public Policy Issues

Since the purpose of an award of punitive damages is to punish and deter, insurance against such an award raises some troublesome public policy issues. If an insured's policy is interpreted to include coverage for a punitive damages award, then the burden of the punitive damages is shifted by the insurance mechanism to all insureds in that particular class. Since the purpose of punitive damage awards is to deter certain kinds of behavior, the existence of insurance might reduce or eliminate that deterrence effect.

For example, assume that the latest light airplane produced by the Flying Saucer Airplane Company has a disturbing habit of having its wings fall off if the plane flies into turbulent air. The resulting crashes significantly reduce the ranks of Flying Saucer's satisfied customers. If, during a trial, plaintiffs seeking damages from Flying Saucer for product liability also ask for punitive damages, the intent is to modify the manufacturer's behavior.

If Flying Saucer's products liability insurance is interpreted to cover the punitive damage award, some would argue that the deterrence effect of the award has been eliminated. In this case, the burden of the punitive damages award would be shifted to the entire class of products liability policyholders.[6]

The Legal Environment

The insurability of punitive damages has been considered by courts in most states. Some courts have held that the insurance of punitive damages does not affect public policy. Other courts have held that to permit the insurability of punitive damages would violate public policy. This issue therefore has been handled differently from state to state. In some cases, courts within the same state have held different views on this issue depending on the facts of each particular case.

Underwriters should be aware of whether or not insurance policies within their territory include coverage for punitive damages. In some cases, there is an exclusion for punitive damages in the policy. The state of Michigan, on the other hand, prohibits the use of such an exclusion within that state.

In 1964, the case of Lazenby v. Universal Underwriters Ins. Co. held that insurance of punitive damages was not against public policy.[7] This Tennessee case involved auto insurance.

Many of the cases which have held that the insurance of punitive damages does not violate public policy have involved auto insurance. Often the Lazenby decision has been cited as a precedent. Some courts have argued that without a specific exclusion for punitive damages, the insured's reasonable expectations are that any damage claim arising from an auto accident should be covered by the insurance policy. Other courts have found that insurance for punitive damages does not violate public policy even for such intentional acts as assault and battery, false arrest, and malicious prosecution. These courts have weighed both the policy language and the particular facts in each case in reaching these conclusions. No attempt is made here to identify specific states since the status of any one state could change as the result of one case.

On the other hand, the 1962 case of Northwestern Nat. Co. v. McNulty held that permitting insurance of punitive damages was against public policy.[8] This court applied the law of both Florida and Virginia to this auto insurance case. The court decided that the state's need to deter reckless driving outweighed the insured's expectations for coverage under the policy. There are about a dozen states prohibiting insurance of punitive damages.

Underwriting Considerations

The first underwriting consideration regarding punitive damages is the determination of whether or not insurance against punitive damages is permitted under the common or statutory law of the states within an underwriter's territory. This is complicated by the fact that, in some states, courts have held that insurance policies can and do provide coverage against punitive damages in certain situations but not in others. Insurer underwriting manuals should provide guidance to the underwriter in such situations.

Award Size Where insurance coverage is provided for punitive damages, the potential size of awards is increased. In products liability cases, the size of punitive damages awards can be many times that of the compensatory damages. Since the purpose of punitive damage awards is to deter and punish, the extent of the defendant's assets and net worth are taken into consideration. The reasoning is that a firm with over a billion dollars in assets would not be deterred by a $5,000 punitive damage award.

Therefore, the existence of potential punitive damage awards should influence the underwriter's thinking in such areas as the appropriate limits of liability and levels of retention. Underwriters should keep the potential for punitive damages in mind when arranging reinsurance. A recent court held that a reinsurer was not liable for punitive damages even though the reinsurance agreement followed the coverage of the underlying insurance.[9]

Evaluation of the Punitive Damages Risk In those states where insurance coverage for punitive damages awards are possible, prudent underwriting practice would include evaluation of this potential risk. In auto insurance, the punitive damages award is likely to occur when wanton and reckless driving conduct has taken place. Standard underwriting procedures are the only safeguards against this type of loss.

In product liability, professional liability, and municipal liability, the types of actions likely to occasion punitive damage awards are also likely to cause sizable compensatory damage awards. Punitive damage award payments simply increase the severity of this type of loss when it occurs.

ASBESTOSIS AND OTHER LATENT INJURY DISEASES

One of the most troublesome issues in insurance in recent years has been the problem of asbestosis and other latent injury diseases. Present and anticipated future losses from asbestos related diseases have already caused the bankruptcy of several major industrial companies.

The most difficult aspect of asbestos related illnesses is their long latency period. Asbestos fibers when ingested into the lungs can cause damage to the lung tissue. The resulting illness may not become evident (manifest is the term used) for forty years or more. Some asbestos related illnesses are only now making themselves manifest when the exposure occurred at the end of World War II.

Insurance of Latent Injury Diseases

An early latent injury disease was "black lung disease" which affected coal miners. Many coal miners who worked for many years in an environment where the air was filled with coal dust, developed serious lung diseases. Since most of these diseases arose out of working conditions, these disabilities were covered by workers' compensation insurance.

The combination of the pervasiveness of black lung disease among coal miners and the long latency period of the disease made coverage of this illness difficult from a workers' compensation standpoint. If a miner had worked for many different employers prior to manifestation of the disease, pro-ration of the cost of the black lung illness among the several employers was difficult to achieve. This problem was addressed by the creation of a special fund to cover black lung disease.

While most of the asbestosis claims involve workers' compensation, some involve third parties such as asbestos installers whose claims fall under the coverage of a third-party liability policy such as the general liability policy.

While the disease of asbestosis has been recognized since the early 1900s, the general danger arising out of prolonged exposure to asbestos fibers was not fully recognized until the late 1960s or early 1970s. Therefore, when general liability coverage was written for asbestos manufacturing and contracting companies during the period from the 1940s through the late 1960s, underwriters did not include within the rating structure a provision for such claims. The general liability rating process bases future rates on an adjusted projection from the loss data from previous time periods.

Further, even assuming that a rate charge had been made for such potential disease claims in the 1945 premium, such a rate would clearly be inadequate to cover a 1985 claim simply considering inflation over the intervening forty years. A further complication arises out of the fact that under the occurrence policy language which was most widely used during this time period, many different policy years might provide coverage for a single claimant. The obvious problem this creates stems from the fact that coverage may have been provided by a number of different insurance companies over the years. Even in a relatively standard policy such as the comprehensive general liability policy, there are differences in policy language from one insurer to another and for the same insurer over time.

Another difficulty occasioned by a long latency period is that a limit of liability which was adequate, given the legal climate and level of awards in 1945, may be inadequate in 1985. Allocation of a particular claim over policies covering many different policy years is further complicated by the existence of different policy limits and the fact that the insured may have been a self-insurer for part of this intervening period.

An additional problem is the "stacking" of the limits of the many different policies in the absence of an aggregate limit. If each policy year is considered separately, each year's limits are available for claims. Thus, if one insurer provides coverage limits of $300,000 for ten years, limits of $3 million are provided and are available. One must also consider that many different persons are filing suit under every policy year.

One final problem examined here is the defense costs issue. The problem of having many different insurers (and self-insurers) with different policy provisions and different policy limits has been addressed. Combine these with the thousands of claimants, the long latency period, and the hundreds of manufacturers and contractors involved, and one should have little problem seeing the legal nightmare presented to insurers. The defense of these cases just from the standpoint of who owes whom what amount is mind boggling. Many persons fear that the legal fees for both the plaintiffs and defense attorneys will eat away at the funds available to pay those victims deserving some compensation. Insurers have the additional headache that most of the policies involved require that the insurer defend the insured and place no limits on the cost of this defense.

From an underwriting standpoint, it is hard to see how a meaningful provision can be made in either rating or risk selection for a latent injury disease that may not manifest itself for forty years.

Asbestosis disease problems were not perceived by underwriters in 1945. It is possible in today's increasingly mechanized society that there are processes or equipment presently in use that will give rise to similar latent injury disease disasters forty years from now. If the CRT on the word-processor on which this is being written is even now giving off some mysterious radiation, for example, the numbers of people affected would be tremendous.

Dealing with the latent injury disease insurance problem must depend more upon changing policy terms and conditions than a reliance upon detection of all such future problems. One approach is the change to claims-made policies. However, even a change in policy language cannot guarantee that underwriters will write such risks or that they can do so profitably.

Occurrence versus Claims-Made Coverage

Occurrence may be defined as an accident, including continuous or repeated exposure to conditions, which results in bodily injury neither expected nor intended from the standpoint of the insured. Under an occurrence policy, a bodily injury, such as the inhalation of asbestos fibers, which occurs during the policy period is covered by that policy, even if the illness manifests itself forty years later.

The essence of occurrence coverage is that it raises the possibility of substantial incurred-but-not-reported (IBNR) losses.

Under a claims-made policy, coverage is triggered only if a claim for damages is first "made" during the policy period. The determination of when a claim is "made" varies by policy form. Further, many claims-made policies state that insurance does not apply to bodily injury or property damage which occurs before the *retroactive date* shown in the policy declarations or after the end of the policy period. This retroactive date may be the inception date of the policy or it may be an earlier date. It is not contemplated that a claims-made policy written today would have a retroactive date of 1945.

There is usually some "tail" provided in the claims-made policy. Some policies include a "mini-tail" in the form of a sixty to ninety day *extended reporting period*. An unlimited extended reporting period can usually be purchased at an additional premium to extend this tail.

The Triple Trigger Controversy

The appellate court in the Keene case found that coverage was triggered by three things:

1. exposure,
2. exposure in residence, and
3. manifestation.[10]

The exposure trigger to coverage occurs when a claimant is exposed to injurious conditions, the inhalation of asbestos fibers in this case, during the policy period.

Since asbestos fibers while in the exposed individual's lungs continue to injure the lung tissues, the term *exposure in residence* was coined. Under the exposure in residence theory, all policies which were in effect during the time period from the claimant's last exposure to asbestos fibers up to the manifestation of the illness must provide coverage. The final trigger cited by the court in Keene is manifestation

Exhibit 12-1
Coverage Theories and Their Effect

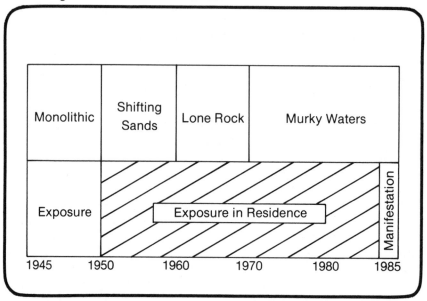

of the disease itself. The court in the Keene case held that all insurers of a risk from the time of exposure until the time of manifestation should respond—thus the term triple trigger.

An example of the impact of the triple trigger approach is shown in Exhibit 12-1. Assume that John B. Dokes was an insulation/asbestos installer using the products of the Lukless Asbestos Company. Dokes worked as an asbestos installer from 1945 to 1950. Then he went back to school and became an insurance professor. In 1985 he was diagnosed to be suffering from asbestosis. Lukless was insured with Monolithic Insurance from 1945 to 1950, Shifting Sands Insurance from 1951 to 1960, Lone Rock Insurance from 1961 to 1970, and Murky Waters Insurance from 1971 to the present. Exhibit 12-1 shows the time periods of the various triggers and the companies affected. Because it is not known in advance which theory will apply, all four insurers would have to respond from a defense standpoint.

EIL (ENVIRONMENTAL IMPAIRMENT LIABILITY)

Currently there exists an insurance crisis in the market for environmental impairment liability (EIL). A good indication of this problem is the decision by Insurance Services Office (ISO) to have a total pollution exclusion in its commercial general liability policy introduced in 1986. Many persons believed it was no longer possible to distinguish between gradual and sudden pollution (from a coverage interpretation standpoint) and therefore the only reasonable alternative was to totally exclude the pollution exposure. This came at a time when many insurers of gradual pollution coverage were either greatly curtailing their offerings or withdrawing from the market altogether. This section provides a study of the effect of changes in the demand for and supply of insurance coverage on the market.

Changes on the Demand Side

Pollution of the environment is an undesirable side effect of the production process in an increasingly technological society. Industrial pollution probably pre-dates recorded history. When early man first started working with metals and clearing land, the result was the degradation of the landscape and the introduction into streams of salts and other pollutants from runoff.

In modern society, construction operations and chemical and other manufacturing processes produce toxic industrial wastes which can pollute the environment unless their disposal is carefully controlled. Increasing societal interest in environmental issues has created strong pressure to eliminate pollution and punish polluters, past and present.

It has been estimated that from 2,000 to 5,000 hazardous waste sites could be included on the EPA National Priorities List of sites requiring clean-up action.[11] In addition to the obvious pollution exposures of the hazardous waste site, manufacturing and processing firms that generate hazardous wastes, and transport firms that move them, also have significant EIL exposures.

Societal interest in this area has resulted in the passage of a number of environmental laws including:

- The Clean Air Act (CAA),
- The Comprehensive Environmental Response, Compensation and Liability Act of 1980 (CERCLA—usually referred to as "Superfund"),
- The Clean Water Act (CWA),
- The National Environmental Policy Act (NEPA), and
- The Resource Conservation and Recovery Act (RCRA).

Financial Responsibility Requirements

RCRA, passed in 1976, requires operators of treatment, storage, and disposal facilities (TSDFs) to demonstrate financial responsibility of

$1 million per occurrence and $2 million annual aggregate for sudden and accidental pollution, and $3 million per occurrence and $6 million annual aggregate for nonsudden accidental occurrences. Financial responsibility requirements have not yet been established for generators (manufacturers/processors) and transporters.

While RCRA deals only with hazardous wastes, Superfund imposes strict liability with respect to all hazardous substances. The Superfund provides federal funds for an emergency response and clean-up with respect to a release or a substantial threatened release of hazardous substances into the environment.

Superfund authorizes the federal government to recover clean-up costs from responsible parties. The strict liability provision of Superfund is generally interpreted as being joint and several. Under joint and several liability, one party can be forced to pay all damages, even though its actions contributed only a small fraction to the cause of injury or damage. Therefore a paint manufacturer dumping paint in the Mississippi River in St. Louis could theoretically be liable for the clean-up costs of the entire river.

Superfund provides for potential bad faith action against insurers acting as guarantors under the still-to-be promulgated financial responsibility requirements. In the event of a finding of potential bad faith, the insurer's liability could be unlimited.[12]

It is likely that the combination of the joint and several liability, strict liability, and potential bad faith provisions of Superfund had an adverse effect upon the willingness of underwriters to write this coverage.

Changes on the Supply Side

While societal pressure has increased demand for EIL coverage, the supply has decreased. Prior to 1982, the only EIL coverage available was in the excess and surplus lines market. In that year some insurance companies began offering the coverage in the standard market.

During 1984 and 1985, capacity in this market dwindled as companies either pulled out of the market or drastically reduced the lines that they would write. In addition to the standard and surplus lines market segments, the Pollution Liability Insurance Association provides pooled coverage for approximately fifty member companies. This association was formed in 1982.

Reinsurers, particularly the London market, play a critical role in the market for EIL coverage. The amount of reinsurance available for this coverage has dramatically decreased, causing sharp drops in capacity. The structure of this market is shown in Exhibit 12-2.

Exhibit 12-2
Pollution Liability Marketplace*

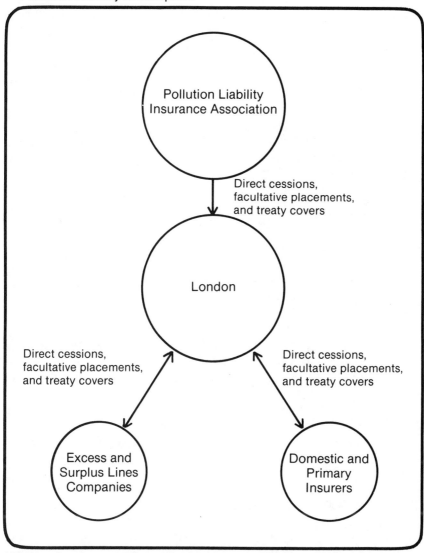

* Reprinted, with permission, from David C. Sterling, CPCU, CLU, ChFC, CIC, in John D. Long and Everett D. Randall, editors, *Issues in Insurance*, 3rd Edition, Volume II. (Malvern, PA: American Institute for Property and Liability Underwriters, 1984), p. 241.

As drastic as these changes in capacity appear, the reduction in coverage is even greater. At least one of the insurers still writing EIL has eliminated coverage for punitive damages and includes defense costs within the policy limits.

Some insureds hope to obtain coverage for EIL losses under their standard comprehensive general liability policies. As mentioned earlier, the 1986 ISO commercial general liability form contains a revised pollution exclusion. The intent of the policy language is to exclude virtually every (there is a minor exception) conceivable type of pollution loss.

This exclusion has two parts. The first part excludes: "Bodily injury" or "property damage" arising out of the actual alleged or threatened discharge, dispersal, release or escape of pollutants:

   (a) At or from premises you own, rent or occupy;
   (b) At or from any site or location used by or for you or others for the handling, storage, disposal, processing or treatment of waste;
   (c) Which are at any time transported, handled, stored, treated, disposed of, or processed as waste by or for you or any person or organization for whom you may be legally responsible; or
   (d) At or from any site or location on which you or any contractors or subcontractors working directly or indirectly on your behalf are performing operations:
      (i) if the pollutants are brought on or to the site or location in connection with such operations; or
      (ii) if the operations are to test for, monitor, clean up, remove, contain, treat, detoxify or neutralize the pollutants.[13]

Coverage is limited further by the second part of the exclusion which eliminates coverage for "any loss, cost or expense arising out of any governmental direction or request that you test for, monitor, clean up, remove, contain, treat, detoxify or neutralize pollutants."[14]

The 1986 ISO commercial general liability program has provision for EIL coverage if the underwriter is willing to endorse the contract. The first provision, designed for those with minor pollution exposure, is an endorsement which can be attached to either the occurrence or claims-made policy deleting the first part of the exclusion. The second provision is a separate coverage part for pollution liability to be available on both a claims-made and occurrence basis with or without coverage for cleanup and related costs. It remains to be seen how much coverage will be provided on either basis, since most treaty reinsurers seem to be unwilling to accept EIL type coverages from their primary insurers.

The Effects

Societal concerns about pollution have been expressed in several federal laws. Both the Resource Conservation and Recovery Act and the Superfund have stimulated the demand for EIL coverage. At the

Exhibit 12-3
The Effect of Demand and Supply Shifts

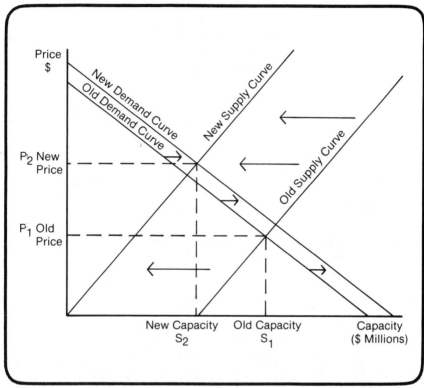

same time, certain provisions in these acts, and the resulting potential for catastrophic losses have restricted the supply of EIL coverage. The result is a classic illustration of the operation of the forces of supply and demand in the market. The interaction of these forces is illustrated in Exhibit 12-3.

The increase in demand for EIL coverage resulted in a shift of the demand curve to the right. At the same time, the decrease in the amount of EIL coverage available in the market resulted in a shift of the supply curve to the left. The result is a sharp decrease in capacity and an increase in the equilibrium price in the market from P_1 to P_2.

There are two troublesome potential consequences of this dramatic decrease in the EIL market capacity in the face of increasing demand.

The first is that the premium for the EIL coverage may become so high that it becomes uneconomic for the insured. This would lead to a complete collapse of the market for EIL coverage and perhaps government intervention. It would leave insureds with no recourse except self-insurance or captive insurers.

The use of self-insurance or captives may be feasible alternatives for large industrial firms, but may not be feasible for smaller firms. These firms may lack the financial capacity to meet the financial responsibility standards of present and pending legislation. Some form of pooling arrangement may be required with governmental approval.

The second potential problem is that if EIL coverage becomes generally unavailable, courts may interpret older comprehensive general liability policies as providing coverage.[15] This would create a situation similar to the asbestos latent injury disease problem in that losses are realized under a coverage although the underwriter never contemplated that exposure.

UNISEX AND SOCIAL PRICING

There is no right more important than equal opportunity for everyone regardless of race, creed, color, gender, or national origin. However, the problem is how to define "equal" in such a way that unfair discrimination is avoided.

Gender as a Classification Factor

In insurance pricing there are some cost-based differences attributable to gender. If these differences are ignored, market distortions result. Historically, life insurance mortality tables have acknowledged the fact that women live longer than men. The underlying fact of women's greater longevity appears to be established by actuarial data and is beyond dispute. In auto insurance, rates for women have traditionally been lower, reflecting lower loss costs.

When society decides that classification systems using gender are inappropriate, the result is social pricing rather than pricing based on cost. In life insurance, a combined male/female mortality table ignores the very real differences between the genders with respect to life expectancy. The major court cases in this area deal with pension funds. Since women have a longer life expectancy than men, a woman earning the same as a man and employed for the same number of years would receive a lower pension amount per month if her longer life expectancy were to be recognized.

Without getting into the complexities of actuarial science, a simple example will show the principle involved. Assume that both the woman and man had accumulated $122,920 in their pension "account." Assume that they are both to receive annual payments with the man expected to receive ten payments and the woman fifteen. Further assume a 10

Exhibit 12-4
A Simple Pension Example

Man — aged 65 — life expectancy — 10 years — 10 percent interest assumption

Fund $122,920/6.145 (PVIF[†] annuity 10 years 10 percent) = $20,000 a year

Woman — aged 65 — life expectancy — 15 years — 10 percent interest assumption

Fund $122,920/7.606 (PVIF[†] Annuity 10 years 10 percent) = $16,161 a year

[†]PVIF = Present Value Interest Factor

percent rate of interest. As Exhibit 12-4 shows, the man would receive $20,000 a year and the woman $16,161.

This example indicates the difference between cost-based pricing and social pricing. Mathematically, at 10 percent interest, a ten year annuity of $20,000 is equal to a fifteen year annuity of $16,161. The difficulty occurs when society proscribes the use of gender as a classification factor.

The use of a combined mortality table which ignores gender means that neither the man nor the woman receives the pension which a cost-based system would have assigned them. The addition of the longer female mortality to the male table will cause the assumed life expectancy to increase for the men and decrease for the women. Therefore the men will get paid less than they would have under a cost-based system, while the women will receive more. This produces a cross-subsidization, with funds flowing from the men to the women.

Social Pricing in Auto Insurance

Auto insurance actuarial data has consistently shown that women under the age of 25 have fewer and less severe auto accidents than males in the same age group. The possible reasons for this difference are many and varied. Perhaps young women do not drive as many miles a year as their male counterparts, resulting in lower accident exposure. Whatever the reason, gender can help predict future auto insurance loss results.

Several states have prohibited the use of gender as a classification factor in auto insurance rating. In most cases the pressure for these changes have come from the women's movement and its supporters. It is important that persons understand the economic consequences of the changes.

These economic consequences are best illustrated by means of a numerical example. Assume that in a certain very isolated rating territory there are exactly 100 young men and 100 young women under the age of 25 applying for auto insurance. Assume further that, based on the historical accident data compiled on the young men alone, their premium should be $1,500. This is their cost-based premium. Assume that the cost-based premium for the young women should be $1,000. Now assume that legislation is introduced eliminating the use of gender as an auto insurance rating factor in the interest of social equality. The result would be a social price premium of $1,250 for both men and women. This result is shown in Exhibit 12-5.

Elimination of gender as a classification factor again leads to cross-subsidization. The addition of the women's better loss results to the combined male/female under 25 class reduces premiums for men; however, women pay a higher premium. Social pricing has introduced heterogeneity into this new rate class.

While legislation may prohibit underwriters from using gender as a classification factor for pricing purposes, it is difficult to block all gender distinctions. In most cases, underwriters can often determine the gender of a particular applicant by something as simple as the name. In the rating example given in Exhibit 12-5, an insurance company will lose money on every male under 25 written and make money on every female under 25 written. The social pricing scheme will not harm the underwriting results of a particular insurer if that insurer's books are perfectly balanced on a male/female basis. If one insurer seeks out young women insureds and shuns young men, an imbalance will result. This happens immediately in the isolated territory visited in the preceding example.

Assume that the above territory is serviced by two insurance companies, Cain and Able. Cain Insurance Company writes sixty women and forty men while Able writes forty women and sixty men. In this theoretical, if imperfect world, the expected loss results are exactly matched by the actual loss results. Therefore, all males have losses and expenses exactly equaling $1,500 while all females have losses and expenses exactly equaling $1,000. As Exhibit 12-6 shows, Cain enjoys an underwriting gain while Able suffers an underwriting loss, because of a gender imbalance alone. Cain would show an underwriting gain of $5,000 and a combined ratio of .96; while Able would show an underwriting loss of $5,000 and a combined ratio of 1.04. The practical result is that the prohibition of the use of gender as a rating factor increases the importance of gender in risk selection. (See Exhibit 12-6.)

Exhibit 12-5
Social Pricing in Auto Insurance

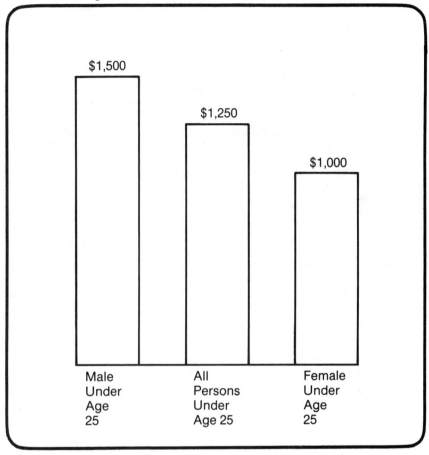

THE UNDERWRITING CYCLE

Webster's dictionary defines a cycle as: "An interval of time during which a sequence of a recurring succession of events or phenomena is completed." The underwriting cycle in property and liability insurance is both persistent and familiar. The cycle starts with a period during which the industry enjoys underwriting gains, resulting in a period of intense competition. This intense competition leads to underwriting losses. At the bottom of the cycle, the market tightens up as capacity disappears and price increases become widespread. These conditions cause improved underwriting results and, finally, the industry again

Exhibit 12-6
Gender Imbalance in Auto Books

Cain Insurance Company	Able Insurance Company
Premium	Premium
100 × $1250 = $125,000	100 × $1250 = $125,000
Loss and Expense Results	Loss and Expense Results
40 male × $1500 = $60,000	60 male × $1500 = $90,000
60 female × $1000 = $60,000	40 female × $1000 = $40,000
Total = $120,000	Total = $130,000
Underwriting Gain	Underwriting Loss
125,000 — 120,000 =	125,000 — 130,000 =
$5,000 gain	$5,000 loss
Combined Ratio	Combined Ratio
120,000/125,000 = .96	130,000/125,000 = 1.04

achieves underwriting gains. The stage is set for the start of the next cycle.

Underwriting cycles for the period 1945-1983 are shown in Exhibit 12-7.

During this time period there have been six cycles. These are:

- 1946—1952
- 1952—1957
- 1957—1964
- 1964—1969
- 1969—1975
- 1975—1985[16]

During the period from 1959 through the present, each cycle has more amplitude than the one preceeding it—that is, the trough is considerably deeper than the corresponding point in the preceding cycle. Exhibit 12-8 shows underwriting gains and losses for the period 1959-1984 and their troughs.

In 1965, the net underwriting loss was $709 million, while in 1969 it was $1.047 billion. Underwriting losses increased to $4.226 billion in 1975 and $21.477 billion in 1984. Over this same time period, investment income has become increasingly important. Throughout all cycles preceding the current one, net investment income has more than offset the underwriting losses. In 1984, for only the second time, combined net income, which is the underwriting gain or loss plus net investment

Exhibit 12-7
Combined Ratio for All Lines of Property-Liability Insurance† 1945-1983*

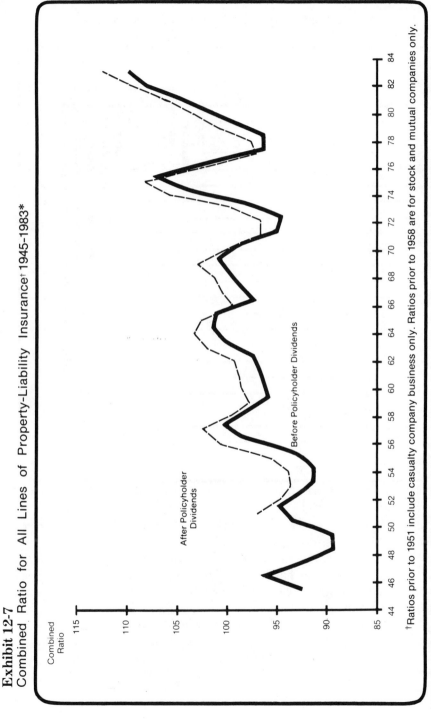

† Ratios prior to 1951 include casualty company business only. Ratios prior to 1958 are for stock and mutual companies only.

* Reprinted with permission from Barbara Stewart, "Profit Cycles in Property-Liability Insurance", in *Issues in Insurance*, 3rd Edition, Volume I, John D. Long and Everett D. Randall, (Malvern PA: American Institute for Property and Liability Underwriters, 1984), p. 279.

Exhibit 12-8
Underwriting Gains/Losses After Policyholder Dividends
Property/Casualty Insurance Business 1959-1984*

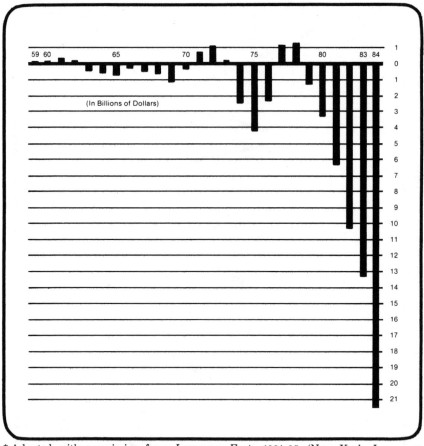

* Adapted, with permission, from *Insurance Facts 1984-85*, (New York: Insurance Information Institute, 1984), p. 21.

income, became negative. In 1984, the property and liability industry lost $3.817 billion before taxes.

While underwriting gains and losses have shown a cyclical pattern, net investment income has followed a path of steady growth. The intricate relationship between underwriting gain or loss, net investment income, and combined net income is shown in Exhibit 12-9.

While a separate cyclical pattern may be traced in the underwriting results for most lines of business, two important types of insurance have different factors causing their cycle. These types are private passenger auto insurance and commercial property and liability insurance.

Exhibit 12-9
Industry Operating Results*

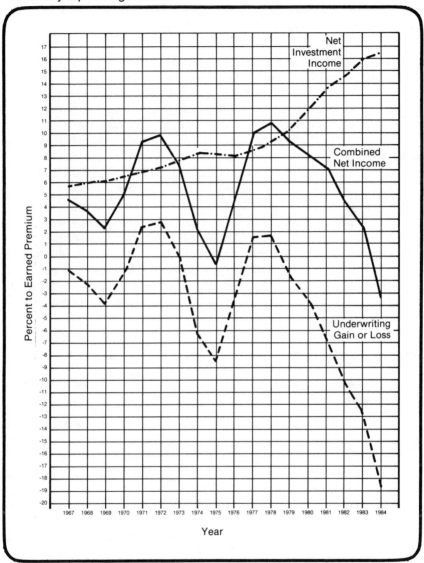

* Reprinted with permission from *Best's Aggregates & Averages 1984*, (Oldwick, N.J.: A.M. Best Co.,) p. 69.

Private Passenger Auto

While private passenger auto insurance is affected to a certain degree by the same factors affecting commercial lines, the cycle in private passenger auto results has additional causes. In many states private passenger auto insurance rates are more closely regulated than any other type of property and liability insurance. The public is very aware of each increase in auto insurance rates and, therefore, regulators are too.

As inflation has increased, the cost of medical care and the cost of auto replacement parts have increased, causing auto insurance rates to increase. Public resentment over these rate increases has been expressed in terms of pressure on legislators and insurance regulators to hold down rate increases. As a result, auto insurers have been subjected to a lag between the time when increasing loss costs begin to influence underwriting results and when necessary rate increases can be obtained. This lag influences the auto underwriting cycle.

An increase in loss costs without a corresponding rate increase leads to a period of underwriting losses. Eventually, auto insurers are able to convince regulators of the requirement for rate increases. When the rate increases are granted, underwriting results improve. If the improved results produce underwriting gains, the combination of competitive forces, the underlying inflationary factors, and additional rate lags combine to erode these gains leading to the next period of underwriting losses. In short, inflation may cause an atypical underwriting cycle in certain lines of insurance.

The Cycle in Commercial Lines

The current underwriting cycle is dominated by the commercial lines sector of the market.

A Model Explaining the Underwriting Cycle The depth of the trough in the current underwriting cycle has given rise to a number of attempts to explain this phenomenon. Barbara Stewart's excellent monograph uses the "cobweb" theory of economics to develop a cycle model based upon expectations.[17] This section focuses more on the specific actions of underwriting management as a cause of the underwriting cycle.

Cycles in most industries are caused by demand. If disposable personal income is up, consumers buy more new cars, and the auto industry has a boom year. If disposable personal income is down, consumers buy fewer new cars, and the auto industry has a bust year with many layoffs.

The demand for property and liability insurance is remarkably constant. Over time, the demand for property and liability insurance shows steady growth as the economy expands.[18]

There are two reasons for this steady demand. First, most persons consider insurance a necessity (and in some cases it is required by law). They feel as though they cannot do without it and there is no readily available substitute for a comparable price. Second, insurance is not like other products in that it cannot be stored or its purchase postponed. For example, when food prices are low, persons tend to "stock up." When auto prices are high (or interest rates are high), persons tend to get "another year" out of their present car. Insurance must be purchased each year and the coverage lasts for only one year (in most cases).[19] As a result of this steady demand, the important factors affecting the property and liability cycle are on the supply side, particularly in commercial lines.

One of the best overall measures of the financial stability of an insurer is its written premiums to policyholders' surplus (often called premiums to surplus) ratio. Very simply, this ratio is an indication of the adequacy of funds available to meet expected future claims and expenses. As more insurance is written, the surplus is exposed to a greater chance of loss variation. If the ratio is too high, an insurer may be overextending itself by writing too much new business. This problem is further aggravated by the surplus drain problem created by the increase in writings, as was described in the reinsurance chapter. A ratio that is too low is generally interpreted as meaning the insurer is not using its capacity to the extent possible.

Although many persons use a premiums to surplus ratio of 2 or 3 to 1 as a benchmark, what should be deemed as a "safe" ratio varies by line of insurance. An insurer writing primarily property insurance can usually safely operate at a higher premium to surplus ratio than an insurer writing primarily third-party liability lines of insurance. Because of the importance of this ratio, management tries to keep it within a fairly narrow range. If "all other things" remain constant, there is little problem with meeting this objective and the objective of maintaining market share. However, when the percentage changes in capacity and demand differ from one period to another, or when an insurer attempts to increase market share while keeping the premiums to surplus ratio stable, cyclical fluctuations in the market for insurance are likely to result.

From 1979 through 1984, there was a rapid increase in net investment income as shown in Exhibit 12-9. This increase would have increased capacity far more than was the case were it not for the substantial underwriting losses which occurred during this period. Underwriting losses cut the rate of increase in capacity. During the period 1979 through 1983, capacity increased despite underwriting losses, and the commercial lines market remained extremely competitive.

The underwriting losses of 1984 were so large that they overwhelmed the still increasing net investment income. The resulting overall losses resulted in a drop in capacity. This set off a "tight" market as prices firmed.[20] As price increases became the rule, capacity decreased still more. The results for 1985 were worse than those of 1984, but there was a tightening of market in commercial lines.

SUMMARY

The theory of concurrent causation holds that if any of a series of concurrent proximate causes is not specifically excluded under an "all-risks" contract, coverage may be provided. This theory has provided coverage for natural disasters such as floods and earthquakes under policies which specifically excluded these perils.

The insurability of punitive damages varies from state to state. In some states insurance of punitive damages is never permitted; in others it depends upon the particular facts in the case. An important public policy consideration is that the existence of insurance for punitive damages might be interpreted as reducing or eliminating their deterrent effect.

The most difficult aspect of asbestos related illnesses and other latent diseases is the length of the latency period. Forty years may pass between the period of exposure to the substance or condition and the manifestation of the illness. This causes problems in allocating claims among insurance companies over the intervening period. This long latency period also creates difficult problems in underwriting and rating under occurrence type policies.

There is currently a crisis in the market for environmental impairment liability (EIL). Societal interest in this area has resulted in the passage of a number of environmental laws which have increased the demand for this coverage. The most important of these are the Resource Conservation and Recovery Act (RCRA) and Superfund. While demand for this coverage has increased, the number of companies offering the coverage has decreased resulting in dramatic price increases, and significant drops in the limits of liability available in the market.

When society decides that classification systems using gender are inappropriate, the result is the substitution of social pricing for cost-based pricing. Social pricing results in cross subsidization as some individuals pay more than their loss costs indicate they should pay while others pay less.

The underwriting cycle in property and liability insurance is both persistent and familiar. The current cycle, which began in 1975 is the sixth cycle since 1946. The current cycle is both longer and deeper than any of those that preceded it. In 1984, for only the second time, underwriting losses exceeded net investment income for the industry as a whole, resulting in negative combined net income.

Chapter Notes

---

1. 10 CAL. 3d 94 (1973).
2. 692 Fed. (2nd) 551 (1982).
3. 140 Cal. App. (3rd) 720 (1983).
4. Insurance Services Office HO-3 policy, April 1984 edition
5. The industry's response to the legislative mandate that all insureds be notified of earthquake coverage had an unintended side effect. Most insurance companies in the state sent certified letters to their insureds notifying them of the availability of earthquake coverage. By chance, two major insurers of the coverage, with a combined book of homeowners business of over 1 million policies sent their certified letters out on the same day.

   Many insureds were not at home when the postal carrier arrived, therefore pink notices were left requiring the addressees to pick up the certified mail at the post office. For most people, the notice that a piece of certified mail awaits your pickup at the post office is a source of anxiety. Literally thousands of insureds descended upon their post offices simultaneously causing lines which were in many cases blocks long. Many postal authorities said that the crush was much worse than Christmas.

   Many insureds were less than delighted that their legislators had decided that they needed their attention so dramatically drawn to the availability of earthquake coverage. On the other hand, the number of insureds purchasing the coverage subsequently doubled to about 15 percent for most insurers.
6. See J. J. Launie, "The Incidence and Burden of Punitive Damages," publication forthcoming in the *Insurance Counsel Journal.*
7. 214 Tenn 639, 383 SW2d1. This and the following section lean heavily on the authoritative discussion of this topic in James D. Ghiardi and John J. Kircher, *Punitive Damages: Law and Practice*, Callaghan & Co., Wilmette, Illinois, 1985, Chapter 7.
8. 307 F2d 432 (CA 5, 1962).
9. American Ins. Co. v. North American Co. for Property and Casualty Insurance 697 F2d 79 (CA 2, 1982). See Ghiardi, op. cit., 1985 Cumulative Supplement, section 7.25, p. 193.
10. Keene Corporation v. INA et al., Aetna Casualty and Surety Company, appellant, 81-1179, Keene Corporation, appellant v. INA, et al., 81-1180, Keene Corporation v. INA, Liberty Mutual Ins. Co. Appellant, 81-1181, US Court of Appeals, District of Columbia, 1981.
11. Rich Janisch, "Protection from Pollution Risk: A Team Effort," *Professional Agent*, June 1984, pp. 26-32. For a definitive treatment of EIL see David C. Sterling, CPCU, CLU, ChFC, CIC, "Environmental Impairment Liability: An Insurance Perspective." in John D. Long and Everett D. Randall,

editors, *Issues in Insurance*, 3rd edition, volume II (Malvern, PA: American Institute for Property and Liability Underwriters, 1984), pp. 217-277.

12. Sterling, p. 232. See also "Refusal to write pollution cover may backfire: Attorney," *Business Insurance*, October 21, 1985, p. 81.
13. *F C & S Bulletins*, Casualty and Surety Volume, Public Liability, p. Aa-7.
14. *F C & S Bulletins*, pp. Aa-7-Aa-8.
15. "Refusal to write pollution cover may backfire: Attorney," p. 81.
16. Barbara Stewart, "Profit Cycles in Property-Liability Insurance," in *Issues in Insurance*, 3rd edition, Volume I (Malvern, PA, American Institute for Property and Liability Underwriters, 1984), pp. 273-331. See also Emelio C. Venezian, "Ratemaking Methods and Profit Cycles in Property and Liability Insurance," *Journal of Risk and Insurance*, September 1985, pp. 477-500 and *Insurer Profitability—The Facts*, Insurance Services Office, Inc., 1986.
17. Stewart, pp. 293-294
18. Stewart, pp. 289.
19. Stewart, pp. 289-290.
20. The terms "tight" and "soft" are often used to refer to the insurance market. A tight market refers to one in which prices are increasing and/or relatively high, strict underwriting standards are being applied, and there is little excess capacity available. Conversely, a "soft" market is one in which there is excess capacity, insurers are cutting prices to attract business, and few risks are declined "for underwriting reasons."

Bibliography

Allen, Tom C. *Risk Management Methodology: A New Journal of Commerce Report.* New York: The Journal of Commerce, 1973.

Barile, Andrew J. *Reinsurance Risk Management Manual, Insurance 6, Supplement 19.* Santa Monica, CA: The Merritt Company, 1976.

Barnard, Chester I. *The Functions of the Executive.* Cambridge, MA: Harvard University Press, 1968.

Bickelhaupt, David L. *General Insurance,* 10th ed. Homewood, IL: Richard D. Irwin, 1979.

Breslin, Cormick L. and Troxel, Terrie E. *Property-Liability Insurance Accounting and Finance.* Malvern, PA: American Institute for Property and Liability Underwriters, 1978.

Buglass, Leslie J. *Marine Insurance and General Average in the United States,* 2nd ed. Centreville, MD: Cornell Maritime Press, 1981.

F. C. & S. Bulletins, Casualty and Surety Volume, Public Liability, p. Aa-7.

Fromm, Erwin F. "The Mechanical Underwriter," *Best's Review,* Property/Liability Insurance Edition, Vol. 76, No. 2., June 1975.

Ghiardi, James D. and Kircher, John H. *Punitive Damages: Law and Practice.* Wilmette, IL: Callaghan & Co., 1985.

Glossary of Insurance Terms. Washington, DC: Reinsurance Association of America, 1972.

Haney, W. V. *Communication and Organization Behavior,* 3rd ed. Homewood, IL: Richard D. Irwin, 1969.

Head, George L. "Fundamentals of Probability Analysis" and "Uses of Probability Analyses in Risk Management," in *Readings on the Risk Management Function.* Malvern, PA: Insurance Institute of America, 1983.

_____and Horn, Stephen, II. *Essentials of the Risk Management Process,* vol. 1. Malvern, PA: Insurance Institute of America, 1985

Heinrich, H. W. *Industrial Accident Prevention,* 4th ed. New York: McGraw-Hill, 1959.

Henderson, Glenn V., Trennepohl, Gary L., and Wort, James E. *An Introduction to Financial Management.* Reading, MA: Addison-Wesley Publishing Co., 1984.

"Hidden Costs—They Can Be Controlled," *NATLSCO Consultant,* September 1980.

Hollingsworth, E. P. and Launie, J. J. *Commercial Property and Multiple-Lines Underwriting,* 2nd ed. Malvern, PA: Insurance Institute of America, 1984.

Holtom, Robert B. *Underwriting.* Cincinnati: The National Underwriter, 1973.

Horn, Ronald C. *On Professions, Professionals, and Professional Ethics,* 1st.

ed. Malvern, PA: American Institute for Property and Liability Underwriters, 1984.

Houston, David B. "Risk, Insurance and Sampling," *The Journal of Risk and Insurance*, December 1964.

Insurance Services Office HO-3 policy, April 1984 edition.

Insurer Profitability—The Facts. Insurance Services Office, 1986.

Janisch, Rich. "Protection from Pollution Risk: A Team Effort," *Professional Agent*, June 1984.

Kimball, Spencer L. and Denenberg, Herbert S. *Insurance, Government, and Social Policy.*

Knight, Frank H. *Risk, Uncertainty and Profit*. Boston: Houghton Mifflin Company, 1921.

Kulp, C. A. and Hall, John W. *Casualty Insurance*, 4th ed. New York: The Ronald Press, 1968.

Lange, Jeffrey T. "General Liability Insurance Ratemaking," *Insurance Insights*. Cincinnati: South-Western Publishing Co., 1974.

Launie, J. J. "The Incidence and Burden of Punitive Damages," publication forthcoming in *Insurance Counsel Journal*.

Magee, John F. "Decision Trees for Decision Making," *Harvard Business Review*, Vol. 41, No. 4, July-August 1964, pp. 126-138.

McNamara, Daniel J., "Discrimination in Property-Liability Insurance Pricing," in John D. Long and Everett D. Randall, eds., *Issues in Insurance*, vol. I, 3rd ed. Malvern, PA: American Institute for Property and Liability Underwriters, 1984.

Mehr, Robert I. and Cammack, Emerson. *Principles of Insurance*, 7th ed. Homewood, IL: Richard D. Irwin, 1980.

Newman, Joseph W. *Management Applications of Decision Theory*. New York: Harper & Row, 1971.

"Refusal to Write Pollution Cover May Backfire: Attorney," *Business Insurance*, 21 October 1985, p. 81.

Reinarz, Robert C. *Property and Liability Reinsurance Management*. Fullerton, CA: Mission Publishing Company, 1969.

Sanders, Donald H. *Computers in Business—An Introduction*, 2nd. ed. New York: McGraw-Hill, 1972.

Sterling, David C. "Environmental Impairment Liability: An Insurance Perspective," in John D. Long and Everett D. Randall, eds., *Issues in Insurance*, vol. II, 3rd ed. Malvern, PA: American Institute for Property and Liability Underwriters, 1984

Stewart, Barbara. "Profit Cycles in Property-Liability Insurance," in John D. Long and Everett D. Randall, eds., *Issues in Insurance* vol. I, 3rd ed. Malvern, PA: American Institute for Property and Liability Underwriters, 1984.

Thayer, Lee. *Communications and Communication Systems: In Organization, Management, and Interpersonal Relations*. Homewood, IL: Richard D. Irwin, 1968.

"The Definition of Risk," *Business Insurance*, 9 May 1983, p. 41.

Venezian, Emilio C. "Ratemaking Methods and Profit Cycles in Property and Liability Insurance," *The Journal of Risk and Insurance*, September 1985.

Webb, Bernard J., Launie, J. J., Rokes, Willis Park, and Baglini, Norman A. *Insurance Company Operations*, vols. I and II, 3rd. ed. Malvern, PA: American Institute for Property and Liability Underwriters, 1984.

Werner, Edgar C. *Fundamentals of Reinsurance*. New York: The College of Insurance, 1964.

Williams, C. Arthur, Jr., Head, George L., Horn, Ronald C., and Glendenning, G. William. *Principles of Risk Management and Insurance*, vol. I, 2nd ed. Malvern, PA: American Institute for Property and Liability Underwriters, 1981.

_____and Heins, Richard M. *Risk Management and Insurance*, 3rd ed. New York: McGraw-Hill, 1976.

Index

F